INDIA POLICY FORUM 2004

VOLUME 1

EDITED BY

Suman Bery
Barry Bosworth
Arvind Panagariya

NATIONAL COUNCIL OF APPLIED
ECONOMIC RESEARCH
New Delhi

BROOKINGS INSTITUTION
Washington, D.C.

Published by

BROOKINGS INSTITUTION PRESS

1775 Massachusetts Avenue, N.W., Washington, DC 20036

www.brookings.edu

ISSN 0972-9755

ISBN 0-8157-0881-5

NCAER

INDIA

POLICY FORUM

VOLUME 1

2004

PURPOSE

India Policy Forum 2004 comprises papers and highlights of the discussions from the first India Policy Forum (IPF) conference, held March 25–27, 2004, in New Delhi. IPF is a joint venture of the Brookings Institution and the National Council of Applied Economic Research (NCAER) that examines India's reforms and economic transition using policy relevant empirical research. The editors acknowledge the generous support of USAID, Citigroup, the State Bank of India, and HDFC Ltd.

The objective of the IPF is to generate theoretically rigorous, empirically informed research on important current and unfolding issues of economic policy. A panel of established researchers has agreed to support this initiative for an initial period of three years through 2006. Overall guidance is being provided by a distinguished international advisory panel.

Papers appear in this publication after presentation and discussion at a yearly conference in New Delhi. During discussions at the conference, the authors obtain helpful comments and criticism about various aspects of their papers. These comments are reflected in the journal as discussants' comments. The papers, however, are finally the authors' products and do not imply any agreement by those attending the conference or providing financial support. Nor do any materials in this journal necessarily represent the views of the staff members or officers of the NCAER and the Brookings Institution.

CORRESPONDENCE

Correspondence regarding papers in this issue should be addressed to the authors. Manuscripts are not accepted for review because this journal is devoted exclusively to invited contributions.

ORDERING

For information onordering, please visit the Brookings website at www.brookings.edu or contact the Brookings Institution Press, 1775 Massachusetts Avenue, N.W., Washington, DC 20036. Telephone 202/797-6258 or 800/275-1447. Fax 202/797-2960. E-mail bibooks@brookings.edu.

STAFF

Martha Gottron, Eileen Hughes, Brenda Szittya, Michael Treadway, editors
  Brookings Institution
Anjali Malhotra   *National Council of Applied Economic Research*
Pradeep Srivastava   *National Council of Applied Economic Research*

GUESTS WHOSE WRITINGS OR COMMENTS APPEAR IN THIS ISSUE

Shankar Acharya   *Indian Council of Research in International
  Economic Relations*
Rajesh Chadha   *National Council of Applied Economic Research*
Shawn Cole   *Massachusetts Institute of Technology*
Ila Patnaik   *National Council of Applied Economic Research*
Sanjeev Sanyal   *Deutsche Bank*
Anil Sharma   *National Council of Applied Economic Research*

Editors' Summary

The *India Policy Forum* (*IPF*) is a new journal, jointly promoted by the National Council of Applied Economic Research (NCAER), New Delhi, and the Brookings Institution, Washington, D.C., that aims to present high-quality empirical analysis on the major economic policy issues that confront contemporary India. The journal is based on papers commissioned by the editors and presented at an annual conference. The forum is supported by a distinguished advisory panel and a panel of active researchers who provide suggestions to the editors and participate in the review and discussion process. The need for such real-time quantitative analysis is particularly pressing for an economy like India's, which is in the process of rapid growth, structural change, and increased involvement in the global economy. The founders of the *IPF* hope it will contribute to enhancing the quality of policy analysis in the country and stimulate empirically informed decisionmaking. The style of the papers, this editors' summary, and the discussants' comments and general discussions are all intended to make these debates accessible to a broad nonspecialist audience, inside and outside India, and to present diverse views on the issues. The *IPF* is also intended to help build a bridge between researchers inside India and researchers abroad, nurturing a global network of scholars interested in India's economic transformation.

The first India Policy Forum conference took place at the NCAER in Delhi on March 26–27, 2004. In addition to the working sessions, the occasion was marked by a public address given by Stanley Fischer, vice chairman with Citigroup International and a member of the *IPF* advisory panel. This inaugural issue of the *IPF* includes the papers and discussions presented at that conference. The papers focus on several contemporary policy issues. The first two papers provide alternative perspectives on the trade policies that would do the most to enhance India's future growth prospects in the context of ongoing developments in the global trading system. The three papers that follow are devoted to an analysis of recent developments in India's balance of payments and their implications for the future exchange rate regime, the integration of exchange rate policy with other aspects of macroeconomic policy, and capital account convertibility, respectively. The sixth paper is devoted to an examination of the performance of the Indian banking system and the implications of the dominant role of government-run banks.

The first paper, by Arvind Panagariya, provides a broad review of India's external sector policies; the impact of these policies on trade flows, efficiency, and growth; and the future direction trade policies should take. Since trade policies are a means to an end, namely faster growth and improved efficiency, and since trade policies support other domestic policies, Panagariya's review necessarily ranges into these areas as well. Finally, to place India's performance in perspective, Panagariya makes extensive comparisons throughout between Indian and Chinese outcomes over the past two decades (1980–2000), a period when both economies have chosen to reintegrate into the world economy.

India's growth experience since 1950 falls in two phases. The first thirty years were characterized by steady growth of around 3.5 percent; thereafter growth has tended to stay in the 5 to 6 percent range. Panagariya links this differential growth performance with the imposition and subsequent relaxation of microeconomic controls, particularly in the external sector. In turn he divides these external sector policies into three phases. Between 1950 and 1975 the trend was toward virtual autarky, particularly after a balance-of-payments crisis in 1956–57. This was succeeded by a period of "ad hoc liberalization" starting around 1976, when reform of quantitative restrictions on trade was complemented by deregulation of industrial licensing in certain sectors. A further balance-of-payments crisis in the period from late 1990 to early 1991, concurrent with a general election, provided the background for a switch to deeper and more systematic liberalization, which, in fits and starts, continues today.

In the merchandise trade area the focus of reform has been to reduce tariff levels, particularly on nonagricultural goods. This has been done by gradually reducing the peak rate and reducing the number of tariff bands. In 1990–91 the peak rate stood at 355 percent, while the simple average of all tariff rates was 113 percent. By early 2004 the peak rate on individual goods was down to 20 percent, though there were notable exceptions, such as chemicals and transport equipment. Similarly, there has been less than ideal progress in reducing end-user and other exemptions. In nonindustrial areas there has been substantial liberalization of trade (and investment) in services, but following the OECD example, less in agriculture.

Panagariya next reviews the impact of this liberalization on trade flows, on efficiency, and on growth, in many cases using China as a benchmark.

India's share in world exports of goods and services—which had declined from 2 percent at Indian independence in 1947 to 0.5 percent in the mid-1980s—bounced back to 0.8 percent in 2002, implying that for roughly twenty years India's trade has grown more rapidly than world trade. In addition, the deeper reforms of the 1990s yielded a pick-up of almost 50 percent over the previous decade, from 7.4 percent to 10.7 percent. Encouraging though these numbers are in light of India's past performance, they pale in comparison with the Chinese record over the same period. Aside from any issues that may arise in the measurement of Chinese GDP at a time of rapid institutional and economic change, the combined share of exports and imports of both goods and services rose in China from 18.9 percent in 1980 to 49.3 percent in 2000, according to World Bank data. For India, the comparable numbers were 15.9 percent (in 1980) and 30.6 percent (in 2000).

The increase in India's trade intensity has been accompanied by significant shifts in composition. The most dramatic has been the increased share of service exports in the 1990s. Within industry, exporting sectors with above-average growth tended to be skill- or capital-intensive rather than labor-intensive, while on the import side the share of capital goods imports declined sharply. In the area of services, rapid growth was exhibited by software exports and recorded remittances from overseas Indians. However, tourism receipts remain below potential. With regard to trade partners, the main shift over the 1990s was a move away from Russia toward Asia, particularly developing Asia. An interesting recent development has been the rapid expansion of India's trade with China.

Panagariya then reviews the evidence on the impact of liberalization on static efficiency and on growth. One common approach is to use a computable general equilibrium (CGE) model to estimate the effects of the removal of trade distortions. The one study cited estimates the impact as raising GDP permanently by 2 percentage points. Additional domestic liberalization could raise this figure to 5 percentage points. Panagariya argues, however, that such models miss some key sources of gains. He cites two in particular: the disappearance of inefficient sectors and improvements in product quality. In addition, disaggregated analysis at the five-digit SITC level reveals far more dynamism in product composition of both exports and imports than is revealed at the two-digit level. This suggests greater gains from trade and improved welfare from enhanced choice than is captured in more aggregate models.

The links between liberalization and aggregate growth—or growth in total factor productivity (TFP)—have been controversial both in India and elsewhere in the emerging economies of Asia. In the case of India, the focus has been almost exclusively on manufacturing. After reviewing several studies, which admittedly differ in methodology and data quality, Panagariya judges that the weight of the evidence indicates that trade liberalization has led to productivity gains. Notwithstanding this reasonably positive assessment, Panagariya reminds us that overall, Indian industry's performance in the 1980s and 1990s has been pedestrian, particularly compared with that of services.

The poor performance of Indian industry and the stronger growth performance of Chinese industry form the backdrop for Panagariya's final section, on future policy. He discusses four issues: domestic policies bearing on trade; autonomous liberalization; regional trade agreements; and India's participation in multilateral negotiations. With regard to the first, the central question for Panagariya is why Indian industry's response to liberalization has been more sluggish than China's. Panagariya attributes this in part to differences in economic structure but also to differences in the two countries' domestic policies. He argues that it is easiest to expand trade in industrial products, and it is easier to do so if the industrial sector represents a large share of national value added. As far back as 1980, the share of industry in China was 48.5 percent, while in India it was half that, at 24.2 percent. Two decades later things are not very different. Panagariya makes a further interesting point: a relatively small industrial sector also reduces the capacity of the economy to absorb imports, leading to a tendency toward exchange rate appreciation (although even China has not been immune from this tendency). He concludes that it is imperative to stimulate industrial growth and cites reform in three areas as being essential: reduction of the fiscal deficit; reduction and ultimately elimination of the list of manufactured products "reserved" for small-scale industry; and reform of the country's labor laws, which make reassignment or retrenchment of workers prohibitively difficult in the so-called formal or organized sector.

Turning next to autonomous trade reform, Panagariya is critical of the view, widely held in India, that the tariff structure ought to favor final goods over intermediates. He also notes that the current tariff structure remains riddled with complexity. He urges the authorities to move quickly to a single uniform tariff of 15 percent for nonagricultural goods and to move to a uniform tariff of 5 percent by the end of the decade. With regard to agriculture, Panagariya points out that India stands to gain from autonomous tariff liberalization given its potential as an agricultural exporter. He also addresses the issue of "contingent protection," wherein India's liberal use of antidumping regulations has clearly had protectionist intent. Panagariya urges changes in the antidumping procedures currently in place and also greater use of safeguard measures, as they are applied on a nondiscriminatory basis to all trading partners.

While India has traditionally taken comfort in a multilateral rule-based system of international trade, it has more recently embarked on an ambitious program of regional trade negotiations. It has signed free trade area (FTA) agreements with Sri Lanka and Thailand and is in the advanced stages of negotiating an FTA with Singapore. Panagariya analyzes the global, regional, and domestic factors that have brought about this shift in strategy—essentially the weakening of the U.S. commitment to multilateral negotiations, together with political imperatives. Panagariya observes that for a relatively protected economy, trade diversion and the associated revenue loss should be important concerns. He is also concerned that preoccupation with FTAs diverts attention from both unilateral liberalization and multilateral negotiations, each of which yields greater return for the effort expended. However, Panagariya concedes that there is a strategic case for FTAs, both to exert leverage in the multilateral sphere and to create a template that reflects India's interests in future bilateral and multilateral negotiations. In this context he is critical of the template developed in the agreement on the South Asian Free Trade Area (SAFTA), which, in his view, is cluttered with many nontrade issues. In the specific case of a U.S.-India FTA, he believes that there is a strong case for an agreement in services, with mutually beneficial exchange of market access.

The paper ends with a discussion of India's interests in ongoing multilateral trade negotiations. Panagariya's main point is that India has a strong interest in successful conclusion of the Doha Round and could agree to the U.S. proposal aimed at eliminating tariffs on industrial goods by 2015. As noted before, India also has interests in improved market access in agriculture; given the considerable water in its bound tariffs, some concessions should be possible, particularly if accompanied by reductions in subsidies by rich countries.

The 1990s and the new millennium have seen a massive proliferation of preferential trade arrangements (PTAs), which typically lead to free trade among two or more countries, as, for example, under the North American Free Trade Agreement (NAFTA). Until recently, Asian countries had more or less stayed away from these arrangements, but this is changing rapidly, with many countries in the region now forging free trade areas. In their paper, Robert Lawrence and Rajesh Chadha assess the likelihood and benefits of the negotiation of a free trade area between India and the United States. Like Panagariya, Lawrence also embeds his discussion of

India's trade policy within the framework of the larger Indian reform effort.[1] Following Ahluwalia, he characterizes Indian reform since 1991 as incremental, not radical.[2] While there has been deepening consensus about the broad direction of reform within the policy elite, excessive clarity on endpoints and on the pace of transition is seen to be politically risky. Trade policy reform has been an important part of this liberalization effort, and it has been similarly characterized by a clear direction but fitful implementation and shifting promises as to endpoints.

Lawrence accepts that this strategy has been relatively successful in producing steady growth without major policy reversals or financial crises over the last decade. Yet, like Panagariya, he notes that trade reform is a job only half done. India's tariff rates remain among the world's highest, and there remain significant barriers to foreign investment. Within India, there continues to be political resistance to liberalization. Lawrence asks what the best trade and reform strategy for India is now, given the tasks yet to be accomplished.

Lawrence articulates three options available to India at this time: continued incremental unilateralism dictated, as in the past, by domestic concerns and feasibility; more active engagement with multilateral negotiations through the World Trade Organization (WTO); and what he calls a multitrack approach, whereby deeper bilateral free trade agreements complement the first two channels. Within this larger context the specific question he explores in depth is what role might be played by an FTA between India and the United States. He recognizes that consideration of such an FTA is at best at a nascent stage in official circles and that it is far from being an idea whose time has come. Nonetheless, his core thesis is that given India's domestic reform goals, a multitrack approach centered on a U.S.-India FTA would be superior to excessive reliance on the WTO, given likely outcomes under the ongoing Doha Round. This is the argument that the paper attempts to substantiate.

Lawrence first considers a purely defensive motive for such a FTA. From this perspective, the key issue is to establish a legal and institutional framework for keeping trade in information technology (IT) services free. Noting the rapid growth in India's export of such services, Lawrence cites studies that suggest that this trade is still in its infancy. Given that the

1. As indicated in the paper, Rajesh Chadha is responsible primarily for measuring the quantitative aspects of a possible India-China free trade arrangement and is not responsible for the qualitative views expressed in the paper. Accordingly, in this summary only Lawrence is referred to, except when the simulations are discussed.

2. M. S. Ahluwalia. "Economic Reforms in India since 1991: Has Gradualism Worked?" *Journal of Economic Perspectives* 16, no. 3 (2002): 67–88.

United States is currently the destination of two-thirds of India's IT services exports—and that this share could well be maintained—trade between the United States and India has the potential to become one of the most dynamic examples of trade in global commerce.

Will this growth be allowed to take place? Protectionist pressures in the United States already are strong. Outsourcing is headline news in the United States, and federal and state governments are taking politically visible stands to restrict the practice under government contracts. While some of this is undoubtedly election year politics, preserving access for India in the U.S. market is a genuine challenge. Lawrence explores various options available to India to preserve its access, including through the General Agreement on Trade in Services (GATS) agreement within the WTO. He notes that GATS operates on a positive list approach, which can create some ambiguity as to what forms of market access have been bound. By contrast, services liberalization in U.S. bilateral agreements already uses a negative list approach: trade is allowed unless it has specifically been prohibited.

Lawrence then explores the possibility, from the U.S. perspective, of an FTA with India. He notes that the United States first moved away from exclusive reliance on multilateral negotiations as far back as the 1980s, when it signed FTAs with Canada and Israel, followed by NAFTA in 1993. Under the Bush administration the pace of negotiation of bilateral agreements has accelerated dramatically. Agreements with Chile, Singapore, and Jordan have been implemented; those involving the Central American Free Trade Area (CAFTA), Morocco, and Australia have been completed; and numerous others are either under active negotiation or planned.

In this environment Lawrence believes that an FTA with India would be seen by the U.S. authorities as being of great strategic interest in the larger U.S. negotiating strategy but also politically difficult to achieve, given the current mood in Congress. But he is skeptical of the possibility that such an agreement could be restricted to services alone—as proposed, for example, by Panagariya and by a recent task force of the Council on Foreign Relations. The United States is unlikely to forgo the opportunity of obtaining preferential access for the exports of its goods to the Indian market. In addition, dropping all goods trade in an agreement with India would create a difficult precedent for the United States in its other FTA negotiations, in which, with few exceptions, there have not been sectoral opt-outs.

Accordingly, in his discussion Lawrence deals with the case for a comprehensive U.S.-India FTA with most of the features of those that the United States already has concluded. These include a negative list for services; investment provisions with a few sectoral exclusions; full national treatment for U.S. companies; intellectual property rules that might be more comprehensive than those in the WTO; and additional provisions relating to labor, environmental standards, technical barriers, and government procurement. While the phase-in periods may differ for the two sides, once the agreement was fully implemented (generally in fifteen years), the obligations would be symmetric.

Lawrence readily concedes that willingness to sign an FTA agreement of this scope with the United States would be a radical departure for India in a number of respects. While much Indian trade liberalization has been unilateral, India has so far been a strong advocate of multilateral trading rules, but there too its efforts have concentrated on obtaining special and differential treatment for developing countries. As Panagariya has also noted, India has only lately entered the game of bilateral FTAs, so far with countries in Asia, but even in terms of goods trade these have not been comprehensive. A U.S.-India FTA would have major implications for India's trade and domestic policies. It is the positive (or offensive) case for such a radical shift that Lawrence next examines.

He starts by offering some hypotheses on the political economy of liberalization. At the beginning, an opportunistic and piecemeal approach may be necessary to create constituencies for liberalization. But unilateralism carries the risk of reversal, and such policy uncertainty can inhibit the private investment decisions needed to shift the economy in the direction of its comparative advantage. Trade agreements, whether bilateral, regional, or multilateral, can impart credibility to commitments by the home government, making it more likely that liberalization will be successful. Such enhanced credibility is not costless, however. In contrast to an incremental approach, a comprehensive agreement means that many political battles have to be conducted simultaneously. This drawback can be offset by the fact of reciprocity, which can be used to develop coalitions of exporters who favor the trade reform. A further set of allies is provided by proponents of domestic reform, who can argue that the domestic reforms necessary for domestic growth can also deliver improved access to international markets. Lawrence believes that such a strategy was followed by the Chinese in connection with their accession to the WTO.

If these are some of the benefits of comprehensive reciprocal agreements, the question of what type of reciprocal agreements, multilateral or bilateral, remains. This is the choice addressed by Lawrence in the remainder of the paper. In making his assessment, Lawrence uses as a yardstick the impact of each of the two routes in assisting India to undertake changes in its own interest while avoiding constraints that have the potential to damage its welfare.

In order to assess the impact of a U.S.-India FTA, Lawrence examines some of the FTAs that the United States has recently negotiated. His review makes it clear that the institutional changes needed in the Indian economy would indeed be deep but in most areas they would prod Indian policymakers to move in directions that are inherently desirable. A particular concern of Indian policymakers is the introduction of labor and environmental standards through an FTA, and Lawrence clears up several misconceptions in this area. Recent bilateral agreements place the emphasis on each government enforcing its own domestic environmental and labor laws and not weakening those laws or reducing protections to encourage trade or investment. While these obligations are backed by the dispute settlement provisions of the agreements, trade measures may not be used to retaliate. On balance, implementing a U.S.-India FTA at this time would probably help to bolster and accelerate many dimensions of economic reform, but Lawrence notes that the benefits depend crucially on taking a range of complementary actions. Failure to do so could lead to conditions that were worse than before.

Lawrence then examines whether a successful conclusion to the Doha Round could deliver equivalent benefits to the cause of Indian reform. In so doing he notes that those who argue for exclusive reliance on multilateral liberalization compare actual FTAs with an idealized version of multilateral liberalization. But actual achievement under multilateral liberalization is heavily conditioned by the specific rules of trade negotiations, which may not actually result in significant domestic liberalization at all. As a developing country, India benefits from the "special and differential treatment" provisions of the General Agreement on Tariffs and Trade (GATT), while benefiting from the most-favored nation provisions of the multilateral system. An additional institutional feature is the gap between applied and bound tariffs, which is particularly large where agricultural goods are concerned. A final feature is what Lawrence (following Jagdish Bhagwati) calls "first difference" reciprocity, where the offers made by each nation are measured against their protection levels at the beginning of the round.

Taking these elements into account and reviewing the actual performance of past rounds in reducing industrial tariffs, Lawrence comes to the strong conclusion that the current WTO system actually impedes a developing country like India from using WTO agreements to support meaningful liberalization; he also believes that the diffuse reciprocity involved in the most-favored nation system is not a strong catalyst for rallying exporter interests in favor of import liberalization.

Having provisionally concluded that an FTA would be of greater assistance than exclusive reliance on multilateral negotiations, Lawrence then explores the benefits to India of blending the two approaches in what he calls a multitrack approach. In his view, a U.S.-India FTA would certainly make India a more attractive negotiating partner for third countries hoping to match the access obtained by U.S. firms. Equally, assuming that it preceded the conclusion of the Doha Round, willingness to sign an FTA with the United States would also improve India's negotiating credibility in the multilateral sphere. India could then challenge developed countries to improve their own offers dramatically by indicating a willingness to engage in extensive multilateral liberalization itself. A comprehensive FTA with India would also be of strategic importance to the United States in its current policy of competitive liberalization. This would strengthen India's hand in its negotiations with the United States, while strengthening the U.S. hand in negotiating with other significant but reluctant partners.

The paper ends with some quantitative welfare simulations undertaken by Lawrence's coauthor, Rajesh Chadha of the NCAER, using a computable general equilibrium model of world production and trade developed by the NCAER and the University of Michigan. The simulations deal only with the impact of liberalization on trade in goods. The model is designed to capture the long-run impact of an agreement. More crucially, it is a real model that holds employment and the trade balance constant; as such it captures the second-round adjustments needed to restore full employment in the economy following an initial trade shock.

A U.S.-India FTA is compared first with the current situation and then with a number of counterfactuals. The results reveal that aggregate welfare gains are greatest under multilateral liberalization, next greatest under unilateral liberalization in each country, and least under a bilateral FTA, but they note that even in the last case the effects are positive. The results also point out asymmetries between the United States and India in unilateral and multilateral liberalization, given the differences in the openness of the two economies. Indian and world welfare both rise significantly when India liberalizes unilaterally, while for the United States the greatest welfare gains flow from multilateral liberalization.

Lawrence concludes that the more difficult decision facing India today is whether to opt for reciprocal approaches in lieu of the unilateral approach that it has traditionally pursued. There are gains in credibility to be achieved, but these could entail reduced policy space and require a significant agenda of complementary reform to achieve their full effect. Should India choose to pursue the reciprocal route, he suggests a U.S.-India FTA as worthy of serious consideration, precisely because of its comprehensive and deep character.

India has had a turnaround in its balance of payments in recent years, with a swing in the current account from a deficit to a surplus and rapid growth in the capital account surplus. It has used those inflows to build up substantial holdings of foreign exchange reserves that now stand at $120 billion. While the initial reserve accumulation was welcome insurance against the risk of unanticipated future outflows, the current level is adequate to meet any foreseeable challenge, and policymakers need to develop an exchange policy that goes beyond simple reserve accumulation. Should India accelerate the process of capital account liberalization, perhaps allowing the export of capital by residents? Should it allow an appreciation of the exchange rate or speed up the liberalization of the trade regime? Above all, how should the exchange policy be integrated with the broader concerns of domestic economic policy?

In their paper, Vijay Joshi and Sanjeev Sanyal provide a broad review of the external aspects of Indian macroeconomic policy over the past decade. They use that review as the backdrop for a discussion of the policy options open to India in the future, posing the question of how economic policy should respond to the continuation of the strong balance-of-payments position of recent years. In their answer, they argue in favor of a combination of accelerated import liberalization on the external side and domestic fiscal consolidation. In particular, they view trade liberalization, which provides a means of absorbing continued capital inflows without constraining the competitiveness of the export sector, as an alternative to exchange rate appreciation.

In reviewing the economic events of the 1990s, they emphasize the degree to which India relied on an extensive system of capital controls. Foreign direct investment and portfolio investment inflows were gradually liberalized and foreign investors could freely repatriate their investments, but capital outflows by residents were prohibited. Offshore borrowing and lending by Indian companies and banks were also strictly limited. The capital controls allowed Indian monetary policy to maintain a relatively fixed exchange rate regime with minimal conflict with domestic economic policy. India's restrictive measures on the capital account, reluctance to permit short-term foreign borrowing, and strong accumulation of foreign exchange reserves allowed it to escape any serious consequences from the Asian financial crises.

By accumulating foreign reserves over the decade, India passed up the opportunity to use capital inflows to finance a larger current account deficit.

Joshi and Sanyal argue that this policy imposed relatively small costs in terms of forgone investment and growth. The reserve accumulation averaged 1.2 percent of GDP annually, and even if all of the accumulation had been used alternatively to purchase investment goods, the incremental impact on economic growth would have been small. This conclusion is in sharp contrast to the claims of others that foreign reserve accumulation imposed large costs in terms of forgone growth.

Overall, Joshi and Sanyal believe that the external aspects of Indian economic policy were well executed during the 1990s. However, the ample level of foreign exchange reserves and the continuation of strong capital inflows present a more difficult policy choice going forward. The current policy of sterilized intervention in exchange markets has outlived its usefulness, and further additions to reserves will impose rising fiscal costs with few benefits. At the same time, the authors oppose exchange rate appreciation because of its negative impact on export competitiveness. An intermediate policy of continued intervention in the foreign exchange market but without any attempt at sterilization would translate into an easing of domestic monetary policy and higher growth in the short run. However, they fear that it would quickly lead to increased inflationary pressures, and the resulting rise in the real exchange rate would be as unattractive from the export perspective as outright nominal appreciation.

Instead, Joshi and Sanyal argue for a mixed strategy that combines a faster rate of import liberalization on the external side with domestic fiscal consolidation. A rise in imports would provide a means of absorbing the excess capital inflows with no loss of export competitiveness. Since India's tariff structure is among the world's highest, the policy would also intensify the competitive pressures on the import-competing industries and strengthen incentives to raise productivity. The constraining factor is the negative public revenue impact of reductions in tariffs, but that is consistent with greater reliance on an expanded value-added tax to meet the revenue needs of both the central government and the states.

They stress the importance of action on the fiscal side because of fear that maintaining the large deficit will crowd out investment and slow the pace of growth in future years. A combination of fiscal contraction and monetary expansion would produce lower interest rates with strong incentives for growth. The greater foreign and public saving would provide the resources necessary to support the higher rate of investment and growth.

Finally, Joshi and Sanyal reflect a strong shift in professional sentiment in their lack of enthusiasm for further liberalization of the capital account.

They argue against liberalization of the restrictions on capital outflows by residents, based on the risks they pose in the event of adverse future shocks. In fact, they conclude with a willingness to use Chilean-type taxes in the event that inflows of foreign capital should intensify.

In a paper that is largely devoted to a positive analysis of the experience with exchange rate management in India, Ila Patnaik examines the reactions of the monetary authority to the changing external environment. The exchange rate plays a central role in the economic policy of most emerging economies, as monetary policy is torn between a focus on stabilizing the domestic economy and maintaining an exchange rate that is consistent with export competitiveness. In a world of capital controls, it is possible to manage both of these goals simultaneously, but once the economy is fully open to the free inflow and outflow of capital, monetary policy must choose between the external and the internal balance. Over the 1990s, Indian monetary policy operated in a transitional phase, as it only gradually reduced its restrictions on capital account transactions. Since 1993, the external value of the rupee has been determined by market forces, but the central bank intervenes extensively to maintain a stable rate vis-à-vis the U.S. dollar. The continuation of partial controls on capital flows provides some room for an independent monetary policy.

Patnaik focuses on two periods of substantial net capital inflows that necessitated large-scale intervention by the central bank to prevent currency appreciation. The first was a relatively short episode extending from June 1993 to November 1994; the second lasted from August 2001 until at least the middle of 2004. Despite official protestations to the contrary, Patnaik's empirical analysis demonstrates that India is best characterized as operating a tightly pegged exchange rate over the full period. Her paper explores the extent to which the focus on the exchange rate limited the operation of a monetary policy directed at stabilizing the domestic economy.

The first period began with an easing of the restrictions on inflows of portfolio capital in early 1993. The result was a sharp surge of capital inflows and private expectations of a rise in the exchange rate. However, the Reserve Bank of India (RBI) chose to purchase a large portion of the inflow to prevent appreciation. The bank also acted to sterilize a portion of the inflow, financing some purchases through the sale of government debt. However, the lack of liquidity in the bond market restricted the efforts at sterilization and led the bank to finance much of its purchases through an expansion of reserve money. It attempted to offset the inflationary effects of a rapid growth in the monetary base through a series of increases in the cash reserve ratio. However, the net result was still a significant acceleration of growth in the money supply and, at least in the early months, a decline in interest rates. Despite the small size of the external sector and the limited openness of the capital account, the episode represented India's first experience with the partial loss of monetary policy autonomy, dictated by the need to intervene in the currency market.

The second episode, beginning in the summer of 2001, was triggered by a swing in the current account from deficit to surplus. Increased capital inflows played a significant role only in later years. Again, the RBI intervened to prevent appreciation, and the exchange rate actually depreciated slightly up to mid-2002. This time around, the market for debt was considerably more developed. The bank was able to finance nearly all of its purchases of foreign currency through the sale of government debt instruments, avoiding use of the currency reserve ratio. There was little or no acceleration of growth in reserve money, and the growth of a broad-based measure of the money supply (M3) actually slowed. However, the RBI did not attempt to hold the exchange rate completely fixed after the summer of 2002, opting instead for a small but steady appreciation. Capital inflows also began to accelerate at the same time, perhaps motivated by currency speculation.

The two episodes differ in the extent to which the RBI was able to engage in sterilizing interventions to avoid any conflict with its policies for domestic stabilization. Patnaik's review suggests that controls on the capital account are still sufficient to permit considerable discretion in the conduct of domestic monetary policy. To date, Indian policymakers have opted to prevent the capital inflow from translating into a current account deficit. However, the sustainability of the bank's interventions in future years is debatable because the fiscal costs of accumulating additional reserves are rising.

The paper by Kenneth Kletzer offers a third perspective on India's exchange rate regime, focusing on the issue of capital account convertibility. Should India accelerate the pace of its liberalization of capital account transactions? Kletzer views this as a particularly critical decision in light of a history of severe repression of domestic financial markets. He points to numerous international examples in which liberalization led to large financial inflows followed by equally abrupt outflows and financial crisis. In his paper, he lays out the conditions necessary to achieve a successful policy for capital account liberalization.

Kletzer begins with a review of the potential benefits and costs of capital mobility. On the benefits side, he points to five factors. First, there are gains from trade in commodities across time, just as there are gains from contemporaneous trade in goods and services. Second, international financial integration, which brings direct foreign investment, may raise the growth rate by raising productivity growth. Third, such integration allows the sharing of risk between savers and investors. Domestic residents are able to diversify risk, which may raise the saving rate. Fourth, the presence of these flows may reduce output and consumption volatility. Finally, capital account liberalization may provide a means for forcing an end to financially repressive policies. The ability of resources to move across borders in response to unsustainable fiscal or financial policies may impose discipline on public authorities.

The principal cost of an open capital account is the possibility that a crisis may occur in the form of capital flight, leading to large depreciation, large-scale bank failures, or both. For example, under a pegged exchange rate regime, a realization or expectation of monetization of public sector budget deficits that is inconsistent with the pegged rate of currency depreciation forces its abandonment sooner or later in a sudden outflow of international reserves. Such depreciations may then spill over into bank failures if the banks have large, unhedged foreign currency–denominated liabilities and home currency–denominated assets.

To date, the international empirical evidence on the growth effects of capital account liberalization for emerging markets is inconclusive. The bottom line is that countries tend to benefit from liberalization when they can better absorb capital inflows by having higher levels of human capital, more developed domestic financial markets, and greater transparency in financial and corporate governance and regulation. On the other hand, the opening of the capital account in the presence of significant macroeconomic imbalances reduces net gains and raises the prospects of subsequent crisis.

Turning to India, Kletzer notes that India had a relatively unrestricted financial system until the 1960s. Starting in the 1960s, interest rate restrictions and liquidity requirements were adopted and progressively tightened. The government established the State Bank of India, a public sector commercial bank, and went on to nationalize the largest private commercial banks toward the end of the decade. Through the 1970s and into the 1980s, credit directed to "priority" sectors constituted a rising share of domestic lending and interest rate subsidies became common for targeted industries.

With the start of economic reforms in 1985, steps were taken toward internal financial liberalization, mainly in banking. The government began to reduce financial controls by partially deregulating bank deposit rates, though that step was partially reversed in 1988. However, in later years the government simultaneously began to relax ceilings on lending rates of interest. Progressive relaxation of restrictions on both bank deposit and lending rates of interest and the reduction of directed lending was under way by 1990.

Liberalization accelerated after the 1991 crisis, when important steps were taken toward external liberalization. Specifically, both direct foreign investment and portfolio investment were progressively opened. A major development was full current account convertibility of the rupee under IMF Article 8 in August 1994. In the subsequent years, sectoral caps on direct foreign investment and restrictions on portfolio borrowing and foreign equity ownership were relaxed. Currently, foreign investment income is fully convertible to foreign currency for repatriation. External commercial borrowing has been relaxed, but it is regulated with respect to maturities and interest rate spreads. Effective restrictions continue on the acquisition of foreign financial assets by residents and on currency convertibility for capital account transactions.

According to Kletzer, there remain four macro-cum-financial vulnerabilities that must be considered in evaluating the case for full capital account convertibility: high public debt and fiscal deficit; financial repression; weakness in the banking sector; and a tendency to peg the exchange rate. India's external debt is low in relation to its foreign exchange reserves, so there is less to fear on that front.

Using two alternative measures of the real interest rate, Kletzer evaluates the sustainability of the current public debt as a proportion of GDP and concludes that without a major reduction in the primary deficit (fiscal deficit minus interest payment on the debt) it cannot be stabilized at its current level of 82 percent. Based on one measure, the current primary deficit of 3.6 percent must be turned into a primary surplus of 0.8 percent for the debt to be sustained at its current level. On the deficit, Kletzer points out that the combined central and state government budget balances understate total public sector liabilities. Unfunded pension liabilities, various contingent liabilities, and guarantees on the debt issued by loss-making public enterprises (most notably state electricity boards) must also be taken into account.

High levels of public debt and deficits have been sustained partially through financial repression, which has been a central aspect of the Indian fiscal system for decades. Capital controls provide the public sector with a captive capital market and allow lower-than-opportunity rates of interest for government debt. Kletzer estimates that the implicit subsidy to the government averaged 8.2 percent of GDP from 1980 to 1993 and 1.6 percent from 1994 to 2002. Thus the liberalization of the 1990s is clearly reflected in the substantial reversal, though not elimination, of financial repression. In the same vein, the government collected seignorage revenues that averaged 2 percent over the entire 1980–2002 period, but 1.4 percent from 1997 to 2002. The decrease in public sector revenue from financial repression is large, indicating some significant progress in financial policy reform.

Policies of financial repression hamper domestic financial intermediation and raise the vulnerability of the banking system to crisis as international financial integration increases. At the end of March 2003, according to the Reserve Bank of India, the gross nonperforming assets of the commercial banks were 9.5 percent of bank advances; taking provisions into account, this figure drops to around 4.5 percent. Directed credit to priority sectors accounted for 31 percent of commercial bank assets but about 40 percent of nonperforming assets of the banks. At 2 percent of GDP, nonprovisioned and nonperforming assets are not large. But some researchers estimate that the actual figure may be twice as large as the official one. Banks also suffer from unhedged interest rate exposure arising from the large holdings of government debt (currently 40 percent of their total assets) and the liberalization of deposit rates.

Finally, capital controls allow policymakers to manage the nominal exchange rate and influence domestic rates of interest as independent objectives of monetary policy. Past exchange rate management in India displays resistance to currency appreciation. The adoption of a floating exchange rate, albeit managed relatively tightly, reduces crisis vulnerability. The government can resist exchange rate movements while not offering any exchange parity guarantee, as under a pegged exchange rate (or crawling peg or narrow target zone). The uncertainty that is induced, especially for short-term rates of change in the exchange rate, could lead to private sector hedging against currency risk. A possible source of concern is the revealed tendency of the government to lean against exchange rate movements that could result in sudden losses of reserves and capital account reversals under an open capital account.

Kletzer concludes that the initial conditions for capital account convertibility in India are strong, with the exception of public finance. India's very low short-maturity foreign debt exposure, low overall foreign debt, large stock of foreign reserves, and flexible exchange rate place the Indian economy in a strong position by international standards. The average maturities of foreign and public debt could be expected to fall with international financial integration, but a prospective rise in short-term debt does not in itself justify capital controls. The stock of foreign reserves exceeds the current level of short-term external debt several fold. Liberalization and further opening of the banking system requires regulatory improvement, but the present level of nonperforming assets in the banking system is not excessive in comparison with the emerging markets.

In concluding, Kletzer notes two aspects of fiscal vulnerability relevant to financial integration. First, the primary deficit and the need to amortize public debt constitute the government borrowing requirement that would need to be financed on international terms under an open capital account. Second, the banking system holds the overwhelming majority of the public debt; with international financial integration, these become risky assets. Any gain to the government from currency depreciation or rising interest spreads on public debt would be matched by losses by the banks. These holdings pose a threat to the banking system, and a capital account crisis could begin with the exit of domestic depositors. In this case, deposit insurance could reduce the exposure of the banking system to crisis. Limiting the contingent liability of the government created by deposit insurance so that it just offsets public sector capital gains requires institutional reform to ensure successful prudential regulation.

The final paper, by Abhijit Banerjee, Shawn Cole, and Esther Duflo, addresses some of the concerns raised above about India's domestic financial system. In comparison with its peers at similar stages of development, India has an advanced and extensive banking system, with branches throughout rural and urban areas, providing credit not only to industry but also to a significant number of farmers. As in many other developing countries, publicly held banks are by far the largest players, and financial sector reforms have become major policy goals. The authors evaluate the performance of India's banking sector in terms of its provision of financial intermediation and its contribution to the achievement of a variety of "social goals." They also offer a comparison of the performance of public and private sector banks.

The paper begins with an overview of banking in India, including the two episodes of bank nationalization in 1969 and 1980. Because the Indian government used a strict policy rule (based on the asset base of banks) to determine which banks were nationalized and which were left in the private sector, India offers an ideal case study in the relative performance and behavior of public and private sector banks.

A primary rationale for bank nationalization was to increase the flow of credit, both in general and to targeted "priority sectors" such as agriculture and small-scale industry. In the first section of the analysis, Banerjee and colleagues use detailed records from a public sector bank to determine whether there is "under-lending" to priority sector firms in the Indian financial system. They define under-lending as a situation in which the marginal product of capital for a firm is higher than the rate of interest it is currently paying. A change in lending regulations that increased the amount of credit issued by banks to one group of firms but not another allowed them to estimate the effect of additional credit on output and profits. They find a strong, positive effect of the change, suggesting that the firms are indeed credit constrained.

Enhancing credit supply was a primary goal of nationalization: while the performance of this public sector bank was not impressive, perhaps private sector banks fared worse? Using a regression discontinuity approach, the authors compared the propensity of public and private banks to lend to borrowers in several sectors of the economy: agriculture, small-scale industry, and the composite sector called trade, transport, and finance. They find that public sector banks did lend substantially more to agricultural borrowers than did private sector banks. Contrary to popular wisdom, however, they find that once bank size is taken into account, public sector banks lend no more to small-scale industry than do private sector banks.

Nor does bank nationalization appear to have increased the overall speed of financial development. The authors find that in the period 1980–91, nationalized and private banks of similar asset size grew at about the same rate. However, in the more liberalized period of 1992–2000, old private sector banks grew 8 percent more than public sector banks. (The lack of attention to new private sector banks is explained by the fact that there are simply not enough data at this stage to allow meaningful analysis.)

To gain further insight into under-lending and a low level of financial development, the authors again study the loan information from the same public sector bank. Under government regulations, loan officers are required to calculate credit limits on the basis of firm size (as measured by turnover) rather than profitability; though the rules do allow for some flexibility on the part of the loan officer, the authors find that in most cases loan officers simply reapproved the previous year's limit. Because of inflation, real credit thus typically *shrinks*. Firms that are growing rapidly or that have profitable opportunities are not rewarded with additional credit, nor are poorly performing firms cut off.

The authors then turn to potential explanations for the reluctance of loan officers to lend. Public employees are subject to strict anticorruption legislation, and bank officers have expressed concern that if they issue a new loan that subsequently goes bad, they could be charged with corruption, denied promotion, fired, or even put in jail. The authors test this hypothesis by examining whether a corruption charge against a bank employee in a specific bank led to a reduction in overall lending by all loan officers in that bank. They find that it did: corruption charges led to a reduction in lending of approximately 3 percent compared with lending of other banks. That decline lasted approximately twenty-four months.

Critics of public enterprises are quick to point out that since employees tend not to have a stake in the performance of the enterprise, they may tend to exert less effort. For public bankers, this may mean making guaranteed safe loans to the government rather than spending time and energy on screening new clients and monitoring existing ones. To test this possibility, the authors compare how public sector banks in low- and high-growth states responded to a change in spread between lending rates and the rate at which the government was willing to borrow. They find that banks in low-growth states were more inclined to make "low-effort" loans to the government when the spread increased.

The final exercise was to examine the contentious issue of nonperforming assets, bank failures, and bailouts. The official rates of nonperforming loans in public sector banks tend to be higher than those in private sector banks, but because those numbers are notoriously unreliable, the authors instead compare the fiscal costs of bailing out failed private banks with the costs of recapitalizing poorly performing public sector banks. Using data starting from the first nationalization, they identify twenty-one cases of bank failure between 1969 and 2000 and compute the costs imposed on the government in rupees at 2000 prices. That sum is compared with the substantial cost of recapitalization of public sector banks in the 1990s. Controlling for size, the cost of the bank failures appears to be slightly higher than recapitalization, implying a small advantage for public sector banks. However, since recapitalization expenses are recurring, in all likelihood the public sector banks represent a greater cost to the treasury.

The authors conclude by arguing that the evidence suggests a tentative case for privatizing public sector banks. Privatization is not a panacea, however, and both public and private sector banks could benefit from significant internal reform. Liberalization and privatization should be accompanied by strong regulation to ensure the continued existence of social banking. But in net terms, the reduction in agency problems, the increased flexibility, and the reliance on private rather than public incentives to limit corruption and NPAs should make for a more dynamic banking system that is more responsive to borrowers' needs.

ARVIND PANAGARIYA

Columbia University

India's Trade Reform

Among developing countries, India's growth experience during the past five decades has been unique. Unlike many of its East and Southeast Asian neighbors, India did not grow at "miracle" rates that exceeded 6 percent and reached as high as 10 percent. Nor, unlike Africa and Latin America, did it suffer periods of prolonged stagnation or decline. For three of the five decades (1950–80), India's economy grew steadily at the so-called Hindu rate of $3\frac{1}{2}$ percent a year in real terms, and during the next two decades it grew at annual rates between 5 and 6 percent.

Although the credit for this steady growth without prolonged stagnation or decline goes to the macroeconomic stability and policy credibility that the government provided, the blame for the relatively low rate of growth, especially during 1950–80, must be assigned to the myriad microeconomic distortions and heavy state intervention that straitjacketed India's entrepreneurs.[1] The government effectively stamped out domestic competition through strict investment licensing and eliminated foreign competition through strict import licensing. It was only during the second half of the 1980s that the government began to loosen its grip on investment and import licensing; this was followed by a more systematic and comprehensive opening up in the 1990s and after.

This paper discusses India's external sector policies, focusing especially on the past two decades; the impact of these policies on trade flows, efficiency, and growth; and the future direction trade policies must take. It begins with a discussion of the major policy developments in trade in both goods and services. This is followed by a discussion of the evolution of trade flows—their growth, composition, and direction. The next section describes the impact of trade liberalization on efficiency and growth.

The author thanks Pranab Bardhan, Suman Bery, Govinda Rao, Jagadeesh Sivadasan, and participants in the India Policy Forum 2004 in New Delhi for excellent comments on an earlier draft.

1. Policy changes, whether good or bad, have been largely predictable in India. Consultations with the relevant parties, extensive discussions, and special committee reports have usually preceded all major policy actions.

The penultimate section considers policy options available to India and the most appropriate course for the country. The final section concludes.

The Reforms to Date

The history of India's external sector policies since independence can be divided into three phases: 1950–75, when the trend was toward tighter controls, culminating in virtual autarky by the end of the period; 1976–91, when some liberalization took place, especially during the last five to seven years; and from 1992 onward, when deeper and more systematic liberalization was undertaken.

Toward Virtual Autarky, 1950–75

Although the history of tariff protection in India goes further back in time, quantitative import controls were introduced in May 1940 to conserve foreign exchange and shipping during World War II.[2] Starting in 1947, however, regulation of the balance of payments became the central concern, and the government introduced explicit restrictions on the rate at which foreign exchange could be run down. From then until the launch of the First Five Year Plan in 1951, India alternated between liberalization and tighter controls. But the period covered by the first plan was one of progressive liberalization. In particular, the India Tariff (Second Amendment) Act of 1954 stepped up tariff rates for thirty-two items and paved the way for the liberalization of import quotas through additional licenses over and above normal entitlements.

A balance-of-payments crisis in 1956–57 led to a major reversal of this liberalization, as India resorted to comprehensive import controls.[3] The crisis left a sufficiently deep impression on the political leadership that it made the allocation of foreign exchange across various activities the central objective of trade and foreign exchange policy. The interaction of this objective with an ambitious, powerful, and self-interested bureaucracy produced a regime that was highly protectionist and without a clear sense of

2. This section draws heavily on part 7, especially chapters 15 and 22, of the most remarkable contribution by Jagdish Bhagwati and Padma Desai (1970), which foresaw the pitfalls of the license raj early on and offered a thorough analytical case for an open, pro-market policy regime, paying due attention to the political economy and institutional context of the time.

3. India's financial year starts on April 1 and ends on March 31. Therefore, 1956–57 covers the period from April 1, 1956, to March 31, 1957; it is also called fiscal year 1957.

economic priorities. The number of criteria to be taken into account was large—private versus public sector, small versus large enterprises, and capital versus intermediate versus consumer goods—and the number of industries across which foreign exchange had to be allocated even larger: within the machinery sector alone they included paper machinery, chemical machinery, mining machinery, tea machinery, and metallurgical machinery, to name just a few. Unsurprisingly, the process quickly degenerated into a system of ad hoc rules. As Bhagwati and Desai describe graphically, "The problem was Orwellian: all industries had priority and how was each sponsoring authority to argue that some industries had more priority than others?"[4] They conclude, "It is not surprising, therefore, that the agencies involved in determining industry-wise allocation fell back on vague notions of 'fairness,' implying *pro rata* allocations with reference to capacity installed or employment, or shares defined by past import allocations and similar other rules of thumb without any clear rationale."[5]

Under the regime that evolved, producers needed to make only minimal effort to get absolute protection against imports. The authorities applied the principle of indigenous availability, according to which the government denied the allocation of foreign exchange for importing a product if domestic import substitutes were available in sufficient quantity. Therefore all a producer needed to do to block the entry of imports of a product was to let the relevant agency know that the producer made a substitute for it in the requisite quantity. The quality of the substitute, the price at which it was supplied, and any delay in delivery were of secondary importance to the authorities.

An important switch in policy came in June 1966, when India undertook a major devaluation from 4.7 rupees to 7.5 rupees to the dollar and, alongside, took steps toward liberalization of import licensing, tariffs, and export subsidies.[6] The liberalization measures gave fifty-nine industries, covering 80 percent of output in the formal ("organized") sector, freedom to import

4. Bhagwati and Desai (1970, p. 288).

5. Bhagwati and Desai (1970, p. 290). The authors quote an unpublished doctoral thesis by Arun Shourie (1966), which offers systematic evidence supporting the hypothesis that, rather than devise a set of priorities based on proper economic criteria, the government agencies essentially fell back on simple rules of thumb. For example, the cuts imposed on various industries immediately following the Sino-Indian war in late 1962 and early 1963 were overwhelmingly uniform.

6. Some industrial de-licensing and limited decontrol of steel distribution on the recommendation of the Swaminathan Committee on Industries Development Procedures had taken place just before and after these steps on the external front. But the de-licensing was mainly aimed at reducing delays in the issuance of licenses. For details see Bhagwati and Desai (1970, p. 477).

their raw materials and components.[7] Paradoxically, however, the need to obtain a license remained. Because the licensing procedures continued to apply the principle of "indigenous availability," the actual liberalization turned out to be very limited ex post.[8]

The impetus for the devaluation and other measures had come from the World Bank, which promised a package of $900 million annually for several years to help finance the expansion of imports that would result from the liberalizing measures.[9] Unfortunately, this policy measure coincided with a second consecutive crop failure, which led to an industrial recession.[10] As a result, a large proportion of the World Bank aid remained unutilized in 1966–67. More important, the timing of the recession gave credence to the widely held and popular view that the measures forced by the World Bank were the wrong prescription in the first place. Intense domestic criticism, a political leadership that was keen to distribute export subsidies, and an industry that had learned to profit from protection came together to reverse the policy in less than two years.[11] Bhagwati and Desai describe the political economy of the reversal:

> In a very real sense, therefore, the timing of import liberalization was not ideal, in retrospect: a burgeoning economy would have increased the chances of making an effective dent in the practice of granting automatic protection to every activity. On the other hand, it was clear that it was quite naïve to expect industrialists . . . to agree to switch over to an efficient system involving competition . . . . In this, the pressure groups were often in the company of disinterested politicians (such as the Finance Minister Morarji Desai) whose thinking had also been conditioned by the planning philosophy of the earlier period: that anything which could be produced and supplied from domestic capacity must automatically be protected from imports.[12]

7. The "organized" sector in India is defined as consisting of central, state, and local administrations and public and private firms with ten or more workers if using electrical power and twenty or more workers if not using power. Firms in the organized sector are required to register with an appropriate governmental agency.

8. Bhagwati and Desai (1970, p. 483).

9. The World Bank had acted on the recommendation of the Bell mission, which also advised a shift away from industry and toward agriculture. Starting in 1960–61, the performance of Indian agriculture had deteriorated rapidly, and the aid consortium had become concerned about an impending "quiet crisis." The Bell mission was a response to that concern. For details see Joshi and Little (1994, chapter 4).

10. Industrial growth fell from 5.6 percent in 1965–66 to 2.6 percent in 1966–67 and 1.4 percent in the first three quarters of 1967–68.

11. Around this time, under pressure from the United States, the World Bank also went back on its promise of $900 million in annual aid; this further strengthened the hands of the protectionist forces, which had more or less full control of the process in any case. See Joshi and Little (1994, chapter 4).

12. Bhagwati and Desai (1970, pp. 486–87).

The late 1960s and early 1970s saw a reversal of the 1966 liberalization measures and a further tightening of the import controls. The U.S. policy of isolating Prime Minister Indira Gandhi immediately before and after the Bangladesh war in 1971 drove her further toward economic isolationism. By the mid-1970s India's trade regime had become so repressive that the share of nonoil, noncereals imports in GDP fell from an already low 7 percent in 1957–58 to 3 percent in 1975–76.

Two factors paved the way for a return to liberalization in the late 1970s, however. First, industrialists came to feel the adverse effect of the tight import restrictions on their profitability and began to lobby for liberalization of imports of the raw materials and machinery for which domestically produced substitutes did not exist. Second, improved export performance and remittances from overseas workers in the Middle East led to the accumulation of a healthy foreign exchange reserve, raising the comfort level of policymakers with respect to the effect of liberalization on the balance of payments.

Ad Hoc Liberalization: 1976–91

The new phase of liberalization began in 1976 with the reintroduction of the Open General Licensing (OGL) list, which had been a part of the original wartime regime but had become defunct as controls were tightened in the wake of the 1966 devaluation. The system operated on a positive-list basis: unless an item was on the OGL list, its importation required a license from the Ministry of Commerce. Inclusion on the OGL list did not necessarily mean that the good could be imported freely, however, since the importer usually had to be the actual user and, in the case of machinery imports, could be subject to clearance from the industrial licensing authority if the sector in which the machinery was to be employed was subject to industrial licensing.

Upon its introduction in 1976, the OGL list contained only 79 capital goods items. But by April 1988 it had expanded to cover 1,170 capital goods items and 949 intermediate inputs. By April 1990 OGL imports had come to account for approximately 30 percent of total imports.[13] Although tariff rates were raised substantially during this period, items on the OGL list were given large concessions on those rates through "exemptions," so that the tariffs did not significantly add to the restrictive effect of licensing. Mainly, they allowed the government to capture the quota rents, thus helping relieve the pressure on the budget. The government also introduced

13. See Pursell (1992).

several export incentives, especially after 1985, which partly neutralized the antitrade bias of import controls. Above all, during 1985–90 the rupee was devalued in nominal effective terms by a hefty 45 percent, leading to a real depreciation of 30 percent.

In addition, by 1990 thirty-one sectors had been freed from industrial licensing. This measure had a trade-liberalizing dimension as well, since it freed machinery imports in these sectors from industrial licensing clearance. Import flows were also helped by improved agricultural performance and by the discovery of oil, which made room for nonoil, nonfood imports, mainly machinery and intermediate inputs. As Garry Pursell, a long-time follower of India's trade regime, notes, "The available data on imports and import licensing are incomplete, out of date, and often inconsistent. Nevertheless, whichever way they are manipulated, they confirm very substantial and steady import liberalization that occurred after 1977–78 and during 1980s."[14] During 1985–90, nonoil imports grew at an annual rate of 12.3 percent.

The liberalization, complemented by expansionary fiscal policy, raised India's growth rate from the Hindu rate of approximately 3.5 percent during 1950–80 to 5.6 percent during 1981–91. The jump in the average annual growth rate was particularly significant during 1988–91, when it reached 7.6 percent. Nevertheless, the external and internal borrowing that supported the fiscal expansion was unsustainable and culminated in a balance-of-payments crisis in June 1991. This time, however, the government turned the crisis into an opportunity: instead of reversing the course of liberalization, it launched a truly comprehensive, systematic, and systemic reform program that continues to be implemented today.

Deeper and Systematic Liberalization: 1992 to Date

The collapse of the Soviet Union, the phenomenal economic rise of China following its adoption of outward-oriented policies, and India's own experience, first with protectionist policies for three decades and then with liberalization in the 1980s, finally persuaded policymakers of the merits of the policy approach that pro-market and pro–free trade economists, most notably Jagdish Bhagwati, had advocated for nearly two decades. Starting with the July 1991 budget, there was a clear switch in favor of a move toward an outward-oriented, market-based economy. The trade liberalization program initiated in the 1991 budget was comprehensive, although the pace remained gradual and there were occasional hiccups.

14. Pursell (1992, p. 441).

MERCHANDISE TRADE LIBERALIZATION. The July 1991 reforms did away with import licensing on all but a handful of intermediate inputs and capital goods. Consumer goods, accounting for approximately 30 percent of tariff lines, remained under licensing. Only a decade later, after a successful challenge by India's trading partners at the World Trade Organization (WTO), were these goods freed of licensing. Today, except for a handful of goods that are disallowed on environmental or health and safety grounds, and a few (including fertilizer, cereals, edible oils, and petroleum products) that are "canalized" (meaning they can be imported by government only), all goods may be imported without a license or other restrictions. As called for under the Uruguay Round Agreement on Agriculture, all border measures on agricultural goods have been replaced by tariffs.

As noted earlier, tariff rates in India had been raised substantially during the 1980s, so as to turn quota rents for industry into tariff revenue for the government. Accordingly, tariff revenue as a proportion of imports rose from 20 percent in 1980–81 to 44 percent in 1989–90. In 1990–91 the highest tariff rate stood at 355 percent, the simple average of all tariff rates at 113 percent, and the import-weighted average of tariff rates at 87 percent.[15] With the removal of licensing, these tariff rates became effective restrictions on imports. Therefore a major task of the reforms in the 1990s and since has been to lower tariffs.

Tariff reductions have been confined to nonagricultural, industrial goods, however. Therefore the liberalization described below applies strictly to these goods. The reduction in tariffs has been accomplished through a gradual compression of the top tariff rates, with a simultaneous rationalization of the tariff structure through a reduction in the number of tariff bands. The top rate fell to 85 percent in 1993–94 and to 50 percent in 1995–96. Despite some reversals along the way in the form of special duties and through unification of two successive bands at the higher rate, the general direction has been toward liberalization. Before the most recent elections in May 2004, the then finance minister announced that the top tariff rate would be lowered from 25 percent to 20 percent and that the Special Additional Duty (SAD), which could be as high as 4 percent, would be eliminated. The incoming government has approved this change, so that the top tariff rate on industrial goods now stands at 20 percent, with no other additional custom duties, such as the SAD, on top of this rate.

There remain exceptions to this rule, however, as evidenced by table 1, which is taken from the latest Trade Policy Review of India by the WTO.[16]

15. WTO (1998) and Panagariya (1999a).
16. WTO (2002)

TABLE 1. Tariff Structure and Average Tariff Rates by Product Type, India

Product type	No. of lines	MFN tariff rates, 1997–98			MFN tariff rates, 2001–02		
		Average (percent)	Range (percent)	Coefficient of variation	Average (percent)	Range (percent)	Coefficient of variation
All products							
By WTO definition							
Agricultural products	676	35.1	0–260	0.9	40.7	0–210	0.7
Live animals and products	81	25.4	15–45	0.6	39.8	35–100	0.4
Dairy products	20	31.5	0–35	0.3	38.0	35–60	0.2
Coffee and tea, cocoa, sugar, etc.	128	37.6	15–192	0.4	39.6	35–170	0.4
Cut flowers and plants	34	25.1	10–45	0.6	29.9	10–35	0.3
Fruit and vegetables	150	32.7	0–127	0.5	36.6	25–115	0.3
Grains	16	0.0	0–0	...	49.4	0–100	0.8
Oils, seeds, fats, and oil products	71	38.9	15–45	0.2	56.2	15–100	0.5
Beverages and spirits	31	114.8	15–260	0.8	96.9	35–210	0.8
Tobacco	9	45.0	45–45	...	35.0	35–35	...
Other agricultural products, n.e.s.[a]	136	27.8	0–45	0.5	28.1	0–50	0.4
Nonagricultural products (excl. petroleum)	4,435	35.4	0–192	0.3	31.1	0–170	0.3
Fish and fishery products	108	20.3	0–65	0.6	35.0	35–35	...
Mineral products, precious stones, etc.	335	37.5	0–45	0.3	30.6	0–55	0.3
Metals	588	32.5	10–45	0.2	32.0	5–35	0.2
Chemicals and photographic supplies	840	34.6	0–192	0.2	33.8	0–170	0.2
Leather, rubber, footwear, travel goods	146	39.8	0–45	0.3	32.1	0–35	0.2
Wood, pulp, paper, and furniture	248	30.1	0–45	0.4	29.3	0–35	0.4
Textiles and clothing	830	43.7	25–55	0.1	31.3	15–35	0.2
Transport equipment	122	41.7	3–45	0.2	40.5	3–105	0.6

Nonelectric machinery	525	27.1	10–45	0.2	25.9	0–35	0.2
Electric machinery	257	34.7	15–45	0.3	26.8	0–35	0.4
Nonagricultural products, n.e.s.	436	37.1	0–55	0.2	30.0	0–35	0.2
Petroleum	2	31.0	37–35	0.2	25.0	15–35	0.6
By sector[b]							
Agriculture and fisheries	289	26.5	0–45	0.6	33.1	0–100	0.4
Mining	105	26.2	0–45	0.5	21.9	5–55	0.5
Manufacturing	4,718	36.1	0–260	0.4	32.5	0–210	0.4
By stage of processing							
First stage	628	25.7	0–127	0.6	29.4	0–115	0.5
Semi-processed products	1,673	35.7	0–192	0.2	32.3	0–170	0.2
Fully processed products	2,812	37.3	0–260	0.4	33.0	0–210	0.5

Source: World Trade Organization (2002).

a. n.e.s., not elsewhere specified.

b. International Standard Industrial Classification, Revision 2; excludes electricity, gas, and water (one tariff line).

The table compares in detail the structure of tariffs in 2001–02 with that in 1997–98, when the top tariff rate was still 35 percent. According to the table, chemicals and photographic supplies were subject to tariff rates as high as 170 percent, and transport equipment to rates reaching 105 percent, both well beyond the official "top" tariff rate applicable to industrial goods. Within transport equipment, automobiles constitute a major potential import and are currently subject to a 60 percent duty. In addition, numerous exemptions remain, based on end-user or other criteria.[17]

In agriculture, India took essentially the same approach as the member countries of the Organization for Economic Cooperation and Development, choosing excessively high tariff bindings, ranging from 100 to 300 percent, to replace border measures agreed to be discontinued under the Uruguay Round Agreement on Agriculture. On some agricultural products such as skimmed milk powder, rice, corn, wheat, and millet, India traditionally had zero or very low bound rates. These were renegotiated under Article XXXVIII of the General Agreement on Tariffs and Trade in December 1999 in return for concessions on other products.[18] According to the WTO, India's average bound rate in agriculture is 115.2 percent.[19] For comparison, the applied most-favored-nation tariff rate was 35.1 percent in 1997–98 and 41.7 percent in 2001–02.

Traditionally, India has also restricted exports of several commodities. As part of its liberalization policy, the government began to reduce the number of products subject to export controls in 1989–90. But until the July 1991 reforms, exports of 439 items were still subject to controls, including (in declining order of severity) prohibition (185 items), licensing (55 items), quantitative ceilings (38 items), canalization (49 items), and prespecified terms and conditions (112 items). The March 1992 Export-Import Policy reduced the number of items subject to controls to 296, with prohibited items reduced to 16. The process continued thereafter, so that today export prohibitions apply to only a small number of items on health, environmental, or moral grounds, and export restrictions

17. According to the WTO (2002), there are more than 100 kinds of exemptions, each running into several pages. The general notification for exemptions has 378 entries. The WTO (2002, p. 35) notes, "The use of such exemptions not only increases the complexity of the tariff, it also reduces transparency and hampers efficiency-increasing tools such as computerization of customs."

18. For example, in its negotiations with the United States, India gave market access in apples. It has been suggested that removing or reducing the exemptions and introducing a lower and uniform most-favored-nation duty structure would be more simple and transparent, with clear implications for governance.

19. WTO (2002, table III.1).

are maintained mainly on cattle, camels, fertilizers, cereals, groundnut oil, and pulses.

The lifting of exchange controls and the elimination of overvaluation of the rupee, both of which had served as additional barriers in the traded goods sector, also accompanied the 1990s reforms. As part of the 1991 reform, the government devalued the rupee by 22 percent, from 21.2 rupees to 25.8 rupees to the dollar. In February 1992, a dual exchange rate system was introduced, which allowed exporters to sell 60 percent of their foreign exchange receipts in the free market; the rest had to be sold to the government at the lower official price. Importers were authorized to purchase foreign exchange in the open market at the higher market price, effectively ending the exchange control regime. Within a year of establishing this market exchange rate, the official exchange rate was unified with it. Starting in February 1994, many current account transactions, including all current business transactions, education, medical expenses, and foreign travel, were also permitted at the market exchange rate. These steps culminated in India accepting the International Monetary Fund's Article VIII obligations, which made the rupee officially convertible on the current account. In recent years, bolstered by the accumulation of approximately $120 billion worth of foreign exchange reserves, India has freed up many capital account transactions. Two provisions are of special significance: first, residents can remit up to $25,000 abroad every year, and second, firms can borrow freely abroad as long as the maturity of the loan is five years or more.

LIBERALIZATION OF TRADE IN SERVICES. Since 1991, India has also substantially liberalized trade in services. Traditionally, the services sector has been subject to heavy government intervention. The public sector presence has been conspicuous in the key sectors of insurance, banking, and telecommunications. Nevertheless, considerable progress has been made toward opening the door wider to participation by the private sector, including foreign investors.

Until recently insurance was a state monopoly. On December 7, 1999, the Indian parliament passed a law establishing an Insurance Regulatory and Development Authority and opening the door to private entry, including entry by foreign investors. Up to 26 percent foreign ownership of a domestic firm was permitted, provided a license was obtained from the IRDA. In the 2004–05 budget this limit was raised to 49 percent.

Although public sector banks dominate the banking sector, private sector banks are permitted to operate. Foreign direct investment (FDI) in private sector banks, up to 74 percent of ownership, is permitted under the automatic route. In addition, foreign banks are allowed to open a specified number of new branches every year. More than 25 foreign banks with full banking licenses and approximately 150 foreign bank branches are in operation today. Under the 1997 WTO Financial Services Agreement, India committed itself to permitting twelve foreign bank branches to be established each year.

The telecommunications sector has experienced much greater opening to the private sector, including foreign investors. Until the early 1990s the sector was a state monopoly. The 1994 National Telecommunications Policy provided for opening cellular as well as basic and value-added telephone services to the private sector, with foreign investors granted entry. Rapid changes in technology led to the adoption of the New Telecom Policy in 1999, which sets the current policy framework. Accordingly, in basic, cellular mobile, paging, and value-added services, and in global mobile personnel communications by satellite, FDI of up to 49 percent of ownership, subject to licensing by the Department of Telecommunications, was permitted until recently. The 2004–05 budget raised this limit to 74 percent. FDI of up to 100 percent ownership is allowed, with some conditions for Internet service providers not providing gateways (for both satellite and submarine cables), infrastructure providers providing dark fiber, electronic mail, and voice mail. Additionally, subject to licensing and security requirements and the restriction that proposals with FDI beyond 49 percent must be approved by the government, up to 74 percent foreign investment is permitted for Internet service providers with gateways, radio paging, and end-to-end bandwidth.

FDI of up to 100 percent of ownership is permitted in e-commerce. Automatic approval is available for foreign equity in software and almost all areas of electronics. Full foreign ownership is permitted in information technology units set up exclusively for exports. These units can be set up under several schemes including export-oriented units, export processing zones, special economic zones, software technology parks, and electronics hardware technology parks.

The infrastructure sector has also been opened to foreign investment. Full foreign ownership under the automatic route is permitted in projects for construction and maintenance of roads, highways, vehicular bridges, toll roads, vehicular tunnels, ports, and harbors. In projects for construction and maintenance of ports and harbors, automatic approval for foreign equity up to 100 percent is available. In projects providing support services to water transport, such as the operation and maintenance of piers and loading and the discharging of vehicles, no approval is required for foreign equity up to 51 percent. FDI up to 100 percent ownership is permitted in airports, although FDI above 74 percent requires prior approval. Foreign equity up to 40 percent and investment by nonresident Indians up to 100 percent is permitted in domestic air transport services. Only railways remain off limits to private entry.

Since 1991, several attempts have been made to bring private sector investment, including FDI, into the power sector, but without perceptible success. The most recent attempt is the Electricity Act of 2003, which replaces the three existing laws on electric power dated 1910, 1948, and 1998. The act offers a comprehensive framework for restructuring of the power sector and builds on the experience in the telecommunications sector. It attempts to introduce competition through private sector entry side by side with public sector entities in generation, transmission, and distribution. The act completely eliminates licensing requirements in generation and freely permits captive generation. Only hydroelectric projects would henceforth require clearance from the Central Electricity Authority. Distribution licensees would be free to undertake generation, and generating companies would be free to enter the distribution business. Trading has been recognized as a distinct activity, with the regulatory commissions authorized to fix ceilings on trading margins, if necessary. FDI is permitted in all three activities.

Impact on Trade Flows

The policy changes discussed above have brought with them important changes in trade flows. These can be discussed under three headings: growth in trade, the composition of trade, and its direction.

Growth in Trade

India's share in world exports of goods and services, which had declined from 2 percent at independence to 0.5 percent by the mid-1980s, bounced back to 0.8 percent by 2002.[20] Thus, since the mid-1980s, India's exports of goods and services have grown faster than world exports. Table 2 offers an overview of the evolution of India's external sector during the 1980s and 1990s compared with that of China. The numbers leave little doubt that the liberalizations of the 1990s have had a more significant impact on India's trade than those of the 1980s. Although trade has performed less

20. Trade in services refers to nonfactor services and does not include remittances.

TABLE 2. **Exports and Imports of India and China, 1980–2000**

Category[a]	Billions of current dollars			Average growth (percent per year)	
	1980	1990	2000	1980–90	1990–2000
India					
Exports of goods and services	11.2	23.0	63.8	7.4	10.7
Merchandise, f.o.b.	8.5	18.5	44.9	8.1	9.3
Manufactures	5.1	13.0	34.5	9.8	10.3
Imports of goods and services	17.8	31.5	75.7	5.9	9.2
Merchandise, c.i.f.	15.9	27.9	59.3	5.8	7.8
Capital goods	2.4	5.8	8.8	9.2	4.2
Fuel and energy	6.7	6.0	15.7	−1.0	10.0
China					
Exports of goods and services	20.2	68.0	279.6	12.9	15.2
Merchandise, f.o.b.	18.3	62.1	249.2	13.0	14.9
Manufactures	9.0	46.2	223.8	17.8	17.1
Imports of goods and services	20.9	55.5	250.7	10.3	16.3
Merchandise, c.i.f.	20.0	53.4	225.1	10.3	15.5
Capital goods	5.1	16.9	91.9	12.6	18.5
Fuel and energy	0.2	1.3	26.0	20.1	35.2

Source: World Bank (2002).
a. f.o.b., free on board; c.i.f., cost including insurance and freight.

spectacularly in India than in China, the claim by some that the 1990s did not see a perceptible shift in the growth of exports and imports is simply wrong.

As table 2 shows, exports of goods and services grew 7.4 percent a year on average in the 1980s but 10.7 percent a year during the 1990s. The pace also picked up on the imports side, with growth rising from 5.9 percent a year in the 1980s to 9.2 percent a year in the 1990s. Thus the growth rates of both exports and imports rose by 3.3 percentage points. Nevertheless, these growth rates are substantially lower than those experienced by China since its opening to the world economy. China's exports of goods and services grew at a 12.9 percent average annual rate during the 1980s and at 15.2 percent a year during the 1990s, and its imports grew at an average annual rate of 10.3 percent during the 1980s and 16.3 percent during the 1990s. These higher growth rates are reflected in the higher degree of openness achieved by China in terms of its trade-to-GDP ratio.

According to table 3, the ratio of total exports of goods and services to GDP in India nearly doubled between 1990 and 2000, rising from 7.3 percent to 14 percent. The rise was less dramatic on the import side but still significant: from 9.9 percent in 1990 to 16.6 percent in 2000. Over these ten

T A B L E 3. Indicators of Trade Openness for India and China,
1980, 1990, and 2000
Percent of GDP

Indicator	1980	1990	2000
India			
Merchandise exports	4.6	5.8	9.8
Merchandise imports	8.7	8.8	13.0
Goods and services exports	6.2	7.3	14.0
Goods and services imports	9.7	9.9	16.6
Total trade in goods and services[a]	15.9	17.2	30.6
China			
Merchandise exports	8.5	17.1	23.1
Merchandise imports	4.2	12.7	20.8
Goods and services exports	9.3	18.7	26.0
Goods and services imports	9.6	15.3	23.3
Total trade in goods and services	18.9	34.0	49.3

Source: World Bank (2002).
a. Exports plus imports.

years the ratio of total goods and services trade to GDP rose from 17.2 percent to 30.6 percent. Although this is substantially lower than the corresponding ratio of 49.3 percent for China over the same period, it is comparable to the ratio that China had achieved twelve years after its opening: 34.0 percent in 1990.

Composition of Trade

Tables 4 and 5 summarize the broad composition of merchandise exports and imports, respectively, in three periods—1987–88, 1992–93, and 2001–02—and table 6 provides details on the composition of services and transfers ("invisibles" in the official Indian terminology) for 1980–81, 1990–91, and 2001–02.[21] Table 7 provides additional details on invisibles receipts for 2001–02 and 2002–03 that are not available for other years. One can draw five important conclusions from these tables together with table 2.

First, services exports have grown more rapidly than merchandise exports. As table 2 shows, the share of services in total exports of goods and services rose from 19.6 percent in 1990 to 29.6 percent in 2000. More

21. Changes in the classification system do not allow one to go farther back than 1987–88 on a comparable basis; 1992–93 has been chosen to represent the baseline at the beginning of the reform, instead of 1991–92, because the latter was off trend as a result of the June 1991 crisis.

TABLE 4. Composition of Merchandise Exports, India,
1987–88, 1992–93, and 2001–02

Percent of total exports except as indicated

	1987–88	1992–93	2001–02
Primary products	26.1	20.9	16.1
Agriculture and allied products	21.2	16.9	13.4
Tea	3.8	1.8	0.8
Coffee	1.7	0.7	0.5
Rice	2.2	1.8	1.5
Cotton raw including waste	0.7	0.3	0.0
Tobacco	0.9	0.9	0.4
Cashews including cashew nut shell liquid	2.0	1.4	0.9
Spices	2.1	0.7	0.7
Oil Meals	1.4	2.9	1.1
Fruits and vegetables	0.8	0.6	0.5
Processed fruits, juices, misc. processed items	1.1	0.4	0.7
Marine products	3.4	3.2	2.8
Sugar and molasses	0.1	0.7	0.9
Meat and meat preparations	0.6	0.5	0.6
Other	0.5	1.0	2.1
Ores and minerals	5.0	4.0	2.8
Iron ore	3.5	2.1	0.9
Mica	0.1	0.0	0.0
Other	1.3	1.9	1.8
Manufactured goods	67.8	75.7	75.6
Leather and manufactures	8.0	6.9	4.3
Chemicals and allied products	4.7	6.6	9.2
Drugs, pharmaceuticals, and fine chemicals	2.1	2.9	4.7
Other	2.6	3.8	4.6
Plastic and linoleum products	0.4	0.8	2.2
Rubber, glass, paints, enamels and products	1.4	2.1	2.2
Engineering goods	9.5	13.4	15.7
Readymade garments	11.6	12.9	11.4
Textile yarn, fabrics, made-ups, etc.	9.0	10.3	10.1
Cotton yarn, fabrics, made-ups, etc.	7.3	7.3	6.9
Natural silk yarn, fabrics, made-ups, etc.	0.9	0.7	0.6
Other	0.8	2.2	2.5
Jute manufactures	1.5	0.7	0.3
Coir and manufactures	0.2	0.2	0.1
Handicrafts	20.2	20.4	18.8
Gems and jewelry	16.7	16.6	16.7
Carpets (handmade exclusive silk)	2.1	2.3	0.8
Works of art (exclusive floor coverings)	1.4	1.5	1.3
Sports goods	0.4	0.2	0.2
Others	0.9	1.3	1.1
Petroleum products	4.1	2.6	4.8
Other	1.9	0.8	3.5
Total exports (billions of dollars)	12.1	18.5	43.8

Source: Author's calculations using data from Reserve Bank of India (2002, table 124).

TABLE 5. Composition of Merchandise Imports, India, 1987–88, 1992–93, and 2001–02

Percent of total imports except as indicated

	1987–88	1992–93	2001–02
Bulk imports	40.9	44.9	39.4
Petroleum, crude and products	18.2	27.9	27.2
Bulk consumption goods	6.6	2.3	4.0
Cereals and cereal preparations	0.3	1.5	0.0
Edible oils	4.4	0.3	2.6
Pulses	1.1	0.5	1.3
Sugar	0.9	0.0	0.0
Other bulk items	16.1	14.7	8.2
Fertilizers	2.3	4.5	1.3
Crude	0.6	0.7	0.3
Sulphur and unroasted iron pyrites	0.8	0.6	0.1
Manufactured	0.8	3.2	0.9
Nonferrous metals	2.9	1.8	1.3
Paper, paperboards, manufactures, including newsprint	1.2	0.8	0.9
Crude rubber, including synthetic and reclaimed	0.5	0.4	0.3
Pulp and waste paper	1.1	0.6	0.6
Metalliferrous ores, metal scrap, etc.	2.2	3.0	2.2
Iron and steel	5.9	3.6	1.6
Non-bulk imports	59.1	55.1	60.6
Capital goods	29.5	20.7	18.1
Manufactures of metals	0.7	0.7	0.8
Machine tools	1.0	0.8	0.4
Machinery, except electrical and electronic	11.8	7.6	5.8
Electrical machinery, except electronic	4.9	3.8	1.2
Electronic goods			7.3
Computer goods			0.4
Transport equipment	3.4	2.1	1.2
Project goods	7.8	5.8	1.1
Mainly export related items	15.1	19.0	16.0
Pearls, precious and semi-precious stones	9.1	11.2	9.0
Organic and inorganic chemicals	4.9	6.5	5.4
Textile yarn, fabrics, made-ups, etc.	0.8	0.7	1.4
Cashew nuts	0.3	0.6	0.2
Other	14.5	15.4	26.5
Artificial resins and plastic materials, etc.	2.5	1.9	1.3
Professional, scientific, and controlling instruments[a]	2.2	2.3	2.0
Coal, coke, and briquettes, etc.	1.0	2.2	2.2
Medicinal and pharmaceutical products	0.8	1.3	0.8
Chemical materials and products	0.9	0.8	0.9
Nonmetallic mineral manufactures	0.5	0.4	0.8
Others	6.6	6.5	18.4
Total imports (billions of dollars)	17.2	21.9	51.4

Source: Author's calculations using data from Reserve Bank of India (2002, table 124).

a. Including photographic and optical goods.

TABLE 6. Composition of Invisibles Receipts and Payments, India, 1980–81, 1990–91, and 2001–02
Percent of total except as indicated

	Receipts			Payments		
Item	1980–81	1990–91	2001–02	1980–81	1990–91	2001–02
Nonfactor services	39.0	61.0	57.0	71.2	46.3	74.6
Travel	17.0	19.5	8.2	5.4	5.1	10.6
Transportation	6.4	13.2	5.5	21.2	14.2	11.0
Insurance	0.9	1.5	0.7	2.0	1.1	1.2
Government, not included elsewhere	1.5	0.2	1.3	2.8	2.2	1.3
Miscellaneous	13.2	26.6	41.2	39.7	23.7	50.5
Investment income	12.8	4.9	7.7	28.0	53.5	25.1
Transfers						
Private	37.7	27.9	34.2	0.7	0.2	0.3
Official	10.5	6.2	1.1	0.2	0.0	0.0
Total (billions of dollars)	7.2	7.5	35.6	2.1	7.7	21.6

Source: Author's calculations using data from Reserve Bank of India (2002, table 137).

TABLE 7. Composition of Invisibles Receipts, India, 2001–02 and 2002–03
Percent of total except as indicated

Item	2001–02	2002–03
Transfers	34.3	35.4
Software services	20.6	22.3
Miscellaneous services other than software	20.4	21.2
Travel	7.9	7.0
Transportation	5.4	5.9
Income	9.4	6.6
Insurance and GNIE[a]	2.0	1.6
Total receipts (billions of dollars)	36.7	43

Source: Reserve Bank of India (2003, table 6.4).
a. GNIE: Government, not included elsewhere

recent data from the World Bank show that this ratio rose further, to 33.1 percent, in 2001.[22] H. A. C. Prasad places India's share of world services exports in 2002 at 1.3 percent.[23]

Second, at the relatively broad level of aggregation shown in table 4, the commodity composition of India's trade has changed only modestly.[24]

22. World Bank (2003).
23. H. A. C. Prasad, *Business Line*, August 27, 2003.
24. The next section will show that in the more finely disaggregated data, changes in the composition of both exports and imports are quite dramatic. Products with no or very low trade initially have grown very rapidly.

During 1992–2002 the share of manufactures in total commodity exports remained unchanged at approximately 75 percent. Within manufactures the sectors that have grown more rapidly than the average for all merchandise exports are the capital- and skilled labor–intensive sectors, including chemicals and allied products and engineering goods. Within the former category, drugs, other pharmaceuticals, and fine chemicals have done especially well; within engineering goods, automobiles and auto parts have lately shown impressive growth. The key unskilled labor–intensive sectors have grown at best at the average pace of all merchandise exports. For example, leather manufactures have grown at rates well below the average, whereas ready-made garments and textiles, yarn, fabrics, and made-up goods have grown at approximately the average rate of all merchandise exports.

Third, on the import side, perhaps the most remarkable observation is that the share of capital goods imports declined drastically during the 1990s (table 5). From 29.5 percent in 1987–88, this share fell to 18.1 percent in 2001–02. In part this decline reflects a bias in liberalization in the 1980s in favor of capital goods over intermediate inputs, whereas in the 1990s both capital and intermediate goods (but not consumer goods) were freed from licensing. But the decline also reflects the general slowdown in private investment activity during the 1990s relative to the late 1980s.

Fourth, on the invisibles account, two key items that have shown very rapid growth are remittances from Indians residing overseas and software exports. The former are reported under "private transfers" in tables 6 and 7. The latter are subsumed within the category "miscellaneous" in table 6 but are reported separately for the last two years in table 7. Software exports (including business process outsourcing) accounts for the greater part of the growth in the miscellaneous category during the 1990s. According to table 7, software exports have risen from $7.6 billion in 2001–02 to $9.6 billion in 2002–03. Interestingly, a substantial part of the growth in remittances has also come from the software industry, since these remittances include the repatriation of earnings by temporary Indian workers in the United States (mainly H1B visa holders). This component rose from $2.1 billion in 1990–91 to $12.2 billion in 2001–02.

Finally, it comes as no surprise that India is far from achieving its potential in tourism. After reaching $3.2 billion in 2000–01, tourism receipts fell to $2.9 billion in 2001–02 in the wake of the September 11 tragedy and recovered only slightly to $3.0 billion in 2002–03. Given

India's attractiveness as a tourist destination and its low costs, this level of tourism is well below what the country could achieve.

Direction of Trade

Table 8 summarizes the direction of India's merchandise trade for 1987–88, 1992–93, and 2001–02. On the export side the major shift has been away from Russia and Japan toward developing Asia. The share of India's exports going to Japan declined from 10.3 percent in 1987–88 to 3.4 percent in 2001–02. The share taken by Russia declined from 12.5 percent to a paltry 1.8 percent over the same period. The share of developing countries as a whole grew from 14.2 percent to 30.9 percent, with each major region—Asia, Africa, and Latin America—absorbing a larger share of India's total exports than before. The share taken by developing Asia rose from 11.9 percent to 23.6 percent. The United States meanwhile has remained a steady trading partner, accounting for approximately one-fifth of India's merchandise exports throughout the period.

On the import side, the major shift has been away from the industrial countries and Russia to the OPEC nations and other developing countries. India's imports from the European Union declined from 33.3 percent of the total in 1987–88 to 22.1 percent in 1999–2000.[25] The decline in the U.S. share over the same years was from 9.0 percent to 7.2 percent, and that in the Japanese share from 9.6 percent to 5.1 percent. Russia also lost share, with imports from that country declining from 7.5 percent to 1.3 percent of India's total imports. OPEC and the other developing countries meanwhile gained share. The share of imports coming from OPEC rose from 13.3 percent to 25.9 percent, and that from developing countries from 17.3 percent to 29.2 percent.

An interesting ongoing development is the rapid expansion of India's trade with China. From just $18 million in 1990–91, India's exports to China rose to approximately $2 billion in 2002–03. India's imports from China similarly expanded from $35 million to $2.8 billion over the same period. India's exports to China have consisted of medium- to high-technology products. In 2002–03 three product groups—engineering goods, iron ore, and chemicals—accounted for more than 70 percent of India's exports to China. On the import side, electronic goods, chemicals, and textiles, yarn, fabric, and made-up articles together accounted for approximately half of the total value of India's imports from China.

25. The available direction-of-trade data on imports for years 2000–01 and after are not consistent with those for the earlier years.

TABLE 8. **Direction of Trade, India, Selected Years**
Percent of total exports or imports except as indicated

Country or group	1987–88 Exports	1987–88 Imports	1992–93 Exports	1992–93 Imports	2001–02 Exports	1999–2000 Imports[a]
OECD countries	58.9	59.8	60.5	56.1	49.3	43.0
European Union	25.1	33.3	28.3	30.2	22.5	22.1
Germany	6.8	9.7	7.7	7.6	4.1	3.7
United Kingdom	6.5	8.2	6.5	6.5	4.9	5.4
North America	19.7	10.3	20.0	11.7	20.8	7.9
Canada	1.1	1.3	1.0	1.9	1.3	0.8
United States	18.6	9.0	19.0	9.8	19.4	7.2
Asia and Oceania	11.6	12.0	9.1	10.6	4.5	7.5
Australia	1.1	2.3	1.2	3.8	1.0	2.2
Japan	10.3	9.6	7.7	6.5	3.4	5.1
Other OECD countries	2.5	4.2	3.0	3.6	1.6	5.5
Switzerland	1.3	1.1	1.1	1.7	0.9	5.2
OPEC	6.1	13.3	9.6	21.8	11.9	25.9
United Arab Emirates	2.0	3.4	4.4	5.1	5.7	4.7
Eastern Europe	16.5	9.6	4.4	2.5	2.9	2.0
Russia	12.5	7.2	3.3	1.2	1.8	1.3
Developing countries	14.2	17.3	22.9	19.6	30.9	29.2
Asia	11.9	12.1	18.8	14.6	23.6	20.0
SAARC members[b]	2.6	0.4	4.0	0.8	4.6	0.8
Other	9.3	11.7	14.8	13.8	19.0	19.2
Hong Kong	2.8	0.5	4.1	0.8	5.4	1.6
South Korea	0.9	1.5	0.9	1.6	1.1	2.6
Malaysia	0.6	3.8	1.0	1.9	1.8	4.1
Singapore	1.7	1.9	3.2	2.9	2.2	3.1
Thailand	0.5	0.3	1.4	0.3	1.4	0.7
Africa	2.0	2.9	3.1	3.5	5.2	7.3
Latin America	0.3	2.3	1.0	1.5	2.1	1.9
Other	0.0	0.0	0.1	0.0	0.2	0.0
Total trade (billions of dollars)	12.1	17.2	18.5	21.9	43.8	49.7

Source: Author's calculations from Reserve Bank of India (2002, table 130).

a. Available direction of trade data on imports for 2000–01 and beyond are not consistent with those for earlier years.

b. In addition to India, members of the South Asian Association for Regional Cooperation include Bangladesh, Bhutan, Maldives, Nepal, Pakistan, and Sri Lanka.

Impact on Efficiency and Growth

The benefits of liberalization may be measured in terms of static efficiency gains and economic growth.[26] This section will discuss each of these approaches briefly.

Static Efficiency

Measurements of efficiency gains inevitably rely on simulations using partial- or general-equilibrium models.[27] The dominant approach today is to construct a general-equilibrium model and parameterize it such that it reproduces the equilibrium in the base year with the existing policy distortion in place. The model is then subjected to a comparative statics exercise by removing specific distortions and solved for the changes in various endogenous variables, including consumption, output, net imports of various goods, and real income. The results of these exercises critically depend on the choice of the model, functional forms, and parameter values.[28] Moreover, the effects on sectoral consumption, output, and trade predicted by these models do a very poor job of tracking the actual outcomes.[29] For these reasons estimates based on these studies must be taken with a grain of salt.

With this caveat, the only comprehensive study that quantitatively measures the impact of India's liberalization on welfare is that by Rajesh Chadha and others.[30] Using the Michigan Computable General Equilibrium model, this study concludes that trade liberalization corresponding approximately to what has been accomplished to date had the potential to raise GDP permanently by approximately 2 percent. If the same liberalization were done after a competitive regime replaced the existing regime, however, the gain from trade liberalization would rise to as much as 5 percent of GDP.

The traditional analyses of the static gains from trade liberalization fail to emphasize some key sources of such gains: specialization in production that eliminates certain sectors entirely and gives rise to new ones; reduced costs due to the availability of higher-quality inputs; and the

26. An examination of the effects on poverty reduction is beyond the scope of this paper.
27. See Panagariya (2002a).
28. Panagariya and Duttagupta (2001) demonstrate this fact in the context of computable general-equilibrium models of preferential trading.
29. See Kehoe (2003).
30. Chadha and others (1998).

availability of new and higher-quality products to consumers.[31] Because these sources are particularly relevant for India, given its regime of across-the-board protection, it is useful here to consider briefly each of these sources of gains.

When a country's production structure is excessively diversified as a result of a policy of wholesale, indiscriminate import substitution, as was the case in India, opening to trade is likely to lead to the disappearance of certain activities and sectors altogether. Conversely, the availability of new inputs and higher-quality substitutes for low-quality inputs produced domestically will likely give rise to new products and sectors capable of competing in world markets. Benefits from these changes can potentially give rise to gains much larger than the traditional triangular efficiency gains from the expansion or contraction of existing activities that are relatively small.

Even in the case of products that continue to be produced domestically, the availability of newer and higher-quality inputs is likely to yield large savings. For years India prohibited imports of machinery and intermediate inputs whenever domestic substitutes were available, even if the latter were of dubious quality. This resulted in low efficiency as well as poor quality of the final product. Vijay Kelkar makes this point forcefully:

> In the manufacturing sector we opted for an across-the-board import substitution strategy where we sought to produce everything in a production chain whether the product was a commercial vehicle or a steel mill. And by this, the weakest link decided the fate of the strength of the whole production chain. We entered into production of a number of activities in which we just did not possess the competitive edge. It resulted in a loss of efficiency for the entire industry. For instance, forcing the Indian fertilizer industry to use only Indian designed catalyst, the entire fertilizer industry's productivity suffered. Same was the case for electronics sector where our software industry took time to take off because of the insistence on the use of domestic computer hardware.[32]

Pursell expresses a similar sentiment when describing India's trade regime until the mid-1970s:

> During this period, import-substitution policies were followed with little or no regard to costs. They resulted in an extremely diverse industrial structure and high degree of self-sufficiency, but many industries had high production costs. In addition, there was a general problem of poor quality and technological backwardness, which beset even low-cost sectors with comparative advantage such

31. Chadha and others (1998) do allow for economies of scale and are thus able to capture some of the pro-competitive effects of reduced protection on production costs. But they apparently hold the numbers of domestic and foreign products fixed.
32. Kelkar (2001, p. 5).

as the textiles, garment, leather goods, many light industries, and primary industries such as cotton.[33]

A final source of static welfare gains is the availability of new and perhaps higher-quality variants of existing products. As Paul Romer has emphasized using an elegant analytical model, when new products become available, the benefits are not limited to the traditional welfare triangles but the entire area under the demand curve.[34] For many years India either prohibited imports of consumer goods or allowed them only under very stringent conditions. As a result, products that were readily available elsewhere commanded a very large premium in India. In addition, the quality of domestically produced counterparts of foreign goods was often extremely poor.[35] This situation changed drastically after the liberalization of consumer goods imports, first through the easing of baggage rules and the issuance of tradable special import licenses for specified consumer goods, and subsequently, in April 2001, through an end to all licensing.[36] The availability of high-quality products has contributed to consumer welfare not only directly but also indirectly, by making consumers more discriminating and therefore forcing domestic manufacturers to upgrade the quality of their products.

Two sectors in which the impact of opening up on the quality and availability of new products is highly visible are automobiles and telecommunications. Indian consumers had long suffered the 1950s models sold by Ambassador and Fiat, and even then they had to wait in queues that were several years long. Today virtually all of the world's major car manufacturers are represented in the Indian market, and consumers have immediate access to a wide variety of models. Continued high tariffs on automobile imports notwithstanding, consumers have reaped large benefits because automobile manufacturers have been able to enter the market through tariff-jumping investments.

33. Pursell (1992, pp. 433–34).
34. Romer (1994).
35. Bhagwati tells an anecdote that aptly captures the deleterious impact that protectionist policies had on the quality of the Indian products. Upon his return from study abroad in the early 1960s, Bhagwati initially shared the intellectual attitudes that helped India turn inward, although he quickly changed his mind in light of the realities on the ground. In a letter to Harry Johnson written during his tenure at the Indian Statistical Institute in the early 1960s, Bhagwati happened to complain about the craze he observed in India for everything foreign. Harry Johnson promptly responded that if the quality of the paper on which Bhagwati had written his letter was any indication of the quality of homemade products, the craze for the foreign seemed perfectly rational to him.
36. "Baggage rules" are those applicable to imports entering India as a part of passengers' baggage.

In the same vein, not too long ago, telephone service was considered a luxury even among upper-middle-class Indians in urban areas, and they had to wait in long queues to obtain it. The few "lucky" ones who did manage to get a telephone usually found that half the time they could not get a dial tone, and the other half of the time they got a wrong number.[37] In contrast, telephone service today, whether it be fixed line or cellular, is available on demand in most regions, and absence of a dial tone and inability to connect to the number dialed are no longer at issue. India has made full use of the rapid advances in technology in this sector, with benefits to consumers that many now take for granted. Had it not freed imports of information technology products (and undertaken other reforms in the telecommunications sector), India could not have taken advantage of these advances.

The benefits of new imported inputs and final products are not limited to these obvious, highly visible examples. In her doctoral thesis, Purba Mukerji analyzes the changes in trade flows during the 1990s at a highly disaggregated level.[38] She finds that, at the five-digit SITC classification, the total number of products imported jumped from 2,120 in 1991 to 2,611 in 1999, or 23 percent, and that of exports from 2,273 to 2,549, or 12 percent, over the same period.

More important, following Timothy Kehoe and Kim Ruhl, Mukerji studies the change in the share of new goods in total merchandise imports and exports using the five-digit SITC data.[39] Contrary to the impression of relatively minor changes in the composition of imports and exports conveyed by the aggregate data, she finds movements in the composition of imports and exports that could not be more dramatic. The available data span the years 1988 to 1999. Mukerji first sorts products in ascending order of the value of their imports. She then divides them into ten categories, with each category accounting for 10 percent of the total imports in 1988. By construction, the first category consists of products that individually

---

37. Prompted by his unhappy experience with the Indian telephone system, Bhagwati once quipped that one way to distinguish between a developed and a developing country is that in the former one gets tired of *receiving* phone calls, whereas in the latter one is exasperated *making* them. Tharoor (1997, p. 167) offers a more direct indictment of the telecommunications sector in India in the early 1980s and the government's attitude toward it: "The government's indifferent attitude to the needs to improve India's communications infrastructure was epitomized by Prime Minister Indira Gandhi's communications minister, C. M. Stephens, who declared in Parliament, in response to questions decrying the rampant telephone breakdowns in the country, that telephones were a luxury, not a right, and that any Indian who was not satisfied with his telephone service could return his phone—since there was an eight-year waiting list of people seeking this supposedly inadequate product."

38. Mukerji (2004).

39. Kehoe and Ruhl (2002).

contributed little or nothing to the volume of imports in 1988 and therefore contains the largest number of products. By the same token, the last category contains products that individually contributed the largest volume of imports in 1988 and hence contains the fewest products.[40] Mukerji then fixes the categories and computes the change in the share of each category in the following years. She does a similar exercise for exports.

Mukerji's results for imports are reproduced in the top panel of table 9. Because so many products were allowed to be imported only in tiny quantities, or not at all, in 1988, as many as 2,312 out of 2,742 importable items accounted for 10 percent of imports in the first category. That is to say, the remaining 429 products, or just 15.6 percent of all importable items, accounted for 90 percent of India's merchandise imports. In the following years, especially after the major liberalization in July 1991, the proportions shifted dramatically. By 1999, products in the first category had increased their share in total imports from 10 percent to 35 percent, with products in most other categories experiencing a declining trend.

A similar if slightly less dramatic story emerges on the export side. According to the bottom panel of table 9, in 1988 only 8.4 percent of all products accounted for 90 percent of India's exports, with the remaining 91.6 percent of products accounting for the remaining 10 percent. By 1999 the share of the products in the latter category had climbed to 27 percent. Again, the pattern is one in which products with zero or minuscule shares initially are the ones that grew fastest. Only the first two categories in table 9, which contain those products with the smallest initial shares, show gains, with the rest experiencing either a decline or no change in 1999.

Growth and Productivity

The bulk of the benefits from liberalization has evidently come from faster growth. Although India has seen a clear shift in its growth rate during the last two decades, its connection to liberalization has been questioned. Bradford DeLong argues that since the shift in the growth rate took place during the 1980s whereas the reforms began only in 1991, reforms cannot be credited with the shift.[41] Dani Rodrik endorses DeLong's view, asserting that "the change in official attitudes in the 1980s, towards encouraging rather than discouraging entrepreneurial activities and integration into the world economy, and a belief that the rules of the economic game had

---

40. The last category contains 20 percent of the imports initially, to overcome a problem posed by a switch in classification in 1992.

41. DeLong (2003).

TABLE 9. Composition of Trade According to New versus Old Products
Percent of total imports or exports

Category[a]	No. of products	1988	1989	1990	1991	1992	1993	1994	1995	1996	1997	1998	1999
Imports													
9	2,312	10	13	15	15	17	20	28	26	28	32	38	35
8	211	10	10	11	9	9	11	11	11	11	11	9	10
7	97	10	10	11	10	11	13	13	14	12	11	10	8
6	49	10	9	9	8	8	7	7	7	6	5	5	4
5	29	10	8	9	9	8	8	9	9	8	7	6	6
4	19	10	9	9	8	7	6	5	5	4	5	3	2
3	13	10	8	7	6	5	5	7	8	8	7	8	8
2	8	10	12	11	10	9	6	6	6	5	5	3	8
1	3	20	21	18	25	26	24	14	14	18	17	18	21
Exports													
9	2,553	10	13	14	18	20	22	23	24	26	27	25	27
8	132	10	10	11	10	10	11	11	12	12	12	12	11
7	52	10	11	10	11	11	8	9	7	8	8	7	8
6	23	10	10	11	10	8	7	7	7	7	7	7	7
5	11	10	10	10	11	10	11	11	11	12	12	11	10
4	7	10	11	11	10	11	10	9	8	9	8	8	7
3	5	11	9	10	11	10	10	11	12	10	10	11	8
2	1	3	3	3	2	2	1	1	1	1	1	1	1
1	1	26	23	20	17	18	20	18	18	15	15	18	21

Source: Mukerji (2004).

a. Products are ranked according to quantities imported or exported and then divided into categories according to import or export quantity in 1988, with the first category including the products accounting for the most imports or exports, and the ninth category the least (the latter including products in which there was no trade in 1988). Thus an increase in the share of trade accounted for by products in a given category indicates an expansion of trade in products in that category or (in the ninth category) the introduction of trade in formerly nontraded products. Category 1 contains 20 percent of imports in 1988 to overcome a problem posed by a switch in classification in 1992.

changed for good may have had a bigger impact on growth than any specific policy reforms."[42]

Elsewhere I have subjected this view to a systematic critique, offering four counterarguments.[43] First, growth during the 1980s was fragile, exhibiting significantly higher variance than in the 1990s. It was the super-high growth rate of 7.6 percent a year during the last three years of 1980s that makes overall growth in the 1980s look comparable to that in the 1990s. Second, growth in the 1980s, especially the extremely rapid growth of the last three years of the decade, took place in the presence of significant liberalization of both investment and import licensing, notably during the second half of the decade. Third, growth during the 1980s was also fueled by fiscal expansion. As such, it was unsustainable, with the result that the economy crash-landed in 1991. Finally, even if DeLong were right that changes in attitudes rather than in policies led to the shift in the growth rate in the 1980s, without further liberalization that growth would not have been sustained. It is on the strength of continued liberalization that India sustained a 6 percent annual growth rate from 1992–93 onward. It is also because of the 1990s liberalization that India has been able to build a foreign exchange reserve of $120 billion, putting it beyond the immediate reach of another macroeconomic crisis despite fiscal deficits that are currently as large as those in the late 1980s.[44]

In assessing the contribution of liberalization to growth more directly, one may ask whether liberalization was accompanied by increased growth in total factor productivity (TFP). Before reviewing the evidence from India in this area, however, it is important to recall that the literature on productivity has been, in general, controversial and inconclusive on the role of policy in stimulating growth. In the context of East Asia, Alwyn Young set off a major debate with his conclusion that the super-high growth rates of the Asian miracle economies were almost entirely due to capital accumulation, and that policies—whether outward-oriented and pro-market, or inward-oriented and interventionist—played no role.[45] Later findings by Jong-Il Kim and Lawrence Lau, Susan Collins and Barry Bosworth, and Ishaq Nadiri and Wanpyo Son have reinforced Young's conclusions, leading Paul Krugman to colorfully describe the East Asian

---

42. Rodrik (2003).
43. Panagariya (2004).
44. Nevertheless, the deficits are not sustainable in the long run and impose a short-term cost by crowding out private investment.
45. See Young (1992, 1995).

growth experience as one of Soviet-style perspiration rather than policy-induced inspiration.[46]

Bhagwati argues forcefully, however, that the traditional measures of TFP fail to capture the effect that policies have on capital accumulation itself.[47] Good policies can raise the rate of saving and therefore of investment. Approaching the issue from the productivity perspective, Charles Hulten has long argued that increased productivity due to innovation raises the return to capital and induces greater capital accumulation.[48] The conventional productivity measures do not take this innovation-induced accumulation into account. For example, Hulten and Mieko Nishimizu study the direct and indirect effects of innovation on growth in nine industrialized countries for the period 1960–73 and find that the conventional TFP measure accounts for 45 percent of output growth, but that when innovation-induced capital accumulation is taken into account, the contribution of innovation jumps to 84 percent.[49]

Empirical studies aimed at measuring TFP in India focus virtually exclusively on manufacturing and may be divided into two categories, those relying on industry-level data and those relying on firm-level data. Their findings are not unambiguous, because of differences in methodology, the unit of analysis, and the quality of the data, but the weight of the evidence is in favor of trade liberalization leading to productivity gains.

Among studies based on industry-level data, the key source of the differences in results is the manner in which gross output and intermediate inputs are deflated. Isher Ahluwalia initially looked for effects of the early reforms on productivity using industry data from 1959–60 to 1985–86.[50] She concluded that although there was no net TFP growth during the entire period, a mildly accelerating pattern of productivity growth did emerge after liberalization began in the late 1970s.

P. Balakrishnan and K. Pushpangandan and J. Mohan Rao rejected this finding, however, on the ground that Ahluwalia had used a "single-deflation" procedure that assumes that prices of output and intermediate inputs grow at the same rate.[51] Instead they used a "double-deflation"

46. See Kim and Lau (1994), Collins and Bosworth (1996), Nadiri and Son (1998), and Krugman (1994).

47. Bhagwati (1999).

48. Hulten (1975).

49. Hulten and Nishimizu (1980).

50. See Ahluwalia (1991). For a discussion of the earlier literature on productivity growth in India, see Bhagwati and Srinivasan (1975).

51. See Balakrishnan and Pushpangandan (1994) and Rao (1996).

method, with separate estimates of prices for final output and for intermediate goods, and found the opposite pattern of TFP growth, with TFP growth collapsing during 1985–92.

More recently, Hulten and Syleja Srinivasan have taken a fresh look at the data for 1973–92.[52] They begin by noting that the finding by Balakrishnan and Pushpangandan and by Rao, that TFP increased rapidly until 1982–83 and then plummeted 35 percent by the end of the period, is rather implausible, and they share the skepticism expressed subsequently by Ahluwalia and by B. H. Dholakia and R. H. Dholakia about the Balakrishnan-Pushpangandan-Rao double-deflation method.[53] They then proceed to recalculate productivity growth applying different and, in their view, superior methods of measurement of output and intermediate input prices. Their price indexes lead to the same results as in the Balakrishnan-Pushpangandan-Rao papers for the entire sample period (1973–92) but yield major differences for the subperiods 1973–82 and 1983–92. In particular, whereas the output price index used by Rao accelerates from the first half of the sample period to the second, the output price index used by Hulten and Srinivasan decelerates. In the same vein, the Hulten and Srinivasan input price index shows a less rapid deceleration between the two subperiods than the Rao index.

These differences in price indexes lead to different productivity outcomes in the two subperiods. They smooth out the TFP path, and the sudden collapse found in the Balakrishnan-Pushpangandan-Rao papers disappears. At the same time, no pickup in TFP growth in the second period is found: the growth rates are 2.2 percent and 2.1 percent in the two subperiods, respectively.

Hulten and Srinivasan argue, however, that the lack of pickup in TFP growth still leaves open the possibility that the surge in investment in the second subperiod reflected an improved investment climate due to reform. Therefore they proceed to make the process of capital accumulation itself endogenous and calculate the total growth in productivity (direct productivity growth plus that through productivity-induced capital accumulation). This leads to estimates of 5.0 percent and 5.7 percent growth in productivity in the two subperiods, respectively, indicating at least a small pickup in productivity growth.

In a more recent study, Satish Chand and Kunal Sen break up the time period more finely and use a different methodology, one that incorporates

52. Hulten and Srinivasan (1999).
53. Ahluwalia (1994) and Dholakia and Dholakia (1994).

TABLE 10. Change in Protection and Growth in Total Factor Productivity, India, 1974–88
Percent

	Industry classification		
	Consumer goods	Intermediate goods	Capital goods
Change in protection			
1974–78	4.5	0.4	–1.8
1979–83	–1.1	1.4	1.7
1984–88	–0.4	–5.4	–4.3
Growth in TFP			
1974–78	–0.5	–1.2	–1.6
1979–83	–1.2	–3.1	–1.5
1984–88	5.1	4.8	3.7

Source: Chand and Sen (2002).

the productivity effects of new inputs made available by trade liberalization.[54] They use three-digit industry data covering thirty industries that account for 53 percent of gross value added and 45 percent of employment in manufacturing over the period under study, 1973–88. The industries are divided approximately equally among consumer, intermediate, and capital goods. Chand and Sen measure protection by the proportionate wedge between the Indian and the U.S. price and estimate TFP growth in the three industry groups averaged over three nonoverlapping periods: 1974–78, 1979–83, and 1984–88. They then relate this productivity growth to liberalization.

Table 10 presents Chand and Sen's findings.[55] By their measure, protection declines over the sample period in the intermediate and capital goods sectors but not in the consumer goods sector. Moreover, all three sectors see a significant improvement in TFP growth in 1984–88 compared with the two earlier periods. Thus the jump in TFP growth coincides with the liberalization of capital and intermediate goods.

Chand and Sen perform further tests by pooling their sample and employing fixed-effects estimators to allow for intrinsic differences across industries with respect to the rate of technological progress. Their estimates show that, on average, a 1 percentage point reduction in the price wedge leads to a 0.1 percent rise in TFP. For the intermediate goods sector, the effect is twice as large. The impact of liberalization of the intermediate

54. Chand and Sen (2002).
55. See Chand and Sen (2002, table 3).

goods sector on productivity turns out to be statistically significant in all of their regressions.[56]

Several studies focus principally on the impact of the 1990s reforms on productivity growth using firm- or plant-level data; these include the contributions by Pravin Krishna and Devashish Mitra; Balakrishna, Pushpangandan, and M. Babu; Petia Topalova; and Jagadeesh Sivadasan.[57] The first three of these studies employ the PROWESS firm-level database maintained by the Center for Monitoring the Indian Economy (CMIE), whereas the last one uses, for the first time, the plant-level data underlying the industry-level data used by earlier researchers, which come from the Annual Survey of the Industries (ASI). The three papers using the PROWESS/CMIE data reach conflicting conclusions, perhaps because they employ different subsets of the dataset or different techniques, but possibly also because of the same differences in price deflators that have been at the heart of the conflict between industry-level studies.

The PROWESS database includes information on a number of variables on an annual basis for all of the roughly 4,000 industrial firms listed on the Bombay Stock Exchange. Krishna and Mitra choose firms in four sectors: electronics (90 firms), electrical machinery (90 firms), nonelectrical machinery (72 firms), and transport equipment (111 firms). They allow for scale economies and imperfect competition and find strong evidence of a pro-competitive effect, as reflected in a decline in the price-cost margin, as well as some evidence of an increase in productivity growth following the 1991 reform. Balakrishna, Pushpangandan, and Babu employ essentially the same methodology as Krishna and Mitra but apply it to a much larger sample of 2,300 firms spanning the period 1988–89 to 1997–98. They fail to find any acceleration in productivity growth following the 1991 reform, however.

Topalova carries out a more comprehensive analysis, with a sample that covers 1989–2001 and includes the largest number of firms (which varies across years) of the three studies using the CMIE/PROWESS database. She

56. Two recent studies by Das (2003) and Unel (2003) extend the industry-level analysis to the 1990s. The results of these two studies contradict each other, however. Whereas Unel finds substantial growth in productivity in the 1980s and 1990s (with the growth rate higher in the latter decade), Das finds the opposite: TFP growth accounts for only 7 percent of the manufacturing growth during the 1980s and almost none of that in the 1990s. Once again, the differences arise from the deflators used. Whereas Unel effectively uses a common deflator for output and intermediate inputs, Das uses separate deflators for each of them.

57. Krishna and Mitra (1998); Balakrishnan, Pushpangadan, and Babu (2000); Topalova (2003); Sivadasan (2003).

finds very strong evidence that tariff reductions have a positive effect on both the level of productivity and its growth rate. The results are highly statistically significant and robust to different specifications.

A criticism applicable to all three of these firm-level studies is that the CMIE/PROWESS data are of poor quality. Often the totals and mean values of several variables do not match those available from other, more reliable sources. There is also the possibility that since firms file the information to the stock exchange as a part of their profit-loss statements, they may misrepresent it in order to influence investors. Most important, however, the CMIE data do not report the number of a firm's employees. This makes it difficult to measure labor input. The usual way around this (as, for example, in Krishna and Mitra, 1998) is to use the deflated wage bill as the labor input, but this suffers from the problem that if TFP growth is shared by workers through higher wages, the change in TFP would be underestimated. These deficiencies of the data make the recent, carefully executed study by Sivadasan using the ASI data particularly important.

Sivadasan estimates the effects of tariff liberalization, FDI, and the removal of investment licensing at the plant level on aggregate productivity, using annual data on 40,000 plants from 1986–87 to 1994–95. A key appeal of his analysis, among many, is that he applies the double-deflation method advocated by Hulten and Srinivasan and experiments with several aggregations for the deflation of inputs, finding the results to be robust across the different deflators.

Sivadasan finds a 30 to 35 percent increase in mean intraplant productivity in those industries subject to tariff liberalization. He also finds a 25 percent increase in aggregate output growth and a 20 percent increase in aggregate productivity growth following tariff liberalization. The change in intraplant productivity growth turns out to be the biggest component of the change in aggregate productivity and output growth. He finds similar results for de-licensing and for liberalization of FDI.

To sum up, the four studies do not uniformly demonstrate an acceleration in productivity growth following the reforms, but the more careful of them, using reliable data, clearly point in that direction. At the industry level, the careful study by Chand and Sen offers clear evidence of the acceleration in productivity that coincided with the reforms in the second half of the 1980s. At the plant level, the careful study by Sivadasan, who is able to exploit the variation within plants over time as well as across plants during a given year, is particularly persuasive. His findings are robust and uniform in the expected direction for the level as well as the growth rate of productivity, and not just for tariff liberalization but also for investment de-licensing and FDI.

Three additional points are worth noting. First, for reasons discussed briefly in the next section, Indian industry was not a stellar performer during either the 1980s or the 1990s, despite the reforms. Average annual growth in this sector was only 6.8 percent during 1981–91 and 6.4 percent during 1991–2001. Therefore, regardless of what view one takes on the productivity story, the bigger puzzle to solve is why industry has grown relatively slowly.

Second, to a considerable degree, the rapid growth during the 1990s was driven by services, which today account for approximately half of India's GDP. In the aggregate, services grew at a 6.9 percent annual rate during 1981–91 and 8.1 percent during 1991–2001. Because of a lack of data, there are no studies on productivity growth in this important sector. But the record of some of the services sectors clearly looks sparkling. According to Jim Gordon and Poonam Gupta, the faster growth in services during the 1990s than during the 1980s was driven mainly by fast growth in communications services, financial services, business services (which include the information technology sector), and community services.[58] Trade liberalization has played a direct role in the growth of at least some of these sectors, namely, telecommunications and business services.

Finally, insofar as output is measured at prereform domestic relative prices, it is likely to be undervalued in a liberalizing environment. The point is readily made with the help of figure 1, which shows the production possibilities frontier between two goods, with good 1 imported. Lines AA' and TT' give the world price. Initially, a tariff keeps the domestic price at AB, with production and consumption taking place at A and C, respectively. Elimination of the tariff changes the domestic price to TT' and moves the output and consumption points to T and C'. If output is measured at prereform domestic prices, however, income is given by line RR', suggesting a *decline* in income. Insofar as a movement toward exportables and away from importables accompanies the growth process, this undervaluation of output will be observed with a changing level of the capital stock as well. Thus the growth rate is likely to be understated in an environment in which domestic prices are being progressively realigned with world prices. In view of the much smaller realignment of the prices during the 1980s than during the 1990s, this fact suggests that the growth rate in the latter period relative to that in the former is understated.

---

58. Gordon and Gupta (2003).

FIGURE 1. GDP at Domestic and World Prices

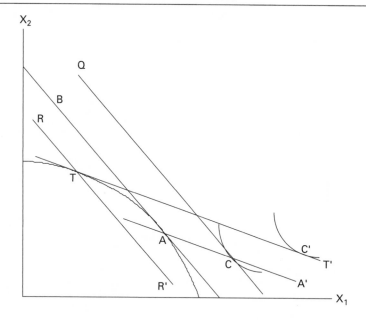

Future Policy

Although this paper focuses only on trade policy, the discussion cannot be totally divorced from some key domestic policy issues that necessarily impinge on trade flows and patterns of specialization. This section is therefore divided into five parts. The first part discusses some key domestic policy reforms necessary to allow the Indian economy to specialize in sectors where India has comparative advantage. The second takes up the issue of autonomous trade policy reform—also called unilateral trade reform—arguing in favor of adopting a uniform tariff regime and lowering the single tariff rate to below 10 percent in the next three years. The third part discusses the reforms necessary in the area of contingent protection—antidumping and safeguards. The fourth part takes up the issue of bilateral trade arrangements, and, the fifth the state of play in the ongoing Doha Round of multilateral trade negotiations under the auspices of the WTO.

Domestic Policy Reforms

Two important related facts emerge from our review of trade flows and growth from the viewpoint of domestic policy reform: the overall response of trade to India's opening up has been weaker than in countries such as China, and the economy has failed to move rapidly into the manufacturing of labor-intensive products. Both facts point to the need for some key domestic policy reforms.

The response of trade to liberalization has been an order of magnitude weaker in India than in China. In China, exports of goods and services grew at annual rates of 12.9 and 15.2 percent during the 1980s and the 1990s, respectively. Imports performed similarly. Consequently, China's ratio of total trade to GDP rose from 18.9 percent in 1980 to 34 percent in 1990 and to 49.3 percent in 2000.

Although foreign investment is not the subject of this paper, it may be noted that the differences between India and China on this front are even starker. FDI into China rose from $60 million in 1980 to $3.5 billion in 1990 and then to a whopping $42.1 billion in 2000. China was slower to open its market to portfolio investment, but once it did, inflows quickly surpassed those into India, reaching $7.8 billion in 2000. Even if one allows for an upward bias in these figures, as some China specialists suggest, and a downward bias in the figures for India, there is little doubt that foreign investment flows into China are several times those into India.

Part of the difference in performance between India and China can be attributed to the presence of Chinese entrepreneurs in Hong Kong and Taiwan, who have been eager to escape rising wages in their home economies by moving to China. However, a more central explanation lies in differences in the composition of GDP in the two countries and the asymmetric responses of their industries to opening up. Among developing countries, India is unique in having a very large share of its GDP in the mostly informal part of the services sector. Whereas in other countries a decline in the share of agriculture in GDP has been accompanied by a substantial expansion of industry in the early stages of development, in India this has not happened. For example, in 1980 the proportion of GDP originating in industry was already 48.5 percent in China, whereas in India it was only 24.2 percent. Services, on the other hand, contributed only 21.4 percent to GDP in China, but as much as 37.2 percent in India.

In the following twenty years, despite considerable growth, the share of industry did not rise in India. Instead the entire decline in the share of agriculture was absorbed by services. In China, in contrast, the share of industry started out very high in 1980, fell to 41.6 percent in 1990, but went back up to 50.9 percent in 2000. Correspondingly, services rose from its low

1980 level of 21.4 percent to 31.3 percent in 1990 and just 33.2 percent in 2000. The key point is that industry already accounted for a large share of GDP in China in 1980, and what it lost during the 1980s it more than recovered in the 1990s.[59]

Why does this matter? Because under liberal trade policies, developing countries are much more likely to be able to expand exports and imports if a large proportion of their output originates in industry. Not only is the scope for expanding labor-intensive manufactures greater in a labor-abundant country, but a larger industrial sector also requires more imported inputs, thereby offering greater scope for the expansion of imports. In India, not only have exports failed to grow rapidly, but the response of imports has been just as muted. Consequently, in recent years the Reserve Bank of India has had to purchase large volumes of foreign exchange to keep the rupee from appreciating. Even then it was unsuccessful and had to let the currency appreciate by 5 to 7 percent against the dollar during 2003. Given the poor performance of industry, imports have simply failed to absorb the foreign exchange generated by remittances and relatively modest foreign investment flows.

This same factor is also at work in explaining the relatively modest response of FDI to more liberal policies. Investment in industry, whether domestic or foreign, has been sluggish. Foreign investors have been hesitant to invest in industry for much the same reasons as domestic investors. At the same time, the capacity of the formal services sector to absorb foreign investment is limited.

Therefore the solution to both trade and FDI expansion in India lies in stimulating growth in industry. Here again this paper's review of the composition of trade flows gives some clear clues. On the export side, as noted above, unskilled labor–intensive sectors such as apparel and footwear have grown at no more than the average rate for total exports, whereas the capital- and skilled labor–intensive sectors have shown above-average growth. This pattern clearly points to bottlenecks facing the labor-intensive sectors. On the import side, machinery imports have seen their share of the total decline during the 1990s relative to the 1980s. Given the removal of trade barriers on both capital goods and intermediate inputs, this fact is also explained by relatively sluggish growth in industry.

If industrial growth is to pick up, three key domestic reforms are essential. First, the fiscal deficit must be brought down, to release funds for investment in the private sector. A major surge in industrial growth

59. These data are taken from World Bank (2002).

will have to come from increased investment, and that will require the availability of savings to the private sector. Because the productivity of private investment depends crucially on public investment in infrastructure, the fiscal deficit cannot be contained at the expense of public investment. Therefore containing the revenue deficit is the only choice. This means cutting and streamlining current expenditure and raising more revenue.

Second, a large majority of labor-intensive manufacturing products still remain on the small-scale industries reservation list. Without an end to this reservation, there is little hope that industry will begin to grow rapidly. The large multinationals that, in China, have driven the growth of labor-intensive industry in sectors ranging from toys to apparel can hardly be expected to enter manufacturing in India on a small scale. Nor can India count on sustained rapid growth of industry on the back of the capital- and skilled labor–intensive sectors, because the scarcity of skilled labor places an automatic limit on the potential growth of these sectors. If India is to transform itself from a primarily agricultural to a primarily industrial economy, rapid growth of labor-intensive industry is essential.

Finally, the end to the small-scale industries reservation is also insufficient by itself to ensure rapid industrial growth. Current labor laws that virtually prohibit even the reassignment of workers, let alone their dismissal, must be reformed as well. The virtual ban on the exit of firms with 100 or more workers is a major disincentive to firms interested in entering the market on a large scale. Reliance on contract labor, the use of capital-intensive techniques, and the concentration of production activity in skilled labor–intensive industries—practices that get around the hiring and firing regulations relating to unskilled workers—have been deployed by many manufacturers. But this solution exacts a heavy toll in terms of drastically reduced employment opportunities or (in the case of contract labor) low worker morale, resulting in low productivity and poor product quality.

The effect of these twin regulations—the small-scale industries reservation and stringent labor laws—is best illustrated by a comparison of the apparel industry in India with that in China. According to a 2001 McKinsey Global Institute report,[60] India's share in apparel imports of the top ten importing countries not constrained by Multifibre Arrangement (MFA) quotas, at 1.6 percent, is less than its share of 3.2 percent among the MFA quota-constrained countries. The reverse holds true for the more competitive China: its share in apparel imports of the top ten non-quota-constrained

---

60. McKinsey Global Institute (2001).

countries is 38.1 percent, and that among the top quota-constrained countries is 11.3 percent. This difference in performance derives to a large degree from the vastly different organization of apparel factories in the two countries. Whereas the average clothing plant in India employs 50 machines, the average Chinese plant employs 500. Without reform of the small-scale industries reservation and of labor law, this organizational difference and the accompanying differences in the cost and quality of production cannot be eliminated.

Some leading economists in India question the importance of reforming the Industrial Disputes Act and related labor laws to give firms the power to retrench workers, subject to appropriate compensation, on the ground that these laws impact less than 10 percent of the labor force that is employed in firms with 100 workers or more. This is a nonsensical argument. The reason the number of firms with 100 or more workers in India is so small is precisely that labor laws remain a major barrier to the entry of firms with 100 or more workers. If India wishes to create a large number of jobs that pay decent wages, it must make the business environment friendly to labor-intensive industries. Labor law reform is a necessary condition for the creation of that environment.

Autonomous Trade Reform

Turning back to trade policy, India's autonomous trade reform program must continue until all tariffs have fallen well below 10 percent. In addition, India must address the issue of its tariff structure, which, despite substantial compression and rationalization, remains complex.

For example, the peak tariff on nonagricultural goods is ostensibly 20 percent. But nearly 10 percent of nonagricultural tariff rates are still not subject to this peak. With respect to complexity, the situation is even grimmer: approximately twenty tariff bands currently exist. As was shown in table 1, tariff rates on chemicals and photographic supplies ranged from 0 to 170 percent in 2001–02, and those on transport equipment from 3 to 105 percent.[61] The situation is not much different today, with the multibillion-dollar automobile industry receiving nominal protection at the ad valorem rate of 60 percent. With lower input tariff rates, the effective rate of protection is even higher.

This tariff structure has little economic rationale but is rather the result of two sets of forces. First, some politically powerful sectors such as chemicals and automobiles have managed to evade the tariff compression

61. WTO (2002).

applied to other sectors during the past decade. Second, the misconception remains among policymakers that somehow final goods must be protected at tariff rates higher than those applied to raw materials and intermediate inputs. As a result, tariffs on final goods have been compressed less than those on inputs. The process has been slowed recently, however: tariff reductions have been largely limited to products subject to the "peak" tariff rate, which happen to be final goods, and some of the lower tariff rates applying to intermediate inputs have been raised as a part of the rationalization process.

As part of further reform, it will be best for India to move to a single uniform tariff of 15 percent for nonagricultural goods starting in financial year 2005–06. This will involve ending the plethora of exemptions and raising tariffs on approximately 5 percent of tariff lines currently subject to tariffs below 15 percent. The uniform tariff should then be lowered to 10 percent and by a further 2 to 3 percentage points in each of the subsequent two years, to achieve a 5 percent uniform tariff rate by the beginning of 2008–09.

The adoption of a uniform tariff has the major advantage that it will take politics out of trade policy. When the government is willing to offer protection at different rates, industrial lobbies have a field day. Politically more powerful sectors such as the automobile and chemical sectors can lobby for sweetheart deals at the expense of the consumer. But once the rule is that all will receive equal protection, the incentive for any single industry to lobby diminishes dramatically. Simultaneously, the government has a logical defense against the demands of specific industries for higher protection: because it must raise the tariff for all if it does so for one, its hands are tied.[62]

The single tariff rate also has the advantage of transparency and administrative simplicity. It eliminates the prospect of industries getting a higher tariff by classifying their product as a finished rather than an intermediate good. It also does away with all kinds of exemptions. As noted earlier, according to the WTO, India's current tariff code has more than 100 kinds of exemptions, each of which runs to several pages. In addition to creating distortions, these exemptions hamper the deployment of efficiency-increasing tools such as computerization of customs.

---

62. Panagariya and Rodrik (1993) present a number of formal models that yield the uniform tariff rule as the optimal outcome. In these models tariffs are determined by lobbying. The adoption of a uniform tariff rule then creates a free rider problem in the lobbying activity, since the protection granted to one industry is automatically granted to all industries. This feature of the uniform tariff rule has a strong dampening effect on incentives to lobby.

A single uniform tariff of 15 percent would also be superior to the two-part structure proposed by the Indian government in a previous budget, with rates of 10 percent on inputs and 20 percent on final goods. A tariff structure that levies a 10 percent tariff on inputs and a 20 percent tariff on final goods grants excessively high effective protection to the latter. For example, suppose the world price of a cell phone is $100 and that its components cost $80. The proposed two-part tariff would raise the prices of the cell phone and its components to $120 and $88, respectively. This would allow domestic value added in cell phone assembly to rise from $20 to $32, thus providing effective protection of 60 percent.

Critics of the uniform tariff may argue that it would fail to minimize the distortion cost of raising revenue. In a strict sense, this is correct. The theory of optimal taxation states that, under certain technical assumptions, goods with inelastic import demand should be subject to higher tariffs than those with elastic demand. The problem, however, is that India's actual tariff structure bears little relationship to this theoretical ideal. The relevant counterfactual is not some optimal tariff structure based on various elasticities about which information is lacking, but rather the one actually in place. Compared with that structure, the uniform tariff is a vastly superior alternative.

A key issue concerning the progressive reduction in tariffs is its connection to government revenue and therefore to domestic tax reform. Even if tariff reductions initially increased tariff revenue as imports rose or compliance improved, eventually tariff revenue must fall. In the extreme case, a zero tariff rate raises no tariff revenue at all.

In India, tariff revenue has been declining for some time, as a proportion both of imports and of GDP. Tariff revenue fell as a proportion of imports from 40 percent to 17.5 percent between 1991 and 2001, and as a proportion of GDP from 3.3 percent to 1.6 percent. On the one hand, this loss of revenue may share some of the blame for the increased fiscal deficit, but, on the other, it may be credited with having forced the government's hand on reforming the domestic tax system, a process that is ongoing. Optimal efficiency dictates that revenue be raised through domestic taxes. This implies that tariff liberalization and domestic tax reform must go hand in hand. Here China provides an interesting contrast to India: tariff revenue in China is currently less than 3 percent of total imports.

India can also achieve—and benefit from—considerable compression of agricultural tariffs through autonomous liberalization. India has export potential in agriculture, but that potential will not be fully exploited without the liberalization of India's own agricultural trade regime. The World

Bank and several influential nongovernmental organizations such as Oxfam have repeatedly asserted in recent years that agricultural protection is a problem of the rich countries, and that it is wrong to ask poor countries to liberalize when rich countries maintain high protection. Their position, however, effectively ties the hands of Indian politicians in this area, who now routinely express the view that, without an end to agricultural subsidies and considerable liberalization by the rich countries, India cannot risk liberalizing its agriculture, which employs 65 percent of its work force. Given this state of political play, liberalization in agriculture will have to be left to multilateral negotiations.[63]

Fortunately, politics is less of a constraint on the autonomous liberalization of services trade. India has the potential to become a major exporter not just of information technology–related services but of health and education services and tourism as well. India's costs in these sectors are relatively low, but in the education sector, considerable internal liberalization will be required. Currently, India does not permit private universities, but without them India cannot hope to become an education hub of Asia. In the health care and tourism sectors, it will be essential to improve the country's infrastructure, including its aviation infrastructure.

On the import side, India will benefit further through liberalization of its FDI rules. Sectoral caps on FDI remain in such areas as insurance, effectively denying foreign investors control of firms. These caps should be simply abolished, to allow foreign investors 100 percent ownership. There also seems little justification in many cases for the requirement that the Foreign Investment Promotion Board approve foreign investments. Indeed, the board should also be disbanded.

Contingent Protection

The WTO permits temporary protection of domestic industry through two main measures: antidumping and safeguard duties. In WTO terminology, dumping is said to occur when one or more foreign firms sell a product for less than fair value, where "fair value" is measured, for example, by the price the exporting firm charges in its home market. If such dumping causes injury to the domestic industry, the country can subject the dumping firms to antidumping duties equal to the dumping margin, measured as the difference between the "fair value" and the price actually charged. Safeguard

63. For reasons to be explained below in the section on a possible India-U.S. Free Trade Agreement, bilateral trade agreements also do not offer an effective channel for the liberalization of agriculture.

duties are permitted if import competition resulting from trade liberalization causes serious injury to the domestic industry. Whereas antidumping duties are applied only to the firms found to be dumping and other firms from the same countries, safeguard duties are applied to all trading partners on a nondiscriminatory basis.

Traditionally, Indian industry enjoyed sufficient permanent protection through tariffs and licensing that it did not require protection through antidumping measures and safeguards. But the end to licensing and the liberalization of tariffs led India to institute administrative mechanisms for these measures. India's first three antidumping cases were initiated in 1992–93. Since then the number of cases has risen steadily, especially following the Asian financial crises in 1997–98 and the end to the Indian licensing regime in 2001. According to the WTO, from July 2001 through June 2002, India was the largest initiator of antidumping cases, with seventy-six, followed by the United States with fifty-eight.[64] In terms of cumulative measures in force, the United States topped the list, followed by the European Union and India, in that order. By far the country most frequently targeted by India has been China. In contrast, India has made only limited use of safeguard measures, having initiated only six cases as of March 1999.

Many of the antidumping measures have been imposed with a clear protectionist intent, hurting buyers of the product subject to the duties. Moreover, insofar as antidumping measures tend to target the most competitive firms, the potential losses from higher domestic prices are likely to be large. It is critical that the use of antidumping measures be restrained considerably if India is to reap the benefits of its liberalization. It makes little sense to replace one instrument of protection with another. An effective remedy to limit the use of antidumping measures would be to make the injury criteria more demanding.

India also needs to streamline its antidumping procedures. Currently, the same agency carries out both the investigation to establish the dumping margin and the investigation to determine injury to the domestic industry. In other countries, such as the United States, the dumping investigation is carried out by the Department of Commerce and the injury investigation by the International Trade Commission. To ensure the independence of the two investigations, it is important that they be carried out by different agencies. The natural agency to be entrusted with the injury investigation in India is the Tariff Commission, which needs to be strengthened and made more independent.

64. WTO (2003).

A final important reform in the area of contingent protection is to encourage the use of safeguard rather than antidumping duties. Because the former are applied on a nondiscriminatory basis to all trading partners, they are inherently more efficient. Moreover, since they cover all potential sources of imports, duty rates can be much lower than the duty rates in antidumping cases, which are often very high.

Replacing antidumping with safeguard duties will require a key change in India's safeguards legislation, however. Currently, unlike the antidumping mechanism, the safeguard mechanism can be invoked only if the domestic industry can provide persuasive evidence that it is capable of restructuring itself during the period when safeguard duties are in force. This requirement is an entirely Indian invention and is not required by the WTO rules. Therefore it would be best to drop it.

Regional Arrangements

Recently, India has embarked upon an ambitious program of regional trade arrangements.[65] It has signed free trade area (FTA) agreements with Sri Lanka and Thailand and is in the advanced stages of negotiating an agreement with Singapore. India has also signed a framework agreement for an FTA with the members of the Association of South East Asian Nations (ASEAN) and an agreement to create a South Asian Free Trade Area (SAFTA). Recently, it has also approached more distant trading partners such as South Africa and Brazil to negotiate FTA arrangements.

A number of mutually reinforcing factors have contributed to this upsurge in FTA activity on India's part. First, the proliferation of regional trade arrangements around the world has made India feel that it is being left behind in this area. In the wake of the failure to make progress in multilateral talks at Cancún in September 2003, the U.S. Trade Representative announced that the United States would now aggressively move to free up trade preferentially with those countries willing to liberalize. This announcement prompted Indian leaders to seek to respond in kind. The framework agreement with the ASEAN members, SAFTA, and the offers for FTA negotiations with Brazil and South Africa are all post-Cancún developments.

---

65. The usefulness of regional trade agreements is a vast and controversial topic, and the discussion here is highly selective. Bhagwati and Panagariya (1996) and Panagariya (1999b, 2000) discuss various analytical and policy issues surrounding these agreements in greater detail.

Second, having seen the Indian economy adjust relatively painlessly to very substantial trade liberalization over the last two decades, Indian leaders have acquired greater confidence in their country's ability to withstand the competition that would result from the complete elimination of trade barriers even against selected trading partners.

Third, India's rising economic strength has made other countries keen to gain preferential access to the potentially large Indian market. This was clearly a factor in the ASEAN members' decision to accept the framework agreement, which India had sought for some time.

Fourth, political factors have been clearly dominant in the decision by India and Pakistan—and perhaps other countries in the region—to sign the SAFTA agreement. Regardless of the economic implications, the leaders foresaw a major payoff to such an agreement in terms of easing tensions between the two rivals.

Finally, during the last year of the National Democratic Alliance government, India had an external affairs minister who had previously served as finance minister for several years and whose heart was more in economic diplomacy than in political diplomacy. In contrast to Jaswant Singh, his predecessor, Yashwant Sinha demonstrated much less interest in political diplomacy and much greater keenness in seeking trade agreements abroad.

The critical question is whether this aggressive pursuit of FTAs is a good idea from the Indian perspective and, if so, what kinds of agreements should be pursued and with which countries. This subsection will consider first the potential downside of these arrangements and then the potential benefits. It will then outline what may be the best and most pragmatic strategy for India.

THE DOWNSIDE. At least three important factors weigh against India proceeding along the route toward preferential trade agreements. First, given its own high external trade barriers, India faces the obvious risk of losses due to trade diversion that preferential liberalization brings with it. Although economists have long recognized and stressed this risk, it continues to be underestimated in policy discussions and is worth spelling out explicitly here.

To make the point most dramatically, consider the proposed India-Singapore FTA. Suppose for the sake of argument that India's tariff on steel imports is 20 percent. If the world price of steel is $500 a ton, the tariff-inclusive price in India would be $600 a ton. An FTA with Singapore would give that country's steel exporters tariff-free access to the Indian market, allowing them to displace some of the steel previously imported from third countries such as South Korea and Russia. A perhaps surprising point is that, despite this "liberalization," as long as some steel continues to be imported from those third countries, the internal price of steel would remain unchanged at $600. The third countries would continue to receive $500 per ton of steel, and the Indian customs authorities would collect $100 in duties on each ton. Since Singaporean steel would be exempt from the duty, however, their exporters would now receive an extra $100 a ton in revenue. What used to be tariff revenue collected by India would now become extra revenue for Singaporean firms.

One might ask why the price of steel in India would not drop to $500 a ton as a result of the FTA. This could happen, but only if Singapore produced enough steel to supply all of India's steel imports at $500 a ton. But as long as even a small quantity of steel continued to be imported from nonmembers, it would have to be sold at $600, and thus the price would not change.

One way around this outcome would be for Singaporean firms to buy steel from Korean and Russian suppliers for $500 a ton and then resell it in India at the higher internal Indian price. If enough Singaporean exporters did this, the price of steel in India would drop to $500. The outcome would be the same as if India removed the duty not just on Singapore but on all its trading partners. However, this type of transshipment is prohibited under most FTA arrangements through what are called rules of origin. For example, to claim duty-free status, Singaporean exporters would have to prove to the satisfaction of a commerce ministry bureaucrat that a minimum, prespecified percentage of value added in each ton of steel being brought into India originated in Singapore. This regulation would eliminate transshipments from third countries.

It is tempting to conjecture that although India might lose on the goods it imports from Singapore, the losses might be offset by tariff preferences received on exports to Singapore. The catch, however, is that Singapore is already a free-trading country. The FTA gives Indian exporters no tariff preference whatsoever in the Singaporean market. More generally, in an FTA, a high-tariff member is likely to lose, since it gives up more in preferences to its partner than it receives in return. The lesson is that it is best to have low external tariffs, as does Singapore, if a country wants to benefit from FTAs.

The second risk of FTAs is their likely adverse effect on autonomous, nondiscriminatory liberalization, as illustrated by the Latin American experience. Several countries in Latin America had already been liberalizing their external trade barriers aggressively before the North American Free Trade Agreement (NAFTA) went into effect in 1994. Following NAFTA, however, they all turned to FTAs with a vengeance, and the move toward nondiscriminatory liberalization came to a standstill. These countries felt they had a better chance of forming FTAs if they kept their external tariffs as a bargaining chip to be exchanged for preferential access to partner-country markets.

Finally, the move toward FTAs may also undermine the Doha WTO negotiations aimed at multilateral liberalization. Because FTAs give exporters of a member country preferential access to the partner country's market, exporters prefer them to multilateral liberalization. This constituency's incentive to push for multilateral liberalization declines even more once preferential agreements with major trading partners are in place. For example, Mexico, which has preferential access to the U.S. and EU markets, is unlikely to push hard for multilateral liberalization, because such liberalization would result in the loss of its preferential access. For India's part, it can scarcely afford to let the multilateral route close. Because of the numerous FTAs that already exist in the Americas and Europe, India faces considerable discrimination against its products in those markets. The only way to end this discrimination is to bring tariffs down to near zero on a multilateral basis in the Doha negotiations.

POTENTIAL BENEFITS. On the benefits side of the equation, two main factors may be noted. First, the strategic issue is of paramount importance: The proliferation of FTAs in the Americas and in Europe and its neighbors has led to increasing discrimination against Asian goods. The countries of Asia have two options: either they can either try to persuade these other countries to put an end to the preferences through a multilateral bargain in the near future, or they can form their own FTAs in an attempt to create discrimination against European and American goods and thereby raise their bargaining power in a future negotiation. The first option is clearly superior, but the second can serve as insurance against failure to end discrimination in the near future. It is also a good way of demonstrating to the Americas and Europe that discrimination is a two-way street.

Second, through its FTAs, the United States is systematically creating an FTA template that makes labor and environmental standards, WTO-plus intellectual property protection, and even restrictions on the use of capital controls a part of the agreements. The eventual objective of such a template is to apply it to a future multilateral agreement. For countries such as India that oppose the inclusion of these nontrade issues in trade agreements, FTAs provide an opportunity to create an alternative template. Confronted by U.S. assertions that nontrade issues already exist in the bilateral trade agreements, and that therefore their inclusion in multilateral agreements is justified, India and other developing countries can point to their own template that does not admit their inclusion.

Some analysts view FTAs as an additional instrument for promoting liberalization. The argument is that a country may find it politically difficult to eliminate tariffs against all trading partners as part of its autonomous liberalization program, but that it may be able to do so against a handful of trading partners on a reciprocal basis. Once this is accomplished, it may find that the pressure against liberalization for the remainder has become muted. This argument is unpersuasive. Logically, the incentive for autonomous liberalization will instead decline, because the existing FTA partners will see such liberalization as an assault on their preferences, and the potential future FTA partners will become reluctant to enter an agreement when they see that the potential preferences to be won are minimal. As noted above, the available evidence from Latin America points in the same direction.

THE PRAGMATIC COURSE. Given the incentives and the pressures they face today, governments find it difficult to restrain the move toward FTAs. If all the big players are chasing every FTA they see, how can smaller players resist the temptation? It is as though the alternative to opt out of such agreements no longer exists. Given this reality, the right question to ask is, How should India approach the FTAs it chooses to seek?

The first point to note is that if India stays the course on its autonomous liberalization program, the risks of preferential liberalization will be considerably ameliorated. After some hiccups during the second half of the 1990s, India has recently been remarkably steady in bringing its external tariffs down. If this process is continued, with the external tariff on industrial goods unified and brought down to between 5 and 10 percent by 2007–08, India will be well positioned to take advantage of the regional approach to liberalization, just as Singapore is today.

In addition, if India wishes to maximize the strategic advantage from FTAs, it must work toward the creation of an Asia-wide FTA. At present, India and China both have separate framework agreements with the ASEAN members to forge FTAs with them. But if India's strategic advantage vis-à-vis the Americas and Europe is to be maximized, India must eventually form an FTA with China, thereby creating pressure for Japan, Korea, and Taiwan to join to create an Asia-wide FTA.

To keep a clean FTA template, India should also be careful to keep nontrade issues, whatever they may be, out of its FTA agreements. For example, the recent SAFTA agreement incorporates many issues that are of mutual interest—infrastructure projects and rules for competition and the promotion of venture capital—but that are unrelated to trade.[66] This practice creates a bad precedent. It also risks making valuable projects of mutual benefit hostage to trade negotiations and trade disputes. The appropriate forum for pursuing these nontrade issues in South Asia is the South Asian Association for Regional Cooperation (SAARC), of which SAFTA should be a distinct part that focuses only on trade.

Because theoretical analysis does not give an unambiguous answer to the question of whether FTAs improve or worsen economic welfare, it is useful to subject any such agreements to quantitative empirical analysis. Unfortunately, much of this type of analysis relies on computable general-equilibrium (CGE) models, which, as mentioned above, have rather poor predictive power. As Kehoe demonstrates, not one of the numerous CGE models of NAFTA came even close to predicting the actual outcome.[67] A key reason, Kehoe notes, is that in reality the most pronounced trade effects of the agreement are in products that are initially traded in small quantities or not at all. The models, in contrast, focus on products that are already extensively traded.

Therefore my own inclination is to encourage future researchers to carry out sectoral studies that are much more deeply grounded in actual data than the CGE models. The benefits from an FTA are likely to arise in sectors where trade with third countries is minimal and the scope for increasing trade with the partner is large. Likewise, the losses are likely to be seen in sectors where trade with third countries is large and may be displaced by the partner. Such studies should focus on identifying these two types of sectors and assessing how the proposed FTA will alter the picture in them.

AN INDIA-U.S. FTA. Many observers, including the Confederation of Indian Industry, have proposed negotiations toward an India-U.S. FTA. Given that India now faces considerable actual or potential discrimination in the North American market vis-à-vis Mexico, Canada, Chile, Central America, Australia, and other countries, the affirmative case for such a move from the Indian perspective is straightforward. I will argue, however, that, so far as an FTA in goods is concerned, the overall case is weak and the political impediments are insurmountable.

First, at current levels of tariffs on industrial goods in India, there is considerable scope for trade diversion and the losses that accompany it. Tariffs in India are still very high compared with U.S. tariffs, so that India stands to experience the tariff revenue loss noted above in the context of

66. Panagariya (2003) discusses the economics of SAFTA.
67. Kehoe (2003).

the India-Singapore FTA. Of course, if India carries out the liberalization outlined above, this objection will lose its force.

Second, in the area of agriculture, even though India stands to benefit from increased imports as well as increased exports, political pressures preclude the inclusion of this sector in a potential India-U.S. FTA. On the import side, benefits arise simply because Indian imports from third countries are currently limited, so that the scope for trade diversion is likewise limited. Moreover, because the United States is a globally efficient producer of agricultural products, opening to it will open India to competition against the world's most efficient producers in many sectors. The difficulty, however, is that with large domestic and export subsidies in place in the United States, which cannot be negotiated within the FTA but only in a multilateral context, any liberalization by India in agriculture is a pipedream. India's position on agriculture even in the multilateral context, with possibilities of substantial reductions in export subsidies and some reductions in domestic subsidies by the rich countries, has been squarely protectionist. The dominant view in the government is that, with 650 million people living on farm income, India cannot afford to open its agriculture to foreign competition.

Finally, the emerging U.S. FTA template, which requires the inclusion of labor and environmental standards and WTO-plus intellectual property rights in its agreements, is yet another insurmountable barrier. The U.S. Congress insists on the inclusion of these provisions in FTA agreements to which the United States is a party. India, on the other hand, is squarely opposed to them. Neither side is likely to compromise: the United States wants to establish as many precedents as possible, so as to make the linkage acceptable in the multilateral WTO agreements, whereas India has the diametrically opposite objective.

A limited case can be made, however, in favor of a mutually beneficial and politically acceptable FTA in *services* between the two countries, although even here the recent acrimonious debate on outsourcing in the United States points to potentially serious political barriers. The WTO General Agreement on Trade in Services (GATS) provides for such agreements, and there are already several precedents. Although a detailed analysis is beyond the scope of this paper, three preliminary points favoring the proposal can be made.

First, looking at the issue from the Indian perspective, to the extent the two countries' barriers in services take the form of anticompetitive regulations that cannot be eliminated on a discriminatory basis, preferential liberalization effectively becomes nondiscriminatory. Moreover, in sectors where no external liberalization has yet taken place, there is no possibility of trade diversion. In many services the United States may well be the most efficient supplier, in which case preferential liberalization will mimic multilateral liberalization.

Against these arguments one must consider that trade diversion of at least two forms cannot be ruled out. In cases where liberalization has already taken place under the GATS, trade from more efficient suppliers could be diverted. For example, India is committed to allowing twelve foreign bank branches to be opened annually as a part of its current GATS obligations. Should U.S. banks, as a result of an FTA, decide to open additional branches in India, India could count these toward fulfilling its GATS obligations. In the extreme case, if U.S. banks opened twelve or more branches a year, other countries would effectively be barred from entry into the Indian market, even if they were more efficient. Trade diversion may also happen in the potential sense in sectors that start from a position of autarky. If an FTA precedes multilateral liberalization, the U.S. firms would acquire an incumbency advantage. This would give rise to a different and inferior outcome than would have prevailed if the FTA had not preceded multilateral liberalization.[68]

Second, within these qualifications, there are several sectors in which the United States and India could benefit from an FTA in services. The U.S. comparative advantage in such sectors as telecommunications, banking, and insurance is well known. Indian firms in these sectors remain inefficient and would benefit from competition from the U.S. firms. An FTA might also spur further reforms, including privatization and the lifting of sectoral caps on FDI on a nondiscriminatory basis.

But there are other, less obvious sectors in which U.S. suppliers might benefit from market access in India. One of these is the "hospitality" sector of the tourism industry. On the one hand, India is beginning to emerge as a major attraction for foreign tourists, while, on the other, rapidly rising incomes are expanding the demand for tourism by the local population. This market could prove lucrative for U.S. suppliers of tourist services. For example, members of the Asian American Hotel Owners Association, most of whom are Americans of Indian origin, own 20,000 U.S. hotels with a total of 1 million rooms, accounting for 37 percent of all hotel properties in the United States, with a market value placed at $40 billion. These Indian American hoteliers could benefit greatly from setting up middle-tier motels

68. Mattoo and Fink (2002) offer a detailed and thoughtful discussion of potential benefits and costs of preferential trade liberalization in services and how they differ from preferential liberalization in goods.

along the national highways being constructed to link India's four major metropolises.[69]

In the same vein, the U.S. hospital and education sectors may benefit from market access in India. India can offer relatively cheap nursing and mid-level medical services, whereas Americans can bring excellent hospital management and top-tier medical skills. Similarly, there may be scope for cooperation in higher education if the FTA can serve to open the Indian market to the entry of private universities.

For its part, India would benefit not only from imports in the areas just described but also from increased exports. The provision of various services to U.S. firms under the broad rubric of "outsourcing" has emerged as a major export area for India. A services FTA could be a useful instrument for cementing market access in this important area. India may also benefit from an increased share of temporary worker visas in the United States. At present India is losing share because the United States is using the fixed number of H1B visas to first make good on its commitments to countries such as Mexico and Chile that already have services FTAs with it. In addition to the workers it provides in the information technology sector, India can offer many professional workers in such sectors as nursing and hospitality.

Finally, in a services FTA it may be possible to set aside the divisive issue of labor standards. In goods trade the United States faces the prospect of increased competition in unskilled labor–intensive sectors such as footwear and apparel. The "fair trade" argument for linking market access to labor standards has greater political salience in these sectors than in the skilled labor–intensive activities likely to be opened up to Indian services suppliers in the U.S. market.

Multilateral Negotiations

This paper would be incomplete without some discussion of the ongoing multilateral trade negotiations at Doha. Perhaps the single most important objective for India in the trade domain is to bring the Doha negotiations to a conclusion. It would be unrealistic to expect the round to close by the end of 2004 as originally planned, but a conclusion by the end of 2006 is both feasible and in India's interest.[70]

---

69. "Indian-American Hotel Owners See Prospects in Hospitality Industry," *News India-Times*, January 23, 2004, p. 16.

70. As discussed in detail in Panagariya (2002b), India has approached the Doha negotiations with great suspicion, which has not served its own best interests. The case for why and how India must support the liberalization agenda of the Doha negotiations is outlined in Bhagwati and Panagariya (2003).

After the failure to make progress in Cancún, the United States has revised its position in favor of a narrower round. India can readily make common cause with the United States around this position. Thus, in a letter dated January 11, 2004, and addressed to the trade ministers of the WTO member countries, U.S. Trade Representative Robert Zoellick expressed willingness to drop all Singapore issues from the agenda except for trade facilitation.[71] India has been willing to negotiate on trade facilitation, so that there is no more disagreement with the United States in this area. Moreover, Zoellick's proposal would considerably narrow the scope of the round, focusing it on trade liberalization just as India had sought originally. And India surely stands to benefit from liberalization in all areas: industry, agriculture, and services.

INDUSTRIAL TARIFFS. In his letter to the trade ministers, Zoellick renewed his proposal to achieve zero tariffs on industrial goods by 2015. Given its own autonomous trade liberalization program, this is a feasible goal for India. But if India wants more of a cushion, it can surely ask for a more relaxed deadline for developing countries, until 2020 or even 2025. The benefits to India from accepting this proposal as is or in modified form are quite unambiguous.

India has long sought to eliminate tariff peaks against labor-intensive products in developed countries. Top World Bank officials and many nongovernmental organizations have recently raised hopes that repeated public exhortations to the effect that developed country barriers cost developing countries more than what they give the latter in aid might shame them into dismantling these barriers unilaterally. But the experience of the last forty years leads to a different conclusion. The U.N. Conference on Trade and Development, the leaders of developing countries, trade and development experts, and even World Bank reports have condemned the barriers against developing country exports for decades. As early as 1965, developing countries successfully deployed moral suasion to add Part IV to the General Agreement on Tariffs and Trade, explicitly committing the developed countries to "accord high priority to the reduction and elimination of barriers to products currently or potentially of particular export interest to less developed contracting parties" and to "refrain from introducing, or increasing the incidence of customs duties or non-tariff barriers on products currently or potentially of particular export interest" to them.

71. The first WTO ministerial meeting in 1996, held in Singapore, introduced four new issues into the WTO study agenda: investment, competition policy, government procurement, and trade facilitation. New issues are initially taken up as study issues, and if there is enough support for them, they may be turned into negotiating issues.

Yet because developing countries insisted on one-way concessions, little progress was actually made. On the contrary, textiles and apparel imports by developed countries came under severe restrictions through no fewer than 3,000 bilateral treaties under the MFA. Likewise, footwear and steel were frequently subject to the imposition of "orderly market arrangements" by the United States, and tariff peaks systematically discriminated against developing country exports. The only "concession" that the developing countries received was the Generalized System of Preferences, which now even Oxfam correctly cites as evidence against the United States' sincerity about opening its markets to developing countries.

The main substantive break that developing countries received in gaining improved market access for themselves in the last forty years was the agreement in the Uruguay Round to end the MFA. India would be deluding itself if it hung onto the notion that hard-core developed country barriers can be eliminated through moral suasion alone, without reciprocity.

India also gains a tactical advantage through the proposed initiative. In one stroke it would knock down its image as an "obstructionist" in the negotiations and announce its emergence as a truly confident player on the world economic stage, as it already has on the world political stage. Indeed, such a move would put the United States on the defensive, since, according to some, the U.S. government put forward the zero-tariff proposal, despite immense political pressure against it from domestic lobbies, precisely in the hope that developing countries would refuse to go along. India can call this bluff and turn the U.S. tactical advantage into its own.

There are two more reasons why India stands to benefit big from the proposed initiative. First, India's own liberalization, to which it would commit itself as a part of the deal, benefits India. India has now fully recognized this fact in its economic reforms program, with the Kelkar task force (the Task Force on Indirect Taxes) recommending that virtually all tariffs be lowered to 10 percent or less by 2006–07.[72] All that India will be doing under the proposed initiative is to bind this liberalization at the WTO and push it to its logical conclusion of zero tariffs by 2025. Second, as noted above, with NAFTA, the European Union, and numerous other preferential trade areas both between the European Union and its neighbors and within Latin America, Africa, and even East Asia already in existence, India's products today face discrimination in virtually every major market. Through the zero-tariff option, India would eliminate this discrimination in one stroke.

72. Government of India (2002).

AGRICULTURE. Effectively admitting his mistake in trying to make common cause with the European Union on agriculture at Cancún, Zoellick made the elimination of agricultural export subsidies a priority in his letter to the trade ministers. This is something India has sought as well. Nevertheless, India remains defensive in this area. India's main concern, as already noted, is that with 650 million or more Indians living on farm income, India cannot afford to open its agriculture.

Agriculture is indeed a politically charged issue in India, but the story is not altogether different in other parts of the world. Therefore, if India seeks agricultural liberalization, including substantial cuts in domestic subsidies by the rich countries, it has to be willing to place its own agricultural barriers on the table. This is not a particularly risky course for two reasons. First, like many rich countries, India has bound its agricultural tariffs at very high levels ranging from 100 to 300 percent. Bringing these bindings down to even 50 percent would lead to minimal effective opening up. All India would be doing is to eliminate the existing headroom in its tariffs. But if, in return, India could win additional market access in rich country markets, it could only contribute to boosting agricultural incomes in India. Second, according to available studies, if the developed country subsidies were substantially reduced, Indian agriculture would be competitive in a large majority of commodities. Thus any loss of market at home could be substantially made up by the market access achieved in the partner countries.

SERVICES. Services negotiations have been relatively less controversial. The discussion above of a possible services FTA between India and the United States illustrates the potential benefits to India from negotiating actively in this area. One priority for India ought to be to seek binding commitments from its trading partners, especially the United States, in those business services that fall under the heading of business process outsourcing. But India can also benefit from negotiations in areas in which it can offer low-cost services, such as health and accounting services. In return, India can offer binding commitments in areas such as banking, insurance, and telecommunications. Many of India's liberalizing measures in services are unbound and therefore can be used as bargaining chips.

Conclusions

This paper has discussed India's record on trade liberalization; its impact on trade flows, efficiency, and growth; and future choices for India's trade policy. It has demonstrated that liberalization has had a major impact on both the volume of trade and its composition. In particular, if one looks at India's trade at a highly disaggregated level, India's opening has led to the emergence of many new products on the imports and exports lists.

Trade liberalization has led to improved static efficiency in production as well as consumption. According to the calculations done by Chadha and others discussed above, total annual gains from these sources may have been as much as 5 percent of India's GDP. Liberalization was a key ingredient in sustaining India's growth rate of nearly 6 percent a year on average during the last two decades. The studies dealing with productivity have produced mixed evidence, but on balance they suggest that a considerable increase in both the level and the growth rate of productivity has accompanied liberalization. Specifically, the recent study by Sivadasan based on plant-level data offers robust evidence of tariff liberalization leading to increased productivity.[73]

To date, liberalization has failed to stimulate India's labor-intensive industries to any great degree. The industries that have shown the fastest export growth are typically capital- or skilled labor–intensive industries. This paper has identified the policy of small-scale industry reservation and stringent labor laws as the key reasons why labor-intensive exports have failed to grow rapidly. Reform in these areas is a necessary condition for the transformation of India from a primarily agricultural to a primarily industrial economy.

This paper has also argued that, by 2004–05, India should adopt a uniform 15 percent tariff rate on industrial goods and then gradually bring this rate down to 5 percent by the beginning of 2008–09. This reform would allow the country to end the plethora of exemptions that currently afflict the tariff regime and would help bring administrative costs down. In agriculture, although unilateral liberalization would still be beneficial, the current political climate seems against it. Therefore the best course is to take a more flexible approach in the Doha negotiations, which may help bring the level of subsidies and protection in the rich countries down quite substantially. Liberalization by India within the context of this rich country liberalization would provide considerable scope for the expansion of agricultural exports.

This paper has taken a generally cautious view on regional arrangements. If India must pursue these arrangements, it should work toward an Asia-wide FTA that includes China. Such an FTA would have strategic value in attracting attention to the diversion of Asian exports from the

73. Sivadasan (2003).

North American and European markets caused by NAFTA and the European Union, respectively. The desirability of smaller arrangements such as the SAFTA rests primarily on their political value. Economically, given the high tariffs in the region, trade diversion is likely to dominate. But the arrangement may prove to be a useful instrument for eventually establishing better political ties between India and Pakistan. All such FTA arrangements, however, should be limited to trade issues. Issues of cooperation in other areas, such as infrastructure projects of common interest, are better handled in the context of the SAARC rather than the SAFTA.

Finally, should India seek an FTA with the United States? A conventional India-U.S. FTA that focuses on goods trade is politically a nonstarter. Such an FTA would have to include agriculture but could not be expected to end agricultural subsidies in the United States (since these subsidies can only be eliminated in the multilateral context), and this would be unacceptable to India. This same issue has marred the current negotiations on the Free Trade Area of the Americas, with Brazil and the United States finding themselves at odds. The United States would also insist on the inclusion of labor and environmental standards and WTO-plus intellectual property protection in such an FTA, which would likewise be unacceptable to India. Therefore this paper has argued for studying the benefits and feasibility of an India-U.S. FTA limited to services trade. Evidence suggests that an FTA in this area could be mutually beneficial and politically feasible, but more work is required before a definitive conclusion can be reached.

Comments and Discussion

M. Govinda Rao: In this paper, Arvind Panagariya provides a comprehensive account of the evolution of India's trade policy in the context of the public sector–dominated, heavy industry–based, import-substituting industrialization strategy that the country followed in the initial phase of planned development and explores its impact on the productivity and growth of the Indian economy. The author shows how the strategy, pursued with vigor during the first twenty-five years of planning, evolved into an autarkic foreign trade and investment regime marked by tight export controls and culminated in economic isolationism. The next phase, which was characterized by ad hoc liberalization (1976–91), saw acceleration in economic growth, but expansionary fiscal policy created an unstable macroeconomic environment. The "progressive liberalization" phase, which began in 1991, has seen the increasing globalization of the Indian economy. The paper analyzes the broadening and deepening process of trade liberalization in terms of commodity composition and the direction of trade; it also reviews available evidence on the impact of liberalization on the efficiency and growth of the economy. The paper explores various policy options and charts an appropriate course for India to follow.

This is a well-researched paper. There can be hardly any disagreement on the various phases of trade policy analyzed, on the asserted impact of trade policy on the productivity and growth of India's economy, or on the policy options recommended. This comment attempts instead to supplement the analysis with some additional issues and argues for greater emphasis with respect to some of the issues discussed.

The author deals with the ill effects of India's autarkic trade policy as well as several microlevel distortions in considerable detail. The important issue, however, is that the country's protectionist trade policy and interventionist domestic policy combine to create adverse growth consequences that are much more than the sum of the impact of the two policies implemented separately. Combined, the two have created havoc with the economic system and the structure of incentives in the economy. Indeed, as the author notes, "the myriad microeconomic distortions and heavy state intervention straightjacketed the entrepreneurs." I would like to add that the ill effects were even more far-reaching. The combination of these policies led to "structural stagnation" by creating powerful special interestgroups, a large rent-seeking society, in every sphere of economic activity.

The issue is important because India's autarkic international trade regime was closely followed by total central control of the banking and financial system in 1969, with the nationalization of fourteen major commercial banks. This, the single most important act of centralization of the financial system, has been, in combination with other dirigistic policies, a cause of several microeconomic distortions and inequities.

While the paper devotes considerable space to the discussion of the microlevel distortions created by various domestic policies, the analysis of total factor productivity (TFP) seems to attribute its growth entirely to trade liberalization. In particular, the evidence cited from the Chand and Sen paper covers only the phase in which trade policies were tinkered with. It may well be difficult to attribute the growth of TFP in 1984–88 to trade liberalization per se because it was a period of significant liberalization of both trade and internal regulation.

The importance of the Panagariya paper lies in highlighting the emerging policy issues. To be sure, tariffs have to be lowered within the next few years to the levels prevailing in the Southeast Asian economies, but it is important to phase out fiscal imbalances before significant external liberalization can be attempted. The task force chaired by Kelkar to achieve the targets set out in the Fiscal Responsibility and Budget Management Act 2003 has laid out a roadmap for augmenting revenues, primarily by levying a national goods and services tax.[1] However, the "grand bargain" required for such a levy is unlikely to materialize in the short, and even in the medium, terms. If containing the fiscal deficit is vigorously pursued, deficit reduction may be achieved at the cost of infrastructure investments. The paper, therefore, emphasizes the need to focus on reducing the revenue deficit in the near term.

Indeed, infrastructure development—particularly of ports, roads, railways, and most of all power facilities—is a critical determinant of the competitiveness of domestic producers. It is also important to provide adequate funds for maintaining physical infrastructure, which is considered as revenue expenditure. In the absence of infrastructure development, a tariff reduction could result in a flood of imports of finished consumer goods from neighboring countries such as China, Thailand, Malaysia, and Singapore. At the same time, it is important that the outlay on education and health care be increased, both to accelerate growth and to reduce poverty.

1. Government of India (2004).

Therefore the focus of fiscal restructuring should shift to the primary deficit rather than to either the revenue or the fiscal deficit.

The paper refers to the need to complement reductions in tariffs with domestic trade tax reforms. In particular, freeing internal trade from impediments to the movement of factors and products is critical in order to take advantage of the large common market. Equally, at the micro level there is too much protection (through exemption from various labor laws and freedom from the plethora of inspectors who implement them) of small-scale industry, which hinders its growth into medium- and large-scale enterprises. Small-scale industry also is exempt from domestic taxes, particularly the central excise duty. Panagariya rightly refers to the distortions and inefficiency created by the policy of reserving items for manufacture in small-scale industries. However, by merely de-reserving the items in the small-scale sector we may not be able to solve the problem, unless there is an incentive for small enterprises to grow into medium- and large-scale industries.

To conclude, the Panagariya paper makes a valuable contribution to the debate on trade policy. Its most important contribution lies in its recommendation for a future course of action, and one hopes that policymakers will heed its sound advice.

Pranab Bardhan: I found the Panagariya paper to be a lucid and fairly comprehensive survey of the main trends and issues of India's trade policy. I also agree with the main thrust of the paper in terms of policy recommendations. I would endorse the author's ideas on trade reform—in particular, on uniform and low tariffs—and I find his thoughts on the regional trade agreements sensible and pragmatic. A few suggestions that I had for the earlier version of the paper have been largely incorporated, so I have very little to say now, except for one minor and one quasi-major point.

It is not central to Panagariya's main empirical discussion on growth and productivity, but it seems to me that the brief discussion of the general literature on the role of total factor productivity growth (with particular reference to East Asia) vis-à-vis capital accumulation is somewhat incomplete. I have always found this literature to be unnecessarily controversial, particularly when much of the technological progress in developing countries (including that in East Asia) results from improved technologies that are embodied in imported capital goods, so that the distinction between TFP growth and investment is necessarily blurred. Also, before deriding

East Asian growth as "Soviet-style perspiration," American commentators should keep in mind that almost all countries, including the United States in large parts of the nineteenth century, have shown a similar pattern in the early stages of industrialization.[2]

I agree with Panagariya on the importance of two key domestic reforms if trade reform is to stimulate industrial growth: containing the public revenue deficit in order to release funds for public investment in infrastructure and dismantling the existing small-scale industries reservation program. But the practical importance of labor reform for industrial growth is a substantive point on which I and the author somewhat disagree. It is clear that the labor laws that are now on the books can hamper flexibility and ultimately harm the unemployed and workers who have to crowd the informal sector, but I would like to see more convincing evidence on how much of a hindrance to business investment they really are. Beyond repeated assertions by pro-reform economists and the "pink" (financial) press in India, there is very little hard evidence to go by.

Most of the anecdotes one hears about inefficient job secure workers in India are based on common encounters with lazy public sector, white-collar workers protected by their unions. However, there are counter-anecdotes that suggest that labor laws are commonly flouted by industrial employers in many states (particularly in west and south India) while the state government looks the other way. Jenkins (2000) has described this as "reform by stealth."

Nagaraj (2004) has raised the question of why, if labor laws made sacking workers and closing plants so difficult, Annual Survey of Industries data show that between 1995–96 and 2000–01 about 15 percent of workers in the organized manufacturing sector (about 1.1 million workers) lost their jobs. This loss of jobs was spread across industries and states in India.

Let me refer now to two careful microeconometric studies that I have seen that may also be relevant to the question of job security laws. One is by Dutta Roy (2004), who fits dynamic labor demand functions for sixteen industry groups (separately for production and nonproduction workers) for the period from 1960–61 to 1994–95. She shows that the impact of job security regulations in India is statistically insignificant, except in the cement industry. The rigidities in the adjustment of labor were about the same even before the introduction of stringent job security clauses in the

---

2. See Eichengreen (2002).

1976 and 1982 amendments to the Industrial Disputes Act. This suggests there are other reasons for any rigidities in the labor market.

The second study, by Daveri, Manasse, and Serra (2003), was part of a joint project with the World Bank on the impact of globalization on industrial labor market outcomes in India. Using a new dataset from a World Bank survey of 895 Indian firms in 1997–99, covering five manufacturing sectors, they find that employees of firms subject to foreign competition face much more uncertainty with regard to their earnings and employment prospects (there is, of course, a positive incentive effect—they are more likely to be involved in training and skill-upgrading programs).

All of this suggests that it is not socially responsible to talk about the beneficial effects of trade reform without at the same time making concrete suggestions for creating social adjustment programs for displaced workers. In a country where social safety nets for poor workers are either nonexistent or extremely inadequate and where authorities often renege on their compensation promises, academic demonstrations of the long-run benefits of trade reform are not going to be convincing. In this respect the attempt, though small scale, of the Department of International Development of the U.K. government in collaboration with a local NGO to financially assist and retrain displaced industrial workers in some bankrupt public sector firms in West Bengal is a step in the right direction. Social protection should be part of a comprehensive trade and labor reform package if reform is to be desirable as well as feasible.

General Discussion

Surjit Bhalla believed that the role of labor reform in explaining India's disappointing industrial performance was overstated. Instead, he felt that macroeconomic policies, particularly tight monetary policy, were more important. As evidence for this view he pointed out that the 1991 reforms had indeed led to a growth spurt in industry in the years immediately following, but that it had petered out in 1996, not to revive until 2002–03. He also felt that India's exchange rate policy had led to a loss of competitiveness, particularly with respect to China. Rajesh Chadha felt that policy uncertainty had been important in depressing industrial activity. He cited the sudden reduction in the customs duty on certain capital goods as an example of policy uncertainty that might dampen the investment intentions of other potential investors. John Williamson noted that there was a tendency to focus on the rupee-dollar rate, while even over 2003 the rupee had continued to depreciate in effective terms. He also queried the concept of the "capital intensity" of Indian exports, citing a recent McKinsey study that found that India's auto industry was much less capital intensive than China's, in part because of the greater skill level and flexibility of the Indian labor force.

Suman Bery asked whether there were any studies on the political economy of trade reforms that could explain both the liberalization episodes and the occasional backtracking. He also asked what the international experience was with a uniform tariff rate: If it is so pure, why is it not adopted more widely? Are the forces that determine more complex tariff structures revenue-driven or the result of lobbying for effective protection? Rajnish Mehra tended to agree with political explanations of industrial sluggishness, attributing it to the power of existing interests to prevent competition and extract rents. Noting Panagariya's caution on free trade agreements, Anil Sharma asked whether there was really any alternative, given the difficulties faced during the Doha Round of trade talks and the reduced appeal of unilateral action. Vijay Kelkar asked how realistic it is to impose a uniform tariff when the taxation of domestic inputs is not properly offset by drawback schemes. A uniform customs tariff would lead to negative rates of protection in a number of activities because the incidence of domestic indirect taxes is not uniform. Given the realities, he believed that a uniform low rate of custom duties in an environment of exchange rate appreciation would lead to a backlash from Indian industry and a possible reversal of the progress made. He agreed with Panagariya that the special and differential treatment provisions of GATT had outlived their utility for India and also that India's antidumping machinery needed review. Montek Ahluwalia and Vijay Joshi both pursued the issue, raised by Bardhan, of the link between India's intellectual property regime and the rise of India's pharmaceutical industry. Ahluwalia believed that the export orientation of the big Indian pharmaceutical firms in the past had as much to do with domestic price controls as with the intellectual property regime. Since these controls affected primarily the large players, these firms found foreign markets more lucrative than the domestic market.

Ahluwalia also concurred that the emphasis on labor reform might be overdone. He noted that import restrictions on labor-intensive sectors had been lifted only recently, as was the case with the liberalization of the small-scale industry regime. He believed that competition in product markets would be reflected in the behavior of the labor force, which would adjust to ensure company survival. Barry Bosworth noted, though, that labor legislation could have a major impact on foreign firms, which do not have the option of entering the informal sector. This could be one reason for the dis-appointing response of foreign direct investment to India's liberalization. Panagariya disagreed with the points made on labor reform and on uniform customs duties, indicating that both industry's stagnant share of GDP and the low share of organized sector employment in the labor force were indicators of serious obstacles to the expansion of modern industrial employment. He also rejected the view that the existing (and proposed) differential customs duty structure had anything to do with distortions in domestic taxation; in his view this structure reflects attempts by lobbies to secure effective protection and would lead only to further rent-seeking behavior and difficulties in implementation.

References

Ahluwalia, Isher J. 1991. *Productivity and Growth in Indian Manufacturing.* Delhi: Oxford University Press.

_____. 1994. "TFPG in Manufacturing Industry." *Economic and Political Weekly,* October 22, p. 2836.

Balakrishnan, P., and K. Pushpangandan. 1994. "Total Factor Productivity Growth in Manufacturing Industry: A Fresh Look." *Economic and Political Weekly,* July 30, pp. 2028–35.

Balakrishnan, P., K. Pushpangandan, and M. S. Babu. 2000. "Trade Liberalization and Productivity Growth in Manufacturing: Evidence from Firm-Level Panel Data." *Economic and Political Weekly,* October 7, pp. 3679–82.

Bhagwati, Jagdish. 1999. "The 'Miracle' That Did Happen: Understanding East Asia in Comparative Perspective." In *Taiwan's Development Experience: Lessons on Roles of Government and Market,* edited by Erik Thorbecke and Henry Wan. Boston: Kluwer Academic Publishers.

Bhagwati, Jagdish, and Padma Desai. 1970. *India: Planning for Industrialization.* London: Oxford University Press.

Bhagwati, Jagdish, and Arvind Panagariya. 1996. "Preferential Trading Areas and Multilateralism: Strangers, Friends or Foes?" In *The Economics of Preferential Trading,* edited by Jagdish Bhagwati and Arvind Panagariya. Washington: AEI Press. Reproduced as chapter 2 in *Trading Blocs: Alternative Approaches to Analyzing Preferential Trade Agreements,* edited by Jagdish Bhagwati, P. Krishna, and Arvind Panagariya. MIT Press, 1999.

_____. 2003. "Defensive Play Simply Won't Work." *Economic Times,* August 29, p. 15.

Bhagwati, Jagdish, and T. N. Srinivasan. 1975. *Foreign Trade Regimes and Economic Development: India.* New York: National Bureau of Economic Research.

Chadha, Rajesh, Alan Deardorff, Sanjib Pohit, and Robert Stern. 1998. *The Impact of Trade and Domestic Policy Reforms in India: A CGE Modeling Approach.* University of Michigan Press.

Chand, Satish, and Kunal Sen. 2002. "Trade Liberalization and Productivity Growth: Evidence from Indian Manufacturing." *Review of Development Economics* 6, no. 1: 120–32.

Collins, Susan M., and Barry P. Bosworth. 1996. "Economic Growth in East Asia: Accumulation versus Assimilation." *Brookings Papers on Economic Activity,* no. 2, pp. 135–91.

Das, Deb Kusum. 2003. "Manufacturing Productivity under Varying Trade Regimes: India in the 1980s and 1990s." Working Paper 107. New Delhi: Indian Council for Research on International Economic Relations.

Daveri, F., P. Manasse, and D. Serra. 2003. "The Twin Effects of Globalization." Turin, Italy: Luca d'Agliano Foundation.

DeLong, J. Bradford. 2003. "India Since Independence: An Analytic Growth Narrative." In *In Search of Prosperity: Analytic Narratives on Economic Growth,* edited by Dani Rodrik. Princeton University Press.

Dholakia, B. H., and R. H. Dholakia. 1994. "Total Factor Productivity Growth in Manufacturing Industry." *Economic and Political Weekly,* December 31, pp. 3342–44.

Dutta Roy, S. 2004. "Employment Dynamics in Indian Industry: Adjustment Lags and the Impact of Job Security Regulations." *Journal of Development Economics* 73, no. 1: 233–56.

Eichengreen, B. 2002. "Capitalizing on Globalization." *Asian Development Review* 19, no. 1: 17–69.

Gordon, Jim, and Poonam Gupta. 2003. "Understanding India's Services Revolution." Paper presented at the IMF-NCAER Conference, "A Tale of Two Giants: India's and China's Experience with Reform," New Delhi, November 14–16.

Government of India. 2002. "Reports of the Task Force on Indirect Taxes." Chairman, Vijay L. Kelkar. New Delhi: Ministry of Finance and Company Affairs.

_____. 2004. "Report of the Task Force on Implementation of the Fiscal Responsibility and Budget Management Act, 2003." Chairman, Vijay L. Kelkar. New Delhi: Ministry of Finance.

Hulten, Charles R. 1975. "Technical Change and the Reproducibility of Capital." *American Economic Review* 65, no. 5: 956–65.

Hulten, Charles R., and Mieko Nishimizu. 1980. "The Importance of Productivity Change in the Economic Growth of Nine Industrialized Countries." In *Lagging Productivity Growth: Causes and Remedies,* edited by Shlomo Maital and Noah M. Meltz. Cambridge, Mass.: Ballinger.

Hulten, Charles, and Syleja Srinivasan. 1999. "Indian Manufacturing Industry: Elephant or Tiger? New Evidence on the Asian Miracle." Working Paper 7441. Cambridge, Mass.: National Bureau of Economic Research.

Jenkins, R. S. 2000. *Democratic Politics and Economic Reform in India.* Cambridge University Press.

Joshi, Vijay, and Ian M. D. Little. 1994. *India: Macroeconomics and Political Economy: 1961–91.* Washington: World Bank.

Kehoe, Timothy J. 2003. "An Evaluation of the Performance of Applied General Equilibrium Models of the Impact of NAFTA." Research Department Staff Report 320. Federal Reserve Bank of Minneapolis.

Kehoe, Timothy J., and Kim J. Ruhl. 2002. "How Important is the New Goods Margin in International Trade?" University of Minnesota.

Kelkar, Vijay. 2001. "India's Reform Agenda: Micro, Meso and Macro Economic Reforms." Fourth Annual Fellows Lecture, Center for the Advanced Study of India, University of Pennsylvania.

Kim, Jong-Il, and Lawrence J. Lau. 1994. "The Sources of Economic Growth of the East Asian Newly Industrialized Countries." *Journal of Japanese and International Economies* 8: 235–27.

Krishna, Pravin, and Devashish Mitra. 1998. "Trade Liberalization, Market Discipline and Productivity Growth: New Evidence from India." *Journal of Development Economics* 56: 447–62.

Krugman, Paul. 1994. "The Myth of Asia's Miracle." *Foreign Affairs* 73, no. 6: 62–77.

Mattoo, Aaditya, and Carsten Fink. 2002. "Regional Agreements and Trade in Services: Policy Issues." Policy Research Working Paper 2852. Washington: World Bank.

McKinsey Global Institute. 2001. *India: The Growth Imperative*. San Francisco.

Mukerji, Purba. 2004. "Essays in International Trade." Ph.D. dissertation, University of Maryland.

Nadiri, M. Ishaq, and Wanpyo Son. 1998. "Sources of Growth in East Asian Economies." New York University (July).

Nagaraj, R. 2004. "Fall in Organized Manufacturing Employment: A Brief Note." *Economic and Political Weekly* 39, no. 30.

Panagariya, Arvind. 1999a. "WTO Trade Policy Review of India, 1998." *World Economy* 22, no. 6: 799–824.

_____. 1999b. "The Regionalism Debate: An Overview." *World Economy* 22, no. 4: 477–511.

_____. 2000. "Preferential Trade Liberalization: The Traditional Theory and New Developments." *Journal of Economic Literature* 38: 287–331.

_____. 2002a. "Cost of Protection: Where Do We Stand?" *American Economic Review, Papers and Proceedings* 92, no. 2: 175–79.

_____. 2002b. "India at Doha: Retrospect and Prospect." *Economic and Political Weekly,* January 26, pp. 279–84.

_____. 2003. "South Asia: Does Preferential Trade Liberalization Make Sense?" *World Economy* 26, no. 9 (special issue on Global Trade Policy): 1279–91.

_____. 2004. "Growth and Reforms During 1980s and 1990s." *Economic and Political Weekly*, June 19, pp. 2581–94.

Panagariya, Arvind, and Rupa Duttagupta. 2001. "The 'Gains' from Preferential Trade Liberalization in the CGEs: Where Do They Come From?" In *Regionalism and Globalization: Theory and Practice*, edited by Sajal Lahiri. London: Routledge.

Panagariya, Arvind, and Dani Rodrik. 1993. "Political Economy Arguments for a Uniform Tariff." *International Economic Review*, August, pp. 685–703.

Pursell, Garry. 1992. "Trade Policy in India." In *National Trade Policies*, edited by Dominick Salvatore. New York: Greenwood Press.

Rao, J. Mohan. 1996. "Manufacturing Productivity Growth, Method and Measurement." *Economic and Political Weekly,* November 2, pp. 2927–36.

Reserve Bank of India. 2002. *Handbook of Statistics on Indian Economy*. Mumbai.

_____. 2003. *Annual Report 2002-2003*. Mumbai.

Rodrik, Dani. 2003. "Institutions, Integration, and Geography: In Search of the Deep Determinants of Economic Growth." In *In Search of Prosperity: Analytic*

Narratives on Economic Growth, edited by Dani Rodrik. Princeton University Press.

Romer, Paul. 1994. "New Goods, Old Theory, and the Welfare Costs of Trade Restrictions." *Journal of Development Economics* 43: 5–38.

Shourie, Arun. 1966. "Allocation of Foreign Exchange in India." Ph.D. dissertation, Syracuse University.

Sivadasan, Jagadeesh. 2003. "Barriers to Entry and Productivity: Micro-Evidence from Indian Manufacturing Sector Reforms." Graduate School of Business, University of Chicago.

Tharoor, Shashi. 1997. *From Midnight to the Millennium.* New York: Harper Perennial.

Topalova, Petia. 2003. "Trade Liberalization and Firm Productivity: the Case of India." Massachusetts Institute of Technology.

Unel, Bulent. 2003. "Productivity Trends in India's Manufacturing Sectors in the Last Two Decades." IMF Working Paper WP/03/22. Washington: International Monetary Fund.

World Bank. 2002. *World Development Indicators 2002.* Washington.

_____. 2003. *World Development Indicators 2003.* Washington.

World Trade Organization (WTO). 1998. "Trade Policy Review—India." Geneva.

_____. 2002. "Trade Policy Review—India." Geneva.

_____. 2003. *Annual Report.* Geneva.

Young, Alwyn. 1992. "A Tale of Two Cities: Factor Accumulation and Technical Change in Hong Kong and Singapore." In *NBER Macroeconomics Annual,* edited by Olivier J. Blanchard and Stanley Fischer. MIT Press.

_____. 1995. "The Tyranny of Numbers: Confronting the Statistical Realities of the East Asian Experience." *Quarterly Journal of Economics* 110, no. 3: 641–80.

ROBERT Z. LAWRENCE
Kennedy School of Government, Harvard University

RAJESH CHADHA
National Council of Applied Economic Research

Should a U.S.-India FTA Be Part of India's Trade Strategy?

I n the current political environment, it is an understatement to say that a U.S.-India Free Trade Agreement (FTA) does not appear to be an idea whose time has come. Slow employment growth in the United States has raised fears about the loss of high-paying jobs to outsourcing, and the jobs lost to India have born the brunt of these concerns. Members of the U.S. Congress would surely not relish the opportunity to vote to endorse such trade. It is also unlikely that Indian politicians would relish the opportunity to cast their lot with the United States and abandon long-held positions on nonalignment, multilateralism, special and differential treatment, and domestic protection. Yet precisely because it challenges views held on these issues, the question posed by the title of this paper is important. It offers an opportunity to reflect on whether current trade rules and policies provide an adequate framework for realizing the full potential of India's global integration and domestic reforms. For example, do current arrangements suffice to ensure that one of the most dynamic global linkages—services outsourcing—will continue to flourish? Should India continue to rely primarily on unilateral trade liberalization? Could it reap even greater reform gains from a multitrack strategy in which the World Trade Organization (WTO) and regional free trade agreements play a greater role? And in such a multitrack strategy, what are the relative merits of multilateral and bilateral approaches? These are questions that this paper explores.

The authors thank Suneet Weling and Devender Pratap for excellent research assistance, and Arvind Subramanian, Suman Bery, and participants in the meeting of the India Policy Forum for their helpful comments. The contribution by Rajesh Chadha has mainly been in measuring the quantitative aspects of the likely U.S.-India Free Trade Agreement discussed in the section on "Comparative Static and Dynamic Considerations." He is not responsible for views expressed in other sections of the paper.

The topic is timely. For most of its existence as an independent country, India had highly protectionist and statist economic policies. Self-sufficiency was an important goal. The domestic market was protected by high tariffs and prohibitions on imports. Foreign investment was restricted. The government occupied the commanding heights of the economy by owning many firms and controlling the price, investment, layoff, and exit decisions made by private firms.

Since 1991, however, these policies have been radically changed.[1] Many nontariff barriers have been eliminated and average tariff rates have been dramatically reduced—indeed more than halved.[2] In addition, foreign investment has been liberalized, exports promoted through a host of special tax, zone, and importation privileges, and the government has privatized and reduced its equity positions in many state-owned enterprises. The permit system for domestic investment has been abandoned, and the number of sectors reserved for small-scale industry reduced.

The policy has been associated with positive outcomes. The acceleration in growth that began in the 1980s has been sustained. Both exports and imports have increased as a share of gross domestic product (GDP). As success stories have accumulated, a growing sense of confidence has burgeoned among Indian entrepreneurs in particular and the public at large.

Yet much remains to be done. On the basis of its tariff rates, which remain among the world's highest, India is still a relatively closed economy, and its domestic reforms are a work in progress. Foreign investment is by no means free, and the rules governing exports remain highly complex and interventionist. Likewise, government ownership and controls remain fairly pervasive in the domestic market. In particular, the policies of reserving certain goods for production by the small-scale sector and a rigid regulatory system in the labor market remain in place. Indian competitiveness in manufactured goods, while improving, still has a long way to go to match its major Asian competitors and provide employment for millions of new entrants to the labor market. Indian infrastructure is sorely in need of major new investments. In addition, within India, there continues to be political resistance to liberalization and a widespread view that a highly interventionist strategy is appropriate for a nation at India's stage of economic development. Given the tasks yet to be accomplished, what is now the best trade and reform strategy for India?

1. For more on these policies, see the paper by Arvind Panagariya in this volume.

2. Tariffs have declined from a weighted average duty of 72.5 percent in 1991–92 to 29 percent in 2002–03. Peak duties were reduced from 150 percent to 25 percent (Ahluwalia 2002, p. 74). On January 8, 2004, the Indian government reduced the peak duty on non-agricultural goods from 25 percent to 20 percent and abolished a 4 percent special additional duty that had been levied.

One option is to follow the gradualist, unilateral approach that has been employed successfully since the early 1990s. India could continue, incrementally, to open up trade and foreign investment and to introduce market-based mechanisms at home. As it has done over the 1990s, India would rely mainly on unilateral trade liberalization. Trade agreements would not play a leading role in reform, although India would participate actively in the WTO and perhaps sign additional free trade agreements with developing countries. At the WTO, India would continue to emphasize its need for special and differential treatment and do its best to avoid binding commitments that require significant changes in domestic policies. Similarly, the preferential arrangements would focus mainly on tariff reductions in goods.

For India this strategy is attractive. It maximizes domestic autonomy and control. It allows India to tailor its policies and institutions to fit its unique circumstances, and it provides the government with the flexibility to time its initiatives when political conditions are most favorable. But this flexibility comes with costs. Policies are less effective when they are not seen as permanent. When reforms confront obstacles, flexibility may encourage backsliding rather than persistence. Opportunities to gain reciprocal access to foreign markets and influence foreign policies may be lost, and the political support from those who have an interest in foreign liberalization may not be effectively mobilized behind domestic reform.

Perhaps, therefore, now that liberalization and reform have taken hold, it may be time to adopt a more radical and comprehensive reform strategy. India could use reciprocal liberalization through trade agreements more aggressively to deepen its global integration and bolster domestic economic changes. In this regard, however, an important question is which kinds of reciprocal agreements are best suited for this role.

One option would be to negotiate deeper bilateral free trade agreements as a complement to unilateral and WTO liberalization. This paper considers the role that a U.S.-India FTA could play as the cornerstone of such an approach. Such an agreement could boost Indian welfare by removing trade barriers and providing a stable framework for the growth of information technology (IT) outsourcing. It could also be an effective mechanism for locking in reform policies, mobilizing domestic political support for liberalization, and spurring additional trade liberalization both multilaterally and bilaterally.

Opposition to such an approach comes from some who support more aggressive liberalization but oppose preferential trade arrangements as a means for doing this.[3] They view preferential arrangements as having several

---

3. For a review of these arguments, see Baldwin and Venables (1995), Bhagwati and Panagariya (1996), Frankel (1997), and Lawrence (1996).

serious deficiencies. These include the efficiency costs of discrimination—trade diversion;[4] the administrative burdens and complexity of having different systems of rules—a phenomenon Jagdish Bhagwati disparagingly calls "spaghetti-bowl regionalism"; the diversion of both political and intellectual capital from attending to other aspects of trade policy, in particular multi-lateral liberalization under the WTO; the dangers that political pressures during bilateral negotiations would force adoption of inappropriate domestic policies, such as labor and environmental standards; the inability to deal with issues that have significant spillovers on third parties such as farm subsidies; and the obstacles such agreements could pose to additional multilateral liberalization by creating vested interests in the preferences. Proponents of this position see merit in reciprocal trade agreements, but they advocate exclusive reliance on WTO negotiations as the mechanism for undertaking such agreements.

In this paper, the case for a U.S.-India FTA is evaluated in the context of these options. In particular, the paper examines how the multitrack approach compares with the multilateral and unilateral alternatives. *The paper's central claim is that if India wishes to use trade agreements to spur reform, a multitrack approach centered on a U.S.-India FTA would be superior to an exclusive reliance on the WTO under a likely outcome in the Doha Round.*

The paper first focuses on the defensive case for such a free trade agreement—its potential role in securing U.S.-India trade in IT services. The rest of the paper then turns to the positive (or offensive) case for negotiating a U.S.-India FTA. The merits of removing trade barriers unilaterally are compared with reciprocal liberalization. The next section considers in some detail how the provisions of a U.S.-India FTA would affect India's domestic policies and institutions. The FTA is then compared with the WTO as the appropriate mechanism for stimulating additional liberalization and reform. Finally, a general equilibrium model is presented to provide quantitative comparisons of unilateral, bilateral, and multilateral liberalization.

Playing Defense

There are defensive reasons for India to consider a free trade agreement with the United States. From this perspective, the key issue is establishing a legal and institutional framework for keeping trade in information

---

4. The paper by Arvind Panagariya in this volume, for example, emphasizes the dangers of trade diversion.

technology services free.[5] IT services comprise high-end software and technology services on the one hand and low-end back-office and call center work on the other. Both activities have enjoyed explosive growth since the late 1990s. Technological advances and investments in telecommunications, computers, and software have enabled multinational firms to tap into a large supply of well-educated English-speaking workers in India who are prepared to work for much lower wages than their foreign competition. Because of these increased service export opportunities, the number of Indians engaged in the industry doubled between 2000 and 2004, and exports have soared.[6]

While this performance is impressive, most analysts believe these developments are still in their infancy. Studies by McKinsey Global Institute and others have emphasized the large cost savings from undertaking these activities in India.[7] Forrester Associates projects that an additional 3 million U.S. jobs will be outsourced by 2015. McKinsey forecasts that IT services and back-office work in India will swell fivefold by 2008, to become a $57 billion a year export industry, employing 4 million people and accounting for 7 percent of India's gross domestic product.[8]

Trade between the United States and India, therefore, has the potential to become one of the most dynamic global linkages in the next decade. But will it be allowed to take place? If the United States continues to account for two-thirds of the most dynamic component of India's exports (IT services), India's bilateral trade surplus with the United States will undoubtedly increase. Yet already, protectionist pressures in the United States are strong. At a time when the U.S. economy is recording large trade deficits and its economic recovery is marked by very sluggish employment growth, outsourcing is headline news in the United States. Concerns about the loss of skilled white-collar jobs have become the focus of increasing amounts of political attention. Many bills to protect U.S. jobs have been introduced in state legislatures and the U.S. Congress.[9] On March 4, 2004, for example,

5. According to estimates made by the Indian National Association of Software and Services Companies (NASSCOM) in its annual strategy report, employment in information technology services in March 2004 stood at about 814,000, up from 284,000 in 1999.

6. According to NASSCOM, between 2003 and 2004, exports from the industry, whose main market is the United States, are expected to grow between 26 percent and 28 percent to around $12 billion, up from $9.5 billion in 2002–03 and three times greater than the exports of nearly $4 billion in 1999–2000.

7. McKinsey Global Institute (2003).

8. "The Rise of India," *BusinessWeek*, December 8, 2003.

9. A provision in the federal government's omnibus fiscal 2005 spending bill would bar companies that bid for certain work done by government employees from moving work offshore. Another bill, backed by Democratic presidential contender John Kerry, would require

the Senate passed a bill, by a 70-26 vote, that barred companies from most federal contracts if they plan to carry out some or all of the work abroad. (It included exceptions only for national security and for countries that are members of the WTO procurement code, an agreement to which neither India nor China belong).[10]

These developments naturally raise questions about whether the current framework of the relationship is adequate to allow trade between the United States and India to realize its full potential. One response is simply to ignore the current protectionist threats in the United States and to hope they will fade away once the economic recovery leads to more robust employment growth. A second response is to try to use the current Doha Round of multilateral trade negotiations to secure U.S. commitments to avoid restraints on outsourcing. It is by no means clear, however, that the United States has yet bound, that is, agreed to liberalize or liberalized, its IT services imports through the WTO General Agreement on Trade in Services (GATS). The problem, according to Mattoo and Wunsch, relates to the basic architecture of the GATS by which countries make their commitments to liberalizing services by sector and by mode.[11] It stems partly from the use of a positive list approach in which explicit commitments must be made before a sector is liberalized, that is, bound. Suppose for example that the United States has bound banking services. Suppose an Indian firm wishes to provide U.S. banks with data processing of their human resource records. Is this activity covered by the commitment, or would it be necessary for the United States to have stipulated that it had bound data processing? There is considerable ambiguity in the current GATS system. Mattoo and Wunsch propose either changing the classification system to make these Business Process Outsourcing (BPO) service commitments explicit or—the option they prefer—moving to a negative list approach, in which trade is allowed unless it has been expressly prohibited. These are sensible proposals, but it is by no means clear that they will be adopted.

---

workers at telephone call centers to disclose their physical locations at the beginning of each call. According to the *Wall Street Journal*, "about 80 bills aimed at keeping jobs in the U.S. by limiting outsourcing have been introduced in about 30 states" (*Wall Street Journal*, March 1, 2004, p. 1).

10. At the same time, General Electric filed an alert with the Securities and Exchange Commission claiming that the backlash to outsourcing poses a threat to its future profits because of the reliance of its insurance division on back-office operations in India (*Financial Times*, March 5, 2002, p. 1).

11. Mattoo and Wunsch (2004).

By contrast, services liberalization in U.S. bilateral agreements already uses a negative list approach. As long as an outsourcing service has not been listed, it is automatically permitted.

A free trade agreement that kept these sectors open would keep protection in check. Such an agreement would also fit into the broader strategy of "competitive liberalization" that the Bush administration has been pursuing.[12] While participating actively in the Doha Round and negotiations for a Free Trade Area of the Americas (FTAA), the Bush administration has dramatically stepped up the pace of negotiating bilateral free trade agreements. (The United States had moved away from exclusive reliance on multilateral liberalization in the 1980s, by signing FTAs with Israel and Canada. The North America Free Trade Agreement, or NAFTA, implemented in 1993, was an even more powerful movement in this direction.) A large number of bilateral agreements have been signed, negotiated, or planned. Agreements with Chile, Jordan, and Singapore have been implemented; those with Australia and Morocco have been passed; and the agreement with CAFTA (Central American Free Trade Agreement involving Costa Rica, El Salvador, Guatemala, Honduras, and Nicaragua) has been completed. In addition, bilateral negotiations have been launched with the Dominican Republic, the South African Customs Union, and three Andean countries (Bolivia, Colombia and Peru), and commitments to begin bilateral negotiations have been reached with Bahrain, Panama, and Thailand.

India surely has much greater economic and strategic potential for the United States and the global trading system than many of these nations. An Indian willingness to sign an agreement with the United States could have an important impact not only on the bilateral trading relationship between the two countries but also in increasing the pressure on other countries to liberalize, both bilaterally and through the WTO. This could help advance America's interest in global liberalization.

Nonetheless, obtaining an agreement in the current U.S. political environment would not be easy. The U.S. Constitution requires congressional approval for all trade agreements. Currently, even when it comes to votes on the less controversial free trade measures, the House of Representatives is fairly evenly divided, split basically along partisan lines, with most Republicans in favor and most Democrats opposed. To be sure, India is not without friends in the current U.S. debate; its most important allies are the U.S. companies that have used outsourcing to boost their bottom lines. Few free-trade members of Congress would welcome the opportunity to cast a

---

12. For an extensive analysis of these agreements, see Schott (2004).

vote on outsourcing in the current political atmosphere, however, and the failure to pass such an agreement could strengthen the hand of those who would seek to impede such trade.

But the merits of an FTA are still worth considering on two grounds. First, by offering to sign an FTA, India might be able to strengthen its political position in the current U.S. debate. Second, political conditions could well change. It would have been far easier to endorse such an FTA a few years ago, when the U.S. economy was enjoying high levels of employment and growth, and skilled high-tech employees were in short supply. It is quite possible that the economic environment could again improve.

From an Indian perspective, secure access to the U.S. market for services is surely desirable. Many Indians might therefore agree to such negotiations in the hope that India would obtain such access without having to do much on the domestic front, particularly in the goods area.[13] In his paper in this volume, for example, Arvind Panagariya argues that a case can be made in favor of "a mutually beneficial and politically acceptable FTA between the two countries in services." He correctly notes that such an agreement is not likely to entail much trade diversion, particularly in sectors where the Indian market is currently closed. He would also favor such an agreement in order to establish an FTA template that did not include labor and environmental provisions. But an agreement that is confined to services is not likely to happen. The United States is unlikely to forgo the opportunity of obtaining preferential access for its goods exports to the Indian market. In particular, the U.S. farm and high-tech lobbies play an important role in securing political support for U.S. FTAs. In addition, although the United States made an exception recently when it dropped sugar from the U.S.-Australia FTA, it has generally resisted making sectoral exceptions in its FTAs. Even though it might be legal under GATS, dropping all goods trade would surely create difficult precedents in other FTA negotiations. Moreover, given political realities in the United States regarding issues like labor and environment, any agreement the United States signs would have to include some provisions on these issues.

India has recently agreed to several free trade agreements with Asian countries, but they are not comprehensive even with respect to trade in goods. By contrast, judged on the precedent of other FTAs involving the United States, the range and extent of commitments relate to far more than goods trade. A U.S.-India FTA, therefore, is likely to have binding commit-

---

13. This view is presented in the paper by Panagariya in this volume and also by the Council on Foreign Relations Task Force on New Priorities in South Asia.

ments through the use of a negative list for services and to contain investment provisions with few sectoral exclusions. It would possibly grant full national treatment for U.S.-owned companies. In could also contain intellectual property rules that are more comprehensive than those in the WTO, and it would also almost definitely have additional provisions relating to labor, environment, standards, technical barriers, and government procurement. While it would probably provide India with more time to phase in its commitments, once the agreement was fully implemented—generally fifteen years—as with other U.S. FTAs, it would most likely entail symmetrical obligations by the developed and the developing country signatories.

For India, accepting an agreement with a developed country that was broad, deep, and symmetrical would represent a radical departure from its current policies and positions on foreign trade and investment. India has been a strong advocate of multilateral trading rules (first under the General Agreement on Tariffs and Trade, or GATT, and later the WTO), which concentrate mainly on developed-country trade barriers to goods and exempt developing countries from its disciplines by granting them special and differential treatment. India, however, has generally resisted new WTO commitments. India has not signed the WTO government procurement code. It strongly opposed the introduction of new agreements on intellectual property (Trade-Related Aspects of Intellectual Property Rights, or TRIPS) and services in the Uruguay Round of trade negotiations. Later it strongly opposed U.S. efforts to introduce labor standards into the WTO. Indian representatives also expended considerable effort resisting the launching of the Doha Round in 2001 on the grounds that developing countries required more time and assistance to implement their Uruguay Round commitments. Although this stance did not succeed, India was more effective in thwarting negotiations on the Singapore issues (particularly investment and competition policy) at Doha and later at Cancún.[14]

Laying out these Indian positions makes it clear that a willingness to sign a free trade agreement with the United States would have major implications for both India's trade and domestic economic policies. This takes us to an evaluation of the offensive case for an agreement—the topic discussed in the rest of the paper.

---

14. Even where it has accepted obligations, India has had some trouble ensuring compliance. In particular, it continued to maintain quantitative restrictions until losing a challenge at the WTO. Likewise, it applied requirements on foreign investors in automobiles until this was found in violation of the Trade-Related Investment Measures (TRIMs) Agreement.

Liberalization Strategies: Unilateral versus Reciprocal

In his review of Indian reforms during the 1990s, Montek Ahluwalia emphasizes their incremental nature. His views are worth quoting at some length:

> The goals [of reform] were often indicated only as a broad direction, with the
> precise end point and the pace of transition left unstated to minimize political
> opposition—and possibly to leave room to retreat, if necessary. . . . The result
> was a process of change that was not so much gradualist as fitful and oppor-
> tunistic. . . . Progress was made as and when politically feasible, but since the
> end point was not always clearly indicated, many participants were unclear
> about how much change would have to be accepted, and this might have led to
> less adjustment than was otherwise feasible. . . . The alternative would have
> been a more thorough debate with the objective of bringing about a clearer real-
> ization on the part of all concerned of the full extent of change needed, thereby
> permitting more purposeful implementation. However, it is difficult to say
> whether this approach would indeed have yielded better results, or whether it
> would have created gridlock in India's highly pluralist democracy.[15]

As these comments indicate, the dominant approach used by India has
been unilateral and incremental. Although India moved further and faster
than required by its WTO commitments, it moved at its own pace, without
committing itself to full liberalization. This allowed India to control the
process itself and proceed in a manner that met the needs of its own policymakers. It also allowed the government to adopt partial measures and to
steer the debate away from the doctrinal issue of "free trade versus protection" to one concerning the right level of protection.

One reason for adopting an incremental approach, particularly when
reform is in its early stages, is that initially the constituents for reform are
weak. The winners from trade liberalization, for example—those who will
succeed in export markets or obtain jobs from increased foreign investment—are not yet known. Yet the losers—those who are vulnerable to
international competition—are only too aware of who they are. Once the
process gets going, however, winners start to emerge, and politically,
implementing additional measures may well become easier.

The adjustment process itself may also build up the constituency for liberalization and weaken the constituency seeking protection.[16] At the start,
majority support for *full* liberalization might not exist, but it might be
possible to obtain agreement for a partial measure that then reduces the
number of people in import-competing activities and builds up the size of

15. Ahluwalia (2002, pp. 86–87).
16. For a more general application of these ideas to reform, see Fernandez and Rodrik
(1991).

the export sector. Once this has happened, additional liberalization might be possible. The key to this approach is ensuring at each stage that the liberalization will expand the sectors with comparative advantage under free trade and contract the sectors that are not.[17]

Another reason is that the attitudes toward liberalization may shift as a country experiences improvements in its competitiveness. This seems to have been India's experience. In a highly protectionist regime, such as prevailed in India before 1991, import barriers raise input costs and place firms at a disadvantage in world markets. Under these circumstances, since they feel uncompetitive, domestic firms with export potential are unlikely to be enthusiastic about trade liberalization. But once liberalization proceeds and equipment and inputs become cheaper, their attitudes could change. As they begin to experience success in exporting, their interests in foreign markets and additional reforms may grow. Conversely, when import barriers are very high, there are likely to be many domestic firms that require protection in order to compete, and they will defend this protection strongly. However, as barriers are brought down, the least competitive firms will exit, while others will become more efficient and thus, over time, opposition to liberalization could subside.

These considerations suggest that over the past decade, India's piecemeal approach to reform in general and to trade liberalization in particular probably had considerable merit.[18] But a key question is whether the time has now ripened for India to shift from an approach that is "fitful and opportunistic" to one that has clearer end-point goals and commitments. While moving in such a direction could entail some short-term political costs, it could also yield greater long-term economic payoffs. Let us consider these economic effects first before turning to politics.

Credible Commitments

The purpose of trade liberalization is to improve resource allocation and enhance welfare. For this to occur, private actors must be prepared to

17. Frankel (1997, p. 219); Wei and Frankel (1995); Levy (1994) establishes that in a median voter model, bilateral agreements will not undermine political support for multilateral liberalization if trade occurs in a standard Hecksher-Ohlin framework but could reduce such support when there are increasing returns and greater product variety.

18. This discussion brings to mind the work of Lindblom (1995), who contrasted the paradigm of comprehensive decisionmaking with a more incremental approach. One paradigm of moving toward full free trade would simply be to announce a program and implement it. An alternative, however, is simply to seize opportunities as they arise. India's economic reform has not reflected an overt commitment to liberal free-market ideology. Instead it has entailed reform by stealth.

undertake investment and adjustment: those who can succeed in exporting should undertake the necessary investments in specific capital required to produce and service foreign markets. Those who will meet increased competition from imports must undertake the necessary steps either to adjust away from these activities or to develop strategies that will make them competitive. If the government can effectively put the private sector on notice that all tariff barriers will be eliminated by a certain date, and if these commitments are viewed as credible, then firms, workers, and farmers can immediately begin to undertake these adjustment strategies. From an economic standpoint, clear final goals thus make it more likely that liberalization will be successful.[19]

Governments, particularly those with a record of policy reversals, need to work to make clear that their plans will actually be implemented. Economic theorists have pointed out that trade policymakers with complete domestic autonomy may face a "time consistency" problem.[20] At some time in the future, after firms have sunk costs, it could be politically advantageous to reverse liberalization. If firms anticipate such reversals, however, they will be less inclined to act on expectations that the market will be opened, and thus the gains from trade could be smaller.

The payoffs from liberalization are likely to be highest, therefore, if the policy is locked in. To be sure, India could simply vote a fifteen-year plan for the elimination of all trade barriers and it could unilaterally relax its rules on foreign investment, but doubts would remain about the sustainability and permanence of these policies. Sovereign governments can, after all, simply change their policies and in democracies, governments can change. There are domestic measures, such as writing the policies into a constitution, that could serve to make them more permanent, but doing so can be cumbersome.

Such doubts could be greatly diminished, however, by signing binding trade agreements that entail reciprocal commitments. To be sure, no government would give up its right to withdraw from an agreement that proved to be a failure. Nonetheless, the prospects of future deviations will be kept in check by the discipline of losing the reciprocal benefits gained from the

19. If the intention is to liberalize fully, economists commonly advocate eliminating trade barriers as fast as possible. As shown by Mussa (1984), the presence of adjustment costs is not a reason for incrementalism. While private actors may choose to adjust slowly, in the absence of considerations relating to income distribution and other market imperfections, the government should eliminate barriers immediately. Externalities associated with adjustment could warrant a slower approach, although in this case, there may be more efficient instruments than tariffs to achieve this goal.

20. For a review of the literature, see Staiger (1995), especially pp. 1516–19.

agreement. This greater lock-in will in turn make policies more credible and hence more effective.

Complete and Comprehensive Agreements

Obtaining political support for a comprehensive agreement, that is, one that requires full free trade, may not be easy. Even when an agreement is implemented over a long period of time, for example "free trade by the year 2020," comprehensive trade agreements telescope all the political battles into the present. Thus while comprehensive liberalization may maximize the economic benefits, it may also increase the political costs.

It is noteworthy that the General Agreement on Tariffs and Trade, for example, did not require its contracting parties to commit to complete free trade by a certain date. Instead the parties moved toward free trade in a series of steps, ratcheting the process up by undertaking measures that were feasible at each point in time. As might be expected, momentum was maintained by reducing barriers most radically in sectors with the least political resistance. Over half a century, the results of this approach were remarkable—tariffs on industrial products in developed countries were brought down from about 40 percent to 4 percent. But the process has also been very protracted and incomplete: there has been far less liberalization, for example, in sectors of interest to developing countries, such as agriculture and textiles, and far less formal liberalization by developing countries themselves at the WTO.[21]

Reciprocity

Nonetheless, if the political conditions allow, it could be worthwhile having the political battles up front in the context of ratifying a trade agreement. In addition to enhanced credibility, reciprocal trade agreements can bring both economic and political benefits. Economically, the advantages come from improved access to foreign markets. If a country can use the opportunity of reducing its own trade barriers to persuade others to reduce theirs, it could add to its welfare.

Politically, the prospect of increased access to foreign markets can help stimulate support from export interests. If they understand general equilibrium economics, exporters should also support unilateral trade liberalization since, as Lerner first pointed out, a tax on imports is a tax on exports

---

21. Developing countries have engaged in considerable liberalization since the late 1980s, but much of it has been unilateral. Bound rates at the WTO remain far higher than those actually applied.

and reducing tariffs is like subsidizing exports.[22] But this relationship is not transparent. Instead, exporters are more aware of the particular tariffs they pay on their imports and, absent a trade agreement, generally devote their efforts to obtaining relief from these costs through duty drawbacks or access to export-processing zones. However, the benefits they can enjoy from access abroad in a reciprocal agreement provide additional incentives for their support. A government could therefore find it easier to liberalize through agreements than it would if it tried to act alone.

Promoting Domestic Reforms

Trade agreements can also help domestic reforms. The politics of reform is often difficult. Reformers who believe their policies will bring benefits domestically may strengthen their hand if they can argue that implementing such policies will also confer the benefits of increased access to international markets. One of the best examples of this was the conditions to which China agreed upon its accession to the WTO. By using the demands of the United States for introducing market-based measures as a condition for accession, reformers in China were able to gain the upper hand. Many in the outside world complained that the agreement with the United States was a painful price imposed by outsiders; in fact, for the most part it was a means by which the Chinese leadership effectively signaled its commitment to an open, market-based system in which private firms would play a major role.

There are many other examples. Currently, Europeans (and Americans) are debating reform of their costly and very inefficient agricultural policies. The negotiations in the Doha Round may help those seeking to reduce the market distortions such policies entail. This use of agreements is not simply practiced by the political right. In the European context, the introduction of a European Social Clause has been used to bolster left-wing policies, and in the United States, unions have tried to use trade agreements to improve their rights domestically.[23]

The fact that trade agreements come as packages may also have disadvantages, however. Countries could find themselves adopting policies that

---

22. Lerner (1936).

23. Indeed, while many view American efforts to include labor standards in trade agreements as a protectionist measure to be used against foreigners, the history of these standards in the United States suggests that an important motivation was to raise these standards in the United States itself. Organized labor in the United States is not very strong politically, and in particular many U.S. states have rules that actually contradict core labor standards promulgated by the International Labor Organization.

they might not otherwise desire. In the Uruguay Round, for example, India was particularly opposed to the agreement on intellectual property. Nonetheless, because the Uruguay Round was presented as a single undertaking, India agreed to the TRIPS measures, presumably because it viewed the package as a whole as in its interest. Similarly, countries acceding to the European Union, such as the Baltic States, may find themselves having to accept higher levels of trade protection as a condition of membership.

In sum, the unilateral incremental liberalization employed by India since the early 1990s has been effective in engineering change. But the use of a binding trade agreement could bring additional benefits. Locking in the policies and making them more credible could lead to larger behavioral responses. This would be particularly true of policies that made commitments to comprehensive liberalization. Undertaking such commitments in the context of a reciprocal trade agreement could provide additional benefits to exporters and help mobilize additional domestic support for reform and liberalization. To be sure, these benefits would depend on the ability to obtain enough domestic support to negotiate an agreement that actually promoted the right kinds of domestic policies and to allow passage of the agreement.

The argument in this section has been couched in general terms. We have considered the general merits of conducting liberalization and reforms unilaterally or in the context of reciprocal agreements. *But the question of what type of reciprocal agreements remains.* In particular, should it be bilateral or multilateral? There are those who claim that the only desirable mechanism for reaping these benefits is through multilateral liberalization through the World Trade Organization and that a preferential agreement with the United States, for example, would provide no additional benefits. To deal adequately with such arguments, it is necessary to present a better idea of the likely contents of a free trade agreement. In addition, it is necessary to consider the feasible role a WTO agreement could play in providing such benefits.

Developing or Constraining the Domestic Policy Space

"By imaginatively using these external commitments and pressures as levers, as China is apparently doing successfully, it is to be hoped that the government, whatever its party affiliation, will be able to push the reforms further"

T. N. Srinivasan and Suresh Tendulkar

*"The yardstick that matters is the degree to which trade reform contributes
to the construction of a high-quality institutional environment at home."*

Dani Rodrik

A trade agreement is not simply about changing relative prices to achieve
a more efficient outcome. Particularly for developing countries, it is also
about achieving institutional reforms. The key question in the offensive
case for a U.S.-India FTA is its likely impact on domestic institutional
arrangements. To what degree will an agreement require India to undertake
changes that are in its own interest and to what extent will it impose new
constraints that could actually damage India's welfare? A complete answer
to these questions will depend on the precise terms of the agreement, but it
is possible to give some idea of the major opportunities and risks.

The list of areas for Indian reform is long. It includes the need for additional liberalization of trade and services; customs reform; measures to
attract foreign investment; privatization and reform of public sector enterprises; adoption of competition and regulatory policies; liberalization of
small-scale sector reservation policies; labor market reforms; reforms of
policies for sick industries; reform of relations between the central and state
governments; changes in the investment environment for power, telecommunications, and transportation; tax reform; and agricultural sector reform.
Aside from specific actions in each area, there is a need to improve government performance by reducing corruption, increasing transparency, and
providing opportunities for judicial review.

The preferential arrangements India has, or is in the process of negotiating with its Asian neighbors, are fairly shallow in the sense that the binding commitments focus mainly on border barriers to merchandise trade and
are unlikely to make a major contribution to these internal reforms. In fact,
even with respect to goods trade, these arrangements will have exceptions
that will only be removed gradually. While they may include hortatory language covering services, investment, and cooperation, it is not clear to what
extent these agreements will achieve full national treatment and rights of
establishment for foreign investment and liberalization of services.[24] By

24. According to the Economist Intelligence Unit (EIU 2003, p. 36), Indian Prime Minister Atal Behari Vajpayee signed two free trade agreements in October 2003, one with
ASEAN and the other with Thailand. The agreements divided commodities into three
groups: a small list liberalized by 2004, another group on which tariff reductions will begin
in 2007, and a third group for which tariffs are to come down by 2007. Some members of
ASEAN were given more time to make the required reductions. India signed FTAs with
Bhutan and Nepal in the early 1990s and with Sri Lanka in 1998 (that agreement took effect
in 2000). It was also announced in October 2003 that an existing trade agreement with

contrast, the obligations in a U.S.-India FTA would be extensive and require action by a date certain. To illustrate this, we select some of the provisions from the recent FTAs the United States has negotiated and consider how these provisions might affect Indian domestic reforms. We draw examples from recent free trade agreements the United States has negotiated with countries or regions such as Central America, Chile, and Morocco.

Tariff Reductions

Tariffs are generally removed on a large percentage of trade as soon as the agreement is implemented. Most of rest are eliminated in the following ten or fifteen years. For example, more than 95 percent of the bilateral trade will become duty free when the U.S.-Morocco agreement enters into force and almost all tariffs between the two countries will be eliminated within nine years.[25] Similarly, when the agreement with Chile was implemented in January 2004, tariffs on 90 percent of U.S. exports to Chile and 95 percent of Chilean exports to the United States were eliminated.[26]

For India, similar undertakings would add to the pressures for tax reform and the adoption of a value added tax system that could replace the revenues lost on tariffs on U.S. goods. An agreement would also allow access to U.S. capital equipment and other products duty free, thereby reducing and possibly eliminating the need for the complex set of duty exemptions currently granted to firms producing for export markets.

Textiles and Apparel

When the Multifiber Arrangement expires in 2005, the United States will eliminate the quotas that currently restrain competition in its market. But products from China and other countries without preferences will continue to be subject to fairly high U.S. tariffs. Under these circumstances, duty-free

---

Bangladesh would be converted into an FTA. In addition, a comprehensive economic cooperation agreement was signed with Singapore in 2003, laying a road map for an eventual preferential trade agreement or FTA. India is also discussing possible FTAs with Afghanistan, Myanmar, South Africa, and Mercosur.

25. United States Trade Representative, "Trade Facts: Free Trade with Morocco," March 2, 2004 (www.ustr.gov).

26. United States Trade Representative, "The US-Chile Free Trade Agreement: An Early Record of Success," June 4, 2004 (www.ustr.gov). No tariffs will be applied to 80 percent of U.S. exports to Central America as soon as CAFTA is implemented, and the remaining tariffs are to be eliminated over ten years. United States Trade Representative, "Trade Facts: Free Trade with Central America," May 25, 2004 (www.ustr.gov).

access to the U.S. market will provide an important competitive advantage. The FTAs with Morocco, Chile, and Central America all allow for immediate duty-free trade in textiles and apparel for products meeting the agreements' rules of origin. A similar agreement would therefore give Indian producers a competitive advantage in the U.S. market.

In recent years Mexico, Central America, and others have taken advantage of the opportunity afforded by such preferences, and their clothing exports to the United States have enjoyed explosive growth. Because of such an agreement, Jordanian textile exports to the United States have increased from $30 million to $674 million in just four years.

This opportunity could similarly be used to stimulate further reforms of the reservation policies, which restrict certain sectors to small firms that have hindered Indian competitiveness in this sector. To be sure, the need to administer similar rules of origin for U.S. clothing sold in India would add complexity to Indian customs procedures, but India could, of course, chose simply not to require or enforce them.

Agriculture

The Moroccan FTA requires the phaseout of all agricultural tariffs under the agreement, most in fifteen years. The Central American agreement (CAFTA) adopts a similar approach, although a few very sensitive sectors retain their protection for longer periods, and indeed in some cases liberalization only begins after the agreement has been in effect for ten years. Both agreements also contain special agricultural safeguards.

A similar agreement would create additional export opportunities for Indian farmers. Indian producers of dairy, sugar, rice, and other crops could all increase their exports. Import-competing sectors might have competitive problems, but for these there are precedents for long periods of transition. The agreement with Morocco keeps restrictions on some especially sensitive sectors for as long as 25 years.[27] In NAFTA, Canada insisted on maintaining some of its agricultural protection, and in the recently signed U.S.-Australia FTA, sugar was actually exempted.

The United States continues to subsidize farmers in ways that distort trade and production, and some argue that until these subsidies are removed, it will not be possible to include agriculture in an FTA. But it is

27. For two poultry products, the agreement sets up two Moroccan tariff rate quotas (TRQs) under which out-of-quota tariffs would be eliminated over nineteen and twenty-five years, respectively. A nineteen-year TRQ has been created for U.S. exports of whole birds, and a twenty-five-year TRQ for exports of U.S. leg quarters, which are the two most sensitive products for Morocco, a U.S. official said.

important to understand that for the most part, American farm products that are exported are sold at world prices. While farmers sometimes receive additional payments, these subsidies only affect the prices to the extent that they lower the world price. Studies suggest that U.S. payments do reduce world prices, but the effects are smaller than many discussions imply. For example, Bruce Gardener of the University of Maryland has estimated that the 2002 farm bill reduced world prices 6 percent overall compared with the prices that would have been in place if the farm bill had not been enacted. The U.S. Economic Research Service has estimated price effects of 1.5 to 4 percent for grain and soybean and up to 10 percent for cotton.[28]

Thus for Indian farmers who are protected with tariffs that are orders of magnitude larger than these effects, the challenge of adjusting to world agricultural prices is far greater than that of dealing with the marginal impact of U.S. subsidies. Nonetheless, both sides could make it clear that they would continue to apply the basic principles of the WTO subsidies and countervailing duties code to all trade.[29] Aside from export subsidies, which the code forbids, the code allows for goods that have been subsidized to be traded unless they cause injury. Where subsidies are injurious, each side would apply countervailing duties commensurate with the subsidies. This would serve to level the playing field.

Services

The free trade agreements the United States has recently negotiated include broad commitments to open services markets. They use a "negative list" approach, meaning that all service sectors are covered unless specifically excluded. Key services covered include audiovisual, telecommunications, computer and related services, distribution, construction, and engineering. They generally include significant market opening measures for opening up financial services such as banks, insurance, and securities and for an open and competitive telecommunications market. These reforms would introduce new competitors and new ideas and technologies into India.

The agreements also provide benefits for businesses wishing to supply cross-border services, for example, by electronic means as well as businesses wishing to establish a presence locally. The secure market access that would be given to these dynamic Indian sectors would help stimulate investments by both Indian and foreign firms. India would also be able to

28. These studies are cited by Hathaway (2002).
29. Under the FTAs signed by the United States, countries continue to apply their antidumping and countervailing duty laws.

secure greater access to visas (such as H1B) for supply of services in the United States.

Many Indian service sectors remain closed, and an agreement would help open them to foreign competition and investment. In these cases, opening up to the United States does not give rise to trade diversion because there is no trade to start off with. Moreover, in sectors in which there already is a foreign presence, if regulations that curtail competition are lifted, all who compete will benefit.

Regulatory Transparency

The Moroccan agreement contains "strong and detailed disciplines" for regulatory transparency. Improving transparency in the Indian governmental regulatory system would be beneficial not only for U.S. exporters and firms but for all domestic and international firms subject to these regulations.

Foreign Investment

Foreign investors bring much-needed capital. The domestic rates of Indian investment, on the order of 23 percent of GDP, are not compatible with a growth rate on the order of 8 percent. In 1998, for example, the economies in the Asia Pacific Region as a whole, and China in particular, invested 37 and 38 percent of GDP, respectively. A key priority therefore must be to stimulate domestic and foreign investment.

The recent FTAs give U.S. investors, in almost all circumstances, the right to establish, acquire, and operate investments on an equal footing with local investors and investors from other countries. These rights are to be reinforced by a transparent, impartial procedure for dispute settlement.[30]

Similar rules changes resulting from a U.S.-India FTA could help India attract much-needed foreign direct investment. In response to the liberalization that has already taken place, foreign investment has increased in

---

30. In its WTO accession agreement with the United States, with respect to foreign investment, "China agreed to eliminate export performance, local content and foreign exchange balancing requirements from its laws, regulations and other measures, and China also will not enforce the terms of any contracts imposing these requirements. China has also agreed that it will no longer condition importation or investment approvals on these requirements or on requirements such as technology transfer and offsets. China has further agreed that it will only impose, apply or enforce laws, regulations or other measures relating to the transfer of technology that are not inconsistent with the TRIMs Agreement (or the TRIPS Agreement)." See http://ustr.gov/regions/china-hk-mongolia-taiwan/accession.shtml.

recent years, but its aggregate level is remarkably small.[31] Foreign investors have faced numerous discriminatory obstacles in addition to those that confront Indian firms. A binding agreement and a permanent commitment to provide national treatment in most sectors could go a long way to eliminating these disadvantages. With secure access to the U.S. market and an improved operating environment, India would begin to be viewed by U.S. firms as a far more attractive base for serving the world market. Having implemented such changes for U.S. investors, India could provide similar benefits to firms and investors from other foreign countries.

Governance

The Moroccan agreement requires publication of laws and regulations governing trade and investment, and publication of proposed regulations in advance to provide an opportunity for public comment. Governments agree to establish criminal penalties for bribery. Combating corruption is also an Indian priority. Again, success in this area would benefit both domestic and foreign participants in the economy.

Government Procurement

The agreement with Morocco imposes disciplines on most government purchases, including requiring national treatment of firms for purchases in excess of certain monetary thresholds. In addition there are strong and transparent disciplines on procurement procedures, such as a timely and effective bid review process and requirements for advance public notice of purchases. By signing such an agreement, India would be able not only to rationalize its own public procurement system, but also to avoid the U.S. government's use of government procurement to discriminate against outsourced services.

State-Owned Enterprises

A crucial area for India's economic reforms relates to "public sector undertakings." The key challenge is to free these state-owned firms from being politically accountable and allow them to operate on a commercial basis.

---

31. The gross product of U.S. majority-owned foreign affiliates amounted to 0.1 percent of GDP in 1994 and 0.4 percent in 2001. According to its most recent survey, the U.S. Bureau of Economic Analysis (2003) reports that in 2001 U.S. firms had majority-owned foreign affiliates with assets of $33.4 billion in China and $13.5 billion in India, sales of $32.5 billion and $7.6 billion, net income of $1.8 billion and $265 million, respectively. The Chinese firms shipped $2.9 billion in exports to the United States, whereas India shipped only $140 million. The Chinese firms employed 273,000; the Indian firms, 77,000.

Privatization is one way to do this, but even in the absence of a change in ownership, these enterprises need to be transformed.[32] A commitment to do this could readily be introduced into the FTA. When the United States negotiated the agreement for China's accession to the WTO, for example, it was forced to deal with the extensive role played by state-owned enterprises in that economy. Accordingly, in its accession agreement, China agreed that laws, regulations, and other measures relating to the purchase and commercial sale and production of goods or supply of services for commercial sale by state-owned (and state-invested) enterprises or for use in nongovernmental purposes would be subject to WTO rules. China also agreed that "state-owned enterprises must make purchases and sales based solely on commercial considerations, such as price, quality, marketability, and availability, and that the government will not influence the commercial decisions of state-owned enterprises."[33]

Standards

The recently negotiated FTAs include provisions for technical standards and sanitary and phytosanitary standards (SPS). Developing countries often view such standards as creating barriers to their exports. But for the most part, meeting such standards is a prerequisite for international competitiveness since developed countries will not relax them for imports. International experience also suggests that deep integration agreements can provide opportunities for major improvements in standards and product quality. Mexico, for example, has been extremely successful in using NAFTA to its advantage in raising domestic standards and improving regulation. Sen emphasizes the extent to which the trilateral Free Trade Commission formed as a result of NAFTA and various other NAFTA committees adopted a problem-solving approach to regulatory issues, obviating the need for using dispute settlement mechanisms. NAFTA established an SPS committee along with nine technical working groups and a Committee on Standards-Related Measures with associated subcommittees that meet regularly to discuss implementation issues. "The mechanism, which has a strong problem-solving ethos, works to support improving the application of SPS provisions and in reducing regulatory discretion," Sen wrote.[34] Similarly, as Salazar-Xirinachs and Granados note, "NAFTA's environmental institutions have been partly responsible for the deepening

32. According to Ahluwalia (2002), privatization is essential because "autonomous commercial operation in the Indian political and bureaucratic culture does not seem possible."
33. See http://ustr.gov/regions/china-hk-mongolia-taiwan/accession.shtml.
34. Sen (2002).

level of technical cooperation on environmental protection between the U.S. and Mexico."[35]

Intellectual Property

The recent agreements require protection for trademarks, copyrights, and patents and call for strict enforcement of these provisions including criminalizing end-user piracy and providing for both statutory and actual damages under law. Governments commit to using only legitimate computer software. Some of these provisions would go further than the WTO TRIPS and could increase Indian obligations in a controversial area that does not necessarily accord with Indian interests or enforcement capabilities.

Labor and Environment

There are many misconceptions about what the labor and environmental provisions of a free trade agreement would include. It is important to emphasize first that none of the agreements signed by the United States require adherence to *specific* environmental and labor standards.[36] Instead, while the agreements generally commit countries to "strive to" promote core workers' rights and protect the environment, the emphasis is placed on each government *enforcing its own domestic environmental and labor laws* and on not weakening environmental laws or reducing domestic labor protections in order to encourage trade or investment.[37]

Moreover when it comes to enforcement, the agreements stress that "the parties retain the right to make decisions regarding the allocation of resources to enforcement with respect to labor (or environmental) matters determined to have higher priorities."[38] To be sure, these obligations are backed by the agreements' dispute settlement procedures, and cases can be brought where enforcement failures affect trade.[39] If one party is found guilty of such infractions and fails to come into compliance, however, the

---

35. Salazar-Xirinachs and Granados (2004, p. 255).

36. The Singapore agreement, for example, states that each party "shall strive to ensure" that its labor laws are enforced and consistent with the right of association, the right to organize and bargain collectively, the prohibition on forced labor, a minimum age of employment, and acceptable work conditions.

37. The CAFTA states, for example, that "a Party shall not fail to effectively enforce its labor laws, through a sustained or recurring course of action or inaction, in a manner affecting trade between the parties." Article 16.2. Par 1 (a).

38. CAFTA Chapter 16, Article 16.2 1 (b).

39. The Singapore agreement requires each party to "not fail to effectively enforce its environmental laws, through a sustained or recurring course of action or inaction, in a manner affecting trade between the Parties. . . ."

other side may not be entitled to retaliate using trade protection. In the CAFTA agreement, for example, a country found to be in violation of its enforcement obligations can be subject to a monetary assessment, but the assessment cannot exceed $15 million and the funds are not necessarily paid to the other party but may instead be used to help improve compliance.

The introduction of labor and environmental standards into trade agreements is extremely controversial. Basic principles of fiscal federalism indicate that the scope of governance should match the scope of the problem and thus that national rather than international rules are best suited to deal with environmental problems that are confined to one nation. This is particularly important when countries at very different levels of economic development might wish to make very different choices regarding standards and rules.[40] Efforts to harmonize or raise such standards could unfairly penalize poor countries with limited means. Moreover, even when environmental problems are international or global in scope, they are better dealt with through explicit environmental agreements, such as the Kyoto Protocols, rather than through trade agreements. Similarly, labor standards are better determined nationally, particularly when these standards only affect domestic workers. Some standards, of course, are so fundamental that they should be matters of international concern, for example, those that relate to genocide, and it may be better to deal with core labor standards through the International Labor Organization rather than through the WTO.

Nonetheless, there is political support in the United States for introducing labor and environmental rules into bilateral trade agreements. Given these pressures, the particular formulation described above has some virtues. First, it encourages but does not require adherence to specific environmental or labor standards and therefore accommodates diverse national circumstances. Second, it allows action when a signatory fails to enforce the standards but only when nonenforcement affects trade, and it provides countries with room to argue that they have limited resources and that they place different priorities on their enforcement efforts. Third, in the event of a breach, it does not lead to trade sanctions and should therefore not become a disguised form of protectionism. Fourth, the monetary assessments are capped and not necessarily paid to the complaining country. Finally, there are usually provisions for cooperation and aid to help improve

40. Ironically, according to Srinivasan and Tendulkar (2003, p. 124), "PC Mahalanobis, the architect of India's development strategy pointed out long ago that India's labor laws imitated those in advanced industrial countries and were out of tune with Indian labor market realities."

domestic enforcement capacity. On balance, therefore, the costs of signing such an agreement are unlikely to be large, and it could help win political support from (and provide cover for) members of Congress with strong labor and environmental constituencies.

Even this partial listing of the essential elements of an FTA with the United States makes clear that India could use an agreement to bolster and accelerate many dimensions of economic reform. These include tariffs, taxes, agriculture, foreign investment, government procurement, regulatory policy, competition policy, and public sector enterprises. In addition, however, India would probably have to accept obligations regarding intellectual property, labor, and environmental standards that it might not welcome. These obligations, however, are likely to relate primarily to enforcement, not to specific rules, and in the event of breach would not give rise to trade sanctions.

We close with two words of caution. The first relates to the importance of complementary action. Signing a trade agreement is not sufficient to ensure that the institutions that are necessary to capitalize on reform will be in place. An agreement can provide an opportunity and stimulus, but domestic policy must follow through. In fact, a failure to do so could lead to conditions that are worse than they were before the agreement was reached. Thus an agreement to place public sector undertakings on a commercial basis must be accompanied by the creation of appropriate institutions and policies to regulate and police competition; an agreement to eliminate small-scale reservations must be accompanied by programs to help small producers become more competitive; an agreement to eliminate or reduce tariffs must be coupled with the implementation of offsetting taxes. Enactment of all these accompanying measures will take time and require financial, political, and intellectual resources. Absent these types of responses, the agreement is unlikely to be implemented effectively. Accordingly, the use of trade agreements as an instrument for reform requires particular preconditions and may not be appropriate for all countries. Even if most of the changes called for in an FTA with the United States are desirable, a crucial issue is whether an agreement requires these changes at the appropriate time. In particular, is sufficient time given to adequately prepare for the required changes. Sometimes, as they say, a kick in the pants gets you going—at other times, it just hurts.

The second type of complementary action that is crucial relates to extending the benefits accorded to the United States to other foreigners. In a free trade agreement, nothing constrains India from avoiding excessive dependence on the United States by additional liberalization. A U.S.-India

FTA should be but one component of a broader strategy to immerse India in the global economy. Opening to the United States should be accompanied by similar measures both unilaterally and through negotiations with other countries.

This second note of caution comes back to the basic issue. Trade agreements may provide benefits, but they also entail constraints on domestic policy action. Only if there is sufficient overlap with the measures India needs to take anyway will an FTA be beneficial.

FTA vs. WTO: Which Is a Better Commitment Mechanism for Indian Reforms?

"It has been claimed that contemporary RTAs [regional trade agreements] provide benefits from deeper integration such as greater national security, greater bargaining power in international negotiations, and the possibility of locking in domestic reforms by invoking commitments undertaken in an RTA. However, no convincing case or evidence has been offered why preferential trading is a prerequisite for these benefits. . . .

The argument that preferential liberalization on a discriminatory regional basis and non-discriminatory multilateral liberalization are reinforcing is utterly (un)[sic] convincing."

T. N. Srinivasan and Suresh Tendulkar

In this section, we dispute these claims. The outcome of the Doha Round could improve Indian access to foreign markets, but it may not be particularly effective in helping India reduce its domestic trade and investment barriers or in promoting domestic structural reforms. India's bound rates, that is, the tariffs ceilings to which it is legally committed, at the WTO are so high that they do not constrain its policies. Even a very successful Doha Round would not require much additional liberalization on India's part. With investment and competition policy apparently off the table, additional opportunities for spurring reform are limited. India could, and should, make bold offers to secure the elimination of tariffs on and the free flow of IT services. But thus far in the talks, it has emphasized reductions in agricultural subsidies, and in any case, as just one of 148 participants, India cannot exert a dominant influence on a WTO agreement.

Those who argue for an exclusive reliance on multilateral liberalization often compare *actual* free trade agreements with an *idealized* version of multilateral liberalization. To be fair, however, today's FTAs should be compared with today's liberalization through the WTO in the Doha Round. This is important, because such a comparison highlights the serious possibility that even with a successful round, multilateral liberalization will almost surely remain incomplete. Indeed, a country like India might not have to undertake any additional liberalization at all!

The multilateral system has enjoyed considerable success in reducing trade barriers. In the late 1940s the world was fragmented by tariff and nontariff barriers; by the end of the Uruguay Round in 1994, the applied and bound tariff rates of the industrial economies were just 2.6 and 3.7 percent, respectively.[41] However, liberalization has been slow and undertaken in relatively small steps.[42] The Kennedy (1963–67), Tokyo (1973–79), and Uruguay Rounds (1986–94) took successively longer to complete, and they achieved average tariff reductions of just 35, 33, and 33 percent, respectively.[43]

On the basis of this record, it is reasonable to expect that the Doha Round negotiations, which began in 2001, could be protracted and in the end again reduce average tariffs by about a third. It is also striking that while GATT and the WTO have brought average tariffs down, many developed countries maintain high tariff peaks for certain products, while many developing countries retain substantial protection.

These outcomes are the predictable consequences of the way the multilateral system works. In particular, negotiations reflect the ability of countries to win concessions from each other by agreeing to reduce barriers on a reciprocal basis.[44] Once concessions are made, they are extended under the most-favored-nation (MFN) principle to all members unconditionally. This has the great virtue of nondiscrimination between members, and it leverages the strengths of the powerful to provide benefits for all. But in a system in which participants view opening markets as a concession, it also creates an incentive for free riding.[45]

A key notion in the WTO system is that concessions are made on a reciprocal basis.[46] What exactly does "reciprocity" mean? According to Kyle

41. Laird (2002, p. 98).

42. As Robert Staiger (1995, p. 1528) observes "A striking feature of the multilateral trade liberalization that has occurred since 1947 is just how long it has taken."

43. Hoekman and Kostecki (2001, p. 101).

44. For an extensive consideration of the role of concessions and reciprocity in the WTO, see Lawrence (2003).

45. Caplin and Krishna (1988) formally illustrate this problem.

46. Kenneth Dam (1970, pp. 58, 59) recalls that the Havana Charter, the precedent to the GATT, emphasized that "no Member shall be required to grant unilateral concessions." He later notes: "From the formal legal principle that a country need make concessions only

Bagwell and Robert Staiger, "the principle of reciprocity in GATT refers to the 'ideal' of mutual changes in trade policy that bring about changes in the volume of each country's imports that are of equal value to changes in the volume of each country's exports."[47] Although it is nowhere defined explicitly, implicitly reciprocity in the WTO is used in a specific sense. WTO members are not required to remove their trade barriers completely, nor are they generally required to have the same tariff levels, either on average or for the most part, on specific commodities. Instead, as a result of each negotiation, members are expected to give, in value, the same *new* trading opportunities as they receive. This is a system based on what Jagdish Bhagwati has termed "first difference" reciprocity.

However, full reciprocity is not required of developing countries. They are provided with "special and differential treatment." The GATT states that the "developed contracting parties do not expect reciprocity for commitments made by them in trade negotiations to reduce or remove tariff and other barriers to the trade of less-developed contracting partners."[48]

The combination of special and differential treatment and MFN status creates a very permissive system for developing countries. Under MFN they obtain market access automatically, but they remain free to keep their own barriers high. For most of the postwar period, India with its very high domestic tariffs was a perfect example.

The predictable result of combining a system based on negotiating power with special and differential treatment is that the barriers that remain today—particularly those in labor-intensive manufacturing and agriculture—happen to be highest in sectors that are of particular interest to developing countries. As the saying goes, "You don't get what you deserve, you get what you negotiate," and because developing countries have smaller markets and incentives not to reciprocate, protection in developed countries remains higher on the products developing countries are particularly interested in exporting.

Consider the U.S. and Indian perspectives on the Doha negotiations on Non-Agricultural Market Access (NAMA). For the United States, whose tariff levels are for the most part very low (see the simulations below), the

when other contracting parties offer reciprocal concessions considered to be mutually advantageous has been derived the informal principle that exchanges of concessions must entail reciprocity." Thus while the GATT does not formally require that negotiations produce balanced concessions, it is implicitly assumed that they have done so.

47. Bagwell and Staiger (2000, p. 37).
48. GATT Article XXXVi.8

principle of "first difference" reciprocity is now a problem, since it could leave the United States without anything to bargain with. The United States has therefore offered to eliminate all its remaining tariffs on non-agricultural products, but only if other countries do the same (although with different phaseout periods for developing countries). For other WTO members, however, this offer violates the principle of (first difference) reciprocity; in addition, from the viewpoint of developing countries, it also violates the provisions for special and differential treatment.[49] As a result, developing countries are likely to reject the U.S. offer and propose something less radical. In response, the United States will seek to keep some of its tariffs.

The result is that if the Doha Round is concluded successfully, it will probably reach a NAMA agreement that looks like the previous rounds. On the basis of the three previous WTO agreements, we should expect that a successful Doha Round will succeed in persuading countries to agree to an average cut in tariffs of around 33 percent, with developing countries agreeing to reductions that are about two-thirds that average, or around 22 percent. A more ambitious 45 percent reduction overall would result in 30 percent average reductions by developing countries.

So how much *additional* liberalization would such an agreement require from a country like India? Not much. Perhaps not any at all. The parameters of any agreement would relate not to the rates that India actually applies now but to those that it has bound. According to WTO estimates, by 2005, India's bound average tariff rate will be 50.6 percent, with an average of 115.7 percent on agricultural and 37.7 percent on nonagricultural products.[50] Compare these average bound rates with Indian applied rates averaging 32.3 percent in 2002.[51] India could thus simply bind its current applied rates today and take credit for a 36 percent reduction. But it is unlikely to do this because it would entail an unreciprocated concession. Moreover, if the developed countries were willing to provide only a 33 percent reduction, a 36 percent reduction by India would be incompatible with special and differential treatment. The result

---

49. According to Laird and others (2003), the Quad countries (Canada, European Union, Japan, and the United States) agreed in the Uruguay Round to ten "zero-for-zero" initiatives (beer, brown spirits, pulp and paper, furniture, pharmaceuticals, steel, construction equipment, medical equipment, agricultural equipment, and toys) and one "harmonization" initiative—chemical products. After the Uruguay Round, the Information Technology Agreement (ITA) used a zero-for-zero approach, by which a critical mass of countries agreed to reduce all tariffs to zero on the selected range of products.

50. WTO (2002).

51. WTO (2002, p. 31).

is that in response to a 33 percent average reduction by developed countries, India's bound rates would be more likely to fall by 22 percent to 44 percent. They would remain far out of line with applied rates that are actually scheduled to be between 10 and 20 percent for nonagricultural products by 2005.

Suppose India wanted to use the WTO to really lock in its tariff reductions. India would have to propose (or at least accept) a variant of the U.S. proposal and agree to eliminate all (or almost all) tariff barriers by a date certain. To be sure, in this case, the WTO would become a far more effective lock-in mechanism than an FTA. But consider the implications. Either all developed countries and most developing countries would have to make similar commitments, or India would find itself in the same position as the United States—it would have eliminated all its bargaining chips without ensuring that others had removed all their tariffs. There may be no harm, and considerable benefit, to India for making such a proposal, but its acceptance certainly should not be counted upon.

The current WTO system generally stands in the way of a developing country such as India using WTO agreements to bring about really meaningful liberalization. At the time of accession, when countries such as China have to obtain the agreement of all other members, countries have been forced to make commitments that go further than commitments made by existing members at similar stages of development. The United States, for example, refused generally to treat China as a developing country and insisted that it join on commercial terms. This allowed China to use the WTO as a device for committing to major reforms.

For those that already have membership, therefore, the leniency embodied in special and differential treatment seriously undermines the use of the WTO as a mechanism for mobilizing the support of export interests for trade liberalization. It is hard to rally export interests to support liberalization in the context of a WTO agreement unless one can argue that the liberalization is required to receive the market access benefits others are offering. To be sure, India could simply announce that it was willing to bind its tariffs at the new applied rates. But again, politically, this would be a hard sell within India, where it would be seen as giving up something for nothing.

One response would be to try to remedy the problems with the WTO system, by eliminating the principle of special and differential treatment or requiring developing countries to bind their applied rates. But this is not politically feasible, and in any case, not desirable for countries that are simply not ready to make such commitments. Even if it felt capable of undertaking such commitments for itself, India would feel the need to protect other developing countries that are not ready to make similar concessions.

How about investment? India could certainly be more forthcoming in liberalizing services investment by making offers under GATS (General Agreement on Trade in Services) mode 3, which relates to services requiring the establishment of firms in the foreign market, presumably in return for liberalization by others under modes 1 and 4, which relate to cross-border services and those requiring labor in the foreign market, respectively. But such liberalization would apply only to certain sectors in services. A more comprehensive commitment to foreign investment through the WTO does not seem possible because efforts at Cancún appear to have succeeded in keeping investment and competition off the agenda.

The argument here should not be misinterpreted. India's participation in the WTO makes eminent sense. India derives considerable benefit from a trading system based on the rule of law. Moreover, its unilateral liberalization places it in a strong position to play an active role in moving the global talks forward. In addition, there is considerable merit for an organization with a membership as diverse as the WTO to focus heavily on market access and rules that outlaw discrimination against foreign goods and services. Other international institutions with more select membership may be better suited to deal with deeper integration relating to issues such as labor standards, the environment, and competition policy. At the same time, however, there is merit in allowing those countries that are prepared to make binding commitments in such areas to negotiate bilateral or plurilateral agreements.

By contrast to the WTO's special and differential treatment, the FTAs signed by the United States *are* based on full reciprocity. Special and differential treatment comes into play only in the length of time required for the agreement to be phased in and not the nature of the commitments assumed by each side. FTAs provide considerable incentives for the support of export interests. For exporters, the carrot is not simply being able to compete free of tariff hindrance against firms in the partner country, but also gaining preferential access to that foreign market and thus an advantage over firms outside the agreement. The connection between liberalization at home and foreign market access is more diffused at the WTO. It depends not only on the actions India takes but also upon those undertaken by the other 147 members of the organization. In a bilateral FTA, the links are direct.

In addition, because they have more comprehensive coverage than the WTO, these FTAs provide greater scope for locking in policies that are not covered in WTO agreements. This more comprehensive coverage may also facilitate agreements. Broad agendas may help to create winners on both sides.[52]

The FTAs' deeper integration gives them advantages in signaling changes in policy direction. This applies particularly to investment. Mexico was spectacularly successful in using its partnership in NAFTA to attract foreign direct investment. India's willingness to sign a binding agreement with the United States would likewise send a powerful signal that it was really open for business.

How would a free trade agreement with the United States affect India's ability and willingness to bargain for reciprocal liberalization through other FTAs and at the WTO? Let us deal with ability first and willingness second.

A U.S.-India FTA would surely make India a more attractive negotiating partner for third countries. The need to remain competitive with U.S. products, services, and investment in India would motivate others to sign similar agreements. Thus the FTA would broaden participation in global integration. It is not a coincidence, for example, that, in the aftermath of NAFTA, Mexico has been able to conclude a large number of FTAs with other nations. The EU, for example, has been eager to eliminate the advantage given to U.S. products by NAFTA and in return has provided Mexican exports with preferential access to its markets. Both the EU and Japan would seek to emulate the U.S.-India agreement.

To bargain effectively in complex negotiations, parties need to tread a fine line between being too eager or too reluctant to conclude a deal. If the other side believes you are very eager, it will take advantage and offer you little; if it believes you are very reluctant, it may also be unwilling to make its best offer, particularly if that offer could be politically costly. India currently has a reputation for being extremely reluctant to make concessions at the WTO, partly because of its long history of protectionist policies. Indicating a willingness to sign an agreement with the United States would change these perceptions. Indications that India was also prepared to make reciprocal concessions in the WTO would be taken far more seriously. At the same time, hints that India was not totally dependent on the WTO and had bilateral options as well could also improve its bargaining ability. India

52. To be sure, the greater diversity of WTO membership may offset this advantage. Just as money is superior to barter because it does not require the double coincidence of wants, so the diversity of WTO membership may make it possible to find deals when two countries alone cannot. B might want something from A but have nothing to give in return. But B might have something C wants and C might have something A wants. Thus a deal can be struck between the three of them (A gives to B, B gives to C, and C gives to A) when bilaterally no trade is possible.

could then credibly challenge developed countries to improve their own offers dramatically by suggesting, on a contingent basis, its willingness to engage in extensive multilateral liberalization of its own.[53]

Moreover, U.S. negotiators would see an FTA with India as the jewel in their crown. It would represent the major achievement in the current policy of competitive liberalization. A free trade agreement with India would have important strategic benefits for the United States. This fact would strengthen India's hand in its bilateral negotiations with the United States. Although the United States already has agreements with a large number of countries, many of them are very small and of little strategic importance. This would not be true of India. An FTA with India would put considerable pressure on other countries to try to regain their relative positions, either by negotiating similar agreements with the United States or by supporting more extensive liberalization at the WTO.

But would entering into a bilateral agreement make either India or the United States more reluctant to liberalize multilaterally or unilaterally? The beauty of an FTA—as opposed to a customs union—is that India would retain control of its trade policy. Nothing could stop India from extending its commitments to the United States to other countries. India could unilaterally eliminate the trade-diverting aspects of rules of origin and preferential tariffs. Similarly, having made its environment more attractive for foreign investors from the United States, India could simply give similar treatment to investors from other countries. Some Americans might try to object to the dilution of their preferences, but the United States has put no pressure on its other FTA partners to avoid other agreements, as the large number of free trade agreements Mexico has signed illustrates.

Preferential access to the U.S. market could make India less eager for the United States to reduce its MFN textiles tariffs. India might be less willing to provide the United States with concessions at the WTO in order to preserve its privileged access. There were rumors, for example, that the Common Agricultural Policy (CAP) countries, motivated by the desire to keep their preferences, used their opposition to the Singapore issues (that is, competition, investment, transparency in government procurement and trade facilitation) to prevent success at Cancún. This kind of behavior might nonetheless be in India's interest even if it did have negative implications for the system.

In this section, we have challenged the idea that an FTA with the United States has no particular advantage over Indian liberalization at the WTO.

---

53. Mattoo and Subramanian (2003).

On the contrary, we have pointed out that features such as special and differential treatment and MFN status have led to a situation in which India's commitments at the WTO are not particularly relevant for its domestic liberalization. In addition, areas such as investment and competition are not on the WTO agenda. As a result, India's ability to use the need for reciprocal concessions to mobilize domestic political support for liberalization and reform has been weakened. By contrast, a free trade agreement with the United States would require virtually complete elimination of barriers and much deeper international integration. As such, it would be more effective as a mechanism for mustering domestic support.

There is, however, no reason why India should have to choose between these approaches. They can be used in a complementary manner to reinforce one another. Deeper integration can be achieved through the FTA route, but at the same time, India could be more forthcoming in the Doha Round. Both these approaches are quite compatible with additional unilateral liberalization. As we show in the next section, for India an even better outcome than eventually eliminating its barriers at home would be simultaneously to have no domestic barriers and preferential access to foreign markets.

Comparative Static and Dynamic Considerations

"In our judgment the discriminatory and trade-diverting aspects of preferential trading arrangements, regardless of whether they are open or not, far outweigh any benefits to be reaped."

T. N. Srinivasan and S. D. Tendulkar

Again, this section challenges the skeptical voices quoted above. The traditional thinking about preferential trading arrangements is often couched in Viner's terms of "trade creation" and "trade diversion."[54] While these terms are somewhat imprecise, they do convey the basic idea that compared with multilateral free trade, preferential trading arrangements are something of a mixed bag. Under competitive market conditions, full free trade creates a market in which price signals lead to an efficient allocation of resources. By contrast, with a preferential system, prices do not necessarily give the right signals, because they are influenced by the barriers that

54. Viner (1950). Trade diversion and creation refer to the impact on production, but as Lipsey (1957) showed, if the consumption benefits are sufficiently large, welfare may be improved even when trade is diverted.

remain on outsiders. The result is that, a priori, a preferential trade arrangement's impact on welfare is ambiguous: it could improve welfare by providing the participants with production and consumption gains attributable to reducing tariff distortions; it could also reduce welfare by inducing members to buy from less-efficient suppliers in partner countries rather than from outsiders. Considerable theoretical effort has gone into establishing criteria for predicting the characteristics that make partners suitable for preferential arrangements. For example, Lipsey argued that preferential systems are likely to be beneficial if the partners initially accounted for a large share of each other's imports.[55] But in the final analysis, in most cases, a definitive answer requires an explicit empirical investigation.

In reality, moreover, markets are not perfectly competitive and firms are not all subject to constant returns to scale. Indeed, imperfect competition and scale economies are quite common. In these circumstances, estimating the impact of trade liberalization becomes even more complicated. There are additional changes brought about by changes in competitive conditions, scale economies, and the number of product varieties that need to be incorporated. These features make the theoretical effects of removing trade barriers (both preferentially and multilaterally) ambiguous and again indicate that empirical evaluation is required. Indeed, empirical studies incorporating these considerations suggest that the welfare effects of a preferential trade arrangement can be many times larger that those considering only competitive effects.[56]

Despite this basic ambiguity, many economists who are predisposed to free trade oppose preferential systems and advocate exclusive reliance on nondiscriminatory liberalization. In India's case, for example, the quote from Srinivasan and Tendulkar at the start of this section and the writings of Panagariya (see his paper in this volume) reflect the view that preferential trade arrangements are undesirable, particularly because of the dangers of trade diversion. But for the most part, their views are based on theoretical and a priori reasoning rather than detailed empirical analysis.

Forswearing preferential trade arrangements under all circumstances may not be the wisest advice. Three sets of considerations merit attention. First, how does a specific agreement affect welfare? As noted, this question requires a detailed empirical investigation. Second, what additional policies will the country take? Countries may have the ability to combine their membership in preferential arrangements with additional liberalization. For example, if trade diversion is a problem, a country that participates in

55. Lipsey (1957).
56. See Baldwin and Venables (1995).

a free trade agreement (rather than a customs union) could lower its external tariffs on the products where there is trade diversion and end up only with trade creation. *Moreover, for a small country, even better than having no trade barriers is having no barriers along with preferential access to all other markets.*[57] This makes the country a hub, and its preferential partners all spokes.[58] Thus complementing full free trade at home with untrammeled access to the rest of the world is surely the best of all worlds. (In fact, this may well be the objective of Singapore's drive to conclude FTAs with almost every country it can find, even though it is almost completely open.) Third, what are other countries doing? The appropriate policy on membership in preferential trade arrangements is surely not independent of the actions of other countries. If the trading system breaks up into trading blocks, or if their most important competitors gain preferential access to major markets, countries may be better off seeking refuge in one or more blocks, rather than trying to go it alone.

In this section, we explore these considerations to understand the impact of a free trade agreement between India and the United States. We provide several simulations, using the NCAER-University of Michigan computable general equilibrium model of world production and trade (see appendix). Our purpose is not to provide an estimate of the aggregate benefits of an FTA that takes into account the gains that would result from improved resource allocation attributable to removing tariffs on goods, liberalizing and securing trade in services, enhancing foreign direct investment, and bolstering Indian domestic reforms.[59] Instead, our purpose is the more modest one of considering the liberalization of trade in goods, precisely because this issue appears to be the major concern of FTA critics.

The model, described in detail in the appendix, is designed to capture the long-run impact of an agreement. It is a real model that holds employment and the trade balance constant. It therefore captures not only the initial impact of the FTA on trade and employment but the additional adjustments that would be required to restore equilibrium. For example, the initial

57. Kowalcyk (2000).

58. Cooper and Massell (1965) said that for a small country, unilateral tariff reduction was always preferable to joining a customs union since trade creation alone was better than trade creation combined with some diversion. But the simplicity of this argument is destroyed once intraunion terms of trade effects are allowed for, even when the assumption of a union of small countries is retained. "If A unilaterally reduced its tariffs . . . it would avoid the trade diversion loss, but would forgo the gain to be had from B reducing its tariffs. When they reciprocally reduce tariffs, the intra-union terms of trade may turn in favor of A and, in spite of the trade diversion loss, joining a union may then be better for A than unilateral tariff reduction by it" (Corden 1984, p. 121).

59. Chadha and others (2003).

impact of removing U.S. and Indian tariffs could be to leave India with a trade deficit. Additional shifts in the relative price of Indian products could then be required to increase Indian exports or reduce imports (or both) to restore the trade balance to its original position. Likewise the agreement could increase or decrease the aggregate demand for labor, requiring wage and employment adjustments to restore labor market equilibrium. Because it is based on full employment and a constant capital stock, the real income changes captured by the model reflect the effects of resource allocation rather than changes in the aggregate level of inputs.

It should be emphasized, therefore, that the simulations reported here relate only to the removal of barriers to trade in goods. Including services and investment would lead to far larger numbers and indicate large benefits. Nonetheless, since the problem of trade diversion is likely to be mainly, although not exclusively, an issue relating to goods trade, the simulations do provide some useful insights on this question.

We first simulate a free trade agreement between India and the United States. We then consider how the impact of such an agreement would be affected if in addition to the FTA, India, the United States, or both removed their remaining barriers. We also present scenarios that allow us to compare the U.S.-India FTA with unilateral liberalization by India, unilateral liberalization by the United States, and multilateral global liberalization.

Finally, we consider the FTA as a response to regional blocks. We simulate the breakup of the world trade system into three large regional trading blocks; and in this world explore the effects of a U.S.-India FTA, Indian membership in the Asian block, and Indian unilateral liberalization.

Results of Liberalization under an FTA

As reported in table 1, trade between India and the United States is relatively small and fairly concentrated. In 2002–03 almost 30 percent of Indian exports to the United States were cut gems and 17 percent were cotton textiles and apparel. Indian imports from the United States were concentrated in electronic goods (23 percent), transportation equipment (12 percent), and nonelectrical machinery (11 percent).

As table 2 shows, a free trade agreement between India and the United States would confer benefits to both sides. Indian welfare improves by $2.4 billion (0.61 percent of GDP) and the United States' by $3.3 billion (0.04 percent of GDP). These effects may appear small relative to the incomes of both countries, but the gains are significant given the value of trade (see table 1). Although the model does not provide a separate esti-

TABLE 1. India-U.S. Trade, 2002–03

India's exports to U.S.	Millions of U.S. $	Share (percent)	India's imports from U.S.	Millions of U.S. $	Share (percent)
All commodities	10,883.76	100.00	All commodities	4,429.00	100.00
Gems and jewelry	3,251.72	29.9	Electronic goods	1,004.89	22.7
Readymade garments of cotton including accessories	1,267.22	11.6	Transportation equipment	530.07	12.0
Cotton yarn fabric, madeups	602.47	5.5	Nonelectrical machinery	470.99	10.6
Drugs, pharmaceuticals and fine chemicals	419.18	3.9	Professional instruments, optical goods	243.79	5.5
Manufacturers of metals	413.56	3.80	Organic chemicals	213.76	4.8
Marine products	386.51	3.6	Pearls, precious and semiprecious stones	167.74	3.8
Handicrafts excluding handmade carpets	298.77	2.8	Chemical material and products	125.60	2.8
Electronic goods	262.55	2.4	Pulp and waste paper	113.44	2.6
Readymade garments of man-made fibers	254.21	2.3	Artificial resins, plastic materials	105.74	2.4
Machinery and instruments	253.29	2.3	Electrical machinery	82.45	1.9
Primary and semifinished iron and steel	238.77	2.2	Metaliferrous ores and metal scrap	70.94	1.6
Cashew	222.76	2.0	Computer software	69.38	1.6
Carpets, handmade	195.45	1.8	Cotton, raw and waste	68.50	1.5
Transportation equipment	187.61	1.7	Manufactures of metals	62.84	1.4
Plastic and linoleum products	131.44	1.2	Vegetable oils (edible)	53.88	1.2

Source: Centre for Monitoring Indian Economy, *Foreign Trade and Balance of Payments*, various issues.

TABLE 2. Liberalization Simulations
Millions of U.S. $

	Impact on		
Type of liberalization	India	United States	Rest of world
1 India unilateral	4,882	4,171	19,471
2 U.S. unilateral	696	6,655	22,664
3 U.S.-India free trade agreement	2,429	3,296	−108
4 Multilateral	7,832	44,567	422,823
5 1 + 3	5,890	5,149	18,351

mate of the negative impact of trade diversion associated with a free trade agreement between the United States and India, *it does suggest that whatever these effects may be, they are more than offset by trade creation and the other benefits such as scale economies and the increased competition that the agreement would induce.*

The impact of the FTA on the rest of the world is relatively small, and trade diversion appears to be minimal for other countries. Welfare in the rest of the world declines by just $108 million. By contrast, Indian imports rise by $1.5 billion and U.S. imports by $1.7 billion. All told, the scenario certainly does not support those who claim such an agreement would reduce Indian welfare. Indian labor and capital both gain.

Table 3 provides a more detailed breakdown of the sector impact of a U.S.-India FTA. As a general equilibrium model designed to estimate impacts over the long run, the model appropriately keeps employment constant, but it does capture shifts in the composition of employment and thus gives an idea of the labor market adjustments a free trade agreement would require. For India the employment gains are largest for agriculture (56,111 workers), textiles (140,107), and apparel (59,926), while employment is reduced in other manufactured goods, trade and transportation, and public administration. The expansion of Indian agriculture is interesting because it suggests that despite U.S. agricultural subsidies, the marginal impact of eliminating trade barriers in both countries is to expand agricultural production in India and reduce it in the United States. Given higher productivity levels, the effects on U.S. employment are considerably smaller. All told, displacement is less than 10,000 jobs and would be imperceptible in the U.S. labor force of 138 million. Sectors losing jobs include agriculture (1,990 jobs), textiles (2,804), apparel (3,959), and leather, wood and paper products (543).[60]

---

60. The Indian labor force numbers about 450 million. The U.S. labor force is about 138 million.

TABLE 3. U.S.-India Free Trade Agreement: Sectoral Impacts in India

Sector	Exports (percent)	Imports (percent)	Output (percent)	Employment (number)
Agriculture	5.0	1.9	0.0	56,111
Mining and quarrying	−0.2	−0.2	−0.4	−8,083
Food, beverages, and tobacco	3.0	7.5	0.2	7,985
Textiles	4.4	2.2	1.5	140,107
Wearing apparel	15.6	4.6	8.5	59,926
Leather, wood and paper products	3.3	2.7	0.2	6,365
Chemicals, rubber, and plastics	1.9	4.1	−0.5	−8,112
Nonmetallic mineral products	1.8	12.9	−0.8	−28,478
Metal and metal products	1.8	1.7	−0.6	−22,234
Transportation and machinery equipment and parts	1.0	7.5	−1.1	−14,796
Manufactures including electronic equipment	1.9	3.8	−0.4	−37,669
Electricity, gas, and water	0.0	−0.2	−0.2	−1,973
Construction	0.1	−0.3	−0.2	−19,166
Trade and transportation	0.1	−0.2	−0.1	−46,395
Financial, business, and recreational services	0.2	−0.3	0.0	−917
Public administration, defense, education, health, and housing	−0.2	−0.1	−0.3	−82,671
Total	3.5	3.2	−0.0	0

The overall impression is that for the United States, the economic impact of an agreement would be positive but small relative to gross national product. For India, the gains are comparatively larger. But the absolute gains are larger for the United States. Moreover, this analysis neglects the additional gains that India would reap through increased investment and services liberalization. It also fails to capture the benefits that could accrue from placing outsourcing activities and IT services in a framework that reduced the possibilities of protectionist responses.

As indicated in table 2 (see also the appendix table), India would gain more from unilateral liberalization than from a free trade agreement with the United States. Under unilateral liberalization, Indian welfare would rise by $4.9 billion, or about 1.2 percent of GDP. Unilateral liberalization and a free trade agreement with the United States are not necessarily mutually exclusive, however. *In fact, India would do even better to combine these approaches.* If instead of liberalizing unilaterally, India first signed a free trade agreement with the United States and *then* liberalized with all its other trading partners, it would boost its income by $5.9 billion, or 20 percent more than under simple unilateral liberalization.

One of the major concerns voiced about preferential trading arrangements is that they could reduce the incentives for additional liberalization. In this case, for example, a preferential agreement between the United States and India could provide incentives for the United States to try to preserve its preferences by preventing India from liberalizing further. To be sure, this concern is less acute for a free trade agreement in which India retains discretion over its trade policy than it would be for a customs union. It is also less likely that India would be able to exert much influence over U.S. policy. But the question of U.S. pressures on India remains.

A free trade agreement with India would raise U.S. income by $3.3 billion. If India then responded with unilateral liberalization, U.S. income would increase by an additional $1.9 billion to $5.2 billion. *The United States therefore has an interest in having India become more open even after the two countries conclude a free trade agreement.* The United States apparently gains more from the improvement in its terms of trade when India liberalizes to the rest of the world than it loses from the erosion of its preferential access to the Indian market. India, by contrast would have a marginal interest in keeping the United States from additional liberalization. If both countries are open, India's gains would be $5.6 billion, just $312 million less than they would be if the United States did not liberalize. If both India and the United States opened to the world, American gains would total $10.8 billion—62 percent more than if the United States simply liberalized unilaterally.

Results of a Multilateral Liberalization

Indeed, this is just one example of why the United States, as a very open economy, has much to gain by encouraging other countries to liberalize. The scenario with global multilateral liberalization provides some fascinating insights in the different interests countries may have in multilateral liberalization. For the United States, these interests are considerable. The gains to the United States from unilateral liberalization would be just $6.7 billion— an amount equal to one-tenth of one percent of U.S. gross national product. By contrast, the United States would gain seven times as much— $44.6 billion—from global multilateral liberalization. India's gains from global multilateral liberalization would be smaller: $7.8 billion, just 60 percent more than from unilateral liberalization. This finding helps explain why the United States chooses never to liberalize unilaterally, whereas India has emphasized this approach. It may also explain India's comparative lack of enthusiasm for multilateral liberalization.

At the same time, while it has a comparatively greater interest in global liberalization, the United States has comparatively little to bargain with, since its barriers are low. Indeed, closed economies have more to offer the world from liberalization than do open ones. *Remarkably, the rest of the world gains about as much from unilateral liberalization by India ($19.5 billion) as it does from unilateral liberalization by the United States ($22.7 billion).* Thus even though it is small, India's relatively closed market gives it quite a lot of bargaining power because by opening it has much to confer on the rest of the world. Those that need the world more have comparatively less to offer.[61]

Results of Increased Regionalization

What impact would increased regionalization have on these conclusions? We have simulated the formation of three blocks, one in Europe, one in Asia, and one in the Western Hemisphere. These simulations are reported in table 1A in the appendix. The major result is that if India is excluded from all three blocks, it is hurt by such a development. Its welfare would be reduced by $900 million (−0.23 percent of GDP) in response. If India were to liberalize unilaterally in such a scenario, its (net) benefits would be just under $4 billion. India could also more than offset this loss by forging a free trade agreement with the United States. In a world of blocks, if it joined an FTA with the United States, India would enjoy net benefits of $1.5 billion. (This compares with Indian benefits of $7.8 billion when there is multilateral global liberalization.) By joining the Western Hemisphere block, India's welfare could be raised by $2.1 billion (0.5 percent of GDP). Membership in the Asian block, however, presents India with the largest benefits—being part of an Asian block in this regional scenario gives India welfare gains of $3.0 billion (0.8 percent of GDP). Joining the European block would be distinctly inferior and do little to offset the effects of the other blocks; India's GDP would decline by 0.2 percent. The most important implication of these regional scenarios is that India can always do better than opening unilaterally by combining its unilateral opening with membership in a regional agreement.

In a world of three blocks, the United States would gain far more than it would through unilateral liberalization. The United States would capture 58 percent of the benefits of global free trade. The EU would enjoy 84 per-

61. In their study of the gains from eliminating the remaining barriers in developed countries, Bradford and Lawrence (2004) find that Japan would capture most of the benefits from liberalization by itself while the rest of the world has a great interest in seeing Japan liberalize.

cent of the benefits it would gain from global free trade and Japan 83 percent of its benefits with global free trade. For several major global actors, therefore, a world of blocks comes close to providing gains that are equivalent to full global liberalization.

Attention Diversion

Opponents of preferential free trade agreements voice several concerns in addition to worrying about the possibilities of trade diversion. One is that preferential arrangements could prevent or reduce the possibility of full multilateral liberalization by diverting relatively scarce policymaker attention. Trade officials with limited time and attention will find it difficult to negotiate simultaneously in several forums. Likewise, policymakers may be less willing to devote their scarce political capital to promoting multilateral liberalization if they have to spend it on the passage of preferential trade arrangements. These points may indeed be valid, but the real issue is surely the relationship between these administrative and political costs and the benefits of these preferential measures. When critics decry the attention devoted to preferential agreements, their implicit assumption is that the benefits of such agreements are likely to be much smaller than those from multilateral liberalization. This could well be the case if separate agreements are negotiated with small trading partners. But our simulations suggest that for India, the impact of a U.S.-India FTA is not small. We find that complete multilateral liberalization would boost Indian welfare by just over three times the gain India would have from a U.S.-India FTA and that full unilateral liberalization would provide twice the benefits. On the basis of achievements in previous rounds, we could expect a successful Doha Round to reduce global barriers by a third (see discussion below). If the model is basically linear, this suggests that for India, the payoff from the FTA would be similar to the results of a typical WTO negotiation and equal to a 50 percent unilateral reduction in Indian trade barriers. Moreover, bilateral FTA negotiations are much simpler and less time-consuming than WTO rounds.

To be sure, when *global* benefits in the simulations are compared, the conclusions are quite different. The participants in preferential trade arrangements may well capture more than all the benefits and outsiders would be hurt. By contrast, outsiders will gain from unilateral and multilateral liberalization. A U.S.-India FTA *reduces* foreign incomes by $108 million. By contrast, unilateral Indian liberalization raises incomes in the rest of the world by $19 billion, while the global gains from multilateral liberalization are $475 billion! From a systemic viewpoint, it is clear where attention should be paid. But our focus here is bilateral.

In sum, India benefits from trade liberalization in goods. Unilaterally removing Indian trade barriers would enhance Indian welfare. A U.S.-India FTA would also benefit both countries. India would become more specialized in agriculture and labor-intensive manufactures—areas in which its long-run comparative advantage lies. Even if it could, the United States would not have an interest in preventing additional Indian liberalization. India has an interest in following an approach that combines the FTA with additional unilateral (and multilateral) liberalization. If it did so, its welfare would improve, even in a world that split into regional trading blocks.

Conclusions

This paper raises two basic questions. Should India depart from its strategy of liberalizing trade incrementally and unilaterally to embrace full trade liberalization and reform? And if the answer is yes, should a new policy be exclusively centered on the WTO, or should it be supplemented with a U.S.-India FTA and perhaps other FTAs seeking deeper integration?

The paper has examined both the benefits and the costs from a change in strategy. The unilateral incremental approach has suited a country in the early stages of reform with strong institutions and interest groups that have vested interests in the status quo. The approach provided the maximum scope for molding institutional changes to fit domestic needs and capabilities. The framework was sufficiently flexible to allow policymakers to take advantage of opportunities and retreat in the face of obstacles. Politically, some opponents of full liberalization could be co-opted by promising limited changes; others could be defeated by proceeding in a piecemeal fashion. Over time, as the policies showed benefits and created new beneficiaries, more could be done. The unilateral approach also suits a country with high trade barriers, since the simulations indicate that by simply removing its own barriers, India would obtain almost two-thirds of what it would gain if all countries eliminated all their trade barriers multilaterally.

But the current approach also has costs. It lacks credibility. By failing to obtain a political commitment to comprehensive change, the payoffs have been reduced. Investors at home and abroad retain doubts that the policy direction will be sustained. In addition, the benefits that might have been obtained by reciprocal liberalization have been lost. Economically, these would come from increased and more secure access to foreign markets; politically, they would come from mobilizing export interests to pressure for reforms. The time may now be ripe for a change in approach that could avoid these costs.

Considering a free trade agreement with the United States helps sharpen these distinctions. An FTA would be attractive for defensive reasons if it could secure an open market for the explosive growth in India's exports of information technology (and its bilateral trade surplus) that is expected to emerge in the coming decade. To be sure, obtaining such an agreement could be difficult in the current U.S. political environment. But circumstances could change, and in any case, this is not an issue that can be kept out of the U.S. public eye.

The simulations indicate that as a relatively open economy, the United States has a great interest in liberalization by its trading partners. This helps explain its almost exclusive reliance on reciprocal liberalization as revealed by its WTO proposals and the large number of FTAs it is seeking. For Americans, a U.S.-India FTA would have the appeal of being probably the most important addition to the strategy of "competitive liberalization."

India also has positive reasons to enter into an FTA, namely, the role the FTA can play in stimulating Indian liberalization and reform. The agreement could be used to propel change in a host of areas including trade policy, tax reform, services, industrial policy, foreign direct investment, regulatory policy, competition policy, customs administration, public sector enterprises, agricultural policy, public procurement, governmental transparency, and technical and sanitary standards.

The prospect of an agreement does raise numerous concerns, however. One is that India could be forced to adopt policies that are not in its interests. Rules for labor and environmental standards are viewed with particular alarm. If a U.S.-India FTA follows recent U.S. free trade agreements, however, it would require no changes in current Indian labor and environmental rules. The binding part of the agreement would relate only to enforcement, and violations would result not in trade retaliation but in the violating party devoting more money to improving enforcement.

FTA opponents raise other concerns. They claim that the WTO offers superior mechanisms for locking in reforms and promoting liberalization. But for a country like India, the WTO is poorly suited to this task for four reasons: India's bound tariff rates are far higher than its applied rates; it is given special and differential treatment; the WTO agreements are far less comprehensive than U.S. free trade agreements have been; and an agreement in the Doha Round to phase out all tariffs is highly unlikely and certainly not something India, as just one of 148 members, can count on.

Opponents also claim that an FTA would result in trade diversion. Our simulations show, however, that the gains from an agreement are positive, suggesting that on balance the agreement is trade creating. Moreover, these gains are about as large as can reasonably be expected to result from a successful Doha Round. For India, the return to investing intellectual and political capital in an FTA with the United States would be as rewarding as investing in negotiating a successful Doha Round. And the negotiations would be far quicker.

The simulations clearly demonstrate the benefits of complete unilateral liberalization. But they also show that India would gain even more with an open home market *and* preferential access to the United States. Moreover, even with a U.S.-India FTA in place, the United States still benefits from additional Indian liberalization. Thus the United States has an interest in promoting additional Indian unilateral liberalization, not blocking it. This supports the idea of building blocks rather than stumbling blocks. A U.S.-India agreement would also provide India with protection against a world of trading blocks.

At the end of the day, India's choice is complicated. There appears to be greater uncertainty about the answer to the first question (unilateral versus reciprocal approaches) than to the second (multitrack vs. multilateral). If India should use trade agreements to bolster its reforms, a U.S.-India FTA appears to be the strongest avenue because of its likely comprehensive and deep character. It would provide significant welfare benefits through both trade and investment and strengthen India's bargaining positions, both bilaterally and multilaterally. It also offers the best chance for combating U.S. resistance to outsourcing. By contrast, the WTO is likely to be less effective even if India is prepared to depart radically from the principles, such as special and differential treatment and first-difference reciprocity, that have been such an important part of its positions in the past.

Moreover, departing from a trade strategy that has worked well for more than a decade would entail more risks and more constraints on the domestic policy front. The trade agreement by itself would not suffice to fully realize the potential economic payoffs from more radical reform. Success would ultimately depend on India's ability to adopt complementary policies and institutions.

Appendix: Overview of the Michigan BDS-CGE Model

We provide a brief introduction to the Brown-Deardorff-Stern (BDS) computable general equilibrium (CGE) Michigan Model in the following paragraphs.[62] The distinguishing feature of the Michigan Model is that it incorporates some aspects of the New Trade Theory (New Trade Theory is different from the Traditional Trade Theory, which assumes, among other assumptions, constant returns to scale, perfect competition, and product homogeneity), including increasing returns to scale, monopolistic competition, and product heterogeneity.

Sectors and Market Structure

The main data source is the GTAP-5 database of the Purdue University Centre for Global Trade Analysis Project.[63] The reference year for this database is 1997. It has sixty-five countries and regions, and fifty-seven sectors of production including fourteen in agriculture, four in minerals and metals, twenty-four in manufacturing, and fifteen in services. We have condensed these into sixteen sectors. The fourteen sectors of agriculture have been grouped into one agricultural sector, as have the four sectors of mineral products. Fifteen service sectors have been condensed into five sectoral categories. The twenty-four manufacturing sectors have been grouped into nine sectors. These nine sectors include food, beverages, and tobacco; textiles; wearing apparel; leather, wood, and paper products; chemicals, rubber, plastic, and petroleum products; nonmetallic mineral products; metal and metal products; transportation and machinery equipment and parts; and other manufactures including electronic equipment.

Sixty-five countries of the GTAP database have been condensed into fourteen countries or regions. Asian countries or regions have been distributed among seven countries or regions, namely India, Rest-of-South Asia, China, ASEAN (Indonesia, Malaysia, the Philippines, and Thailand), NIEs (Hong Kong, South Korea, Singapore, and Taiwan), Japan and Australia-New Zealand. USA, Canada, and Mexico have been taken as separate countries. The remaining four regions include Central and South America (Central America and the Caribbean; Columbia; Peru; Venezuela; Rest-of-Andean Pact; Argentina; Brazil; Chile; Uruguay; Rest-of-South America);

---

62. A complete description of the formal structure and equations of the model can be found online at www.Fordschool.umich.edu/rsie/model/. Also see Brown, Deardorff, and Stern (2001).

63. Dimaranan and McDougall (2002).

TABLE A-1. Percent Change in Welfare under Various Trade Scenarios: Computational Scenarios

Countries or regions	Code	Simulation											
		1	2	3	4	5	6	7	8	9	10	11	12
India	**Ind**	**0.61**	**-0.23**	**0.4**	**1.2**	**1.0**	**1.3**	**1.4**	**2.0**	**1.5**	**0.8**	**0.5**	**-0.2**
Rest of South Asia	Rsa	0.00	3.99	4.0	0.3	4.3	2.9	1.0	5.3	0.2	4.6	4.0	4.0
China	Chn	0.00	1.80	1.8	0.1	1.9	0.2	0.6	2.9	0.1	1.9	1.8	1.8
ASEAN	Asn	0.00	3.15	3.1	0.2	3.4	0.3	0.4	4.1	0.2	3.4	3.1	3.2
NIEs	Nie	0.00	3.11	3.1	0.2	3.3	0.3	0.2	3.8	0.2	3.3	3.1	3.1
Japan	Jpn	0.00	2.95	3.0	0.1	3.0	0.2	0.3	3.6	0.1	3.1	3.0	3.0
Australia & New Zealand	Anz	0.00	0.00	0.0	0.1	0.1	0.1	0.2	1.8	0.1	0.0	0.0	0.0
United States	**Usa**	**0.04**	**0.33**	**0.4**	**0.1**	**0.4**	**0.1**	**0.1**	**0.6**	**0.1**	**0.3**	**0.4**	**0.3**
Canada	can	0.01	1.23	1.2	0.1	1.3	0.1	-0.6	1.6	0.1	1.2	1.3	1.2
Mexico	mex	0.00	1.68	1.7	0.1	1.7	0.1	-0.6	2.5	0.0	1.7	1.7	1.7
Central & South America	a_n	0.00	-0.07	-0.1	0.1	0.0	0.1	0.3	0.8	0.1	-0.1	-0.1	-0.1
European Union	eun	0.00	1.12	1.1	0.1	1.2	0.2	0.2	1.3	0.1	1.1	1.1	1.3
EU accession candidates	eua	0.00	1.72	1.7	0.1	1.8	0.1	0.1	3.0	0.1	1.7	1.7	1.9
Rest of EFTA	eft	0.00	3.63	3.6	0.4	4.0	0.5	0.5	4.8	0.4	3.6	3.6	4.1

Note: The twelve simulations are as follows:
1. The United States and India eliminate all tariffs against each other.
2. Asia (excluding India), Free Trade Area of Americas (FTAA, that is, United States, Canada, Mexico, and Central and South America), and Europe (European Union, EU accession candidates, plus rest of European Free Trade Area, or EFTA) form a free trade area.
3. Simulation 2 plus India and the United States also form an FTA.
4. India unilaterally eliminates all import tariffs.
5. Simulation 2 plus simulation 4.
6. India and Rest of South Asia form an FTA and eliminate import tariffs against rest of the world.
7. India and the United States form an FTA and adopt a policy of extending the same benefits to all other countries on MFN basis.
8. Multilateral liberalization: All the countries and regions eliminate import tariffs against each other.
9. India and and the United States form an FTA with India adopting open regionalism through extending the same benefits to all other countries on MFN basis (India's open liberalization).
10. Simulation 2 plus India also joins the rest of South Asia in an FTA.
11. Simulation 2 plus India also joins the Free Trade Area of the Americas.
12. Simulation 2 plus India also joins European free trade agreements (EUN, EUA, and EFT).

European Union - Fifteen; EU accession countries (Hungary; Poland and Rest-of-Central European Associates).

Agriculture and service sectors are modeled as perfectly competitive, and all the manufacturing sectors as monopolistically competitive with free entry and exit of firms.

Expenditure

Consumers and producers are assumed to use a two-stage procedure to allocate expenditure across differentiated products. In the first stage, expenditure is allocated across goods without regard to the country of origin or producing firm. At this stage, the utility function is Cobb-Douglas, and the production function requires intermediate inputs in fixed proportions. In the second stage, expenditure on monopolistically competitive goods is allocated across the competing varieties supplied by each firm from all countries. In the case of sectors that are perfectly competitive and individual firm supply is indeterminate, expenditure is allocated over each country's industry as a whole, with imperfect substitution between products of different countries. The aggregation function in the second stage is a constant elasticity of substitution (CES) function.

Production

The production function is separated into two stages. In the first stage, intermediate inputs and a primary composite of capital and labor are used in fixed proportion to output.[64] In the second stage, capital and labor are combined through a CES function to form the primary composite. In the monopolistically competitive sectors, additional fixed inputs of capital and labor are required. It is assumed that fixed capital and fixed labor are used in the same proportion as variable capital and variable labor so that production functions are homothetic.

Supply Prices

To determine equilibrium prices, perfectly competitive firms operate so that price is equal to marginal cost, while monopolistically competitive firms maximize profits by setting price as an optimal markup over marginal cost. The numbers of firms in sectors under monopolistic competition are determined by the condition that there are zero profits.

---

64. Intermediate inputs include both domestic and imported varieties.

Capital and Labor Markets

Capital and labor are assumed to be perfectly mobile across sectors within each country. Returns to capital and labor are determined so as to equate factor demand to an exogenous supply of each factor. The aggregate supplies of capital and labor in each country are assumed to remain fixed so as to abstract from macroeconomic considerations (such as the determination of investment), since our microeconomic focus is on the intersectoral allocation of resources.

World Market and Trade Balance

The world market determines equilibrium prices so that all markets clear. Total demand for each firm's or sector's product must equal total supply of that product. It is also assumed that trade remains balanced for each country or region, that is, that the initial trade imbalance remains constant as trade barriers are changed. This assumption reflects the reality of mostly flexible exchange rates among the countries involved. Moreover, this is a way of abstracting from the macroeconomic forces and policies that are the main determinants of trade imbalances.

Trade Policies and Rent or Revenues

We have incorporated into the model the import tariff rates as policy inputs that are applicable to the bilateral trade of the various countries and regions with respect to one another. These have been computed using the GTAP–5 database provided in Dimaranan and McDougall.[65] We assume that revenues from import tariffs are redistributed to consumers in the tariff- or tax-levying country and are spent like any other income. When tariffs are reduced, income available to purchase imports falls along with their prices, and there is no bias toward expanding or contracting overall demand.

Model Closure and Implementation

We assume in the model that aggregate expenditure varies endogenously to hold aggregate employment constant. This closure is analogous to the Johansen closure rule.[66] The Johansen closure rule consists of keeping the requirement of full employment while dropping the consumption function. Consumption can thus be thought of as adjusting endogenously to ensure

---

65. Dimaranan and McDougall (2002).
66. Deardorff and Stern (1990).

full employment. In the current model, however, we do not distinguish consumption from other sources of final demand. That is, we assume instead that total expenditure adjusts to maintain full employment.

The model is solved using GEMPACK.[67] When policy changes are introduced into the model, the method of solution yields percentage changes in sectoral employment and certain other variables of interest.

Salient Features

It is useful first to review the features of the model that serve to identify the various economic effects that are being captured in the different scenarios.[68] This helps us explain and interpret the results of this exercise. Although the model includes the aforementioned features (increasing returns to scale, monopolistic competition, and product heterogeneity) of the New Trade Theory, it remains the case that markets respond to trade liberalization in much the same way that they would with perfect competition. That is, when tariffs or other trade barriers are reduced in a sector, domestic buyers (both final and intermediate) substitute toward imports and the domestic competing industry contracts production while foreign exporters expand. With multilateral liberalization reducing tariffs and other trade barriers simultaneously in most sectors and countries, each country's industries share in both of these effects, expanding or contracting depending primarily on whether their protection is reduced more or less than in other sectors and countries. At the same time, countries with larger average tariff reductions than their trading partners tend to experience a real depreciation of their currencies in order to maintain a constant trade balance, so that all countries therefore experience mixtures of both expanding and contracting sectors.

The effects on the welfare of countries arise from a mixture of these terms-of-trade effects, together with the standard efficiency gains from trade and also from additional benefits resulting from elements of the New Trade Theory. Thus we expect on average that the member countries (countries participating in the liberalisation process) would gain from mutual liberalization, as resources are reallocated to those sectors in each country where there is a comparative advantage. In the absence of terms-of-trade effects, these efficiency gains should raise national welfare measured by the equivalent variation for every country, although some factor owners within a country may lose, as is noted below. However, it is possible for a particular

67. Harrison and Pearson (1996).
68. See Brown, Deardorff, and Stern (2001) for details.

country whose net imports are concentrated in sectors with the greatest liberalization to lose overall, if the worsening of its terms of trade swamps these efficiency gains.

At the same time, although the New Trade Theory is perhaps best known for introducing new reasons why countries may lose from trade, in fact its greatest contribution is to expand the list of reasons for gains from trade. It is these that are the dominant contribution of the New Trade Theory in our model. That is, trade liberalization permits all countries to expand their export sectors at the same time that all sectors compete more closely with a larger number of competing varieties from abroad, resulting from import liberalisation. As a result, countries as a whole gain from lower costs due to increasing returns to scale, lower monopoly distortions due to greater competition, and reduced costs and increased utility due to greater product variety. All of these effects make it more likely that countries will gain from liberalization in ways that are shared across the entire population.

In perfectly competitive trade models such as the Heckscher-Ohlin model, one expects countries as a whole to gain from trade, but the owners of one factor—the "scarce factor"—to lose through the mechanism first explored by Stolper and Samuelson.[69] The additional sources of gain from trade attributable to increasing returns to scale, competition, and product variety, however, are shared across factors, and we routinely find in our CGE modeling that both labor and capital gain from liberalization. That is often the case here.

In the real world, all of these effects occur over time, and some of them occur more quickly than do others. This model is static, however, based upon a single set of equilibrium conditions rather than on relationships that vary over time. Our results therefore refer to a time horizon that is somewhat uncertain, depending on the assumptions that have been made about which variables do and do not adjust to changing market conditions, and on the short- or long-run nature of these adjustments. Because our elasticities of supply and demand reflect relatively long-run adjustments and because we assume that markets for both labor and capital clear within countries, our results are appropriate for a relatively long time horizon of several years—two or three at a minimum.

Nonetheless, this model does not allow for the very long-run adjustments that could occur through capital accumulation, population growth, and technological change. Our results should therefore be thought of as being superimposed upon longer-run growth paths of the economies

---

69. Stolper and Samuelson (1941).

involved. To the extent that these growth paths themselves may be influenced by trade liberalization, therefore, our model does not capture that.

As a result of trade liberalization, there are changes in member and non-member (non-participating) countries' terms of trade that can be positive or negative. Those countries that are net exporters of goods with the greatest degree of liberalization will experience increases in their terms of trade, as the world prices of their exports rise relative to their imports. The reverse occurs for net exporters in industries where liberalization is slight, perhaps because most liberalization already happened in previous trade rounds.

The Data

Needless to say, the data needs of this model are immense. Apart from numerous share parameters, the model requires various types of elasticity measures. Like other CGE models, most of our data come from published sources.

The main data source, the GTAP-5 database, provides us with an approximate picture of what the world looked like in 1997, that is about three years down the time of commencement of the Uruguay Round (UR) negotiations. The reference year for this database is 1997. From this source, we have extracted the following data, aggregated to our sectors and regions:

—Bilateral trade flows among fourteen countries or regions, decomposed into sixteen sectors. Trade with the rest-of-world (ROW) is included to close the model.

—Input-output tables for the fourteen countries and regions, excluding ROW.

—Components of final demand along with sectoral contributions for the fourteen countries and regions, excluding ROW.

—Gross value of output and value added at the sectoral level for the fourteen countries and regions, excluding ROW.

—Bilateral import tariffs by sector among the countries and regions, including ROW.

—Elasticity of substitution between capital and labor by sector.

—Bilateral export-tariff equivalents among all fourteen countries and regions, decomposed into sixteen sectors.

The monopolistically competitive market structure in the manufacturing sectors of the model imposes an additional data requirement of the number of firms at the sectoral level. These data have been drawn from the United

Nations Industrial Development Organization (UNIDO), *International Yearbook of Industrial Statistics, 1998*. We also need estimates of sectoral employment for the countries and regions of the model. These data have been drawn from UNIDO, *International Yearbook of Industrial Statistics, 1998*, and International Labor Organization, *Year Book of Labor Statistics, 2000*. The employment data have been aggregated according to our sectoral and regional aggregations to obtain sectoral estimates of workers employed in manufactures. The *World Development Report* was used to obtain data for the other sectors.

Comments and Discussion

Shankar Acharya: This very interesting and stimulating paper by Robert Lawrence and Rajesh Chadha really makes one "think outside the box." In some ways, the argument of the paper is more compelling since it comes from an established and reputable "free trader" who normally advocates multilateral trade liberalization. The paper also provides useful benchmark estimates of the gains from liberalization of trade in goods under alternative scenarios. Although the paper advances a bold and stimulating thesis, my comments may serve to dampen the enthusiasm for the strategy advocated.

Let me start with the basic questions posed and the answers given by the authors. First, they ask whether India should depart from its incremental, unilateral strategy toward trade liberalization and reforms generally? Their basic response is that after a dozen years, reforms seem to have taken hold (that is, there are enough vested interests in proceeding with economic reforms), and now is the time for a "big push." Second, that being the case, should the thrust of further trade liberalization come through the WTO or a U.S.-led FTA? Their answer is that the big push will be best served by a multitrack approach that accords primacy to an India–U.S. FTA. This is so, they argue, because such an FTA will mean "full reciprocity" and "deeper integration" than is likely to be forthcoming through the WTO Doha Round negotiations, which are likely to trundle along and entail weak reciprocity and weak integration. Let me assess each of these answers and offer a few more comments.

India's Approach to Reforms

I would suggest that the correct characterization of India's economic reforms over the last dozen years or so is not "incremental" or "gradualist" as maintained by some,[1] but rather "medium bang," followed by sporadic and discontinuous spurts of reform activity. The medium bang was in the early 1990s, under the hammer of an old-fashioned balance-of-

---

1. For example, Ahluwalia (2002).

payments crisis. The systemic or medium-bang nature of the reforms "may be gauged from the fact that within a few months the following steps had been taken: virtual abolition of industrial licensing; rupee devaluation by 20 per cent; the complex import licensing replaced by a system (EXIMSCRIPS) of tradable, import entitlements earned through exports (later replaced by a dual, and then, market-determined exchange rate); phased reduction of customs duties; fiscal deficit cut by 2 per cent of GDP; foreign investment opened up; banking reforms launched; capital market reforms initiated; initial divestment of public enterprises announced and major tax reforms outlined."[2]

After the early 1990s, economic reforms have tended to come in fits and starts (partly driven by opportunism), not as part of an incremental execution of a master plan. Indeed, the somewhat half-hearted commitment to reforms after 1994 has been correctly described by some analysts as evidence that "India shows a strong consensus for weak reforms." The bottom line seems to be that there is no serious political appetite for strong economic reforms and that there is little evidence (at least in the last half-dozen years) of a technocratically crafted, conscious strategy for implementing economic reforms. If this assessment is true, then there is little chance of a bold trade reform strategy in the immediate future.

The Revenue Problem

There is one other important obstacle to trade reform, which tends to be ignored or downplayed by trade economists, especially those from foreign shores. This is the problem of a low and stagnant tax-GDP ratio in the context of huge fiscal deficits (running at 10 percent of GDP on a general government basis) and inflexible expenditure commitments. A major failure of India's tax and trade reforms over the last dozen years has been the inability to substitute *domestic* taxes for declining customs revenue. Constitutional, technical, and political weaknesses have precluded establishment of a broad-based, elastic, consumption value-added tax. As a result, customs revenues still account for 20 to 25 percent of central government tax revenues. The revenue loss that would result from further reductions in customs tariffs has become increasingly difficult to justify on economic and fiscal grounds. The past failure in restructuring the tax system has now become a serious impediment to further substantial tariff cuts, whether unilateral or reciprocal.

2. Acharya (2004).

Feasibility of an FTA-Based Big Push

Let us review the areas in which India will have to reform (or give concessions) to successfully negotiate an FTA with the United States. According to the excellent analysis by Lawrence and Chadha, these areas can be expected to include agriculture, financial services, intellectual property rights, investment, regulatory transparency, public sector enterprises, and capital account controls. To me, the politics of "conceding" in these areas to achieve closure of an India-U.S. FTA does not look at all promising. Lawrence and Chadha talk of such concessions as a case of reforms being "locked in." Given the Indian political establishment's aversion to conducting economic policy under external "pressures," especially from the United States, this may be more a case of locking out reforms.

Furthermore, the approach recommended by the authors involves a direct link between trade policy reforms and treaty commitments. Lawrence and Chadha see this as a virtue. I am not at all sure. Indeed, I would suggest that much of the success of India's trade policy reforms in the 1990s can be attributed to the *decoupling* of trade reforms and treaty commitments. During the decade, the Finance Ministry undertook a series of unilateral tariff reductions, leaving it to the Commerce Ministry to negotiate the levels of tariff bindings in the WTO. In this way, the process of unilateral trade liberalization was successfully insulated from the politics of "concessions" in WTO negotiations.

Thus the feasibility of a big push in trade policy reform based on a U.S. FTA appears very slight. Much more likely is a combination of gradual unilateral tariff concessions and slow and complex "reciprocal" agreements negotiated through the Doha Round of trade talks. It is true that the past year has witnessed a surge in India's apparent desire to participate in various preferential trading arrangements, including ones with Thailand, ASEAN, Singapore, China, and so forth. But thus far these agreements-in-process appear to be cases of "shallow integration" driven by a combination of neighborhood politics and a post-Cancun search for alternatives. There is nothing there that at all resembles the bold gamble outlined by Lawrence and Chadha.

Kenneth Kletzer: Robert Lawrence and Rajesh Chadha advocate the negotiation of a free trade area (FTA) between India and the United States, arguing that it would complement multilateral and unilateral trade liberalization, deepen international market integration, and reinforce domestic policy reforms. Their paper divides its theoretical arguments into a defensive and offensive case for a U.S.-India FTA, but we might also interpret the arguments as both an offense and a defense against critics of the multitrack approach to trade liberalization and integration. Lawrence and Chadha offer a rebuttal to Srinivasan and Tendulkar in the debate over whether regional free trade agreements aid or impede global trade liberalization.[3] I begin with this argument, highlighting the points made by Lawrence and Chadha.

One point that is well appreciated by both sides is that trade liberalization takes place in an otherwise distorted world economy. The analysis of trade liberalization in a second-best economic environment is well known, but the application here is a bit different from the textbook one.[4] The main point made by Lawrence and Chadha is that multitrack and multilateral liberalization under the WTO are themselves incomplete policy reforms. They argue that any comparison between multilateral liberalization and a U.S.-India FTA must take into account a nonidealized version of WTO liberalization in the Doha Round of talks. The paper goes beyond this point by arguing a defensive political-economy case for pursuing a U.S.-India FTA and a case for FTAs as a means of moving multilateral liberalization forward.

The defensive case seems straightforward: a free trade agreement with India could secure the continued openness of the United States to outsourcing in information technology and back office services as a condition of liberalizing U.S. access to Indian markets. Placing an FTA with India on the U.S. legislative agenda would put the gains for some industries and losses for others on the table at the same time. It would also bring the discussion over job losses from outsourcing into an open legislative debate, risking an adverse outcome. Job displacement has largely concerned manufacturing workers in the United States, but outsourcing to India seems to capture disproportionate attention as a small number of white-collar, high-wage workers face the threat of losing their jobs to foreign competition. However, I agree with the authors that defending India against U.S. protection is a sensible motive for Indian policymakers.

The first aspect of the offensive argument for the FTA is that India will receive net gains from an FTA with the United States. The best way to make an argument for a second-best policy in a distorted world is to use a quantitative model. The paper offers estimates that are reasonable and con-

---

3. Srinivasan and Tendulkar (2003).
4. I use the modifier "second-best" in reference to an economy with any number of distortions greater than the one being addressed.

sistent with those in other studies that show significant net gains for both India and the United States from either an FTA or unilateral Indian liberalization. The estimates also reveal small costs for the rest of the world from trade diversion under an FTA. However, that is not enough to answer critics, since multilateral liberalization is an alternative, and unilateral liberalization produces greater gains for all concerned. Perhaps a justification for an FTA can be found in the combination of the estimates (from a static model with full employment) and the reasoning behind the defensive case. There is no reciprocity under unilateral liberalization, so it offers no defense against protectionist pressures in the United States. The argument of Lawrence and Chadha is that by securing a trade agreement with the United States, India will secure its access to U.S. markets and retain the freedom to unilaterally reduce its barriers to trade with the rest of the world. Interestingly, the quantitative analysis shows larger gains for India from combining an FTA with the United States and unilateral liberalization than from unilateral liberalization alone. This implies that U.S. concessions over the status quo are also welfare improving.

At this point, the argument turns to the critics of bilateral and regional free trade arrangements. I think that the point made by Lawrence and Chadha that an FTA is not the textbook version of a preferential trading arrangement should be well taken. The negotiation of an U.S.-India FTA would not preclude either unilateral liberalization or the negotiation of other bilateral and regional arrangements by either country. I agree that the enthusiasm of recent U.S. administrations for FTAs reflects a deliberate effort to use this route to accelerate global trade liberalization.

A value of the FTA, in the authors' argument, is that it can lead to deeper liberalization in India than either the unilateral or multilateral route in the near term. For example, gaining access for agricultural exports to the U.S. market should be an incentive for political support for liberalization in India, which is unlikely to be achieved in the near term through multilateral trade negotiations. However, an FTA between the United States and India may not achieve the level of bilateral integration of other U.S. FTAs; for example, the prospects for negotiating the protection of intellectual property in a U.S.-India FTA are low.

One of the counterarguments to critics of multitrack liberalization is that comparisons must be made to realistic outcomes of multilateral trade negotiations rather than to idealized global liberalization outcomes. This is sound reasoning, and I agree with it. The essential part of the argument is that bound tariff rates for India are much higher than current tariff rates for the most part, and the completion of the Doha Round is unlikely to lower bound rates to current rates. The authors' forecasts are based on previous rounds; in the current global policy environment, these could be optimistic.

Thus far, I have not taken issue with either the paper or the literature. As represented by the authors, the debate over multitrack or multilateral trade liberalization focuses on an idealized version of multilateral liberalization and a mischaracterization of FTAs. In the paper, the case for a U.S.-India FTA rests on a static comparison of an FTA and a round of multilateral negotiations, using a characterization of each that is based on recent experience. I am not concerned about these representations or the quantitative comparisons, but the real case for multitrack liberalization and the crux of the debate over bilateralism versus multilateralism should be dynamic. Which will lead to broader and deeper international integration in a reasonable period of time? Will individual FTAs encourage or inhibit the extension of preferences to others and eventual unification around a common set of rules and procedures?

The argument in favor of multitrack liberalization should consider whether a bilateral FTA increases or decreases the incentives for extending trade preferences to new partners or for unilateral liberalization. The quantitative part of this paper does address this point and shows that the additional net gains from unilateral liberalization by India decrease with an FTA, although they remain positive. At the same time, the losses to those that lose from further liberalization may also decrease, lowering the resistance to unilateral liberalization or the extension of the terms of the U.S. agreement to other trading partners. If so, this supports the argument that an FTA can catalyze wider liberalization.

One of the arguments against the multitrack approach is that the combination of various regional and multilateral agreements will leave a complex system of rules and procedures (Jagdish Bhagwati's "spaghetti bowl liberalization") that reduces welfare. One hypothesis is that after the individual losses and gains from liberalization have been realized through a hodgepodge of agreements, negotiating uniform rules in a multilateral round may be politically uncontroversial, and the task of tidying things up could be left to bureaucrats. The political heavy lifting could be done by taking advantage of each opportunity to negotiate freer trade, leaving the job of negotiating final multilateral agreements for later, when the redistributive effects are minor. Against this vision must be set the alternative: that multilateral trade negotiations could achieve liberalization more rapidly if they were the only agenda pursued. Without development of the argument within a theoretical model and empirical support, these alternatives cannot be compared.

The quantitative—and theoretical—support for either multitrack or multilateral liberalization depends on a comparison of steady state alternatives, just as is offered in this paper.

In theory, multilateral trade liberalization applies the same reforms to all countries at once and proceeds through successive reductions in barriers to trade. Trade liberalization through FTAs and unilateral liberalization proceeds by expanding the number of countries party to a free trade agreement. The two approaches move in different dimensions. At each round, the multilateral route seeks the greatest reform that is acceptable to all countries, while the FTA route seeks the largest number of countries that accept the most liberal agreement. In practice, multilateral trade liberalization is more complex, and the multitrack route is opportunistic and proceeds in both dimensions. Without an analysis that gives a quantitative answer to the question of which is superior—or of whether the two even end up at the same place—how should policy advice be given? I think that the arguments against the multitrack approach are incomplete and inadequate, as are the arguments in favor of it.

Lawrence and Chadha do just what can be done at this stage: they calculate the effects of a U.S.-India FTA, showing them to be positive. They also estimate that the proposed FTA will not create disincentives for further liberalization. It might have been useful if they had made a direct comparison by also estimating the gains from completion of the Doha Round under their assumption that the outcome will proportionately match those of past multilateral agreements.

General Discussion

Arvind Panagariya raised the issue of the growth effects of preferential trading areas. He noted that while there is an enormous literature relating growth to unilateral liberalization in developing countries across the globe, there is no such clear-cut case for free trade areas (FTAs). While much good has happened to Mexico following NAFTA, the growth response has been disappointing. After the presentation of the Lawrence-Chadha paper, Panagariya was more, not less, convinced that the economic and political realities pointed toward exploring a limited services agreement rather than a comprehensive treaty. The simulation results gave him some concern. He was surprised that the United States gained significantly through unilateral liberalization. Given the extremely low level of existing U.S. tariffs, he found that implausible. He noted also that the largest gains for all concerned were in multilateral liberalization. If that was so, then why not move aggressively along that track? Picking up on Panagariya's points, Williamson first pointed out that the European Union was one example of a preferential trade area (PTA), in this case a customs union, that had certainly benefited a number of countries on the periphery. He, too, felt that the simulations pointed strongly in favor of multilateral liberalization, including the welfare of third countries that clearly appeared to suffer from trade diversion under a bilateral U.S.-India FTA. However, in contrast to Panagariya and consistent with Lawrence-Chadha, he agreed that there was little to fear from the typical labor and environmental provisions found in other bilateral U.S. FTAs. He felt, however, that there was greater cause for concern in two other areas: intellectual property and capital account convertibility. Were these elements to be insisted on by the United States, there would be an enormous, and not necessarily desirable, change in policy for India.

Ila Patnaik noted that there had been scant public discussion in India regarding the FTAs that India had recently concluded, and she welcomed the paper as an example of the sort of debate that should take place. On the simulations, she wanted to see both more detail on where the gains were coming from and some extension to services. Montek Ahluwalia had the same concern regarding capital account convertibility and also asked what analytic framework could be used to gauge the welfare consequences of a move to convertibility. While he remained a multilateralist, the paper raised provocative questions on how India could gear itself for such a sweeping set of negotiations, given its proclivity for incremental change. Surjit Bhalla observed that in India laws often were adopted with no intention that they be enforced. More broadly, he was skeptical about the relative importance of negotiated trade agreements in the face of the larger forces unleashed by globalization, which are unstoppable and will be the true shapers of the India of the next decade. He was also not too concerned about the revenue loss associated with trade liberalization, as he saw considerable buoyancy in direct tax collections. Barry Bosworth pointed out that given the full-employment assumptions underlying the model, most of the domestic conflict and short-term labor adjustment issues are omitted, and it is assumed that macro policies are successful at restoring full employment. Shankar Acharya returned to the revenue issue, pointing out that at 2 percent of GDP, customs revenue still accounted for a quarter of central government tax revenues. In his view, this added to the attraction of a multilateral agreement, since India could agree to a reduction in bound rates within the WTO without affecting applied rates and therefore customs revenue. He also wondered how great the value was of preferential access to the U.S. market, given that U.S. tariff rates were in general very low. Would India actually suffer significantly in comparison with countries that enjoyed preferential access?

Responding to these comments, Lawrence said that the FTA could act as a stimulus for efficient tax reform, freeing India from dependence on second-best revenue mechanisms like customs duties. He also thought there were limits to reform by stealth; there had been a sea-change in public confidence in India that ought to make comprehensive reform more feasible now. He also felt that the welfare gains from multilateral liberalization were overstated, since full liberalization was extremely unlikely. If trade barriers were reduced by 30 percent, as was more realistic, then the gains would not be very different from those from an FTA with the United States. He also noted that the simulation results showed rather large terms-of-trade benefits from India's liberalization, which he found to be an interesting insight. He felt that the pressure to include capital account liberalization in FTAs with the United States was outrageous, but that this could be handled within larger negotiations that were calibrated to India's specific circumstances. With regard to the benefits to Mexico from joining NAFTA, he felt there had been enormous dynamic gains, including much closer official cooperation. Commenting on the modeling issues, Chadha agreed that at the end of the day full employment was assumed, but noted that the models still helped provide a sense of how much adjustment was required in individual sectors. He also noted that the models did not try to capture the additional short-term costs needed to administer an FTA, nor the social costs associated with the reallocation of labor.

References

Acharya, Shankar. 2004. "Why Did India Reform?" *Business Standard* 24 (February).

Ahluwalia, M. S. 2002. "Economic Reforms in India Since 1991: Has Gradualism Worked?" *Journal of Economic Perspectives* 16 (3): 67–88.

Bagwell, K., and R. Staiger 2000. "GATT Think." NBER Working Paper 8005. Cambridge, Mass.: National Bureau of Economic Research.

Baldwin, R. E., and A. J. Venables. 1995. "Regional Economic Integration." In *Handbook of International Economics,* edited by G. M. Grossman and K. Rogoff. Amsterdam: Elsevier.

Bhagwati, J., and A. Panagariya, eds. 1996. *The Economics of Preferential Trade Agreements.* Washington: AEI Press.

Bradford, S., and R. Z. Lawrence. 2004. *Has Globalization Gone Far Enough?* Washington: Institute for International Economics.

Brown, Drusilla, Alan Deardorff, and Robert Stern. 2001. "CGE Modeling and Analysis of Multilateral and Regional Negotiating Options." In *Issues and Options for U.S.-Japan Trade Policies*, edited by Robert M. Stern. University of Michigan Press.

Bureau of Economic Analysis, U.S. Department of Commerce. 2003. "U.S. Multinational Companies: Operations in 2001." *Survey of Current Business* 83 (11): 85–105.

Caplin, A., and K. Krishna.1988. "Tariffs and the Most-Favored-Nation Clause: A Game Theoretic Approach." *Seoul Journal of Economics* 1: 267–89.

Chadha, Rajesh, and others. 2003. "Computational Analysis of the Impact on India of the Uruguay Round and the Doha Round of Negotiations." In *India and the WTO: A Strategy for Development,* edited by Aaditya Mattoo and Robert M. Stern. Washington: World Bank.

Cooper, C. A., and B. F. Massel. 1965. "A New Look at Customs Union Theory." *Economic Journal* 75: 742–47.

Corden, W. Max. 1984. "The Normative Theory of International Trade." In *Handbook of International Economics*, edited by R. Jones and P. Kenen, chapter 2. Amsterdam: North Holland.

Council on Foreign Relations. 2003. *New Priorities in South Asia: U.S. Policy toward India, Pakistan, and Afghanistan.* Chairmen's Report of an Independent Task Force, Council on Foreign Relations and Asia Society. New York.

Dam, K. 1970. *The GATT: Law and International Economic Organization.* University of Chicago Press.

Deardorff, Alan V., and Robert M. Stern. 1990. *Computational Analysis of Global Trading Arrangements.* University of Michigan Press.

Dimaranan, Betina, and Robert McDougall, eds. 2002. *Global Trade, Assistance, and Production: GTAP-5 Database.* Purdue University.

EIU (Economist Intelligence Unit). 2003. *Country Report: India.* London.

Fernandez, R., and D. Rodrik. 1991. "Resistance to Reform: Status Quo Bias in the Presence of Individual-Specific Uncertainty." *American Economic Review* 81 (5): 1146–55.

Frankel, J. A. 1997. *Regional Trading Blocs in the World Economic System.* Washington: Institute for International Economics.

Harrison, Jill, and Ken Pearson. 1996. "Computing Solutions for Large General Equilibrium Models Using GEMPACK." *Computational Economics* 9: 83–127.

Hathaway, Dale. 2002. "The Impacts of U.S. Agricultural and Trade Policy on Trade Liberalization and Integration via a US-Central American Free Trade Agreement." Paper prepared for the Inter-American Development Bank Seminar, Washington, October 1–2.

Hoekman, B., and M. Kostecki. 2001. *The Political Economy of the World Trading System: The WTO and Beyond.* Oxford University Press.

Kowalczyk, C. 2000. "Welfare and Integration." *International Economic Review* 41 (2, May).

Laird, S. 2002. "Market Access Issues and the WTO: Overview." In *Development, Trade and the WTO,* edited by B. Hoekman, A. Mattoo, and P. English. Washington: World Bank.

Laird, S., and others. 2003. "Market Access Proposals for Non-Agricultural Products." United Nations Conference on Trade and Development, Geneva.

Lawrence, R. Z. 1996. *Regionalism, Multilateralism, and Deeper Integration.* Brookings.

———. 2003. *Crimes and Punishments? Retaliation under the WTO.* Washington: Institute for International Economics.

Lerner, A. P. 1936. "The Symmetry Between Import and Export Taxes." *Economica* 3: 306–13.

Levy, P. I. 1994. "A Political-Economic Analysis of Free Trade Agreements." In Political Economy and Free Trade Agreements. Phd. dissertation. Stanford University.

Lindblom, C. E. 1995. "The Science of 'Muddling Through.'" In *Public Policy: The Essential Readings,* edited by S. Theodoulou and M. Can, pp. 113–27. New York: Prentice Hall.

Lipsey, R. G. 1957. "The Theory of Customs Unions: Trade Diversion and Welfare." *Economica* 24: 40–46.

Mattoo, A., and A. Subramanian. 2003. "India and the Multilateral Trading System Post Doha: Defensive or Proactive?" In *India and the WTO: A Strategy for Development,* edited by M. Aaditya and R. Stern. Washington: World Bank.

Mattoo, A., and S. Wunsch. 2004. "Securing Openness of Cross-Border Trade in Services: A Possible Approach." Unpublished manuscript. Washington: World Bank and Institute for International Economics.

McKinsey Global Institute. 2003. *Offshoring: Is It a Win-Win Game?* Washington, D.C.

Mussa, M. 1984. *The Adjustment Process and the Timing of Trade Liberalization.* Cambridge, Mass.: National Bureau of Economic Research.

Rodrik, D. 2002. "Trade Policy Reform as Institutional Reform." In *Development Trade and the WTO: A Handbook,* edited by B. Hoekman, A. Mattoo, and P. English, pp. 3–10. Washington: World Bank.

Salazar-Xirinachs, J. M., and J. Granados. 2004. "The United States–Central America Free Trade Agreement: Opportunities and Challenges." In *More Free Trade Areas?* edited by J. Schott. Washington: Institute for International Economics.

Schott, J. J., ed. 2004. *Free Trade Agreements: U.S. Strategies and Priorities.* Washington: Institute for International Economics.

Sen, J. 2002. "A NAFTA Model for the Americas?" In *Regionalism, Multilateralism and Economic Integration: The Recent Experience*, edited by S. Woolcock and G. Sampson. United Nations University Press.

Srinivasan, T. N., and S. D. Tendulkar. 2003. *Reintegrating India in the World Economy.* Washington: Institute for International Economics.

Staiger, R. 1995. "International Rules and Institutions for Cooperative Trade Policy." In *Handbook of International Economics*, vol. 3, edited by G. M. Grossman and K. Rogoff, pp. 1497–547. Amsterdam: Elsevier.

Stolper, W., and P. A. Samuelson. 1941. "Protection and Real Wages." *Review of Economic Studies* (November): 58–73.

Viner. J. 1950. *The Customs Union Issue.* New York: Carnegie Endowment.

Wei, S.-J., and J. Frankel. 1995. "Can Regional Blocs Be Stepping Stones to Global Free Trade?" *Review of International Economics and Finance* 5 (4).

WTO (World Trade Organization). 2002. *Trade Policy Review: India.* Geneva.

VIJAY JOSHI
Merton College, Oxford

SANJEEV SANYAL
Deutsche Bank

Foreign Inflows and Macroeconomic Policy in India

How should macroeconomic policy in India respond to the dramatic strengthening of the balance of payments in the current decade? This controversial subject of contemporary Indian debate is addressed below. The paper begins with an assessment of the external aspects of India's macroeconomic management in the 1990s. It proceeds to examine the sources of the recent balance-of-payments improvement, then to analyze various relevant policy alternatives, and finally to delineate the contours of the optimal policy mix. We argue that the appropriate response to the strength of the balance of payments is a judicious combination of policies rather than a "corner solution," particularly one in which appreciation of the real exchange rate is used exclusively. In particular, we recommend accelerated import liberalization and fiscal consolidation accompanied by monetary expansion. Such a strategy would achieve the needed adjustment without undermining the competitiveness of the export industries, which is essential for rapid growth.

Management of the Balance of Payments in the 1990s

The decade of the 1990s began with a balance-of-payments crisis caused primarily by weak fundamentals, in particular large fiscal and current account deficits throughout the second half of the previous decade. The trigger for the crisis was the brief spike in oil prices that followed the Iraqi invasion of Kuwait, combined with an unsettled political situation in India.

The authors are grateful to Barry Bosworth and John Williamson for their penetrating comments on the first draft of this paper and to Maurice Scott and David Vines for stimulating conversations.

TABLE 1. Major Macroeconomic Indicators, India,
Fiscal Years 1990–91 to 2003–04[a]
Annual percent increase unless otherwise specified

Fiscal year	GDP (overall)	GDP (industry)	Broad money	Reserve money	Wholesale prices	Fiscal balance (percent of GDP)	Current account (percent of GDP)
1990–91	5.6	7.7	15.1	13.1	10.3	–9.4	–3.1
1991–92	1.3	–0.6	19.3	13.4	13.7	–7.0	–0.3
1992–93	5.1	4.0	14.8	11.3	10.1	–7.0	–1.7
1993–94	5.9	5.2	18.4	25.2	8.4	–8.3	–0.4
1994–95	7.3	10.2	22.4	22.1	12.5	–7.1	–1.0
1995–96	7.3	11.6	13.6	14.9	8.1	–6.5	–1.7
1996–97	7.8	7.1	16.2	2.9	4.6	–6.4	–1.2
1997–98	4.8	4.3	18.0	13.2	4.4	–7.3	–1.4
1998–99	6.6	3.4	19.4	14.5	5.9	–8.9	–1.0
1999–00	6.4	6.4	13.9	8.2	3.3	–9.4	–1.0
2000–01	5.2	6.6	16.2	8.1	7.0	–9.1	–0.5
2001–02	5.6	3.2	14.2	11.4	3.6	–9.9	0.1
2002–03	4.3	6.2	12.8	9.2	3.4	–10.1	0.7
2003–04	8.1	6.6	16.4	18.3	5.4	–9.5	[0.8]

Sources: Government of India, Ministry of Finance, *Economic Survey* (various years); Reserve Bank of India, *Handbook of Statistics on the Indian Economy 2002–03;* Reserve Bank of India website.
a. The fiscal balance figures relate to the central and state governments combined. The numbers for GDP, fiscal balance, and current account balance in 2003–04 are provisional.

When the crisis broke, there was an outflow of nonresident deposits and a cut-off of short-term loans, and for a time the country teetered on the edge of default. The crisis was resolved fairly rapidly (fiscal years 1991–92 and 1992–93) and in an orthodox manner by a combination of devaluation, deflation, and borrowing from the International Monetary Fund. Simultaneously with this stabilization effort, the government embarked on a policy of economic reform.[1]

During the rest of the decade, India's GDP grew at the very respectable rate of 6 percent a year without any major crisis. Even so, there remained a sense that economic growth was lower than it might be. In this section, we critically examine the external aspects of macroeconomic management during the decade and assess their influence on economic performance. Some relevant macroeconomic data are given in tables 1, 3, and 4.

1. For an analysis of the causes of the 1991 crisis, see Joshi and Little (1994), and for an account of its resolution, Joshi and Little (1996). For a critical evaluation of India's reforms, see Joshi and Little (1996), Joshi (1998a), and Ahluwalia (2002).

External Payments Regime

A convenient starting point for an analytical review of the decade is March 1993, when, as part of economic reform, the Indian government inaugurated what was officially called a "market-determined unified exchange rate." "Market-determined" should not be understood to mean a clean float. The Reserve Bank of India (RBI) intervened actively, often heavily, in the foreign exchange market. In practice, exchange rate management appears to have been guided by the aim of keeping the nominal exchange rate reasonably stable vis-à-vis the U.S. dollar but with occasional bouts of crawling depreciation to correct overvaluation of the real effective exchange rate. In other words, the authorities certainly had exchange rate targets in mind though the targets shifted from time to time. One could call this arrangement a "managed float," but "dirty crawl" would be more accurate. The smooth management of this system was greatly helped by capital controls. India's payments regime was thus firmly in the "intermediate exchange rate with capital controls" category.[2]

DISCRETIONARY CRAWL OF THE EXCHANGE RATE. How dirty was India's dirty crawl? Casual eye-balling is sufficient to reveal that the rupee-dollar rate was rather stable or, more accurately, that there were extended periods of stability, punctuated by crawling depreciations. For example, the rate barely moved between mid-1993 and mid-1995, mid-1996 and mid-1997, mid-1998 and mid-1999, and December 2000 and September 2001. The impression of a "dirty crawl" is confirmed by statistical measures of exchange rate volatility, given in table 2. The table shows that the rupee's volatility was significantly lower than that of the currencies not only of the G-3 countries but also of relevant emerging markets. The table also indicates that India exhibited higher volatility of interest rates, monetary base, and foreign exchange reserves than the G-3 countries and relevant emerging markets. This evidence strengthens the presumption that India's exchange rate regime was de facto toward the fixed rather than the floating end of the spectrum of regimes.

2. Note that the IMF's *Annual Report on Trade and Exchange Restrictions* classified India's exchange regime as an "independent float" rather than a "managed float" throughout the 1990s. This was a patently inaccurate description. The strong version of the "bipolar view" says that with financial globalization any country is restricted to the following choice: exchange rate stability by fixing the exchange rate or monetary policy autonomy by floating the exchange rate. See Eichengreen (1994). Fischer (2001) takes a more moderate position. India's experience has shown that it may be feasible and desirable for an emerging country to adopt an *intermediate* exchange rate regime buttressed by selective capital controls.

TABLE 2. Measures of Exchange Rate Volatility, Various Countries

Country	Regime description[a] (IMF)	Probability of monthly changes within +/–1 percent			Probability of monthly change in interest rate being less than 50 basis points
		Exchange rate (against U.S. dollar)	Foreign exchange reserves	Monetary base	
United States, 1973–99 ($/DM)	Float	26.8	28.6	42.1	80.7
Japan, 1973–99	Float	33.8	44.8	22.7	86.4
India, 1993–99	Float	82.2	21.6	27.4	15.9
Mexico, 1994–99	Float	34.6	13.2	5.7	9.4
Philippines, 1988–99	Float	60.7	9.7	12.5	38.9
Chile, 1982–99	Mgd Float	45.5	21.3	29.2	11.1
Korea, 1980–97	Mgd Float	80.1	16.1	12.3	51.9
Malaysia, 1992–98	Mgd Float	59.4	34.3	24.3	83.3
Indonesia, 1978–97	Mgd Float	96.4	22.8	16.9	46.8
Brazil, 1994–98	Mgd Float	64.3	22.2	16.7	20.4
Argentina, 1991–99	Fix	97.9	15.3	14.3	31.6
Thailand, 1970–97	Fix	93.6	21.3	19.8	41.2

Source: Calvo and Reinhart (2002).
a. The regime description is that given by the IMF in its *Annual Reports on Trade and Exchange Restrictions*. It should not be read as a description of the de facto regime.

The natural next question is what were the objectives of exchange rate policy? Though the Indian authorities were at pains to stress that the exchange rate was "market determined," they also articulated other objectives that were incompatible with clean floating. These were to iron out day-to-day volatility to prevent disorderly markets and to maintain a competitive exchange rate.[3] The desire, on prudential grounds, to accumulate

3. The authorities were careful not to define an explicit numerical target for the real effective exchange rate though it is pretty clear that the 1993–94 level was used as the implicit target. The RBI's *Annual Report* for 1995–96 states, "The broad objective of

**TABLE 3. Nominal and Real Exchange Rate, India,
Fiscal Years 1990–91 to 2003–04**
Base: 1993–94 = 100

Fiscal year	Rupees per U.S. dollar	NEER[a]	REER[b]
1990–91	17.94	175.0	147.7
1991–92	24.47	131.5	116.5
1992–93	30.65	117.8	112.3
1993–94	31.37	100.0	100.0
1994–95	31.40	96.1	105.8
1995–96	33.45	87.7	102.3
1996–97	35.50	86.4	103.4
1997–98	37.17	86.4	105.8
1998–99	42.07	76.5	97.8
1999–2000	43.33	74.2	96.7
2000–01	45.68	73.8	100.8
2001–02	45.69	73.2	102.1
2002–03	48.39	68.8	97.9
2003–04	45.60	67.4	99.6

Source: Reserve Bank of India (May 2004), *Bulletin*.
a. NEER: nominal effective exchange rate. NEER is a five-country export-weighted index. The countries in the index are United States, Japan, United Kingdom, Germany, and France.
b. REER: real effective exchange rate. REER is a five-country export-weighted index. The countries in the index are United States, Japan, United Kingdom, Germany, and France.

sizable foreign exchange reserves was also clearly discernible. Evidence in support comes from the following points. First, the objective of preventing excessive short-term volatility is evident in the low volatility of the rupee-dollar rate. Second, as regards "competitiveness," the rupee-dollar rate and the nominal effective exchange rate followed a depreciating trend, so as approximately to maintain the real effective exchange rate at the 1993–94 level (see table 3).[4] Third, in general, during the decade, market pressure was toward nominal rupee appreciation. Moderate trade deficits were

exchange rate policy will be to ensure a reasonably stable real effective exchange rate." The objectives of exchange rate policy were frequently articulated in speeches of high officials of the RBI (for example, see Reddy 1997). The approach of the authorities with regard to the external payments regime as a whole originated in the landmark Rangarajan report (see Government of India 1993).

4. This is based on a five-country index, which we believe was used in making policy. The ten-country index reported in the *Economic Survey* of the Government of India shows a real appreciation of about 5 percent from 1993–94 to the end of the decade. So does a broader thirty-six-country index reported in the RBI *Bulletin*.

outweighed by a combination of invisible inflows (mainly private remittances) and capital account surpluses. As table 4 shows, reserves increased substantially, from $5.8 billion in March 1991 to $42 billion in March 2001 (eight months import cover). And, fourth, notwithstanding the previous point, there was significant downward pressure on the exchange rate from time to time. The authorities resisted such pressures; their intention, largely successful, appears to have been to allow nominal depreciation but no more than to correct any previous real overvaluation.

Thus the exchange rate was heavily managed. With what instruments? Apart from conventional methods, namely, market intervention and monetary policy, India was notable for using capital controls, or more accurately, for not dismantling them when that was fashionable. The purpose of controlling capital flows was (a) to make it possible to target the exchange rate and (b) to reduce vulnerability to exchange rate and macroeconomic crises.

CAPITAL CONTROLS. Capital account controls were imposed in the late 1950s and became comprehensive and draconian in 1973. The controls were *selectively* liberalized during the early 1990s, when the reform process began. (The word selectively must be stressed. In the 1980s, controls on external borrowing, including short-term borrowing, were relaxed to finance current account deficits. In the 1990s, controls on debt-creating inflows, particularly short-term inflows, were tightened while those on non-debt-creating inflows were liberalized.) These controls acquired their bite not so much from variations in their intensity as from the limits they set on activity and expectations in the foreign exchange market. The highlights of the system are given below.

Foreign direct investment. Before 1991, restrictions operated on a case-by-case basis and were so strict that inflows of direct foreign investment (FDI) were reduced to a trickle. In the reforms of fiscal year 1991–92, automatic approval of foreign investment of up to 51 percent of shareholding was allowed for a wide range of industries. Proposals for a higher share of foreign ownership were considered by a Foreign Investment Promotion Board. In 1996 the list of industries in which FDI is permitted was further widened, with foreign equity up to 74 percent allowed in a few.[5]

---

5. In practice, however, the system was more restrictive than it sounds, because there still remained numerous hurdles to jump, erected by state governments if not by the center. FDI inflows rose from an annual average of about $150 million in the 1980s to about $3 billion in the late 1990s. The latter figure is still very small compared with the inflow into East Asian countries. The cumulative inflow of FDI in the 1990s was about $19 billion but its "bolted down" nature meant that it was not a source of crisis vulnerability.

TABLE 4. Balance of Payments, India, Fiscal Years 1990–91 to 2003–04

Percent of GDP at current market prices

Item	1990–91	1991–92	1992–93	1993–94	1994–95	1995–96	1996–97	1997–98	1998–99	1999–2000	2000–01	2001–02	2002–03	2003–04[a]
Exports, f.o.b	5.8	6.9	7.3	8.3	8.3	9.1	8.9	8.7	8.2	8.3	9.5	9.3	10.4	9.3
Imports, c.i.f.	8.8	7.9	9.6	9.8	11.1	12.3	12.7	12.5	11.4	12.3	12.5	12.0	12.8	12.2
Trade balance	−3.0	−1.0	−2.3	−1.5	−2.8	−3.2	−3.9	−3.8	−3.2	−4.0	−3.0	−2.7	−2.4	−2.9
Invisibles, net	−0.1	0.7	0.6	1.1	1.8	1.6	2.7	2.4	2.2	2.9	2.5	2.8	3.1	3.7
Current account balance	−3.1	−0.3	−1.7	−0.4	−1.0	−1.7	−1.2	−1.4	−1.0	−1.0	−0.5	0.1	0.7	0.8
Capital account surplus	2.3	1.5	1.6	3.5	2.8	1.3	3.0	2.4	2.0	2.3	1.9	2.2	2.3	3.6
Foreign investment	0.0	0.1	0.2	1.6	1.5	1.4	1.6	1.3	0.6	1.2	1.2	1.5	0.9	2.0
External assistance	0.7	1.1	0.8	0.7	0.5	0.3	0.3	0.2	0.2	0.2	0.1	0.2	−0.5	−0.4
Commercial borrowing	0.7	0.6	−0.2	0.2	0.3	0.4	0.7	1.0	1.1	0.1	0.9	−0.3	−0.5	−0.7
Nonresident Indian deposits	0.5	0.2	0.8	0.4	0.1	0.3	0.9	0.3	0.2	0.3	0.5	0.6	0.6	0.8
IMF, net	0.4	0.3	0.5	0.1	−0.4	−0.5	−0.3	−0.2	−0.1	−0.1	0.0	0.0	0.0	0.0
Memo items														
Foreign exchange reserves, year end (billions of U.S. dollars)	5.8	9.2	9.8	19.2	25.2	21.7	26.4	29.4	32.5	38.1	42.3	54.1	75.4	111.0
Foreign exchange reserves (months of import cover)	2.5	5.3	4.9	8.6	8.4	6.0	6.5	6.9	8.2	8.2	8.6	11.3	13.8	18.0
Net foreign investment inflow (billions of U.S. dollars)	0.1	0.1	0.6	4.2	4.8	4.8	6.2	5.4	2.4	5.2	5.9	6.7	4.5	12.6
Direct	0.1	0.1	0.3	0.6	1.0	2.0	2.9	3.6	2.5	2.1	3.3	4.7	3.6	3.4
Portfolio	0.0	0.0	0.3	3.6	3.8	2.8	3.3	1.8	−0.1	3.1	2.6	2.0	0.9	9.2

Sources: Reserve Bank of India, *Handbook of Statistics on the Indian Economy 2002–03*. Reserve Bank of India, *Annual Report* (various years).
a. Estimated.

Foreign portfolio investment. Before 1991, foreign portfolio investment was not allowed, apart from some trivial exceptions. In 1992, foreign institutional investors (FIIs) such as pension funds and mutual funds were permitted to invest in listed securities in primary and secondary markets in equities and bonds (other than government bonds), subject only to some regulatory requirements. In 1997 investment permission was extended to cover government securities and treasury bills. Repatriation of capital, income, and capital gains was freely allowed at the market exchange rate.[6]

External commercial borrowing. Offshore borrowing by Indian companies (commercial bank loans, Eurobonds, and the like) was under the jurisdiction of the Ministry of Finance, which exercized careful control on a case-by-case basis. Controls governed not only the amount of each loan but maturity and end-use (priority was given to projects in the energy and infrastructure sectors).[7] Short-term borrowing apart from normal trade credit was strongly disfavored. There was also an overall annual ceiling on approvals for external commercial borrowing.

Bank deposits of nonresident Indians. Conscious efforts had been made during the 1980s to attract bank deposits from nonresident Indians (NRIs) by offering both higher interest rates and exchange rate guarantees. These deposits proved to be highly volatile in the crisis of 1991, so the exchange guarantee was withdrawn and interest rate incentives were progressively reduced.

Commercial banks and financial markets. Banks were not allowed to accept deposits or extend loans denominated in foreign currencies, and controls on their foreign asset and liability positions were strict. It goes without saying that this was a critical element of the system of capital controls. Internationalization of the currency was strongly discouraged. Offshore trading of the rupee was not permitted (though a limited offshore market did exist). There were restrictions on domestic currency lending to nonresidents, so opportunities for direct short-selling of the rupee were very limited. The swap and forward markets were also tightly controlled because these markets could be used to speculate against the rupee by circumventing the restrictions on direct lending in rupees to nonresidents. Thus the overall policy thrust was to limit forward trading in foreign exchange to hedging current account transactions. Of course, there was a price to pay: the forward market lacked adequate liquidity and depth.

---

6. The cumulative book value of foreign portfolio investment from 1991 to 2001 was about $21 billion. This stock is potentially more volatile than FDI.

7. In some years, borrowed funds were required to be kept outside the country until they were committed to a specific investment use.

Capital outflows. Repatriation was freely permitted for foreign institutional investors and nonresident Indian investors who had invested in the country under recognized schemes. But capital outflows by residents were prohibited, apart from some minor exceptions.

In sum, India had a comprehensive system of capital controls that was *selectively* liberalized in the 1990s. The liberalization was focused on direct and portfolio investment by nonresidents. In these areas, free entry and exit was the normal rule. Debt-creating external borrowing was tightly controlled (indeed more tightly controlled than during the 1980s), particularly if it was short-term. Banks and money markets generally faced significant restrictions on their foreign operations. Capital outflows by residents were forbidden.

Regime Performance in the 1990s

The above regime enabled India to moderate a capital-inflow surge from 1993 to 1995, avoid contagion from the East Asian (1997) and other currency crises (Brazil and Russia in 1998 and 1999), and attenuate an industrial slowdown toward the end of the decade. These shocks were handled by a mixture of monetary policy (including sterilized and unsterilized intervention) and moderate exchange rate changes. This tightrope walk would not have been possible without capital controls. They enabled the authorities to pursue a flexible monetary policy, geared to low inflation and internal balance, while simultaneously targeting the exchange rate to preserve international competitiveness.[8] It is suggestive in this context that over much of the decade the covered interest differential between India and the United States was large and varying (see figure 1).

The performance of India's external payments regime has been examined in some depth by Joshi, who concludes that it was, on balance, very satisfactory.[9] We do not repeat that analysis here. We concentrate instead on two relevant issues. First, we examine the apparent puzzle of why India, unlike many emerging countries, did not succumb to contagion from the East Asian crises. This is an issue that is clearly relevant to judging regime performance. Second, we analyze in some detail the strong claim made by

---

8. Note that in India monetary policy autonomy was critically important because the flexibility of countercyclical fiscal policy was limited by high fiscal deficits.

9. Joshi (2003) considers counterfactual scenarios and argues that the payments regime actually adopted in the 1990s produced better economic performance than alternative regimes.

FIGURE 1. Covered Interest Rate Differential, India, January 1993 to January 2004

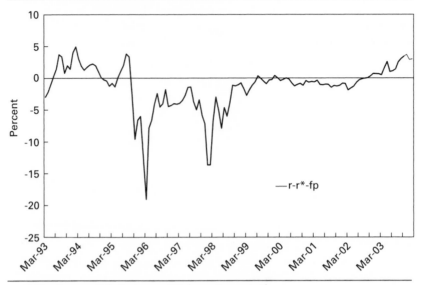

r: yield on three-month Indian treasury bills (percent per annum)
r*: yield on three-month U.S. treasury bills (percent per annum)
fp: three-month forward premium on the U.S. dollar (percent per annum)
Sources: Reserve Bank of India, *Handbook of Statistics on the Indian Economy 2002–03;* IMF, *International Financial Statistics.*

Deepak Lal, Suman Bery, and Devendra Pant that India's payments regime and the manner of its operation (specifically, exchange rate targeting and accumulation of foreign exchange reserves) led to a substantial *reduction* in GDP growth.[10]

WHY DID INDIA ESCAPE THE EAST ASIAN CRISIS AND CONTAGION? A comparison of India and the East Asian countries in 1996, just before the East Asian crisis of 1997, is highly instructive and indicates why India escaped crisis and contagion during that crisis (see table 5). It is clear from the first six columns of the table that in most respects, India's "fundamentals" (fiscal balance, inflation, current account balance, nonperforming assets, debt-exports ratio, and debt-service ratio) were worse or no better than the crisis countries'. Exchange rate policy too was not a distinguishing feature. All these countries were on a loose dollar peg, though the precise mechanism, whether band, crawl, or crawling band, varied. India's

10. Lal, Bery, and Pant (2003).

TABLE 5. **Indicators of Crisis Vulnerability, Various Countries, 1996**

Percent

Country	FB/GDP[a]	ΔP/P[b] (percent a year)	CAB/ XGS[c]	NPA[d]	NCEDT/ XGS[e]	TDS/ XGS[f]	SDT/ EDT[g]	SDT/ RES[h]
India	−9.0	9.0	−11.7	17.3	103.6	21.2	5.3	27.1
Indonesia	−1.0	8.0	−13.0	8.8	180.5	36.6	25.0	166.7
Korea	0.0	4.9	−14.6	4.1	82.0	9.4	49.4	192.7
Malaysia	0.7	3.5	−6.4	3.9	40.4	9.0	27.9	39.7
Philippines	0.3	8.4	−9.9	n.a.	80.1	13.4	19.9	67.9
Thailand	0.7	5.8	−19.5	7.7	110.9	12.6	41.5	97.4

Sources: FB/GDP, NPA: Bank of International Settlements, *Annual Reports*, 1997–98 and 1999–2000, and Government of India, *Economic Survey*, 1999–2000; CAB/XGS, NCEDT/XGS, TDS/XGS, SDT/EDT, SDT/RES: World Bank, *Global Development Finance*, 1999; ΔP/P: IMF, *International Financial Statistics*.
  a. FB/GDP: fiscal balance as a proportion of GDP.
  b. ΔP/P: rate of consumer price inflation.
  c. CAB/XGS: current account balance as a proportion of exports of goods and services.
  d. NPA: Nonperforming assets of commercial banks as a proportion of total advances.
  e. NCEDT/XGS: Non-concessional external debt as a proportion of exports of goods and services.
  f. TDS/XGS: Debt service as a proportion of exports of goods and services.
  g. SDT/EDT: Short-term external debt as a proportion of total external debt.
  h. SDT/RES: Short-term external debt as a proportion of foreign exchange reserves.

exchange rate was no more volatile than those of the crisis countries, so the incentive for unhedged borrowing was similar.[11]

The critical difference between India and the crisis countries can be seen in the last two columns of table 5. India managed to keep short-term debt under control, in relation both to total debt and to foreign exchange reserves. Thus India avoided the crisis by avoiding an unstable debt structure, an outcome that was the direct result of controls on debt-creating short-term inflows.

A relevant political-economy question is why India was able to resist the concerted pressure (until 1997) on emerging countries to adopt capital account convertibility (CAC). One reason is that the ideology of *laissez faire* did not have a constituency in India, and economic reform was quite explicitly of the gradualist variety. It is important also that foreign banks, normally a strong pressure group in favor of CAC, had a very small presence in the country. Last but not least, India was "too big to be bullied" into adopting CAC by Wall Street, the IMF, and the U.S. Treasury.

11. See Joshi (2003). India's exchange rate policy was, however, better in one respect. When the dollar began to appreciate in 1995, the Indian authorities allowed the rupee to depreciate against the dollar. So, unlike the crisis countries, India's real effective exchange rate did not appreciate in 1996.

DID INDIA SACRIFICE GROWTH BY ACCUMULATING FOREIGN EXCHANGE RESERVES IN THE 1990S? In a recent article D. Lal, S. Bery, and D. Pant argue that India paid a heavy price in terms of investment and growth by accumulating foreign exchange reserves in the decade of the 1990s.[12] Indeed, they make the strong claim that India's growth rate during that decade could have been up to 2.7 percent a year higher if the foreign exchange inflows had been fully absorbed.[13] If true, this would be a truly remarkable finding. But their argument is deeply flawed, indeed wholly incorrect.

Absorbing net inflows means increasing domestic spending rather than accumulating foreign exchange reserves. Reserves as a proportion of GDP rose over the decade of the 1990s by an average of about 1.2 percent a year. If the entire increase in reserves had been absorbed into investment each year, the ratio of investment to GDP averaged over the decade would thus have been 1.2 percent higher than it actually was. The incremental net capital output ratio (ICOR) in the 1990s was 2.8. This implies, assuming a constant ICOR, that the increase in India's growth rate of GDP would have equalled 1.2/2.8, or 0.4 percent a year (approximately) over the decade, a far cry from the Lal, Bery, and Pant estimate of 2.7 percent. India's actual growth rate during the 1990s was 5.8 percent. The above argument shows that if reserves had been fully absorbed into investment, India's growth rate would have been at most 6.2 percent, not 8.5 percent as the authors conclude.[14]

This commonsense argument is enough to knock down the authors' claim. How then did they arrive at their extraordinary conclusion? The answer is that their theory and econometrics are based on a simple but devastating analytical error. The underlying fallacy is contained in their assertion that "If the capital inflows had been fully absorbed, the trade deficit and hence the $S - I$ gap [in each year] would have increased by B [where B equals $K + R$, namely, the net inflow of capital (K) and private remittances (R) in that year]. Hence, assuming unchanged domestic

12. Lal, Bery, and Pant (2003).
13. See Lal, Bery, and Pant (2003), p. 4968, table 3, cols. 1 and 2. The authors also claim that there would have been a further 1 percent boost to the rate of growth over and above the 2.7 percent if, in addition to absorbing foreign exchange inflows, bond-financed fiscal deficits had been eliminated: see table 3, col. 3. We do not examine this further claim here.
14. The argument in this paragraph is elaborated in Joshi (2004). The ICOR referred to is the average incremental net capital-output ratio in the 1990s, leaving out the outlier year 1991–92 (when growth fell sharply and the ICOR was 10.7). Lal, Bery, and Pant define investment as net investment and output as GDP at factor cost, both at constant prices. The ICOR is thus the ratio of these two magnitudes. We follow the same (odd) definition of ICOR to stick as closely as possible to their methodology.

savings, and no sterilisation of the capital inflows, an upper bound of the estimate of the investment foregone, by not absorbing the inflows, will equal *B*."[15] This is nonsense. Capital and remittance inflows *were* absorbed, except to the extent of foreign exchange accumulation. It is precisely through the absorption of these inflows that India's current account deficits and the corresponding investment-saving gaps were covered.[16] So if the balance of payments had been differently managed, by floating the exchange rate or by unsterilized intervention with a fixed exchange rate, the maximum potential increase in investment would have equaled the reserve accumulation that took place instead. Hence the forgone investment, as stated above, was at most equal to 1.2 percent a year. In contrast, Lal, Bery, and Pant's estimate of forgone investment is huge. They claim that maximum forgone investment was equal to *B*. In their table 2, *B* averages 4.3 percent of GDP a year during the decade.[17] In their calculations, they use an even higher figure for *B*, namely, $(I^\wedge/Y - I/Y)$ in their table A-3, which averages 5.7 percent of GDP a year.[18] Thus they overestimate the upper bound of investment sacrificed by a massive $(5.7 - 1.2) = 4.5$ percent of GDP a year.

The authors' fallacy can be pinpointed with the aid of their equations and notation. Denote output by Y, total expenditure or absorption by E, domestic saving by S, domestic investment by I, exports of goods and services by X, imports of goods and services by M, increase in reserves by ΔNFA, capital inflows by K, and inflows of remittances by R. Domestic investment equals domestic saving plus the current account deficit; and the current account deficit is covered by capital and remittance inflows, net of reserve accumulation.

$$(1) \qquad \begin{aligned} I - S &= E - Y = M - X = (K + R) - \Delta NFA \\ &\rightarrow I = S + (M - X) = S + (K + R) - \Delta NFA. \end{aligned}$$

Assume, as the authors do, that Y, S, K, and R in any particular year are given. It then follows that the upper bound of I sacrificed in any year

15. Lal, Bery, and Pant (2003), p. 4969.

16. Note that Lal, Bery, and Pant define the current account deficit as exclusive of remittances. They treat remittances as a financing item, along with net capital inflows.

17. Lal, Bery, and Pant (2003), p. 4967.

18. $I^\wedge/Y - I/Y = B = (K + R)/Y$, where $I^\wedge/Y$ is hypothetical investment with full absorption of inflows and the other items are as defined earlier. Note that while estimating B in this manner, Lal, Bery, and Pant follow, without mention let alone explanation, the illegitimate procedure of dividing $(K + R)$ at current prices by Y at constant prices. This naturally inflates B and compounds the upward bias in the estimate of maximum forgone investment. Lal, Bery, and Pant (2003), p. 4974.

is simply ΔNFA in that year. If foreign inflows were fully absorbed into investment and net imports, I would rise to $(I + \Delta NFA)$, E would rise to $(E + \Delta NFA)$, and $(M - X)$ would rise to $(M - X) + \Delta NFA$, and we would have

$$(2) \quad \begin{aligned} (I + \Delta NFA) - S = (E + \Delta NFA) - Y = (M - X) + \Delta NFA = K + R \\ \rightarrow I + \Delta NFA = S + (M - X) + \Delta NFA = S + (K + R). \end{aligned}$$

Investment would now be $(I + \Delta NFA)$, and the new current account deficit $(M - X) + \Delta NFA$ would be covered by the continuing inflow $(K + R)$. Lal, Bery, and Pant argue, instead, that investment could rise to $I + (K + R)$. But if that were so, the left-hand side of equation 2 would have to increase by $(K + R - \Delta NFA)$. To make that possible, the current account deficit in equation 2 would have to widen by $(K + R - \Delta NFA)$, covered by an *extra* inflow of $(K + R - \Delta NFA)$ *over and above* the existing inflow of $(K + R)$. But this cannot happen since K and R are given. That means there would be an *unfilled* current account gap of $(K + R - \Delta NFA)$, clearly an impossible outcome. By the same argument, no increase in investment greater than ΔNFA can be sustained. On the stated assumption that Y, S, K, and R are given, investment therefore *cannot* rise by more than ΔNFA. We conclude that the upper bound of investment sacrificed each year is ΔNFA. The authors' claim that the upper bound is $(K + R)$ is based on false reasoning.[19]

We have shown above that 1.2 percent of GDP a year is the correct maximal estimate of the investment sacrificed by accumulating foreign exchange reserves, with an implied growth sacrifice of at most 0.4 percent a year, not 2.7 percent as Lal, Bery, and Pant claim. But the *actual* sacrifice of growth was surely much less than 0.4 percent. Indeed, it is highly likely that there was gain rather than sacrifice of growth. In other words, India's growth rate would probably have been *lower* than the actual 5.8 percent if reserves had been fully absorbed. The substantive reasons are as follows.

First, even our estimate of 0.4 percent a year as the upper bound of forgone growth is excessively generous to Lal, Bery, and Pant, since it is based

---

19. The wild exaggeration of investment sacrificed is not the sole reason for Lal, Bery, and Pant's incredible result. It is also based on a highly implausible implicit assumption that the ICOR of the extra annual investment of 5.7 percent of GDP would have been 2.1. (They estimate growth sacrificed as 2.7 percent a year and investment sacrificed as 5.7 percent of GDP a year. So the implicit ICOR is 5.7/2.7 = 2.1.) They must surely open their econometric black box and explain why the ICOR of the extra investment made possible by absorbing the inflows would have fallen to 2.1 from its decadal average of 2.7 in the 1980s and 2.8 in the 1990s.

on the assumption of a constant ICOR. The normal assumption of diminishing returns to capital accumulation would produce a much lower estimate of growth sacrificed.[20]

Second, there is no good reason to think that reserve accumulation could have been fully absorbed into domestic investment, whatever the exchange rate regime. Part of the extra absorption, arguably most of it, would have resulted in an increase in aggregate consumption. There is some presumption that inflows of direct foreign investment lead to higher domestic investment overall. With other types of inflow, the outcome is more indirect and more uncertain.

Third, accumulating reserves was in fact a wise policy choice, given their rock-bottom level in 1991. In the absence of reserve accumulation, India would have been highly vulnerable to adverse external shocks. Though, in general, market pressure during the decade was for appreciation, the rupee was under severe downward pressure during several episodes, such as late 1995 and early 1996, late 1997 and early 1998 (the East Asian crisis), and late 1998 and early 1999 (India's nuclear tests followed by currency crises in Brazil and Russia). Without the cushion of adequate reserves, the shelter of capital controls, and the reassurance they provided to the authorities and the market, the exchange rate could have spun out of control and caused severe damage to companies and the financial sector. In principle, a clean float of the exchange rate can enable a country to do without reserves. But the price to be paid is the possibility of a highly unstable or inappropriate exchange rate. India's policymakers were wise to reject this regime and opt for managed floating combined with selective controls on capital flows. It is relevant also that India's float was managed so as to keep the rupee mildly undervalued in real effective terms. There is plenty of empirical evidence that undervaluation boosts growth of GDP through growth of exports, though the exact mechanism is imperfectly understood. Appreciation of the exchange rate would have discouraged the growth of exports in the vital early years of reform. It would have also made it politically more difficult to liberalize imports and to achieve the consequential gains in productivity.[21]

In sum, India sacrificed little, if any, growth of income and output as a consequence of its exchange rate policy in the decade of the 1990s. Indeed,

---

20. This is so a fortiori, because Lal, Bery, and Pant assume that labor force growth *fell* in the course of the 1990s. (See their table A.3, p. 4974.)

21. This argument is elaborated in Joshi (2003).

absorbing net inflows fully could well have made the economy unstable and *reduced* growth. This is not to deny that the appropriate response to inflows is currently a tricky issue. Since 2000, the balance of payments has strengthened significantly. Reserves are now at a very comfortable level but are continuing to rise at a rapid pace. The question of whether and how to absorb foreign inflows is far more pertinent now than it was during the 1990s.

Balance-of-Payments Policy, 2001–04

Since 2000, India's external macroeconomic policy has maintained a continuity with the past, despite changed circumstances. This is particularly true of the exchange rate regime, which continues to be a "dirty crawl." Table 3 shows that since 2000, despite the large changes in the nominal and real exchange rates of the currencies of the major countries, the real exchange rate of the rupee has been broadly constant.[22] Moreover, the authorities have clearly resisted market pressures for an appreciation, as evinced by the rapid accumulation of foreign exchange reserves. Between March 2001 and March 2004, India's reserves rose nearly $70 billion (see table 4).

Despite the continuity, there have been two dissimilarities in the external payments regime in comparison with the previous decade. First, the capital account has been selectively further liberalized. Restrictions on inward FDI, portfolio equity inflows, and external commercial borrowing have been diluted. Resident banks are also now allowed to borrow abroad subject to individual bank ceilings of $25 million. There has also been some capital outflow liberalization. Outward FDI by Indian companies and portfolio investment by domestic mutual funds are now permitted subject to individual and aggregate ceilings. Resident banks too can invest in overseas money markets subject to individual bank ceilings. Resident and nonresident individuals have been allowed limited facilities to transfer their Indian wealth abroad. Despite these changes, the new arrangements fall far short of capital account convertibility. Quantitative restrictions on debt-creating inflows (particularly short-term) remain in force. Banks continue to be severely restricted as regards foreign borrowing and lending; and bank deposits and other domestic assets remain

---

22. Note, however, that the RBI's thirty-six-country index (base 1985) shows a real appreciation of about 8 percent from 2001–02 to 2003–04.

TABLE 6. Sources of Reserve Money Growth, India,
Fiscal Years 1990–91 to 2003–04
Billions of rupees

Fiscal year	ΔRM^a	ΔNFA^b	ΔNDA^c	NDA/RM (Percent)
1990–91	101.9	19.1	82.8	90.9
1991–92	117.3	108.6	8.7	81.1
1992–93	112.7	38.1	74.6	79.6
1993–94	278.9	287.8	−8.9	62.9
1994–95	306.1	233.0	73.1	55.9
1995–96	251.8	−6.3	258.1	61.9
1996–97	55.2	207.3	−152.0	52.6
1997–98	264.2	210.7	53.5	48.8
1998–99	328.2	220.6	107.6	46.8
1999–2000	213.0	279.0	−66.0	40.8
2000–01	227.0	313.0	−86.0	35.0
2001–02	347.0	668.0	−321.0	21.9
2002–03	309.0	942.0	−633.0	2.9
2003–04	673.7	1261.7	−588.0	−11.0

Sources: Reserve Bank of India, *Handbook of Statistics on the Indian Economy 2002–03*; Reserve Bank of India (May 2004), *Bulletin*.
a. ΔRM: increase in reserve money.
b. ΔNFA: increase in net foreign exchange assets of RBI.
c. ΔNDA: increase in net domestic assets of RBI.

largely inconvertible into foreign currency, notwithstanding some limited relaxation.[23] The implication is that although capital mobility has to be factored into macroeconomic policy decisions to a greater extent than hitherto, it is still possible to combine exchange rate targeting with monetary autonomy.

The second dissimilarity with the previous decade is that reserve accumulation since 2000 has been sterilized to a substantial degree. During the 1990s, there was net sterilization in only three out of ten years (see table 6). The cumulative increase in the RBI's net foreign exchange assets in the 1990s was 79 percent of the increase in reserve money. In contrast, since 2000, the same ratio is 205 percent. In the decade of the 1990s taken as a

23. For further details on Indian capital controls, see Jadhav (2003). Recent liberalization of the capital account has been generally in line with that suggested by the Tarapore Committee (see Reserve Bank of India 1997). The recommendations of the Committee were shelved in the immediate aftermath of the East Asian crisis but were later revived.

whole, net sterilization was probably negative.[24] In the current decade, it has been positive and very substantial: 51 percent of reserve accumulation was sterilized from April 2000 to March 2004.

Should external payments policy depart from its current stance of resisting exchange rate appreciation and sterilizing the accumulation of reserves? This is one of the burning questions facing Indian macroeconomic policymakers today.

Sources of the Recent Balance-of-Payments Improvement

Since 2001, there has been a dramatic improvement in the balance of payments. In 2001–02, the current account, traditionally in deficit, moved into surplus. In the same year, foreign exchange reserves began to rise significantly faster than before. We now examine the evolution of the balance of payments in the past three years (beginning fiscal year 2001–02), to identify the sources of strength, and to assess their durability. This is obviously pertinent to deciding the policy response. Tables 4, 7, and 8 contain the relevant data. Balance-of-payments figures are available until December 2003, or the first nine months of fiscal year 2003–04. We have estimated the annual figure for 2003–04 as a whole. The salient points are as follows.

Merchandise trade. The trade deficit fell from 2000–01 to 2002–03 but not significantly. The decline appears to be largely cyclical, related to lower-than-trend growth of national income. Nothing in the export data of the past few years suggests a sustained boom in visible exports. (The dollar value of Indian exports grew at about 10 percent a year in the 1990s. The growth in the current decade is not much higher.) The recent recovery in 2003–04 has increased the trade deficit sharply, as one would expect.

Invisibles. The rapid rise in invisible earnings jumps out of the tables. Two components are particularly important: private remittance inflows and earnings from software services. Remittances were about $15 billion in 2002–03 and even higher in 2003–04. But they were virtually flat at about $12 billion a year from 1996–97 to 2001–02. The recent increase may have been caused by an expectation of rupee appreciation and a "feel-good" factor. Software exports are quantitatively smaller than remittances

---

24. Table 6 shows that over the decade of the 1990s as a whole, domestic assets of the RBI rose. So, there was no net sterilization by this measure. However, there may have been some sterilization caused by a rise in the cash reserve ratio (and a corresponding fall in the money multiplier). In the present decade, the cash reserve ratio has fallen, so that source of sterilization is absent.

TABLE 7. Balance of Payments, India, Fiscal Years 2000–01 to 2003–04
Billions of dollars

Item	2000–01	2001–02	2002–03	April–Dec. 2002	April–Dec. 2003	2003–04[a]
Exports, f.o.b.	44.9	44.9	52.5	38.4	43.2	57.6
Imports, c.i.f.	59.2	57.6	65.4	48.2	58.2	75.6
Merchandise trade balance	−14.3	−12.7	−12.9	−9.8	−15.0	−18.0
Invisibles	10.8	13.5	17.1	12.6	18.2	23.0
Software	5.8	6.9	8.9	5.8	9.1	12.4
Private remittances	13.0	12.1	14.8	10.8	14.5	17.9
Income	−4.8	−3.6	−5.0	−2.7	−5.2	−7.0
Current account	−3.6	0.8	4.1	(2.9)	3.2	5.0
Foreign investment	5.9	6.7	4.6	3.1	10.1	12.6
Direct	3.3	4.7	3.6	2.7	2.5	3.4
Portfolio	2.6	1.9	0.9	0.4	7.6	9.2
Loans	4.3	−1.4	−3.8	−2.9	−3.0	−3.7
External assistance	0.4	1.1	−2.5	−1.3	−1.7	−2.4
External commercial borrowing	3.7	−1.6	−2.3	−2.0	−3.7	−4.1
Short-term capital	0.1	−0.9	1.0	0.4	2.4	2.9
Banking capital	0.8	5.6	8.4	6.8	5.6	7.5
Nonresident Indian deposits	2.3	2.7	3.0	2.4	3.5	4.7
Other net assets of banks	−1.5	2.9	5.4	4.4	2.1	2.8
Rupee debt service	−0.6	−0.5	−0.5	−0.4	−0.3	−0.4
Other capital	−0.3	0.2	3.4	3.0	5.1	6.4
Capital account	10.0	10.6	12.1	9.7	17.5	22.4
Errors and omissions	−0.6	0.4	0.7	0.1	0.3	0.2
Overall balance	5.9	11.8	17.0	12.6	21.0	27.6
Valuation change	−1.7	0.0	4.3	3.7	5.4	8.0
Increase in reserves	4.2	11.8	21.3	16.3	26.4	35.6

Sources: Reserve Bank of India, *Currency and Finance Report* (various years); Reserve Bank of India website.
a. Estimated.

($8.9 billion in 2002–03), but they are growing much faster, at about 30 percent a year in the current decade. Other evidence also suggests that this is a dynamic export sector that has discovered the secret of capturing foreign markets. This improvement is almost certainly durable.

Current account. The current account improved by $7.7 billion from 2000–01 to 2002–03; the current account surplus was $4 billion in 2002–03, or 0.7 percent of GDP. But, as explained above, the trade deficit has started to rise. The current account surplus is expected to be about the same in 2003–04. Part of the current account surplus is undoubtedly spurious, caused by leads and lags in response to the possibility of rupee appreciation.

Foreign investment. Despite much loose talk about buoyant capital inflows, foreign investment actually *fell* from some $6 billion in 2000–01 to some $4.5 billion in 2002–03 as a result of a flat trend in FDI and a decline in portfolio investment. Thus the strength of the capital account in these two years lay elsewhere, as explained below. In 2003–04, however, foreign investment rose very sharply, largely because of portfolio equity inflows. Foreign direct investment showed little change. Net portfolio equity inflows amounted to some $9 billion in the year as a whole.

Medium- and long-term loans. Net inflows of official and private medium- and long-term loans turned into net outflows in 2001–02 and 2002–03. The outflow increased in 2003–04, because the government decided, in view of the strong balance of payments, to prepay some past international borrowing.

Short-term loans, "banking capital," and "other capital." Despite capital controls, recorded short-term debt inflows rose in 2002–03, and rose even faster thereafter. They were estimated to be about $3 billion in 2003–04. Inflows classified under "banking capital" increased sharply from 2001–02 onward, with roughly one-third of the increase due to NRI deposits. "Other capital" inflows also rose in 2001–02, rose sharply in 2002–03, and continued to rise rapidly thereafter. Notably, short-term loans, "banking capital," and "other capital" together constituted 75 percent of the capital account surplus in 2002–03. These are all short-term and highly reversible inflows. Some of the inflows may decelerate: for example, banks will now have exhausted their foreign borrowing limits, and arbitrage funds disguised as trade credit may also slow down. But obviously, the incentive for short-term inflows will remain as long as the covered interest differential in favor of India is significantly positive. The latter was about 3 percent a year in 2003–04.

Accumulation of reserves. As a consequence of the above developments (and the policy of managing the exchange rate), reserve accumulation accelerated. In the ten years from March 1991 to March 2001, foreign exchange reserves increased $35 billion. Roughly the same increase took place in *two* years from March 2001 to March 2003, when reserves reached $75 billion, and in *one* year to March 2004, when they reached $111 billion (about eighteen months import cover).

The Sources of Inflow Acceleration

In examining the character of inflows, it is illuminating to focus on the share of the *increase* in various inflows in the *increase* in reserve

**TABLE 8. India: Increase in Foreign Exchange Inflows,
Fiscal Years 2000–01 to 2003–04[a]**
Billions of dollars

	Increase 2000–01 to 2002–03	Increase 2002–03 to 2003–04[a]	Increase 2000–01 to 2003–04[a]
Trade balance	1.4 (12)	−5.1 (−48)	−3.7 (−17.1)
Net invisibles	6.4 (57)	5.9 (56)	12.2 (56.2)
Software	3.2 (29)	3.5 (33.0)	6.6 (30.4)
Remittances	2.0 (18)	3.1 (29)	4.9 (22.6)
Current balance	7.6 (67)	0.9 (9)	8.6 (39.6)
Foreign investment	−2.0 (−18)	8.0 (75)	6.7 (30.9)
Direct	0.5 (4)	0.0 (0)	0.0 (0.0)
Portfolio	−1.9 (−17)	8.3 (78)	6.6 (30.4)
Loans	−8.4 (−75)	0.0 (0)	−8.0 (−36.9)
External assistance	−3.0 (−21)	−0.4 (−4)	−2.8 (−12.9)
External commercial borrowing	−6.0 (−53)	−1.8 (−17)	−7.8 (−35.9)
Short-term loans	1.0 (9)	1.9 (18)	2.8 (13.0)
Banking Capital	7.0 (62)	−1.1 (−10)	6.7 (30.9)
NRI deposits	0.8 (7)	1.7 (16)	2.4 (11.1)
Other net assets of banks	6.2 (55)	−2.6 (−24.5)	4.3 (19.8)
Other capital	3.8 (34)	3.0 (28)	6.7 (30.9)
Capital account	2.0 (18)	10.3 (97)	12.4 (57.1)
Errors & omissions	1.2 (12)	−0.4 (−4)	0.8 (3.7)
Overall balance	11.2 (100)	10.6 (100)	21.7 (100.0)

Source: Table 7.
a. Figures in parentheses are percentage shares of the increase in the balance-of-payments surplus (overall balance).

accumulation. This perspective is somewhat different from that in the standard RBI calculation of the "sources of accretion of reserves," which emphasizes levels rather than rates of change (see table 8).

It is clear from column 1 of table 8 that the trade balance was a very minor element in the acceleration of reserves during 2001–02 and 2002–03. The acceleration was driven by invisibles (remittances and software exports), "banking capital," and "other capital." Notably, the latter two items taken together were even more significant than invisibles. Other components of the capital account were either stagnant (for example, foreign direct and portfolio investment) or falling (for example, medium- and long-term loans). As column 2 of the table indicates, the pattern changed somewhat in 2003–04. The contribution of the trade balance became significantly negative, and that of invisibles remained high. There was a sharp rise in the contribution of portfolio investment and to a lesser extent of short-term loans.

Overview

The balance of payments has strengthened significantly since April 2001, manifested by the increase in reserves by about $70 billion in the ensuing three years. The evidence in column 3 of table 8 inclines us to the following three conclusions about the nature of the increased inflows from 2000–01 to 2003–04.

First, the inflows were partly real (invisible receipts, especially software exports) and partly financial (especially "banking capital" and "other capital"), but the latter were quantitatively much more important. (The distinction between "real" and "financial" inflows should be understood to turn on whether the increase in inflows directly affects the goods, or "real," market or the money and securities, or "financial," markets.) If we count the entire change in the trade balance, software exports, and FDI and two-thirds of the change in remittances as "real" and the rest of the change in the balance of payments as "financial," then real inflows comprised 28 percent and financial inflows 72 percent of the increased inflows.

Second, the inflows have mostly not been of a kind that would directly increase real investment, because FDI has been stagnant.[25] Software exports could, however, provide some boost to investment in the information technology sector. There is some evidence that remittances boost investment in construction activity, but they also flow into increased consumption and acquisition of financial assets.[26] External commercial borrowing, which is mostly for real investment, has fallen but may rise in the future. Items in the capital account that have been buoyant, such as inflows of portfolio equity and short-term loans, have an indirect and uncertain connection with real investment.

Finally, as regards the *durability* of the inflows, only the increase in software exports can be confidently classified as durable. If we reckon that, in addition, half of the increase in remittances and half of the increase in portfolio equity inflows are "permanent," we arrive at a figure of 55 percent as

25. International evidence suggests that FDI is strongly associated with an increase in domestic investment. That is not the case with inflows of portfolio equity or short-term debt. See Bosworth and Collins (1999) and World Bank (2001). Note that even FDI does not necessarily give additionality of real investment since it may consist simply of foreign acquisition of domestic companies.

26. Not much is known about the disposition of remittances. International evidence indicates that they go largely into consumption and financial assets. See Chami, Fullenkamp, and Jahjah (2003).

the share of durable inflows.[27] A sizable but unquantifiable portion of the remaining inflow acceleration can be attributed to arbitrage activity arising from a covered interest differential in favor of India. It is likely that this will now unwind as interest rates rise in the advanced countries. The stock market boom of 2003–04 has probably run its course, and portfolio equity inflows are now likely to slow down.

In sum, we guess that up to three-quarters of the recent acceleration has directly affected the financial rather than the goods markets; only a minor part of the acceleration has contributed directly to increasing real investment; and about half of the acceleration was of a durable character.

Macroeconomic Policy Options

This section on policy options should be read along with the appendix, which contains some relevant theory, based on the simplest version of the Mundell-Fleming model, well-known even to beginners in economics. The model is distant from reality; nevertheless, it identifies some essential points. Here, we go beyond the appendix model and make judgments that are likely to be controversial.

We begin by identifying policy objectives. It would be widely agreed in India that macroeconomic policy should aim to keep current output close to capacity, keep inflation low (say, at or below an annual rate of 5 percent), insure against the possibility of financial and currency crises, and increase the rate of growth of national income by stepping up investment and productivity.

The first objective, keeping output close to capacity, is noncontroversial. The second, low inflation, has traditionally had and continues to have very high salience in India's democratic politics because a large part of the economy is non-indexed. The third objective, avoiding crises, points to erring on the side of caution as regards the size of foreign exchange reserves and the advance toward capital account convertibility. The fourth, raising investment, is crucial. The rate of investment in India (about 25 percent of GDP) is low compared with that of the successful performers among developing countries and must evidently be increased if the growth rate is to rise. Macroeconomic policy has to be consistent with this objective. If produc-

---

27. Arguably, in a crisis, outflows of portfolio investment should be deterred by falling bond and equity prices, but this a priori argument is not entirely supported by the East Asian experience in 1997 and 1998.

tivity is to rise, it must also be consistent with the agenda of economic reform. Two aspects of reform are particularly germane in the context of increasing investment while responding to foreign inflows, namely, fiscal consolidation and import liberalization.

Alternative responses to (an increase in) foreign inflows can be usefully classified into those that allow the inflows to enter the economy but block balance-of-payments adjustment; those that allow the inflows to enter the economy and enable balance-of-payments adjustment; and those that repel the inflows by direct measures. We term these categories "sterilization," "adjustment," and "capital controls," respectively.

Sterilization

This option describes India's present policy. It consists of fixing the nominal exchange rate or managing it to resist a market-driven exchange rate appreciation and preventing the consequent reserve accumulation from increasing the supply of money. The classic technique of sterilization is open-market operations: the central bank sells government bonds to mop up (or "sterilize") the increase in base money caused by reserve accumulation. But sterilization can also be pursued by changing the money multiplier: for example, the central bank can increase the cash reserve ratio of the banking system.

Sterilization has been the principal response to foreign inflows in the current decade. Table 6 shows that in every year since 1999, growth in the RBI's net foreign exchange assets has exceeded the increase in reserve money. Correspondingly, the RBI's stock of salable domestic assets has fallen; indeed, as of December 2003, it was completely exhausted.

Sterilization can be contrasted with adjustment and increased absorption. Adjustment involves reallocation of resources and changes in the composition of output, with concomitant frictional costs (for example, transitional unemployment or inflation) and unpredictable effects on expectations. Sterilization can therefore be beneficial if the inflows are judged to be temporary, that is, likely to reverse; in that instance, sterilization not only enables the reversal of the inflows to be financed but makes it possible to avoid the costs of unnecessary adjustment and readjustment. Note, however, that sterilization may have some role to play even in the case of durable inflows since it can help with the optimal timing of adjustment. The authorities may be able to influence the outcome of adjustment better if it is gradual; sterilization may be useful in slowing down the adjustment when inflows accelerate rapidly. (Arguably, a gradual adjustment increases the chances of the inflows ending up in extra investment rather than in extra consumption.)

But sterilization has costs. These do not principally relate to the technical difficulty of continued sterilization. Though the RBI has exhausted its stock of salable government bonds, it would be technically possible for it to issue its own bonds (though that would require an amendment of the RBI Act) or for the government to manufacture another security that the RBI could sell to soak up reserve money. Indeed, the latter alternative has recently been put into effect. In March 2004, the government created new "market stabilization bonds" that can be sold by the RBI. (Interest on these bonds will be a charge on the budget.)

The true costs of continued sterilization are of two kinds: economic and quasi-fiscal. (These costs are not additive.) The economic cost pertains to domestic consumption and investment forgone by tying up resources in reserves. The quasi-fiscal cost relates to the adverse impact of sterilized reserves on the fiscal position of the government and the central bank as a combined entity. Each has a *stock* and a *flow* aspect. Back-of-the-envelope reckoning of these costs is given below. We assume the following ball-park figures for India circa December 2003: GDP, $600 billion; foreign exchange reserves, $100 billion; rate of return on investment, 10 percent; government's borrowing rate, 5 percent; rate of return on foreign exchange reserves, 2 percent. Therefore, national income forgone by the stock of sterilized reserves is 100 (.1) − 100 (.02) = 100 (.08) = $8 billion a year, or 1.3 percent of current GDP a year, with a present value of $80 billion at a 10 percent discount rate.[28]

But the *net* economic cost is surely much lower as a result of the offsetting benefits of reserve accumulation. Old benchmarks such as "reserves should equal three months imports" have been rendered irrelevant in a world of high capital mobility. Recent emerging-country experience indicates that a reserve this size would be too small to ensure against the risk of substantial volatility of the exchange rate (including the possibility of large exchange rate changes with destabilizing effects)

28. A more sophisticated treatment would ask whether the opportunity cost of reserve accumulation is forgone consumption or forgone investment. Suppose the marginal social value of investment is twice that of consumption. (In other words, the rate of return on investment is 10 percent but the social discount rate is 5 percent.) Then the economic cost of sterilization would have a present value of $80 billion if reserve accumulation led to a sacrifice of consumption, $160 billion if it led to a sacrifice of investment, and somewhere in the range of $80–$160 billion for intermediate cases. Note that the economic cost of *unsterilized* reserves would be lower. Unsterilized reserves will be expected to be documented over time, in tandem with real exchange rate appreciation. To that extent, absorption is not forgone; it is postponed.

or lengthy periods of exchange rate misalignment. As for capital mobility, this could in principle reduce the need for reserves. But again, recent experience indicates that developing countries cannot borrow when they most need to (in a crisis) and can suffer harmful economic and political consequences thereby. Once we accept that an intermediate exchange rate regime suits India's interests for the near-term future, we must also accept the corollary that the country must maintain a cushion of high reserves (and, in addition, some focused capital controls). In practice, there is no "scientific" way of estimating the optimum reserve level. In our judgment it would not be excessively risk averse, in the light of emerging-country currency crises in the past ten years, to maintain the ratio of reserves to GDP or imports at around the current level. Reserves are now about 16 percent of GDP and cover about eighteen months of merchandise imports.

At the same time, further large increases in these ratios on grounds of precaution and safety would surely be unwise. There is such a thing as being over-insured! India's reserves are now approximately equal to its total external debt; well above 50 percent of total external liabilities (including the accumulated stock of foreign direct and portfolio equity investment); fifteen times the stock of short-term debt; larger than base money; and around 25 percent of broad money. Even if we assume that half the accumulation of reserves in the current decade is caused by potentially volatile inflows, the reserve cushion is clearly perfectly adequate. We assume below that maintaining the present ratio of reserves to GDP would satisfy all reasonable canons of prudence.

The implication of the above argument is that carrying the current stock of reserves does not impose a net economic cost. There remains, however, the future flow cost of continued sterilization. Annual reserve accumulation is now about $30 billion, or about 5 percent of GDP. If we assume that the dollar value of GDP will grow at 6 percent a year, then an addition to reserves of 1 percent of GDP would be required to maintain the ratio of reserves to GDP. That implies "excess" reserve accumulation of around 4 percent of GDP if inflows continue at today's rate. The cost of sterilization in the first year would then be $(.04)(.08) = 0.32$ percent of GDP. But this cost would cumulate rapidly. In the second year it would be 0.64 percent, in the third year 0.96 percent of GDP, and so on. This is clearly not a recipe for a sensible economic policy.

We now turn to the quasi-fiscal flow cost of sterilization. (It is assumed that the quasi-fiscal cost of the present stock of reserves is worth bearing in view of the offsetting benefits outlined above.) The interest differential between the government's borrowing rate and the yield on reserves is 3 percent. If excess reserve accumulation is 4 percent of GDP in the first year, the quasi-fiscal cost is $(.04)(.03) = 0.12$ percent of GDP. But this too can cumulate rapidly if reserves continue to rise at the same rate. In the second year the cost is 0.24 percent of GDP, in the fourth year it is 0.48 percent of GDP.[29]

A word must be said about sterilization by changing the money multiplier, say by raising the cash reserve ratio. In this case, the quasi-fiscal cost of open market operations is substituted by a tax on the banking system. This may lead to disintermediation from the banking system; it may also reduce private savings through a reduction in deposit rates offered by the banking system. Another method of sterilization is to require government-controlled institutions to switch their deposits from commercial banks to the central bank. But this does not avoid the quasi-fiscal cost if the central bank deposit rate is equal to the government's borrowing rate; and if it pays a lower deposit rate, it shifts the costs to savers. There is not much mileage in substituting the above techniques of sterilization for open market operations.[30]

The upshot of the above discussion is as follows. We think that it would be sensible on prudential grounds to maintain the current rather generous reserves to GDP ratio. But if reserves continue to increase at today's rate, they would be excessive to requirements and increasingly expensive to hold. Thus, even if we allow that the present level of reserves in India is optimal, future sterilized reserve accumulation at the present rate would be unwise. India's policymakers must urgently consider how to utilize the continuing "excess" foreign inflows productively. This takes us naturally to various options of adjustment.

Adjustment

The main general point we wish to make about adjustment is that the usual discussion of methods of adjustment is too narrow in its scope and focuses only on adjustment through real appreciation. Adjustment could also be

---

29. Calculations of both the economic and quasi-fiscal costs must in principle allow for expected exchange rate changes (and expected changes in interest rates). We do not pursue the matter here.

30. The RBI may be tempted, at the margin, to use the cash reserve ratio (CRR) for sterilization in preference to open market operations because bank profits have increased in the recent past. But this is only a short-term tactic. The RBI has announced its intention to bring the CRR down over time to 3 percent, as part of the program of financial liberalization. It now stands at 5 percent.

undertaken, wholly or in part, by the use of other methods. The main adjustment options are as follows.

NOMINAL EXCHANGE RATE APPRECIATION. One option is to allow the rupee to appreciate. A free float is theoretically possible.[31] (Note that it would have to be accompanied by full or near-full capital account convertibility if it is to make any sense. A float cannot operate satisfactorily in a thin foreign exchange market.) But a free float is not a relevant alternative in practice. India has not reached the stage when such a regime could be safely adopted. So appreciation should be taken to mean a controlled nominal appreciation, within the context of India's "intermediate exchange rate plus capital controls" regime. The consequent real appreciation would absorb the inflows and promote the transfer of foreign resources by squeezing out net exports. But it may also contract output. This suggests that monetary policy would have to be simultaneously deployed to reduce interest rates. With an active monetary policy, a recession could be prevented. At the same time, the composition of national income would change toward higher consumption, investment, and imports, as well as lower exports.[32]

What if the inflows have a substantial "temporary" component? Adjustment through appreciation involves a significant reallocation of resources away from the tradable sector. If the inflows stop, the process would have to be reversed. Export markets, once lost, are not easy to recapture. In other words, if the inflows are temporary, the costs of adjustment may outweigh the benefits of a temporary increase in absorption. It could be argued that a temporary appreciation would be correctly forecast to be temporary by rational agents, so there would be no significant effects on resource allocation or investment in the tradable sector. But it is surely unwise for policymakers to act on the *assumption* that expectations are rational, if the consequences of the assumption being false would be seriously adverse. In practice, whether inflows are temporary or durable is a hard judgment to make for both public and government. One possible rule of prudence is that

31. If the exchange rate is allowed to float freely, the level to which it would appreciate is bound to be a matter of some uncertainty. Models that incorporate exchange rate expectations work out the short-run dynamics by tying down the long-run exchange rate (say, by purchasing power parity). But this is a theoretical construct. During a time-horizon relevant for policy, the exchange rate can settle for substantial lengths of time at misaligned levels. The danger of prolonged excessive appreciation is thus a danger. This suggests that the authorities should manage the appreciation. That is difficult without some capital controls. Fortunately, India has them in place.

32. In the adjustment outlined, *private* investment increases. One could alternatively envisage adjustment through higher *public* investment. But that would increase the fiscal deficit, which is already excessive.

policy should be biased toward treating positive shocks as temporary and negative shocks as permanent unless proved otherwise.

If the inflows are judged to be durable, there is a case for nominal appreciation and, on the orthodox view, a very good case. We disagree. Mild undervaluation may be good for growth. Our view is that there should be a policy bias against exchange rate appreciation, even in responding to inflows judged to be "permanent," because of the close connection between the level of the real exchange rate and the rate of growth of output through the growth of export demand.

Historically, super-fast growth has been based on harnessing a labor surplus to produce labor-intensive manufactured goods for the world market. This was true of Japan in the 1950s and of several countries in East and South-East Asia, including China, since then. The basic reason goes back to Sir Arthur Lewis's famous closed economy model of a growing economy with "unlimited supplies of labor."[33] In the Lewis model, the modern (mainly industrial) sector can grow rapidly because labor is available at a constant real wage, so capital accumulation is not subject to diminishing returns. The share of profits, and therefore of saving and investment in national income, rises continuously, and growth accelerates until the labor surplus is exhausted. This tendency is reinforced by the fact that all the fruits of technical progress add to profits.

The main problem with the Lewis scenario is that the presence of "surplus labor" in the traditional (mainly agricultural) sector is not enough to ensure the constancy of the real wage. If (food) production in the traditional sector is inelastic, the terms of trade will turn against the modern sector, raising the real wage. (In practice, this may take the form of an "inflation barrier" to industrial expansion.) A further consequence of this tendency would be that in the modern sector the incentive to save and invest would be impaired.

In this context, openness of the economy can dramatically alter the picture. If a growing country can export labor-intensive industrial products at roughly constant terms of trade, the real wage constraint is lifted and the incentive to save and invest is restored. Labor-demanding growth would also reduce poverty directly without having to rely on "trickle-down."

If rapid export growth is important for the above reasons, it makes sense to err on the side of undervaluation of the exchange rate because growth of export demand is related to the level of the real exchange rate. An undervalued exchange rate enables a country to capture a larger share of world

33. Lewis (1954).

markets. (If world markets are growing at x percent, then the country's exports can grow faster than x percent during an adjustment period that can be quite long.) Growing exports, in turn, raise the incentive to invest. Extra domestic savings come from the rise in profits in export activities and the rise in incomes of the recruits to the industrial labor force. An undervalued exchange rate is likely to boost saving by raising the share of profits in national income. (Note that if investment demand outruns available domestic and foreign savings at the target exchange rate, the government would have to restrain consumption by fiscal policy in order to maintain internal balance.) This argument should not be read as implying that unlimited real depreciation is feasible or desirable. It clearly is not. What is being claimed is that there should be a bias toward mild undervaluation because it can play a supportive role to complementary outward-oriented trade policies in generating a virtuous circle of higher saving, investment, and growth. Thus the motivation of this export-led strategy is not mercantilism or "exchange rate protection" but moving the economy to a higher growth path. Import demand would grow concomitantly, and there may or may not be a current account surplus.[34]

How do these considerations bear on Indian macroeconomic policy? It is obvious that if India is to reduce poverty rapidly, it is imperative to raise the rate of growth from 6 percent a year to 8 percent or more. In addition to the existing potential reserve of "surplus labor," India also faces another potentially favorable development, namely, the "demographic bonus." India's working-age population is due to rise sharply over the next two decades in absolute terms and as a share of total population. This will help keep real wages down and also raise the rate of private saving. It is clear, however, that this opportunity can be exploited only if the growing labor force is productively employed and the inducement to invest is maintained at a high level so that the potential savings do not run to waste. In this context, it will be important both to lower real interest rates and to ensure that labor-intensive exports grow rapidly.[35]

---

34. We think this argument could be formalized but have not yet done so. See Little (1981, 1996) and Bhagwati (1996) for illuminating interpretations of the East Asian "miracle" as export-led growth. For an early, forceful advocacy, in a different context, of export-led growth through a competitive exchange rate, see Kaldor (1971). For an insightful model of exchange rate policy and export-led growth, see Williamson (2003). For an empirical cross-country demonstration of the link between undervaluation and growth, see Bhalla (2004).

35. We must note also that if the economy starts to grow at 8 percent rather than 6 percent, the safe limit for monetary expansion will increase, so unsterilized intervention in response to balance of surpluses can play a larger role.

Rapid export growth is necessary not only to sustain the inducement to invest but also to ensure that India's growth is *labor demanding*. This is crucially important. India's recent employment record has been dismal. In the organized sector (even in the organized manufacturing sector), employment barely changed between 1991 and 2001; since 1997 it has actually fallen. Data from the National Sample Survey indicate that total employment (organized and unorganized) is growing at about 1 percent a year, half the projected growth rate of the labor force.

In some quarters, it is thought that employment could grow rapidly on the back of exports of software services. But current employment in that sector is about 700,000; on optimistic assumptions, it may rise to 2 million by 2010. But India's labor force is set to grow by about 8 million per annum for the next twenty years. Thus, it is most unlikely that India could grow fast without rapid growth in exports of labor-intensive manufactured goods. Maintaining a competitive exchange rate is one of several policy measures that are relevant for this purpose (others include trade liberalization, labor market reform, abolition of small-scale industry reservations, and provision of primary education).[36]

FIXED (OR TARGETED) NOMINAL EXCHANGE RATE WITH UNSTERILIZED INTERVENTION. Another policy option is to fix or target the nominal (effective) exchange rate (say, to keep the real effective exchange rate at today's level) and allow the accumulation of reserves to increase the money supply. This would be a continuation of India's present exchange rate policy but with unsterilized intervention.

There may now be some scope to pursue such a policy and enjoy a Keynesian "free lunch." The economy has grown strongly in 2003–04, largely because of a rebound in agriculture, but there is probably still an output gap in the industrial sector since industrial growth has been below trend in the past five years. (The extent of the gap is hard to pin down because estimates of capacity utilization in India are unreliable.) The RBI has permitted both reserve money and broad money to accelerate in 2003–04, which seems sensible given the existence of slack and the comfortable food and foreign exchange position. Even so, although there may be some further room for experimentation to test the margin of slack, the

36. Note that the share of industrial output in GDP is extraordinarily low in India (around 25 percent) and has not increased much in the past forty years. In the fast-growing countries (for example, China, South Korea, Malaysia, Indonesia, Thailand) it has doubled or more over the same period and is now around 40 percent. The view that India can skip the stage of rapid export-led industrial growth is a dangerous illusion. For a similar view, see Acharya (2003).

scope for noninflationary increases in money supply growth is likely to be limited. In our judgment, India's policymakers would rightly be unwilling to undertake inflationary policies on the dubious ground that a highly elastic supply response would eradicate inflation within a reasonably short span of time.

In the absence of output slack, the real effects of a nominal fix are in abstract theory exactly equivalent to those of a nominal exchange rate appreciation. Adjustment and resource transfer are brought about by a rise in prices that leads to a *real* appreciation and widens the current account deficit. Even so, this option is not in practice likely to be quite the same as nominal appreciation. The dynamics may work in a variety of ways. Prices may rise slowly. It may be that the slow transfer of foreign resources has a greater chance of being translated into domestic investment than the rapid transfer engineered by appreciation. But the danger is that what should be an "equilibrium" rise in prices may set off an inflationary spiral, which may be hard to extinguish. If that happens, the real effects would be unpredictable, possibly highly adverse. As with appreciation, if the inflows are temporary but perceived to be permanent, the real adjustment that takes place would have to be reversed; and there may in addition have to be a painful disinflation. If the inflows are "permanent," the above problem does not arise. But a long-lasting real appreciation, as argued earlier, could have adverse growth effects.

We note here that given India's intermediate exchange rate-cum-capital controls regime, it would be possible to combine both options, in other words, to obtain real appreciation partly by nominal appreciation and partly by higher inflation. But there are severe constraints in India on the acceptable rate of inflation. So in practice this compromise is likely to be heavily biased toward nominal appreciation. Moreover, a substantial real appreciation would be undesirable, whichever way it is obtained.

IMPORT LIBERALIZATION. Import liberalization would absorb foreign inflows through an increase in the current account deficit but, unlike appreciation, it would do so without reducing the incentive to export. In common with appreciation, it would reduce aggregate demand, so it would have to be combined with monetary expansion to stabilize output and encourage investment. It would also put particular pressure on industries that produce import-substitutes. But it is a declared objective of Indian reform to reduce tariffs significantly. India's average tariff rate of around 25 percent on industrial goods is still among the highest in the developing world. The current inflows thus provide a window for pursuing a policy that is beneficial in its own right for increasing productivity.

Two other concerns about import liberalization are more pertinent but are based on assuming that the tax structure cannot be rationalized. First, tariff reduction would have a negative impact on government revenue.[37] Import liberalization would thus have to be accompanied by measures to offset the revenue impact. But there is plenty of scope for desirable widening of the tax base and reduction in dysfunctional exemptions. (For example, services are virtually untaxed.) Second, in addition to a central value added tax, India has state taxes that are not rebated on exports. If tariffs were drastically reduced, there is a danger that domestic industry would receive negative effective protection. But state taxes are not an impediment to a substantial reduction of import duties from the current average of 25 percent to (say) 10 percent. Further import liberalization would require a move to an integrated center-state VAT.

FISCAL CONSOLIDATION. A tighter fiscal policy can promote adjustment to foreign inflows in two ways. First, it can create space in the economy to accommodate the increased pressure of demand resulting from inflows that have a direct impact on the goods market (for example, exports, FDI). Second, when combined with monetary expansion, it can reduce interest rates while maintaining output constant. The interest rate reduction would reduce the incentive for interest-sensitive capital inflows, while simultaneously changing the composition of output toward private investment. The critical point is that both these aspects of fiscal contraction promote adjustment *without* significant exchange rate appreciation. (Another way of putting this point is that increased foreign inflows permit fiscal contraction and monetary expansion to crowd in investment *without* the large, and possibly destabilizing, exchange rate depreciation that would otherwise be required to achieve the same result in the absence of inflows.) Adjustment with exchange rate appreciation is likely to result in a lower rate of investment than adjustment with fiscal contraction and monetary expansion with a competitive exchange rate.

The need for fiscal consolidation is not in dispute. The small reduction in the fiscal deficit in the first half of the 1990s was lost in the ensuing years, and the deficit has averaged roughly 9.5 percent of GDP since then. The public debt-GDP ratio has risen about 20 percent (from about 65 percent to 85 percent of GDP) in the past eight years. (External public debt has fallen, so *domestic* public debt as a proportion of GDP has risen by even more over the same period.)[38] Without fiscal consolidation, there is a serious risk of

37. But import liberalization is no worse than sterilization in this respect. Both involve a fiscal cost.
38. See Kapur and Patel (2003), Pinto and Zahir (2004).

lower growth through crowding out of private investment. Indeed, this may already be happening.[39] Fiscal consolidation (like import liberalization) thus has special significance in the context of responding to foreign inflows, since it is independently highly desirable, even essential.

Of course, fiscal consolidation should consist not only of reducing the volume of the deficit but also of improving its quality. What is required is an increase in public investment (especially in infrastructure) and in social sector expenditures, combined with a reduction in unproductive public consumption and subsidies that is big enough to reduce the overall deficit.[40] Such a program would be fully consistent with what we propose. Admittedly, it could not be implemented without political will, which may be hard to muster in an atmosphere of complacency generated by strong foreign inflows.

THE ROLE OF MONETARY POLICY. It is clear from the above discussion that monetary policy is an essential ingredient of optimal policy. With a floating or managed exchange rate, an active monetary policy is required to maintain internal balance and increase the share of investment in national income, while achieving external adjustment.

Capital Controls

This option consists of repelling capital inflows by direct measures, thus avoiding the need for sterilization or adjustment.

This is not the place to rehearse the costs and benefits of capital controls save to note that the academic consensus no longer supports a doctrinaire position in favor of capital account convertibility.[41] India already has capital inflow controls, though they have been diluted in recent years. The practical question is whether to tighten them in response to the current "problem of plenty."

In the present context, the argument for tightening is as follows. If inflows continue at the current rate, or grow even faster, sterilization will become technically more difficult and cumulatively more expensive, and the pressure for adjustment will grow. Adjustment through fiscal consolidation

39. Note that corporate investment *halved* as a proportion of GDP in the second half of the 1990s. Public sector investment also fell. A fall in aggregate investment was avoided by rising household investment. See table 2.7 in Reserve Bank of India (2004).

40. There is plenty of scope for carrying out such a program, see Joshi (1998a, 1998b). Only the nature of the political system and the balance of forces prevent India from achieving it. The future of reform will be endangered, indeed brought to nought, unless the fiscal deadlock is broken.

41. See Williamson (1993), Bhagwati (1998), Cooper (1999), Prasad and others (2003).

and import liberalization can proceed at only a moderate pace. If the inflows are large, the government would therefore be forced willy-nilly to allow real appreciation. But a sizable real appreciation would have adverse consequences for growth for reasons advanced earlier.

Thus, a case can be made for intensification of controls, especially if they are of a market-oriented variety (for example, a tax on capital inflows, Chilean-style). Even so, we think the government should be wary of tightening controls, because the financial markets may interpret the move as a signal that the government is diluting its commitment to reforming the financial sector and integrating with the world economy. Moreover, we doubt such a measure is necessary. It is likely that capital inflows will slow down naturally with the recent turn in the interest-rate cycle in the advanced countries. It is also likely that if the government undertakes the measures we suggest, the expectation of exchange rate appreciation will abate and moderate inflows. Even so, the possibility must be faced that we could be wrong. The weapon of capital controls must therefore be kept in the armory of policy instruments, to be used in extreme circumstances.

Finally, a word is necessary about the suggestion sometimes heard that the right response to the acceleration of inflows is to liberalize controls on capital *outflows* by residents. We do not agree. Capital outflow liberalization could *increase* net inflows and the "embarrassment of reserves" in the short-term. But if there are adverse shocks, confidence could seep away. In that case, an open capital account would be dangerous. The government could face strong competition in the market for funds and may have to borrow in foreign currency. The banks would have to compete for deposits with overseas banks. Given India's unsound fiscal position and weak banking system, this could be a recipe for a fiscal, financial, and currency crisis.

Optimal Policy

We now draw the threads of the argument together and consider the nature of the optimal policy response to the acceleration of foreign inflows. Each policy alternative has its strengths and weaknesses in relation to policy objectives and constraints. It would therefore be sensible to think in terms of policy packages. Different adjustment packages can be envisaged that can give internal balance and balance-of-payments equilibrium but with different effects on the *composition* of output and the balance of payments. (This point is made in the simple appendix model, but it applies more generally.) Policy packages weighted toward fiscal contraction and monetary expansion would tend to produce relatively lower interest rates. Those weighted toward real exchange rate appreciation would involve relatively larger current account deficits. Real appreciation, in turn, could be secured by nominal appreciation or by permitting higher inflation. Policy packages that use import liberalization would, like real appreciation, permit higher absorption through higher current account deficits but without penalizing exports. The optimal package is a judicious combination of these various policies. But what is "judicious" in the Indian context? We think that for reasons already given, the policy package should be biased toward fiscal consolidation and import liberalization, rather than real exchange rate appreciation through nominal appreciation or inflation. Our policy recommendations are thus significantly different from those of Lal, Bery, and Pant (see section IV of their paper).

Our views on future policy can be further amplified as follows. Sterilization has outlived its usefulness. Some sterilized reserve accumulation can continue to maintain the present ratio of reserves to GDP. Further increases in the ratio should be avoided except as a purely short-term response to manifestly short-term inflows. The normal response should be to adjust to the "excess" inflows in the manner described above. Our favored policies have the advantage that in addition to promoting balance-of-payments adjustment, they are also desirable independently of the balance of payments and of the "temporary" or "permanent" character of the inflows. Naturally, because of political and other constraints, these policies could be pursued only at a moderate pace. That leaves the question how policymakers should react in the (in our view unlikely) event of a continued acceleration of inflows, despite the inauguration of the suggested strategy. We think that in such a situation, the government should be prepared to tighten capital inflow controls (for example, by a Chilean-style tax) so that the strategy is not derailed.

We are not arguing that India should resist an exchange rate appreciation forever. After the completion of economic reform and a decade or two of super-fast growth, India would reach the stage at which both a floating exchange rate (accompanied by inflation targeting) and capital account convertibility could be contemplated.

Concluding Remarks

In this paper, arguments have been advanced to support the following propositions.

First, India's policymakers score high marks for their conduct of the external aspects of macroeconomic policy in the 1990s. The "intermediate exchange rate plus capital controls" regime was the right one to adopt and served the country well. It enabled policymakers to combine exchange rate targeting with some monetary autonomy. It also reduced India's vulnerability to currency crises in the decade. Contrary to Lal, Bery, and Pant, there is no evidence that the external payments regime reduced the growth rate of the economy.

Second, the stance of policy so far in the current decade has been more questionable but can nevertheless be defended. The balance of payments has strengthened significantly, but policymakers were understandably uncertain of the durability of the inflows and wished to accumulate reserves up to a manifestly safe level.

Third, if the surge in foreign inflows continues, it would now be wise to depart from the strategy of accumulating and sterilizing foreign exchange reserves on the basis of sterilized intervention. Sterilized intervention would in the future be increasingly costly, in both fiscal and broader economic terms.

Fourth, the options for moving away from the strategy of sterilized intervention should not be formulated as a choice between floating the exchange rate on the one hand and fixing the exchange rate without sterilization on the other hand. Adjustment to foreign inflows can be secured with different policy packages incorporating different combinations of monetary fiscal, trade, and capital account policies.

Finally, in the current situation, the policy response to balance-of-payments surpluses should be biased in favor of fiscal consolidation and import liberalization and against real exchange rate appreciation through nominal appreciation or inflation.

APPENDIX

External Shocks and Policy Response: Analytical Notes

Policy responses to positive balance-of-payments shocks can be analyzed using the Mundell-Fleming model ($IS/LM/BP$).[42] See figure A-1. We assume, realistically, that capital mobility is fairly high but less than perfect, so the BP curve is upward sloping and relatively flat but not horizontal;

---

42. The model is expounded in all standard textbooks. It has deficiencies, in particular its assumption of static exchange rate expectations, but it nevertheless remains the basic "workhorse" model in international economics.

FIGURE A-1.   Mundell-Fleming Model: Effects of Positive External Shocks

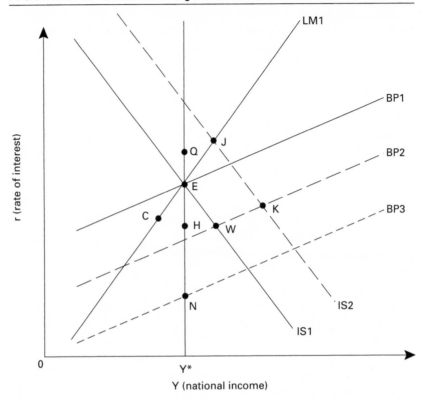

in particular, it is flatter than the *LM* curve.[43] Two kinds of shocks are analyzed: a goods-market shock, such as a boom in exports or foreign direct investment (FDI), and a shock in the market for bonds.[44] In this simple model, "bonds" include all financial assets such as bills, bonds, and equities. A goods-market shock is a simultaneous rightward shift in the *IS* curve and downward shift in the *BP* curve. A bond-market shock is a downward shift in the *BP* curve. It could be caused, for example, by a fall in world interest rates.

43. The assumption of moderately high but less-than-perfect capital mobility is representative of the current Indian situation. Capital mobility is less than perfect because risk makes Indian securities imperfect substitutes for foreign securities, and India has capital controls. The *LM* curve is steep since the interest elasticity of the demand for money is low. For a brief survey of the empirical studies on the demand for money in India see Kulkarni (1999). The analysis would remain relevant *mutatis mutandis,* even if the *BP* curve were steeper than the *LM* curve.

44. It is assumed that FDI has a direct link with domestic real investment. See, however, note 25 above.

We first examine the effects of these shocks in the following policy regimes: a floating exchange rate, a fixed exchange rate with unsterilized intervention, and a fixed exchange rate with sterilized intervention. We then consider the consequences of the application of discretionary policies, in particular, monetary policy, fiscal policy, import liberalization, and capital controls. Two possibilities are allowed as regards the initial preshock equilibrium of the economy: Keynesian excess capacity (hereafter "unemployment") and Keynesian full capacity (hereafter "full employment").[45] We make the simple Keynesian assumption that as long as output is below or at full employment, money wages and prices are constant. Beyond full employment, money wages and prices rise, but output does not.

The initial equilibrium is at E (income Y^*) where $IS1$, $LM1$, and $BP1$ intersect.

Positive Goods Market Shock

Consider first a positive external shock in the goods market, for example, an increase in foreign demand for exports or an increase in inward FDI. Such a shock can be represented by a rightward shift in the IS curve from $IS1$ to $IS2$ and a simultaneous downward shift in the BP curve from $BP1$ to $BP2$.

Floating Exchange Rate

If the exchange rate is floating, the supply of money is exogenous. So LM remains at $LM1$. Suppose export demand (for example, for software exports) increases. The exchange rate appreciates, which offsets the expansionary effect of the shock. The IS and BP curves move back from $IS2$ and $BP2$ to their original positions, and the initial equilibrium E is re-attained. Net exports (other than software exports) are fully crowded out. In the final equilibrium, national income, the interest rate, and the trade deficit are unchanged. If the shock is increased FDI, the consequences for national income and interest rate are exactly the same as above. But aggregate investment will rise and the trade deficit will widen by the full extent of the extra FDI.

45. Strictly speaking, the IS, LM, and BP curves do not exist at levels of output beyond full employment. This does not matter for our analysis. In the "overfull employment" region, prices rise, so the IS, LM, and BP curves shift. Thus the entire analysis could be carried out with IS, LM, and BP curves drawn only up to and including full employment income.

Note that the above analysis is unaffected by the initial position of the economy. The analysis is the same, whether there is "full employment" or "unemployment" at Y^* in the pre-shock equilibrium.[46]

Fixed Exchange Rate plus Unsterilized Intervention

Consider the effects of the same shocks with a fixed exchange rate regime in which the central bank allows balance-of-payments imbalances to affect the money supply. In this case, the outcome depends greatly on the starting position.

If there is "unemployment" in the initial equilibrium at Y^*, an increase in exports or FDI is expansionary, indeed highly expansionary. We may think of the economy moving first to J, but here there is a balance-of-payments surplus. Consequently, the money supply increases (the LM curve shifts to the right) endogenously, and the economy ends up at K. The effects on aggregate investment and the trade deficit would depend on whether the shock is increased FDI or increased exports.

If there is "full employment" in the starting position at Y^*, the final outcome is exactly the same as with a floating exchange rate. The expansionary effect of the shock goes wholly into a rise in prices, so the real money supply is constant, that is, LM remains at $LM1$. The rise in prices causes a real exchange rate appreciation, so the IS curve moves back to $IS1$ from $IS2$, and the BP curve moves up to $BP1$ from $BP2$, exactly as with a floating rate. The economy returns to E. Of course the process takes time; foreign exchange reserves rise at first and then decline.[47] In the final equilibrium, national income is unchanged, prices are higher, and the other effects on investment and the trade balance are exactly as with a floating exchange rate.

Fixed Exchange Rate Plus Sterilized Intervention

With a fixed exchange rate and sterilized intervention, the money supply is kept constant (by the sale of government bonds) despite the increase in reserves that results from the favorable external shock. So $LM1$ does not move.

46. Even if there is unemployment, an equilibrium between E and J is not possible. At any such point there would be an incipient balance-of-payments surplus, so the exchange rate would appreciate further, returning the economy to E.

47. In practice, there may be also some output expansion beyond "full employment" in the short run, which is later undone.

If there is "unemployment" at Y^*, the economy moves to J. National income is higher, but the expansion is limited by the increase in the interest rate, which crowds out some pre-existing domestic investment. If there is initial "full employment" at Y^*, national income remains unchanged in the final equilibrium. Despite a constant money supply, prices will rise because of the higher pressure of demand in the goods market. This moves LM to the left from $LM1$. The real exchange rate appreciation moves IS to the left from $IS2$ and BP upwards from $BP2$. The economy will end up at a point such as Q (national income constant, interest rate higher). The higher interest rate crowds out some investment, so aggregate investment could fall if the shock was increased exports. The domestic-foreign interest rate differential rises because Q is above the BP curve (which will end up somewhere between $BP1$ and $BP2$). This means there will be a persistent incentive for inflows into the domestic securities markets, and foreign exchange reserves will continue to rise.

Positive Shock in the Bond Market

Consider now a positive external shock in the bond market caused, for example, by a decline in world interest rates. This leads to an inflow of portfolio capital into the domestic bond market. Such a shock is depicted by a downward movement in the BP curve from $BP1$ to $BP2$.[48] IS stays put at $IS1$.

Floating Exchange Rate

The exchange rate appreciates because of capital inflows. This worsens the trade balance and moves the IS curve to the left from $IS1$ and the BP curve upward from $BP2$. With a floating exchange rate, the money supply is constant, so LM remains at $LM1$. The IS and BP curves now intersect at a point such as C on the $LM1$ curve. Thus the capital inflow is *contractionary*. There is a fall in income and employment.[49]

48. Alternatively the shock could arise from an increase in expected returns in domestic securities. In this simple model, this is equivalent to the shock discussed here.
49. If the government wanted to preserve full employment, it would have to ease monetary policy, as discussed below. That capital inflows can be contractionary if the exchange rate is floating is a standard result in international economics, but it is often ignored in Indian policy discussions.

Though national income is lower at C, the interest rate is also lower, so investment should rise.[50] The trade balance worsens (the appreciation effect outweighs the effect of the fall in national income) but is of course covered by capital inflows.

Fixed Exchange Rate Plus Unsterilized Intervention

If there is Keynesian unemployment at Y^*, the inflow creates a balance-of-payments surplus. So the supply of money rises endogenously and the economy ends up at W with a higher national income, a lower interest rate, and a higher trade deficit (financed by capital inflows). If there is "full employment" initially at Y^*, the eventual effect will be as with a floating exchange rate. Balance-of-payments surplus followed by monetary expansion raises prices, so the real money supply is constant ($LM1$ does not move), and the real exchange rate would appreciate (so IS moves left from $IS1$, and BP moves up from $BP2$). The economy ends up at C, with a reduction in income and employment.[51]

Fixed Exchange Rate Plus Sterilized Intervention

In this case, the money supply is constant, so LM does not move from its initial position of $LM1$, though BP moves to $BP2$. National income, investment, and the interest rate stay unchanged. Reserves continue to rise because there is a "permanent" rise in the interest differential. This result obtains in both the "unemployment" and "full employment" situations. Note that while the *interest differential* rises, the *level* of the home interest rate is unchanged.

The Case of Increased Remittances

What happens in the case of a favorable shock in the form of increased inward remittances is complex. The remittances could increase real investment, increase consumption, or increase demand for financial assets. The

---

50. Note, however, that the interest rate effect may be outweighed by the effect of recession-induced adverse expectations.
51. It is possible that if prices do not initially rise as fast as the money supply, there would be some increase in the real money supply and the new IS and LM curves could intersect at say H, thus maintaining full employment but with a higher price level. But in a dynamic process, this could only happen by fluke.

effects of increased remittances will vary depending on how the recipients dispose of them.[52]

Simultaneous Positive Shocks in Goods and Bond Markets

We now consider the consequences of positive external shocks to goods and bond markets simultaneously. (As explained in the text, this is representative of the current Indian situation.) We assume that there is "full employment" in the initial equilibrium at Y^*. (As above, the analysis can easily be extended to cover the case of initial unemployment.) The goods market shock moves the *IS* curve from *IS1* to *IS2* and the *BP* curve from *BP1* to *BP2*. In addition, the bond market shock moves the *BP* curve further to *BP3*.

If the exchange rate is floating, the appreciation has to go far enough to burn out *both* the shocks. So the economy will end up at a point such as *C* with lower income and employment. We have the same result if the exchange rate is fixed and intervention is unsterilized.[53] If the exchange rate is fixed but intervention is sterilized, the economy will end up at a point such as *Q* but with a larger interest differential than in the initial situation, and persistent capital inflows. (The *BP* curve will be somewhere between *BP1* and *BP3*.) It is noteworthy that with both a float and a fix (with unsterilized intervention), the bond market shock dominates the overall result, though there are simultaneous shocks in goods and bond markets.

Discretionary Policies, Internal Balance, and Balance-of-Payments Equilibrium

Now consider how full employment and balance-of-payments equilibrium can be attained with discretionary macroeconomic policy. We assume ini-

52. Consider situations where the initial position is one of "full employment" and the exchange regime is either a clean float or a fixed exchange rate with unsterilized intervention. If remittances flow entirely into investment, then their impact will be similar to that of increased FDI, discussed under "goods market shock" above. Investment rises and net exports are crowded out. If the increased remittances flow entirely into consumption, then the effects on net exports are the same as above, but the composition of output will be different. Increased consumption will crowd out net exports, and investment is unchanged. If remittances flow entirely into the bond market, then the effects will be as discussed above under "bond market shock." In practice, the impact of remittances is likely to be felt partly in the goods market and partly in the bond market, and in the goods market, partly on consumption and partly on investment.

53. As before, this assumes that prices rise immediately, so *LM* does not move. The dynamic process may or may not lead to a more favorable result.

tial full employment Y^* and a simultaneous favorable shock in the goods and bond markets as in the previous section. The essential point can be briefly stated: macroeconomic equilibrium can be achieved by different policy combinations.

One such combination is a floating exchange rate with an active monetary policy (this moves the LM curve). We saw that a float on its own will lead to unemployment (a move to C). This can be avoided by a simultaneous monetary expansion.[54] If the authorities get it right, the economy will end up at a point such as H where there is full employment and balance-of-payments equilibrium. The interest rate will be lower than at C or E, so the share of investment in output will be higher than in the pre-shock situation. How the extra absorption is divided up between investment and consumption will depend on the relevant interest elasticities.

But appreciation with an active monetary policy is not the only policy combination that can achieve full employment and balance-of-payments equilibrium. Many other policies can be brought into play, such as fiscal policy, trade policy, and capital account policies. Fiscal policy moves the IS curve. For example, fiscal retrenchment moves the IS curve to the left. Trade policies affect both the IS and the BP curves. For example, import liberalization moves the IS curve leftward and the BP curve upward. Capital account policies affect the BP curve. For example a tax on capital inflows moves the BP curve up. In the presence of capital account restrictions, an intermediate exchange rate regime is feasible. This means that the government can have an independent exchange rate policy (which moves the IS and BP curves) and an active monetary policy (which moves the LM curve). For example, exchange rate appreciation moves the IS curve to the left and the BP curve up; an expansionary monetary policy moves the LM curve to the right. Many different policy combinations can be envisaged which would give full employment and balance-of-payments equilibrium (intersection of IS, LM, and BP somewhere along EN, vertically above Y^*). But they would imply different combinations of the interest rate and the exchange rate and therefore different effects on the *composition* of output and the balance of payments.

Choosing the *optimal* policy mix requires going beyond the above model to bring in policy preferences pertaining to the composition of output and the balance of payments, derived from wider considerations. Moreover, policy formulation has to take place in a dynamic setting, with due regard to expec-

---

54. It could be argued that a central bank that targets inflation (say, follows a Taylor rule) would do this automatically. But it is a point worth making in the Indian context.

tations effects and to political constraints. The above rudimentary model is nothing more than a starting point for policy analysis, but we believe that it nevertheless usefully identifies the range of relevant policies and makes the basic point that the menu of policy options for adjustment to positive balance-of-payments shocks is much wider than a simple choice between a fixed and a floating exchange rate. A qualitative analysis of the optimal policy mix is attempted in the latter part of the paper.

Comments and Discussion

John Williamson: Vijay Joshi and Sanjeev Sanyal present an admirable survey of balance of payments developments in India since the great reform initiative of 1991, and of the policy issues currently confronting India in this field. They use the most standard workhorse models available, notably the Domar model of growth and the Mundell-Fleming model of the macroeconomics of an open economy, and combine them with sensible quantitative estimates to generate judgments on policy issues. I have a great deal of sympathy for both the methods and the conclusions of the paper.

First, I agree with Joshi and Sanyal's critique of Lal, Bery, and Pant, who argued that India had paid a steep price in terms of 2.7 percent a year forgone growth for its reserve accumulation of the 1990s. Joshi and Sanyal note that India's sterilized reserve accumulation averaged 1.2 percent of GDP each year. If all those resources had instead been funneled into investment, they estimate that growth would have been 0.4 percent higher, that is, 6.2 percent instead of 5.8 percent, as opposed to Lal, Bery, and Pant's estimate of 2.7 percent higher. But, of course, part of the addition to absorption—the greater part, according to the standard finding—would have been devoted to additional consumption rather than additional investment.[1] Moreover, if growth is in reality better described by the neoclassical model than by the Domar model, then the marginal return would be less than the average return, and once again one would get a lower estimate of the growth sacrifice implied by reserve accumulation. The only reason I can see for questioning the Joshi-Sanyal conclusion that the growth sacrifice is a *maximum* of 0.4 percent is that they calculate the investment loss as a maximum of the *sterilized* intervention of 1.2 percent of GDP. I would argue that the *entire* reserve buildup preempted real resources that could potentially have been funneled into investment, because the money supply increase that was "bought" by the unsterilized reserves could perfectly well have been provided by bigger domestic credit expansion instead.

---

1. Joshi and Sanyal note that the funds might all have flowed into investment if the capital inflow had taken the form of FDI. Empirical evidence is also fairly clear that inflows of portfolio equity serve to increase investment.

But Joshi and Sanyal argue not only that Lal, Bery, and Pant are in error quantitatively, which seems to me incontrovertible, but also that Indian growth may in fact have been aided rather than depressed by the reserve buildup. One argument is that the reserve accumulation (along with capital controls) served the economic function of protecting India from the East Asian crisis, and that had India got sucked into that maelstrom it could well have ended up with a lower growth rate than the 5.8 percent it actually had. I imagine most people would find that convincing. Maybe their other argument, that a mildly undervalued exchange rate is good for growth because it stimulates investment desires, is less widely accepted, but my own view is that they are completely right in this argument too. Indeed, it is precisely this point that I develop in the 2003 paper that they cite. In that paper I built a model that seeks to investigate the impact of the exchange rate on the growth rate. I argue that one needs to incorporate two factors. One is the impact that a competitive exchange rate has in motivating entrepreneurs to want to go and sell on the world market, and therefore to invest to make that possible. Historically, the economist who most emphasized this consideration was Bela Balassa, although in the last few months Michael Dooley, David Folkerts-Landau, and Peter Garber have made waves by using the argument to defend the undervaluation of the renminbi.[2] If this demand factor were the only consideration, then the more undervalued the exchange rate, the faster would be the rate of growth (which is precisely what Dooley and his coauthors argue, since they do not acknowledge supply constraints, just like other ultra-Keynesians). But while the *desire* to invest is magnified by a more undervalued exchange rate, the resources to make investment *possible* are diminished when a country runs a larger current account surplus (or a smaller deficit), which is the result of a more undervalued rate. (This is the factor that lay behind Lal, Bery, and Pant's analysis). The growth rate is maximized when this supply-side consideration is balanced at the margin against the demand-side impact of a more competitive exchange rate in motivating increased investment. Joshi and Sanyal are arguing that India would probably have suffered from lower rather than higher investment if it had allowed the reserves it sterilized to appreciate the exchange rate instead, because the desire to invest would have been reduced by more than the ability to invest would have been increased.

A second strategic point made by Joshi and Sanyal is that the dilemma identified by Lal, Bery, and Pant, although a mirage so far as the past

2. Dooley, Folkerts-Landau, and Garber (2003).

decade is concerned, has now become a reality. Additional reserves added to the Indian hoard now really do have a low productivity. Unless India wants to depress its growth rate below what is potentially possible, it needs to allow an expansion of absorption ("adjustment") and to stem the reserve increase. Personally, I would have judged that this became a reality several years ago; that is, that Indian reserves are already excessive, rather than that the present level can reasonably be considered optimal, but the point that it is time to contemplate adjustment remains valid.

Joshi and Sanyal go on to argue that the right response to this is a judicious combination of policies rather than a corner solution, particularly one that involves strong appreciation of the real exchange rate, and that also seems to me convincing. Specifically, they argue for a strategy that includes accelerated import liberalization and strong fiscal consolidation. This would permit additional absorption without undermining the competitiveness of the export sector. Once again, I am in complete sympathy with their argument. Perhaps the argument that in these circumstances it would be good for growth can add weight to our longstanding advocacy of fiscal consolidation on the grounds that it will diminish the likelihood of a crisis and thus help make the political case for the drastic reorientation of Indian fiscal policy that most of us believe to be essential.

In sum, I find much to agree with in this paper. If the India Policy Forum maintains this standard of policy relevance and good sense, it deserves to be listened to by Indian policymakers.

Arvind Virmani: The Joshi-Sanyal paper covers a very diverse set of issues. One of the novel topics is the discussion of basic macroeconomic theory in the context of actual balance-of-payments developments in India, a discussion that would be useful for many readers. Given the diversity of topics, however, the interlinkages between the topics is not clearly spelled out. A more explicit discussion of how they all fit together would have been helpful.

In my comments, referring largely to the version presented at the conference, I address some important issues raised in the paper. These are the evolution and performance of the payment regime, the effect of reserve accumulation on growth, and recommended policy approach. There were three important milestones in the evolution of the policy on external commercial borrowing. Until 1980 virtually all external borrowing was related to foreign aid. During the 1980s the policy was gradually liberalized to allow borrowing by companies from foreign private sources (for example, banks). There was consequently a substantial increase in public sector and government-guaranteed debt, whose productivity is questionable.[3] The problems to which this gave rise were clearly recognized in the report of the Eighth Plan Working Group on Balance of Payments (1989), which noted that the ratios of external debt to GDP and of the short-term to total debt were too high. It recommended that the country's ratio of external debt to equity be raised through greater flow of foreign direct investment (liberalization of FDI) and that short-term debt be lowered. Unfortunately, no further action was taken on the report because the new government that came to power after the election disowned the earlier plan approach.

Even though external and internal shocks triggered the crisis of 1990–91, subsequent analysis shows that the current account deficit was rising and reserves had been declining since the mid-1980s. The shocks accentuated the problem by giving rise to adverse expectations among nonresident Indian depositors, resulting in net outflows. One of the lessons learned by the new government in 1991–92 was that timely depreciation was a solution to negative balance-of-payment shocks. Subsequent analysis of the crisis confirmed that the fiscal deficit played a key role in raising current account deficits and that exchange rate rigidity was also an important factor.

The Mexican, Brazilian, and Russian crises also taught us the role of monetary tightening and interest rate increases in stabilizing exchange rate expectations. In my view, however, the wrong lessons were learned from the Asian crisis, as controls regained respectability in India and exchange rate management again veered toward excessive use of controls on exchange futures and forwards, nonresident Indian deposits, and external commercial borrowings. Such controls are a bad idea, except under crisis conditions, which have not occurred in India since 1990–91 and will not happen as long as the exchange rate is allowed to depreciate in response to negative shocks.

If the exchange rate had been depreciated in 1990, the crisis could have been prevented.[4] The surge in equity inflow (stock adjustment) during 1993–93, after foreign institutional investor (FII) entry was allowed in 1991–92, also provided lessons. The analytical approach recommended for managing these flows was to deal with the (estimated) temporary and permanent components differently. The former should be dealt with through sterilized intervention (purchase), and the latter through acceleration of trade and current account liberalization and

3. Virmani (2001).
4. Virmani (2003).

through unsterilized purchase. I argued that in contrast to the policy of nominal appreciation (full employment, rational expectation model), this would result in lower real interest rates and higher investment and growth in India (labor surplus, dual economy). The operational and management rules that emerged were also conditioned by political sensitivity and fear of destabilizing expectations. These were to reduce volatility in the rupee-dollar exchange rate in the short term by immediate purchase or sale of foreign exchange (very short term) and tightening or loosening monetary policy thereafter. The medium-term goal was to sustain exports through a stable real exchange rate (subject to data lags). In this policy, reserve accumulation is an outcome of an asymmetric exchange rate management policy in which the nominal exchange rate is allowed to depreciate over the medium term in response to adverse trends in balance of payments, but nominal appreciation in response to favorable balance-of-payments trends is resisted. This view is in consonance with the conclusions of the Joshi-Sanyal paper on the effect of reserve accumulation on growth.

In recommending a policy approach, I note some recent developments, including an appreciation of the real effective exchange rate and a fall in the inflation differential (India-U.S.) since 1999–2000, as well as a narrowing of the real interest differential (U.S.-India three-month t-bills) and a reduction in its volatility. A study by the Indian Council on Research for International Economic Relations has also shown that tariff reductions during the 1990s have had positive effects on net exports in many three-digit manufacturing industries, while the overall impact has been mildly positive. In the light of these observations, I would recommend the following policies. First, accelerate the tariff reduction to achieve a 5 percent peak rate by 2007–08, instead of in 2011–12, as recommended in an earlier planning commission working paper. Second, pursue further current and capital account liberalization, excluding short-term debt (below one year) for the time being. Third, pursue interest rate decontrol and flexibility, through an active search for hidden controls. Fourth, privatize a few public sector banks (as a start) to break the public sector bank oligopoly (coordinated by the RBI for the government). Finally, pursue unsterilized intervention in response to continued high inflows, followed by nominal appreciation only if inflation rises sharply (from 4–5 percent) and the underlying growth trend goes well above the twenty-four-year average of 5.8 percent.[5]

---

5. *Postscript.* Inflation has now gone above 8 percent as a result of a sharp rise in prices, and allowing nominal appreciation must be among the policies followed if capital inflows continue strongly.

General Discussion

A large portion of the general discussion focused on the question of whether the exchange rate was currently undervalued. Montek Singh Ahluwalia argued that perspectives on the exchange rate were often asymmetric in that it is easier to obtain a consensus in favor of a more flexible exchange rate regime when the rate is thought to be overvalued. A depreciated exchange rate was viewed as positive from a growth perspective, and policymakers would be unwilling to risk appreciation. Several persons expressed the view that the exchange rate was likely to be determined by developments in the capital account, but because the exchange rate would affect the current account, the authorities should have a clear notion of a target or desired exchange rate.

Surjit Bhalla suggested that the risks of a financial crisis also were asymmetric: the probability of a crisis is high in the presence of an overvalued rate, but undervalued exchange rates seldom result in sudden reversals. Thus he thought that India should follow China in targeting an undervalued rate. Vijay Joshi pointed out, however, that a sustained capital inflow could lead to excessive monetary growth and inflation, and ultimately to an overvalued real exchange rate.

John Williamson expressed concern over the notion of a fully flexible exchange rate. He believed that India was still in a transitional phase in which foreign exchange markets and institutions were not sufficiently developed to support a move to a fully flexible exchange rate regime. In particular, it would be some time before residents should be allowed to freely move capital in and out of the country. He worried about a sequence in which large capital inflows led to exchange rate appreciation and a severe contraction of the tradable goods industries. Such damage cannot be easily undone, even if the capital inflows subsequently reversed. Emerging markets were seen as particularly vulnerable to this type of adverse cycle.

Montek Singh Ahluwalia questioned the sustainability of a pegged exchange rate policy and argued that India was basically moving in the right direction, toward a more flexible regime. However, he wondered how to establish priorities. He favored the liberalization of capital outflows as a response to increased inflows, and he thought it would be a good idea to allow a limited amount of foreign investment by resident individuals and mutual funds. In response, Sanjeev Sanyal noted that foreign investment was now permitted but that with a strong domestic equity market, no one was interested in investing abroad.

Several participants spoke in favor of the authors' suggestion of a mixed strategy but wondered how far to pursue some of the policy measures. Would the authors favor tariff cuts even if the cuts could not offset the fiscal revenue loss? Could the reserve bank engage in less sterilization, allowing faster growth of the money supply? Was there adequate capacity to avoid any inflationary consequences?

References

Acharya, Shankar. 2003. "Services as Saviour." In *India's Economy: Some Issues and Answers*, by S. Acharya. New Delhi: Academic Foundation.

Ahluwalia, Montek. 2002. "Economic Reforms since 1991: Has Gradualism Worked?" *Journal of Economic Perspectives* 16(3): 67–88.

Bhagwati, Jagdish. 1996. "The 'Miracle' That Did Happen: Understanding East Asia in Comparative Perspective." Cornell University. [Reprinted in J. Bhagwati, *The Wind of a Hundred Days* (MIT Press, 2000).]

————. "The Capital Myth: The Difference between Trade in Widgets and Dollars." *Foreign Affairs* 77(3): 7–12.

Bhalla, Surjit. 2004. "Wealth Generation from Mercantilism: How Undervaluation of the Exchange Rate Matters for Growth." Paper presented at the NCAER/NBER conference at Neemrana, India.

Bosworth, Barry, and Susan Collins. 1999. "Capital Flows to Developing Economies: Implications for Saving and Investment." *Brookings Papers on Economic Activity*, no. 1: 143–80.

Calvo, Guillermo, and Carmen Reinhart. 2002. "Fear of Floating." *Quarterly Journal of Economics* 117 (2): 379–408.

Chami, Ralph, Connel Fullenkamp, and Samir Jahjah. 2003. "Are Immigrant Remittance Flows a Source of Capital for Development?" IMF Working Paper WP/03/189. Washington: International Monetary Fund.

Cooper, Richard. 1999. "Should Capital Controls be Banished?" *Brookings Papers on Economic Activity*, no. 1: 89–125.

Dooley, Michael P., David Folkerts-Landau, and Peter Garber. 2003. "An Essay on the Revived Bretton Woods System." Working Paper 9971. Cambridge, Mass.: National Bureau of Economic Research.

Eichengreen, Barry. 1994. *International Monetary Arrangements for the 21st Century*. Washington: Brookings.

Fischer, Stanley. 2001. "Exchange Rate Regimes: Is the Bipolar View Correct?" *Journal of Economic Perspectives* 15: 3–24.

Government of India. 1993. *Report of the High-Level Committee on the Balance of Payments*. New Delhi: Government of India.

Jadhav, Navendra. 2003. "Capital Account Liberalisation: The Indian Experience." Available at http://www.imf.org/external/np/apd/seminars/2003/newdelhi/jadhav.pdf.

Joshi, Vijay. 1998a. "India's Economic Reforms: Progress, Problems, Prospects." *Oxford Development Studies* 26(3): 333–50.

————. 1998b. "Fiscal Stabilisation and Economic Reform in India." In *India's Economic Reforms and Development: Essays in Honour of Manmohan Singh*, edited by Isher Ahluwalia and Ian Little. Delhi: Oxford University Press.

————. 2003. "India and the Impossible Trinity." *The World Economy* 26(4): 555–83.

————. 2004. "The Real Exchange Rate, Fiscal Deficits and Capital Flows: A Refutation." *Economic and Political Weekly* 39 (13): 1434–36.

Joshi, Vijay, and Ian Little. 1994. *India: Macroeconomics and Political Economy 1964–1991.* Washington: World Bank, and New Delhi: Oxford University Press.

————. 1996. *India's Economic Reforms 1991–2001.* Delhi: Oxford University Press.

Kaldor, Nicholas. 1971. "Conflicts in National Economic Objectives." *Economic Journal* 81 (321): 1–16.

Kapur, Devesh, and Urjit Patel. 2003. "Large Foreign Currency Reserves: Insurance for Domestic Weaknesses and External Uncertainties?" *Economic and Political Weekly* 38 (11): 1047–53.

Kulkarni, Kishore. 1999. *Modern Monetary Theory.* New Delhi: Macmillan India Ltd.

Lal, Deepak, Suman Bery, and Devendra Pant. 2003. "The Real Exchange Rate, Fiscal Deficits, and Capital Flows: India, 1981–2000." *Economic and Political Weekly* 38 (47): 4965–76.

Lewis, Arthur. 1954. "Economic Development with Unlimited Supplies of Labour." *Manchester School* 22(2): 139–91.

Little, Ian. 1981. "The Experience and Causes of Rapid, Labour-Intensive Development in Korea, Taiwan, Hong Kong and Singapore, and the Possibilities of Emulation." In *Export-Led Industrialisation and Development,* edited by E. Lee. Geneva: ILO.

————. 1996. *Picking Winners: The East Asian Experience.* London: Social Market Foundation.

Pinto, Brian, and Farah Zahir. 2004. "Why Fiscal Adjustment Now?" *Economic and Political Weekly* 39 (10): 1039–48.

Prasad, Eswar, Kenneth Rogoff, Shang-jin Wei, and Ayhan Kose. 2003. "Effects of Financial Globalisation on Developing Countries: Some Empirical Evidence." IMF Occasional Paper 220. Washington: International Monetary Fund.

Reddy, Y. Venugopal. 1997. "Exchange Rate Management: Dilemmas." Speech to the Forex Association of India. Available on Reserve Bank of India website.

Reserve Bank of India 1997. *Report of the Committee on Capital Account Convertibility.* Mumbai: Reserve Bank of India.

————. 2004. *Report on Currency and Finance 2002–03.* Mumbai: Reserve Bank of India.

Virmani, Arvind. 2001. "India's 1990–91 Crisis: Reforms, Myths and Paradoxes." Working Paper 4/2001-PC. Planning Commission website (December).

————. 2003. "India's External Reforms: Modest Globalisation Significant Gains." *Economic and Political Weekly* 37 (32, August 9–15), 3373–90.

Williamson, John. 1993. "A Cost-Benefit Analysis of Capital Account Liberalisation." In *Financial Opening: Policy Issues and Experiences in Developing Countries,* edited by B. Fischer and H. Reisen. Paris: OECD.

————. 2003. "Exchange Rate Policy and Development." Paper presented to a conference of the Initiative for Policy Dialogue, Barcelona. June.

World Bank. 2001. *Global Development Finance.* Washington: World Bank.

ILA PATNAIK
National Council of Applied Economic Research

India's Experience with a Pegged Exchange Rate[1]

According to the Reserve Bank of India (RBI), the exchange rate of the Indian rupee is "market determined," in the sense that it is set in a currency market and is not administratively determined. However, the RBI actively trades in the foreign exchange market with the stated goal of "containing volatility" and influencing the market price. Recent research on the Bank's interventions has demonstrated that the rupee is effectively pegged to the U.S. dollar. That link to the dollar, combined with the easing of restrictions on India's current account and capital account during the 1990s, suggests a potential conflict with Bank efforts to conduct an autonomous monetary policy directed toward stabilizing the domestic economy.

A key insight of open economy macroeconomics, newly prominent in recent decades, is the idea of the "impossible trinity."[2] The theory is that no country can simultaneously have an open capital account, a fixed exchange rate, and a monetary policy targeted on the domestic economy. Specifically, once the capital account is open and the exchange rate is fixed, monetary policy is driven solely by the need to uphold the fixed exchange rate.

To review the logic of the impossible trinity, suppose a central bank begins to tighten monetary policy in the presence of an open capital account and a fixed exchange rate. Tight monetary policy raises interest rates, which attract capital inflows. The central bank must therefore buy foreign currency to prevent a currency appreciation. Financing the purchases requires an increase in the monetary base, reversing the earlier effort to tighten monetary policy. As an alternative, the bank might seek to finance the purchase of foreign currency by offsetting sales of other domestic assets, such as its holding of government debt (a process known as sterilization);

1. This paper grew out of conversations with Ajay Shah. The views in this paper are my own. I would like to thank Rajnish Mehra, Indira Rajaraman, Shankar Acharya, Arvind Virmani, Suman Bery, and Barry Bosworth for many improvements to the paper. I am grateful to CMIE and Golak Nath of NSE for help on data.
2. Mundell (1961).

but those actions will exacerbate the rise in interest rates, attracting further inflows.

Few countries today adhere to the extreme position of having a fixed exchange rate. But many countries that try to "manage" a "market determined exchange rate" face similar conflicts. And the more the central bank focuses on currency policy, the more it loses monetary policy autonomy.

In the years after World War II, many countries chose to have autonomy in both currency policy and monetary policy and did so successfully by closing the capital account. With a closed capital account, even if economic agents have speculative views about future fluctuations of the currency, they cannot express these views by taking positions in the foreign exchange market. With a more open capital account, however, when economic agents have speculative views about the future, they are able to move capital across borders and vary their net currency positions. For example, an importer who expects a rupee appreciation may choose to delay payments in order to convert into U.S. dollars at a more attractive exchange rate. The steady increase in openness on the capital account in recent decades is forcing many countries now to grapple with the trade-off between having a currency policy and having monetary policy.

Until the past decade, India had a system of strong capital controls. In the spirit of the impossible trinity, these controls made it possible for India's central bank to operate a fixed exchange rate regime and have monetary policy autonomy. During the 1990s, however, restrictions on the current account and the capital account were substantially, though not completely, eased. (A later section of this paper describes capital mobility in India in more detail.)

As the conceptual framework of the impossible trinity implies, India's liberalization of the current account and the capital account should have steadily tied monetary policy to the need to maintain the currency regime.[3] Although currency flexibility in India appears to have been unchanged in the past twenty-five years, the monetary policy consequences of upholding this currency policy are likely to have changed substantially.

It is important to emphasize that India has neither a completely open capital account nor a completely fixed exchange rate. The current policy framework comprises partial controls on capital, a pegged (but not fixed) exchange rate with extremely low volatility, and an effort at monetary policy autonomy. The policy framework in India today is hence an interesting gray area, one not well illuminated by theory.

---

3. Joshi (2003).

This paper seeks to shed some light on the extent to which India's choice of a pegged currency regime has attenuated monetary policy. It addresses four questions. First, where does India stand in terms of opening the capital account? Second, what has the RBI's stance of sterilization been? Third, is it possible to isolate episodes of large-scale currency trading by the central bank? And finally, what were the monetary consequences of currency trading?

The following sections provide a brief summary of recent research on India's currency regime, an overview of the implications of capital controls for the operation of the currency forward market, and an examination of the extent to which the RBI has sought to sterilize the domestic monetary implications of its exchange market interventions. These discussions provide the context for the analysis of two episodes of large-scale RBI intervention in currency markets, one in 1993–94 and the other after June 2001. In both episodes the RBI accumulated foreign currency reserves in an effort to resist an exchange rate appreciation. The analysis highlights the growing conflict for India between implementing a pegged exchange rate and operating an autonomous monetary policy.

Recent Research on India's Currency Regime

Several recent research papers have focused on the question of how to characterize a country's de facto currency regime, as opposed to the regime that the central bank claims is in operation. G. A. Calvo and C. M. Reinhart propose a metric of currency flexibility that combines volatility of the exchange rate, volatility of foreign exchange reserves, and interest rate volatility.[4] Within this context, they find that the Indian exchange rate exhibits extremely low flexibility and that the degree of flexibility did not change during 1979–99.

Reinhart and K. S. Rogoff propose a data-driven algorithm for identifying the de facto currency regime.[5] First, they examine the monthly absolute percentage change in the exchange rate. If the change is equal to zero for four consecutive months or more, they classify that episode (however long it lasts) as a de facto peg if no dual or multiple exchange rates are in place. This approach allows them to identify relatively short-lived de facto pegs as well as longer-lasting pegs. Second, they compute the probability that the monthly exchange rate change remains within a 1 percent band over a

---

4. Calvo and Reinhart (2002).
5. Reinhart and Rogoff (2002).

rolling five-year period. If the probability is 80 percent or higher, they classify the regime as a de facto peg or crawling peg over the entire five-year period. If the exchange rate has no drift, they classify it as a fixed parity; if it has a positive drift, they label it a crawling peg. If it goes through periods of both appreciation and depreciation, it is a moving peg. Based on these methods, Reinhart and Rogoff classify the current currency regime in India as a "peg to the US dollar" (in various forms) since August 1979.

In a working paper last year I examined in more detail the question of how to characterize India's currency regime.[6] In summary, I found that India's enormous reserves buildup after mid-2002 cannot be explained as a quest for reserves as insurance. In addition, extending Calvo and Reinhart's metric of currency flexibility beyond 1999 shows no change over 1979–2003. A variety of tests betray symptoms of pegging the rupee to the U.S. dollar. The volatility of the rupee-dollar exchange rate, for example, is extremely low while that of the exchange rate of rupee and the euro or the yen is high. Tests based on a methodology devised by J. Frankel and S.-J. Wei show that the dollar is overwhelmingly the dominant currency in explaining fluctuations of the Indian currency.[7]

India's Openness on the Capital Account

It is widely believed that India opened up to capital inflows beginning in 1991. But as table 1 shows, total inflows dropped from 11.6 percent of GDP in 1991–92 to 9.7 percent of GDP in 2002–03. Nonofficial flows stagnated at roughly 9 percent. How can this picture be reconciled with India's substantial capital account liberalization during the 1990s?

Understanding the Elements of Openness

One explanation for this seeming contradiction lies in the way capital flows are measured. They can be measured in terms of gross inflows, or net inflows, or gross flows (inflows plus outflows), just as trade openness can be measured in terms of the trade balance, or exports, or exports plus imports. In the case of trade, or the current account, the most meaningful measure, which is universally used, is exports plus imports as percentage of GDP. Similarly, I will use capital account inflows plus outflows as percentage of GDP to measure the extent of capital account openness.

6. Patnaik (2003).
7. Frankel and Wei (1994).

TABLE 1.   Capital Inflows into India, 1991–92, 1995–96, 2002–03
Percent of GDP

Year	Total	Nonofficial
1991–92	11.59	8.81
1995–96	7.22	6.34
2002–03	9.75	9.19

Source: Reserve Bank of India, *Monthly Bulletin,* various issues.

The second explanation involves thinking carefully about the nature of capital controls in India today. It proves useful to think in terms of a hierarchy of openness of the different channels through which capital now flows both inward and outward. The following discussion touches briefly on the channels in this hierarchy, running from the most open to the most controlled.

CURRENT ACCOUNT. Since India's current account was sharply liberalized during the 1990s, trade in both goods and services has grown enormously. As table 2 shows, trade, as a share of GDP, grew from 21.3 percent to 36.8 percent from 1991–92 to 2002–03.

The current account is one of the most open channels for cross-border capital movements because government inspectors are unable to measure accurately the value of goods and services, such as shipments of diamonds or email attachments containing software. The current account is also a well-known channel for evading capital controls. During the 1990s, for example, trade misinvoicing on the current account was a significant route for capital flows.[8] Hence the growth of the current account should be interpreted as an effective easing of capital controls. Since 1991, RBI regulations on the current account have not been used to implement currency policy.

INVESTMENT FLOWS. Investment flows involve some capital controls. India has steadily eased restrictions on foreign direct investment, foreign institutional investors engaging in portfolio investment, and outward flows by Indian firms seeking to build international operations, so that investment flows are a relatively open channel for cross-border capital flows. Nevertheless, government regulations for foreign direct investment involve restrictions in certain industries—such as that foreign investors cannot own more than 24 percent of an insurance company. And rules for foreign institutional investors have caps for the ownership of any one stock and ceilings for the total ownership by all such investors in a

8. Patnaik and Vasudevan (2000).

TABLE 2. Growth of India's Current Account, 1991–92 to 2002–03

	Amount (billions of dollars)		Share (percent of GDP)	
Trade account category	1991–92	2002–03	1991–92	2002–03
Merchandise				
Exports	18.3	53.0	6.9	10.4
Imports	21.0	65.5	7.9	12.8
Invisibles				
Exports	9.5	43.0	3.6	8.4
Imports	7.9	26.9	2.9	5.2
Total	56.7	188.3	21.3	36.8

Source: Author's calculations based on data from Reserve Bank of India, *Monthly Bulletin,* various issues, and Centre for Monitoring Indian Economy.

stock. Foreign investors are essentially prohibited from buying government bonds.

At the same time, these channels constitute effective capital account convertibility for these classes of investors, who are free to move capital in and out of India and who are permitted access to the currency forward market. As with the current account, tactical changes in these rules have not been used by the government or RBI as an instrument of implementing currency policy.

OTHER CAPITAL FLOWS. Balance-of-payments statistics show an entry for "other capital flows," which consist of delayed export receipts, advance payments against imports, and loans to nonresidents by residents. These offer a channel for capital flows that are not restricted by official controls.

LOANS. Although Indian firms can borrow from overseas, the borrowing involves significant restrictions, and the Ministry of Finance and RBI have attempted to use changes in these capital controls as a way to implement currency policy.

BANKING FLOWS. Capital flows through the banking system are influenced by a very detailed set of regulatory restrictions operated by RBI. As both the central bank and the banking regulator, RBI uses banking regulation to implement capital controls. For example, RBI sets the interest rate at which banks borrow from foreigners (labeled "nonresident Indians"). Hence it is useful to think of all capital flows through the banking system as being highly controlled.

OFFICIAL FLOWS. These flows are, by definition, not available to private economic agents and are excluded from consideration.

As table 3 shows, the least-controlled capital flow channel, investment flows, increased from less than 1 percent of GDP to 3.9 percent of GDP

TABLE 3. Private Capital Flows as Percent of GDP, India, 1991–92, 1995–96, 2002–03
Percent of GDP

	1991–92	1995–96	2002–03
Investment flows	0.08	1.99	3.91
Other capital flows	2.43	1.20	1.82
Loans	4.19	4.62	4.41
Banking flows	10.07	3.63	5.52
Total	16.76	11.43	15.36

Source: Author's calculations based on data from Reserve Bank of India, *Monthly Bulletin,* various issues, and Centre for Monitoring Indian Economy.

over a decade. The most-controlled channel, banking flows, dropped from 10 percent of GDP to 5.5 percent of GDP. Overall, private capital flows saw no trend increase.

With the current and capital account combined, India's total private external transactions rose from roughly 35 percent of GDP to more than 50 percent of GDP from 1991–92 to 2002–03. Over this decade, both the foreign exchange market and private participation in it increased considerably.

Restrictions on the Currency Forward Market

One element of the capital controls now in place is barriers to arbitrage on the currency forward market. In a conventional forward market, arbitrage defines the forward rate. Even if strong speculative views and positions on the market exist, in a normal forward market no interesting interpretation can be attached to the level of the forward premium because the premium is determined purely by covered interest parity. When violations of market efficiency arise, near-infinite capital comes into play in arbitrage. Through this process, arbitrageurs restore the forward price to its fair value.

In India, RBI rules sharply restrict the ability of banks to engage in covered interest parity arbitrage, thus breaking the link between the spot market price and the price of the derivative.[9] In addition, although the RBI trades extensively to manipulate the spot market, the observed forward price tends to be a market-determined rate.

Interestingly, the RBI rules that inhibit covered interest parity arbitrage combine with the relatively undistorted forward market to generate a

9. Currency derivatives can either trade OTC or on exchange. At present, currency derivatives are only traded OTC; there is no exchange. Hence, my treatment is limited to currency forwards and does not use data from a currency futures market.

remarkable information source. When arbitrage does not determine prices, information from the forward market conveys expectations about the future. If economic agents expect the rupee to depreciate, they grow more interested in selling rupees forward. Exporters stay unhedged, and importers are likely to hedge. Conversely, if economic agents expect the rupee to appreciate, they grow more interested in buying rupees forward.

The arithmetic of forward pricing, as noted, is based on covered interest parity, which involves comparing two routes for riskless dollar investment. An investor could convert \$1 into $(1 + r_u)^T$ through r_u, which is obtained from the U.S. zero coupon yield curve for T years. Or the investor could convert into rupee at the spot price (S), invest in the Government of India (GOI) zero coupon yield of comparable maturity, and obtain a locked-in cash flow of $S(1 + r_i)^T / F$ by converting back into dollars at the exchange rate F at date T. Under no-arbitrage, these two investment strategies have to yield an identical return, through which the fair value for F can be computed. Once we know the fair value, we can measure the error when compared with the observed market price.

If RBI rules did not restrict arbitrage, the forward premium would not be informative. Under the existing policy framework, however, it is a uniquely useful market-based measure of future expectations, one that is not available in most countries where regulators do not inhibit arbitrage.

Internationally, empirical research related to currency expectations uses data based on surveys.[10] Market participants, central bankers, multinational companies, and economics departments of banks are interviewed on a weekly or monthly frequency. Survey data such as the *Currency Forecasters' Digest*, now known as the *Financial Times Currency Forecast*, form the basis of empirical research on currency expectations.[11]

Although no such data are available for India, the daily data from the forward market on the deviation of the forward-market rate from covered interest parity are a unique high-frequency source of information about currency expectations. As shown in figure 1, in the rupee-dollar forward market, deviations from the covered parity conditions have tended to persist over many years. In an open market, arbitrage would have wiped out such deviations almost instantly.

Apart from conveying expectations of the market, the error between the observed forward premium and its fair value also shows the arbitrage opportunity available to those who are allowed to participate in the forward market.

10. Frankel and Okongwu (1996).
11. Chinn and Frankel (1994).

FIGURE 1. Rupee-Dollar Forward Premium: Market Price and Fair Value, January 1993 to February 2004

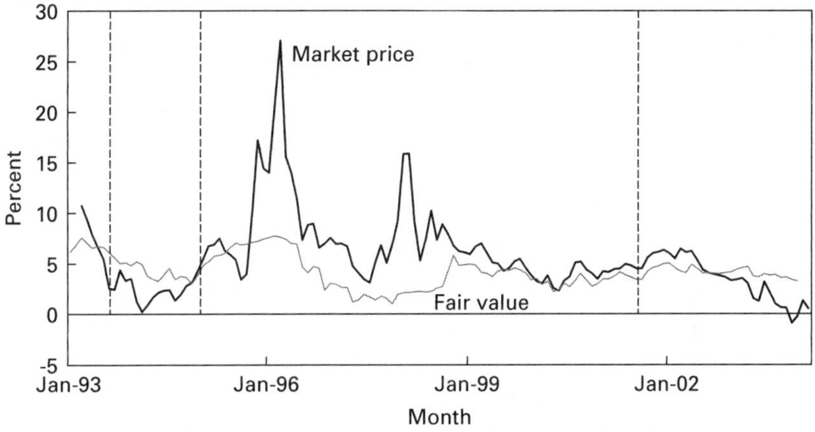

Source: Author's calculations based on data from Federal Reserve Board, National Stock Exchange, Telerate, and ABN Amro. Fair value is the interest rate on 91-day treasury bill in India minus that on the 3-month treasury bill in the United States.
Full Period: Vertical lines are placed at "06/01/93" and "11/01/94" and "08/01/01."

Extent of Sterilization

A central bank has several options in responding to variations in the volume of net capital inflows. One is simply to allow the market for foreign exchange to clear through changes in its price. But if the central bank is committed to a specific exchange rate, it can finance its purchases of foreign exchange either by expanding the monetary base or by selling other domestic assets, normally government debt. Concern that large expansions of the monetary base could worsen inflation pressures often leads to efforts to "sterilize," or offset, the monetary implications through the sale of other assets in the bank's portfolio. The extent of sterilization by the central bank can differ, depending on both the need to sterilize and the ability to do so. It is also possible to distinguish between "narrow" sterilization, involving the sale of other domestic assets, and "broad" sterilization, involving levers like changes in reserve requirements.

In what follows I estimate an offset coefficient that measures the extent to which the addition to net foreign exchange assets (NFA) is sterilized by the central bank. The central bank offsets the change in NFA by changes in net domestic assets (NDA), where NDA is a policy variable. My work is based on a monetary model, which includes a simple money demand function and a money supply function. The reduced form expression assumes that NDA is responsive to demand conditions in the economy, determined by output growth. Changes in NDA take into account the changes in the monetary base due to changes in NFA or to changes in reserve requirements.[12] When the central bank fully offsets changes in NFA, in the limit, the offset coefficient is −1. Partial sterilization generates values of the coefficient between 0 and −1.

The model is estimated for the period April 1993 to December 2003 using monthly data. Net domestic assets of the RBI are adjusted to reflect net non-monetary liabilities. For comparability, the index of industrial production (IIP) is re-expressed in nominal terms using the wholesale price index. This yields a time-series of the nominal IIP (IIPn), which is used as a proxy for nominal output. The cash reserve ratio (CRR) is used to measure bank reserve requirements.

The series NDA, NFA, and IIPn are non-stationary. Unit root tests indicate that they are I(1). Further, both the Johansen cointegration tests and standard tests for stationarity suggest that the series are cointegrated. Consequently, the model for estimating the offset coefficient is set up as an error-correction model. The first stage is specified in levels, and the second stage in first differences with the lagged residual term as an additional variable and with monthly dummies:

(1) $$NDA = \alpha_0 + \alpha_1 NFA + \alpha_2 IIPn + \alpha_3 CRR + \varepsilon_t$$

(2) $$\Delta NDA = \beta_0 + \beta_1 \varepsilon_{t-1} + \beta_2 \Delta NFA + \beta_3 \Delta IIPn + \gamma_t$$

The empirical results are

(3)
$$NDA = -0.822 \ NFA + 841.6 \ IIPn + 360.4 \ CRR,$$
$$(30.7) \qquad (17.7) \qquad (0.4) \qquad R^2 = 0.93$$

and with error correction,

(4)
$$\Delta NDA = -0.271 \ \varepsilon_{t-1} - 0.602 \ \Delta NFA + 375.2 \ \Delta IIPn$$
$$(4.5) \qquad (5.4) \qquad (5.8) \qquad R^2 = 0.38$$

The results suggest that RBI directly sterilized its currency intervention by a reduction in net domestic assets. However, though the extent of sterilization

12. Schadler and others (1993) estimate an offset coefficient that measures the degree to which capital inflows offset the changes in net domestic assets in a fixed exchange rate regime. My model is similar to the one used by them, but is motivated by a different question.

FIGURE 2.   Foreign Exchange Assets of the Reserve Bank of India, 1993–2003

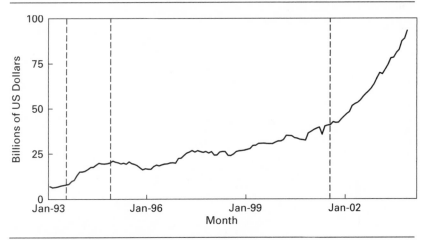

Source: Reserve Bank of India, *Monthly Bulletin,* various issues.
Full Period: Vertical lines are placed at "06/01/93" and "11/01/94" and "08/01/01."

was large, it was not complete. The offset coefficient is estimated to be –0.8 in levels and 0.6 in the error-correction estimate.

The relationship with output growth was found to be positive and highly significant. In other words, growth in net domestic assets was higher when output growth was faster. The coefficient of CRR was found to be insignificant and is excluded in the error-correction estimate.

Analyzing Major Episodes of RBI Currency Trading

To understand the consequences of the impossible trinity, as well as issues in the implementation of the rupee-dollar peg, it is interesting to focus on the periods when the RBI has engaged heavily in currency trading. Figure 2 shows the time-series of India's foreign currency reserves from January 1993 to November 2003. Based on the rate of reserve accumulation, two episodes merit attention. Episode I runs from June 1993 to November 1994 (eighteen months). Episode II runs from August 2001 onward. Both episodes happen to involve a sharp increase in reserves. There is no comparable episode of a sharp drop in reserves.

Reserves increased because the central bank was purchasing dollars to prevent an appreciation of the rupee. Figure 3 shows the time-series of daily volatility of the rupee-dollar exchange rate during the period in question.

FIGURE 3. Rolling Window Estimates of Rupee-Dollar
Daily Volatility, 1993–2003

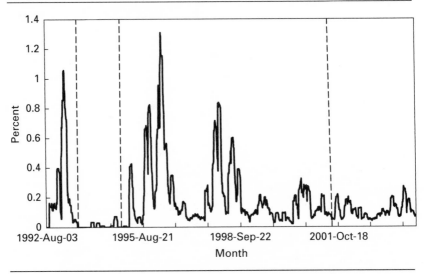

Source: Author's calculations based on data from Centre for Monitoring Indian Economy.
Full Period: Vertical lines are placed at "06/01/93" and "11/01/94" and "08/01/01."

In both Episodes I and II, the standard deviation of daily returns attains low values like 0.1 percent.

I propose to understand both these episodes using the following framework. First, how did the episode commence? Second, what were the fluctuations of the currency in the episode? How tightly did RBI peg the currency? Third, what was the currency forward market thinking? Fourth, how large was RBI's currency trading, compared with reserve money? Fifth, how did RBI offset the monetary implications of currency trading? Sixth, what was the trajectory of money supply and interest rates in the episode?

Episode I

In 1993–94 India began liberalizing portfolio inflows. From near-zero levels, portfolio inflows rose sharply to $307 million in the second quarter of 1993–94, to $935 million in the third quarter, to $2283 million in the fourth quarter. The shift marked the beginning of a capital surge into the country.

TABLE 4. **Balance of Payments in Episode I**

Billions of U.S. dollars

Year	Current account balance	Net capital inflows	Change in net foreign assets
1991–92	−9.6	3.7	5.71
1992–93	−1.2	2.9	−1.25
1993–94	−1.2	9.6	7.45
1994–95	−3.4	9.1	7.10
1995–96	−5.9	4.7	−0.19
1996–97	−4.6	11.5	4.78

Source: Reserve Bank of India, *Monthly Bulletin,* various issues.

Table 4 shows the evolution of balance of payments around Episode I. The current account was unchanged from 1992–93 to 1993–94. Net capital inflows, however, rose sharply from $2.9 billion to $9.6 billion. My dating of Episode I, from June 1993 to November 1994, is squarely in this period of high capital inflows.

Faced with a capital surge, RBI chose to prevent the rupee from appreciating. The rupee-dollar rate was kept largely fixed, as shown in figure 4. Between July 1993 and December 1993, the dollar was fixed at Rs. 31.42. In January 1994, it moved to Rs. 31.37.

FIGURE 4. **Expectations of Rupee Appreciation, Episode I**

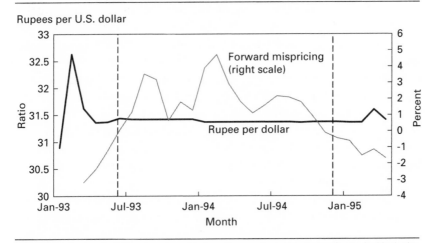

Source: Author's calculations based on data from Reserve Bank of India and Centre for Monitoring Indian Economy.

Episode I: Vertical lines are placed at "06/01/93" and "11/01/94."

As noted earlier, covered interest parity violations on the currency forward market are a source of information about the speculative views of private market participants. In a longer time-series beginning from 1993, the errors are typically negative, reflecting expectations of rupee depreciation.[13]

As figure 4 shows, the speculative views of the market swung into positive terrain at the start of Episode I. That is, private market participants appear to have believed that the rupee was a "market determined exchange rate," so the capital surge would lead to a rupee appreciation.

With the benefit of hindsight, we know that these expectations were incorrect. Nevertheless, this information about expectations shaped contemporaneous investment decisions of economic agents and thus the capital flows.

Figure 5 shows the time-series of RBI purchases of foreign currency during Episode I. Because the exchange rate was fixed, the data on currency intervention serve as a proxy for the capital inflow into the economy, for which monthly data are not available.

The similarity between the fluctuations of RBI purchases of foreign currency and the mispricings on the currency forward market is striking. This is consistent with my argument that such mispricings reflect the then prevalent currency views of private market participants, which would have shaped their decisions on short-term capital flows.

When a central bank engages in currency trading, the trading affects reserve money. If the capital account is highly open, the scale of currency trading required to distort the price on the currency market is larger. In the case of Episode I, the purchases of foreign assets by RBI led to a rise in net foreign assets from 20 percent of reserve money to 45 percent of reserve money.

As noted, the central bank has several options in sterilizing this impact. One would be the sale of government bonds that are part of reserve money. Data for open market operations in this period have not been released, but at the time of Episode I the bond market was highly illiquid, which may have placed constraints on the RBI's use of open market operations in sterilization. Another option would have been the weaker lever of not replacing maturing government bonds.

Figure 6 shows the growth of net foreign assets and net domestic assets in Episode I. Net foreign assets rose sharply, reflecting currency trading.

---

13. The "typical" configuration in India has been one where domestic inflation is higher than worldwide inflation, and the rupee has steadily depreciated.

FIGURE 5. **RBI Net Purchases of Foreign Currency, Episode I**

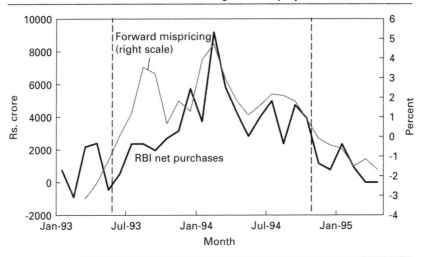

Source: Reserve Bank of India, *Monthly Bulletin,* various issues.
Note: 1 crore is 10 million.

FIGURE 6. **Central Bank Assets and Reserve Money, Episode I**

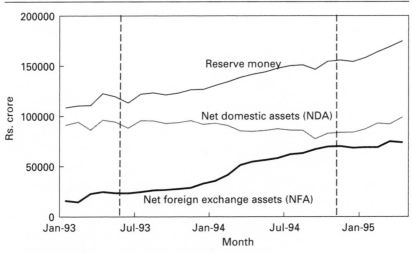

Source: Reserve Bank of India, *Monthly Bulletin,* various issues.
Note: 1 crore is 10 million.

TABLE 5. RBI Use of Reserve Requirements for Sterilization in Episode I

Date	Action
June 11, 1994	Cash reserve ratio raised from 14% to 14.5%.
July 9, 1994	CRR raised to 14.75%.
Aug. 6, 1994	CRR raised to 15%.
Oct. 29, 1994	CRR for foreign currency nonresident accounts raised from 0% to 7.5%.
Jan. 21, 1995	CRR for nonresident accounts raised from 0% to 7.5%; CRR for FCNR accounts raised to 15%.
July 17,1995	Conditions for overdraft facility to stock brokers to draw money from banks made more stringent.

Source: Reserve Bank of India, *Monthly Bulletin,* various issues.

Sterilization is "partial," in that NDA fell, but the drop in NDA was not as large as the rise in NFA.

By my dating, Episode I started in June 1993. One year into the episode, the growth of reserve money, M_0, had touched 30 percent. Beginning on June 11, 1994, RBI embarked on monetary tightening by using reserve requirements (see table 5). These policy decisions marked a reversal of RBI's earlier policy of phasing out the cash reserve ratio (CRR), which was seen as a component of financial repression and a tax on banking. The use of reserve requirements as a tool for currency policy has been observed to affect interest rates in many developing countries.[14]

Figure 7 summarizes the monetary consequences of the pegged exchange rate regime in Episode I. Reserve money grew at rates as high as 30 percent annualized. The RBI muted the impact of reserve money growth on M_3 growth through the use of reserve requirements. Interest rates during the period of the capital surge declined slightly, as may be expected if sterilization is incomplete. The decline can be attributed to the higher growth of money supply. Toward the end of the period, when reserve requirements were raised and as output growth in the economy picked up, short-term interest rates rose (figure 8).

To summarize, Episode I began as a surge in capital inflows. Although the exchange rate was fixed, the market expected the rupee to appreciate against the dollar. The months when the market expected rupee appreciation saw a sharp inflow of dollars. To prevent the appreciation, the RBI actively purchased dollars, pushing net foreign assets as a share of reserve money up from 20 percent to 45 percent. Because the bond market was relatively illiquid, the opportunity for doing open market operations was limited. Although net domestic assets growth slowed, the shift did not offset the sharp growth

14. Reinhart and Reinhart (1999).

FIGURE 7. Growth of Reserve Money and M_3, Episode I

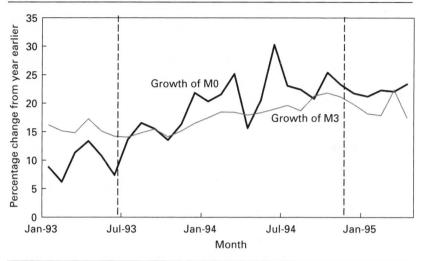

Source: Reserve Bank of India, *Monthly Bulletin,* various issues.
Note: M_3 includes currency, demand deposits, and saving accounts.

FIGURE 8. The 91-Day Treasury Bill Rate and the Cash Reserve Ratio, Episode I

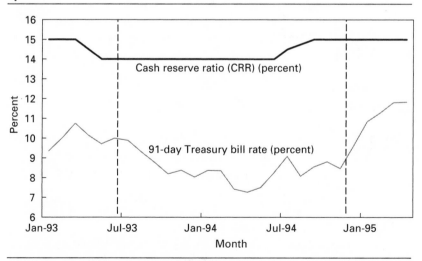

Source: Reserve Bank of India, *Monthly Bulletin,* various issues.
Episode I: Vertical lines are placed at "06/01/93" and "11/01/94."

TABLE 6. Balance of Payments in Episode II
Billions of U.S. dollars

Year	Current account balance	Net capital inflows	Change in net foreign assets
1999–2000	−4.7	10.2	2.26
2000–01	−2.6	9.0	6.14
2001–02	1.4	9.5	12.32
2002–03	3.7	13.3	17.50
2003–04	n.a.	n.a.	37.38

Source: Reserve Bank of India, *Monthly Bulletin,* various issues.

in NFA, and reserve money grew at rates as high as 30 percent. Short-term interest rates fell for roughly a year, reflecting only partial sterilization. After that, reserve requirements were tightened, and interest rates rose. At the same time, M_3 growth accelerated.

In Episode I, the near-fixed exchange rate during a period of large dollar inflows necessitated massive RBI currency trading, which led to rapid growth of reserve money and to a temporary reversal of the phase-out of CRR. Although RBI raised reserve requirements, M_3 growth accelerated significantly. The monetary tightening, which began in month twelve of this eighteen-month episode, led to a period of rising interest rates. Episode I was, hence, India's first experience with the loss of monetary policy autonomy.

The experience was particularly striking given that during Episode I, openness on the capital account was limited and the external sector was small relative to the Indian economy. Nevertheless, the logic of the impossible trinity was powerful enough that the pursuit of currency pegging led to an economically significant attenuation of monetary policy.

Episode II

Unlike Episode I, Episode II did not begin with a capital surge. In 2000–01 and 2001–02, India's capital account (table 6) was remarkably stable. From 1999–2000 to 2001–02, net capital inflows into India were roughly $10 billion a year. Instead, Episode II began with a dramatic shift in the current account— from a deficit of $4.7 billion (1999–2000) to a surplus of $1.4 billion (2001–02)—that affected the currency market.

Figure 9 underlines this difference between Episode I and Episode II. Early in Episode II, the current account turned from a deficit into a surplus; later, large capital inflows began.

FIGURE 9. Current Account Surplus and Capital Inflows in Episode II

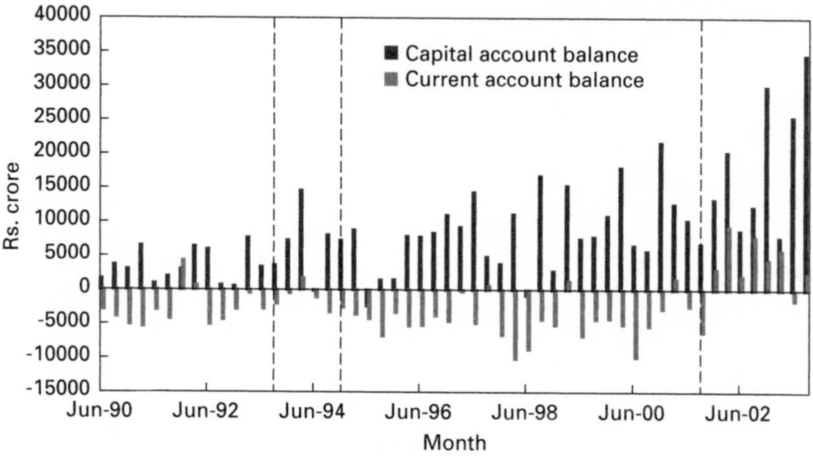

Source: Reserve Bank of India, *Monthly Bulletin*, various issues.
Note: 1 crore is 10 million.
Full Period: Vertical lines are placed at "06/01/93" and "11/01/94" and "08/01/01."

Currency Spot and Forward Markets

In Episode II, the central bank at first prevented the rupee from appreciating. In June 2002, however, with foreign exchange reserves exceeding $55 billion, the rupee was allowed to appreciate.

Figure 10 shows that currency expectations had started turning around even before the rupee began appreciating. After June, when the rupee was allowed to start appreciating, private forecasts of the rupee changed sharply.[15] After July, the observed forward premium was lower than the fair value, reflecting expectations of a currency appreciation.

Currency Expectations and Capital Flows

Foreign exchange reserves with the RBI started growing sharply in 2001–02, that is, before the increase in capital inflows in the following year. The implementation of the pegged exchange rate, coupled with the strengthening current account, led to a sharp increase in currency trading by RBI (figure 11).

15. There was a sharp decline in the forward premium during Episode II, from March 2003 onward. This partly merely reflected a change in the fair value (that is, changes in the 90-day rate in India and in the United States). However, there was also a widening of the gap between the two series, which is shown in figure 10, which shows the mispricing on the forward market.

FIGURE 10. **Expectations of Rupee Appreciation, Episode II**

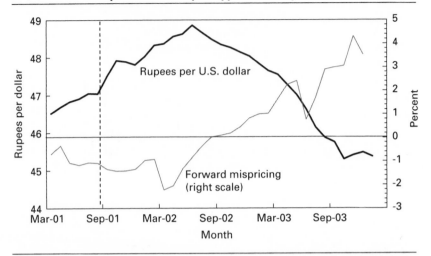

Source: Author's calculations based on data from Reserve Bank of India and Centre for Monitoring Indian Economy.
Episode II: The vertical line is placed at "08/01/01."

As noted earlier, apart from conveying expectations of the market, the error between the observed forward premium and its fair value also shows the arbitrage opportunity available to foreign investors. In December 2003, the error between the observed forward premium and its fair value exceeded 350 basis points.[16] A foreigner who bought GOI bonds and had a locked-in repatriation into U.S. dollars at a future date using the forward market was thus earning a return of over 350 basis points. Not surprisingly, the period after July 2002 witnessed a sharp inflow of dollars, both on the current and capital account (figure 9). The capital surge thus began in 2002–03.

Tools for Sterilization

In terms of sterilization, Episode II also differed from Episode I. This time, the institutional infrastructure for conducting open market operations was in place. By 2000–01, the turnover ratio in the bond market had risen to 100 percent, making the market sufficiently liquid for the

---

16. Strictly, the observed forward premium should be slightly higher than that computed from covered interest parity, owing to the country credit risk premium required for India exposure. However, the failure probability of a GOI bond on a 90-day horizon is likely to have been negligible through this period. Hence, this is unlikely to be an important issue in my analysis.

FIGURE 11. Currency Trading of the Reserve Bank of India, Episode II

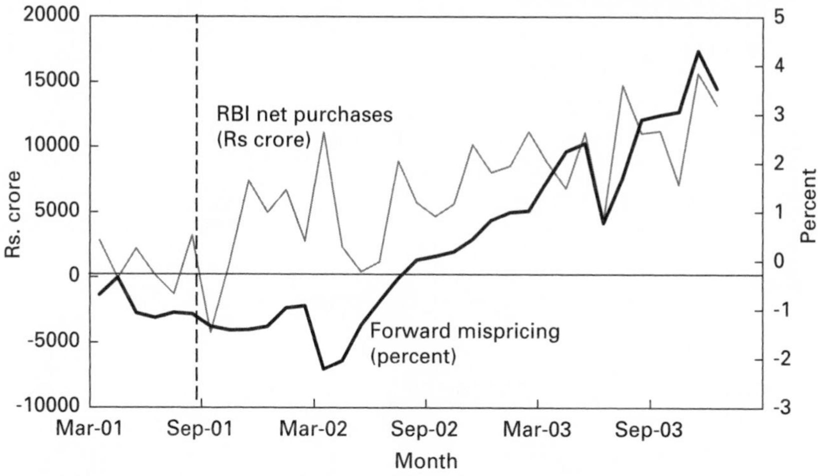

Episode II: The vertical line is placed at "08/01/01."

government to be able to conduct substantial open market operations (figure 12).[17]

Figure 13 shows that the increase in net foreign exchange assets was sterilized by open market operations. In a striking and inverse relationship, the months with high purchases of U.S. dollars were months with substantial sale of GOI bonds.

Table 7 shows that the stock of government bonds with the RBI was reduced to barely Rs. 274 billion, or about $6 billion, by March 2004. That same month, a new category of bonds, Market Stabilization Bonds, was designed to be used solely as an instrument of sterilization. The cash reserve ratio stood at 4.5 percent in March 2004. The existing legal framework prevents the CRR from being cut below 3 percent.

Money Growth

Because of sterilization, reserve money did not grow despite the increase in net foreign assets. Instead, the share of net foreign assets in reserve money increased sharply from 65 percent in 2001 to 78 percent in 2002 to more than 100 percent in January 2004. Figure 14 shows the sharp decline in the

17. While data are not available for the first episode, there is a consensus that the bond market was even more illiquid in the preceding years.

FIGURE 12. Turnover Ratio of Government Bonds, January 1993–February 2004

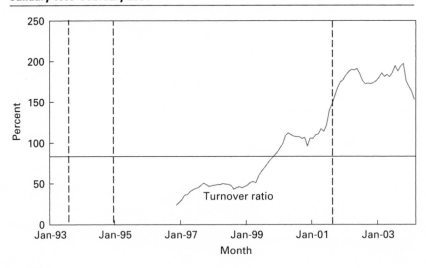

FIGURE 13. Currency Trading and Open Market Operations, 1993–2003

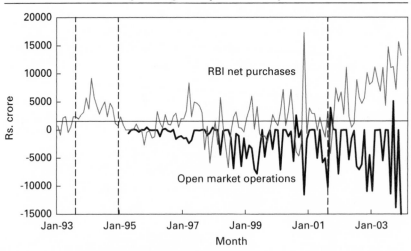

Source: Reserve Bank of India, *Monthly Bulletin,* various issues.
Full Period: Vertical lines are placed at "06/01/93" and "11/01/94" and "08/01/01."

TABLE 7.   Sources of Reserve Money, March 19, 2004

Source	Billions of rupees
Net RBI credit to government	274.83
RBI credit to banks	39.17
Net foreign exchange assets of RBI	4974.02
Government's currency liabilities to the public	72.40
Net nonmonetary liabilities of RBI	1277.73
Reserve money	4082.70

Source: Reserve Bank of India, *Weekly Statistical Supplement,* March 27, 2004.

share of RBI credit to the government in reserve money. As a consequence, growth of reserve money remained under control.

Because sterilization was possible through the simplest route, open market operations, it was not necessary for the RBI to reduce money supply through changes in reserve requirements, as in the first episode. On the contrary, CRR was steadily reduced.

As a consequence, the money multiplier increased in value during this period. Despite that, as a result of the large scale of sterilization and the low

FIGURE 14.   Net Foreign Assets, Net Domestic Assets, and Reserve Money of the Reserve Bank of India, Episode II

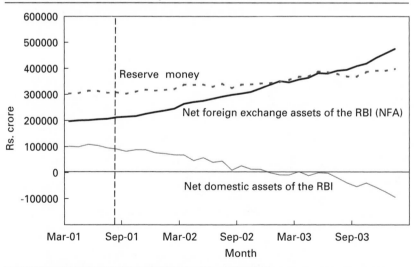

Source: Reserve Bank of India, *Monthly Bulletin,* various issues.
Episode II: The vertical line is placed at "08/01/01."

growth of reserve money, the growth of money supply remained under control (figure 15).

Stance of Monetary Policy

The unprecedented drop in interest rates that India experienced in Episode II reflects a combination of developments. The first was the partial sterilization of capital inflows, which open economy macroeconomics expects to lower domestic interest rates. The second was the steady pace of CRR reductions. And the third was slow output growth during this period, which led to slow growth in demand for capital.

Summary

To summarize, Episode II began as a surge in the current account. Capital account openness in this episode was greater than it was in the first episode. After June 2002, the rupee began to appreciate, the forward market forecasted further appreciation, and a capital surge began. Net foreign assets as a share of reserve money went up from an already high 70 percent to 120 percent. The RBI actively used the bond market for open market operations. The program for phasing out the cash reserve ratio stayed on course;

FIGURE 15. **Growth of Reserve Money and the Money Supply, Episode II**

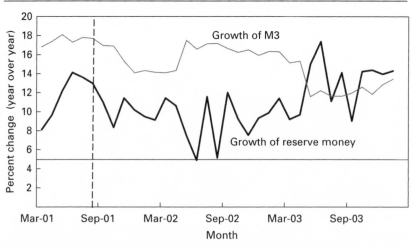

Source: Reserve Bank of India, *Monthly Bulletin,* various issues.
Note: M3 is the sum of currency, demand deposits, and savings accounts.
Episode II: The vertical line is placed at "08/01/01."

FIGURE 16. The 91-Day Treasury Bill Rate and the Cash Reserve Ratio, 1993–2003

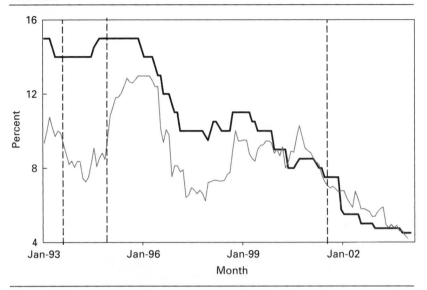

Source: Reserve Bank of India, *Monthly Bulletin*, various issues.
Full Period: Vertical lines are placed at "06/01/93" and "11/01/94" and "08/01/01."

the money multiplier kept rising. M_3 and M_0 growth did not accelerate. The CRR was steadily cut. Interest rates declined sharply through a combination of partial sterilization of capital inflows and a steady pace of CRR reduction.

In contrast with Episode I, when the rupee was kept largely fixed, Episode II saw a slow appreciation of the rupee. The daily volatility of the rupee-dollar exchange rate remained very low, at around 0.1 percent, and the rupee-dollar rate was not a random walk. Once the rupee started appreciating, currency expectations turned around, followed by a sharp inflow of capital, which may have been motivated by either covered interest parity arbitrage or currency speculation.

Comparing the Two Episodes

Did the stance of direct sterilization change in Episode I or Episode II? To address this question, I introduce slope dummies d_1 and d_2 for the two episodes. The model may now be expressed as follows:

(5)
$$NDA = \alpha_0 + \alpha_1 NFA + \alpha_2 d_1 * NFA + \alpha_3 d_2 * NFA$$
$$+ \alpha_4 IIPn + \alpha_5 CRR + \varepsilon_t.$$

Three α coefficients are of interest: α_1, the "normal" level of sterilization; α_2, which tests for a change in stance in Episode I; and α_3, which tests
for a change in stance in Episode II.

The estimated equation when slope dummies for the each of the episodes
are introduced is

(6)
$$NDA = -0.67 \ NFA + 0.039 \ d_1 * NFA - 0 \ 072 \ d_2 * NFA$$
$$(11.3) \quad (0.6) \qquad (3.4)$$
$$+ 701.9 IIPn + -517.7 \ CRR.$$
$$(10.8) \quad (0.5) \qquad R^2 = 0.93$$

The coefficient of NFA is estimated to be –0.67, suggesting that, in general, the RBI sterilizes roughly two-thirds of its trading in the foreign
exchange market. This result is broadly consistent with previous RBI study
results on sterilization by Sitikantha Pattanaik and Satyananda Sahoo that
RBI undertook large-scale but not full sterilization.[18]

The coefficient for the dummy for Episode II is negative and significant,
showing a change in the stance of the RBI. The coefficient for Episode I is
not found to be significant.

Table 8 summarizes the differences between the two episodes. In
some senses, the outcomes in Episode II were more benign than those in
Episode I. Given access to a more liquid bond market, the RBI was able
to sterilize to keep the monetary base under control. It could continue to
cut the cash reserve ratio steadily and prevent interest rates from rising.
In Episode I, the central bank's inability to use open market operations
led to a sharp rise in the monetary base that was followed by a rise in
the CRR and interest rates. So far Episode II has been spared these
developments.

Both episodes featured a tightly pegged exchange rate and partial sterilization of capital inflows. Hence, the surge in capital inflows was expansionary and helped to generate a drop in interest rates.

All through Episode I, a current account deficit offset capital inflows.
In contrast, in Episode II, the current account has turned positive.

The most important difference is that Episode I ended in 1.25 years,
while Episode II had been under way 2.5 years as of the time of writing.

18. Pattanaik and Sahoo (2001).

TABLE 8.   **Comparing Features of Episodes I and II**

Feature	Episode I	Episode II (thus far)
Initiation	Capital account	Current account
Exchange rate	Mostly fixed	Slight appreciation
Forward market	Expected appreciation	Expected appreciation
Net foreign assets as share of reserve money	21% → 45%	70% → 120%
Cash reserve ratio phase-out	Reversed	Unaffected
Bond market	Weak	Much improved
Use of open market operations	Data not disclosed	Strongly visible
M_0 and M_3 growth	Accelerated	Unaffected

How Episode II unfolds further is one of the most interesting questions in Indian macroeconomics today.

Conclusion

The reforms of the 1990s in India saw a significant opening of the current and capital accounts and created new challenges for the implementation of the pegged exchange rate regime.

Faced with a surge of capital inflows soon after the rupee had been made "market determined," the RBI followed a policy of a fixed exchange rate, which implied large-scale trading in the currency market. That trading led to an acceleration in reserve accumulation that was partly sterilized and that partly spilled over into an expansionary monetary policy. Despite the small capital account, pegging to the U.S. dollar led to an attenuation of monetary policy autonomy.

The second major episode of currency trading took place in 2000–01 with a surplus on the current account. Faced with pressure on the rupee to appreciate, the RBI traded extensively on the currency market. This time, the rupee-dollar exchange rate was not fixed. From June 2002 onward, RBI permitted some appreciation.

This appreciation might have been motivated by the RBI's desire to reduce the extent of trading required to implement the peg. However, as soon as the rupee started appreciating, currency expectations changed: instead of depreciating, the rupee was expected to appreciate. The full impact of a more open capital account, with a smaller set of capital controls, led to a surge of inflows on both the current and capital account. The following twenty months have been spent trying to curb the inflows, maintain the currency peg, and cling to monetary policy autonomy.

In conclusion, Episodes I and II both highlight the extent to which implementing a pegged exchange rate comes at the cost of autonomy in monetary policy. As India continues on the path of eliminating currency controls, it appears that implementing the pegged regime will increasingly crowd out monetary policy autonomy.

Comments and Discussion

Rajnish Mehra: Ila Patnaik presents an excellent case study of a country in the process of moving from a regime of strict capital controls to one with a relatively open capital account. The degree of capital account control in India is very different today from what it was in the early 1990s. As a measure of openness, the differential (premium) between the "unofficial" and official rupee-dollar rate has dramatically declined over the past fifteen years. It is now less than 0.5 percent.

The paper begins by citing convincing evidence that the rupee is pegged to the U.S. dollar. Taking Robert Mundell's 1961 insight into the "impossible trinity" as a starting point, Patnaik goes on to argue that the consequences of a pegged exchange rate are likely to be very different with and without capital controls. Specifically, a fixed exchange rate coupled with free capital movements implies a loss of monetary policy independence. Monetary policy in such a setting is entirely determined by the exchange rate system. As India continues on the path of eliminating currency controls, it appears that implementing the pegged regime will increasingly reduce its monetary policy autonomy.

Patnaik identifies two empirically significant periods during the years from 1990 to 2003, when there was a sharp increase in reserves: June 1993–November 1994 (Episode I) and August 2001–present (Episode II). The metric used is the observed increase in the gross reserves measured in dollars.

I will present a somewhat different perspective. Rather than focusing on the level of foreign reserves, I examine the data using the relative shares of foreign reserves to GNP. Here, figure 17, which displays the gross level of foreign currency assets, is the counterpart of figure 2 in the Patnaik paper, except that I have used data expressed in rupees, whereas her figure 2 is expressed in dollars. To the extent that the rupee-dollar rate has fluctuated, the figures are not affine transformations of each other. A potentially more useful way of looking at these data is captured by figure 18, which graphs

I especially thank John Donaldson and Barry Bosworth for their insightful comments. I am grateful to the participants of the India Policy Forum conference for a stimulating discussion. Finally, I thank D. K. Pant and K. A. Siddiqui for their meticulous research assistance.

FIGURE 17. Gross Level of Foreign Currency Assests

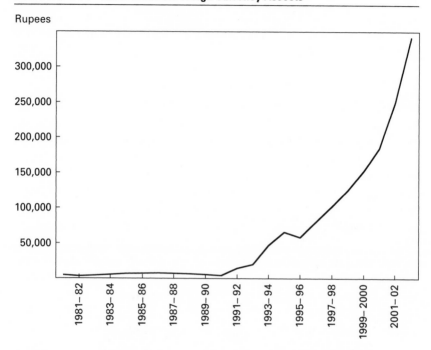

FIGURE 18. Foreign Currency Assests as Share of GDP, 1980–2003

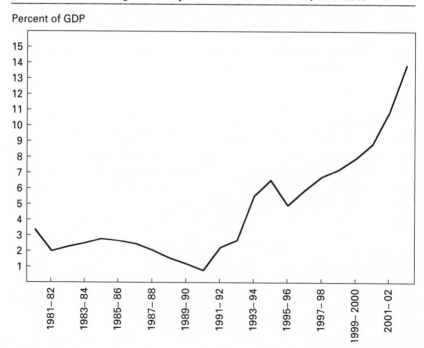

foreign currency reserves as a share of GDP.[1] It is clear that the post-1990 period is very different from the pre-1990 period. After 1990, two periods of rapid change in reserves stand out: 1990–95 (+5.75 percent of GDP) and 1996–present (+8.93 percent of GDP).

While these time periods do not correspond precisely to those identified in the paper, the exact periods are unimportant for the observations made there. Patnaik is agnostic about the costs and benefits of a fixed exchange rate regime and hence does not make a policy recommendation. In my discussion below I will address this and other related issues.

Clearly, a part of the post–1990 reserve accumulation is a rational response to the foreign exchange crisis in 1990–91. Demand for reserves held by Central Banks is similar to the demand for inventories and, like optimal inventory accumulation, depends on: *demand uncertainty* (+), *reorder costs* (+), *stock-out costs* (+), and the opportunity *cost of funds* (–).

Various heuristics have been proposed for optimal reserve accumulation. "Import cover," defined as twelve times the ratio of reserves to merchandise imports is one such heuristic. It is an ad hoc proxy for "demand uncertainty."[2] The RBI achieved this target in mid-2002.

The RBI attained this level of reserves by engaging in a classic sterilization policy—buying foreign currency and bonds and offsetting these purchases by issuing domestic bonds, while leaving M0 remarkably stable at about 15 percent of GNP, as shown in figures 19 and 20. (Figure 19 is the counterpart of figures 6 and 14 in Patnaik's paper, with the modification that I have expressed all quantities as a share of GDP.)

What are the costs of such a policy? This clearly depends on what is used as a benchmark for the "optimal level" of reserves. Using "import cover" as a measure of reserve adequacy, anything more than about 10 percent of GDP would classify as an unnecessary "cost."

Getting an estimate of this cost requires an estimate of the real interest rate differential between U.S. and Indian assets held by the RBI. As of mid-2002, about 95 percent of foreign assets held by the RBI were in the form of liquid assets. Since theoretically the equity premium is negligible, an estimate for the equilibrium risk free rate along a balanced growth path is

$$r = \rho + \gamma E(dc/dt),$$

---

1. These series appear to co-integrated.
2. "Stock out" costs are harder to measure but these became very real in the case of India in 1990–91. An adequate import cover will ensure that these costs are never incurred.

FIGURE 19. NFA, NDA, and MO as Share of GDP, 1981–2003

Percent of GDP

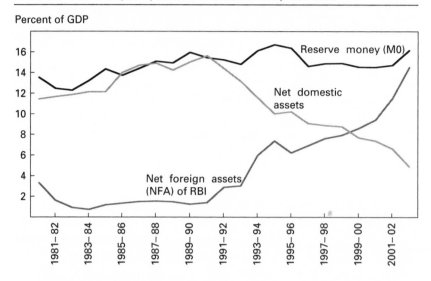

where r is the risk free rate, ρ is a measure of the time preference, γ is a measure of risk aversion, and $E(dc/dt)$ is the expected growth rate of consumption.

For India, a reasonable calibration results in a figure of about 6 percent. For the United States, this figure is about 4 percent. Thus an estimate of the cost of the current policy of holding reserves more than 10 percent of GNP, because of the differential yield on domestic and foreign assets, is between 0.1 percent and 0.2 percent of GNP annually. An additional cost arises because of the increase in the domestic cost of capital and the consequent effect on corporate investments and valuations. Although these numbers are not excessively large at the moment, the cost of such interventions can, and will, mount in the future. In addition, potentially more serious costs may arise because of the distortion of price signals, as discussed below.

Implications for Equity Markets

Without appreciation of the rupee, Indian stocks will appear progressively cheap by international standards. Furthermore, the inevitable speculation about future appreciation may result in an influx (and subsequent withdrawal) of portfolio investments by foreign institutional investors. This process may already be under way and could impose a major cost, as it could destabilize financial markets. A glimpse of such a scenario was seen in the sharp decline in the stock market on the day of the Congress-led gov-

FIGURE 20.   **Market Value of Equity as Share of GNP**

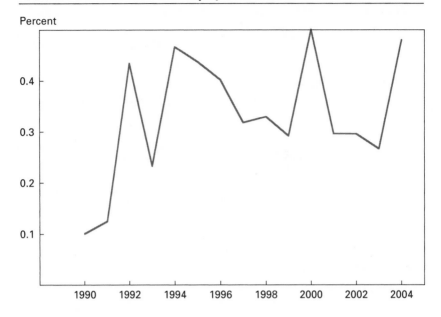

ernment takeover in May 2004. Figure 20 shows that Indian equity valuations are again comparable to their level during the "tech bubble," in sharp contrast to those in other developed capital markets, which are well below their pre-crash levels.

Issues of Interest Rate Differential Parity and Forward Contracts

Selective restrictions on different players can lead to undesirable outcomes and skewed incentives. For example, a situation such as that depicted in Patnaik's figures 4 and 10 cannot arise unless investors have some restrictions on them. For the price of forward contracts to be different from that implied by the interest rate differential parity, there have to be restrictions such that no player has the ability both to buy and sell local currency *and* at the same time to buy and sell foreign currency in unlimited amounts. Domestic players may have their ability to borrow foreign currency restricted, while foreign players have their ability to sell local currency restricted.

To illustrate, if the rupee spot price was 50 per dollar, the one-year forward price implied by the interest rate differential 55 per dollar, and forward price 53 per dollar, foreign investors, in the absence of any restriction, would avail themselves of a "free lunch": borrow dollars, buy rupees spot, and sell rupees one year forward.

The difference between the forward price and that implied by interest rate parity would be a function of two factors. The first is market expectations of future movements of spot. The second is the relative strength of the restrictions that tend to strengthen the currency forwards relative to spot (for example, foreign borrowing restrictions on domestic players) compared to the restrictions tending to weaken it (for example, restriction on foreign players' forward buying of domestic currency).

It is difficult to disentangle these two effects. However, I believe that the forward prices clearly contain some information, not necessarily about the future spot movements but about market players' expectations for such movements, and that these could be exploited by coalitions not subjected to restrictions. For example, in China (domestic) coalitions of individual agents subject to different partial restrictions are able, as a unit, to circumvent most restrictions.[3] Clearly this does nothing to enhance investor confidence.

Concluding Comments

There is a vast literature on the merits of different exchange rate regimes with which the reader is undoubtedly familiar. I believe that the operating characteristics of flexible exchange rate regimes have been shown to be superior to those of fixed rate regimes, particularly in the long run. Economic history reinforces these conclusions. Countries that had abandoned the gold standard typically recovered quicker after the Great Depression.[4] A disproportionate number of recent financial crises have involved countries with fixed rate regimes. (Stanley Fischer's 2001 Lionel Robbins Lecture at the London School of Economics elaborated well on these issues). Under floating rate regimes, price signals are less distorted, resulting in better investment and allocation decisions. In China, with big capital inflows and no currency float, the influx of capital has apparently driven the cost of capital for the "well connected" to zero. This may result in a misallocation of capital and provides no market discipline for industry to gradually become more competitive. I stress these aspects especially because in

---

3. These observations arise from my conversations with Chinese doctoral students in the United States.

4. Eichengreen and Sachs (1985).

developing countries there has been a tendency to emphasize the development of the domestic industry.

Recent actions of the RBI suggest that it wishes to avoid the financial excesses that many observers believe may shortly plague the Chinese economy.

Indira Rajaraman: Ila Patnaik contrasts two episodes of foreign exchange surge in India. Episode I covered a fifteen-month period during 1993–94. Episode II began in August 2001 and finally came to an end in May 2004. Patnaik contrasts the first, moved by a capital inflow surge, with the second, which she characterizes as having been initiated by a current account surge. She sees the attempt to hold the currency value stable in the face of the surge, using sterilization, as having seriously eroded monetary policy autonomy.

The evidence in favor of Patnaik's thesis that Episode II was precipitated by a current account surge is presented in table 6. Although it is true that the current account balance went from negative in 2000–01 to positive in 2001–02, at a time of stable net capital inflows, there were convulsions within the capital account in these two years that are not shown in the table. I present in table 9 the latest figures for the current and capital accounts over the years 2000–01, 2001–02, and 2002–03 (which differ from the unrevised figures in table 6 of the paper). It is clear that while investment inflows, both direct (FDI) and portfolio (FII), remained largely stable between 2000–01 and 2001–02, net loans from abroad declined very sharply indeed, with a sharp corresponding increase in banking capital. This increase in turn consists of two components, bank deposits in special schemes for nonresident Indians (NRI deposits) and other inflows through commercial banking channels. While NRI deposits remained stable over all three years, other commercial banking inflows increased sharply, from negative $1.5 billion in 2000–01 to positive $2.8 billion in 2001–02 and further to $5.4 billion in 2002–03. The increase in banking inflows by $4.3 billion in 2001–02 relative to the previous year was as large as the turnaround in the current account. In the face of this evidence, it is difficult to characterize Episode II as having originated in the current account. The commercial banking channel is subject to very detailed regulatory restrictions, as the author states quite clearly in discussing table 3. That table gives a misleading picture of the magnitude of these flows by comparing 2002–03 to 1991–92, leading the author to conclude that the most controlled component of capital inflows, through the banking channel, has shrunk over the years as a percent of GDP.

TABLE 9. Current and Capital Accounts, India, 2000–03
Billions of dollars

	Periods		
Current and capital accounts	2000–01	2001–02	2002–03
Current account	−3.59	0.78	4.14
Capital account	10.02	10.57	12.11
FDI	3.27	4.74	3.61
FII	2.59	1.95	0.94
Loans	4.25	−1.35	−3.83
Other capital	−0.91	−0.36	2.98
Banking capital	0.81	5.59	8.41
NRI deposits	2.32	2.75	2.98
Other	−1.51	2.84	5.44
Current account	−3.59	0.78	4.14
Merchandise	−14.37	−12.70	−12.91
Invisibles	10.78	13.49	17.05
Services	2.48	4.58	6.77

It is clear that banking inflows increased precipitously in 2001–02 relative to the previous year, and that in turn could only have been because they were *officially sanctioned and permitted*. Thus monetary policy, defined broadly to include the whole panoply of regulatory and administered instruments of control, could actually and quite justifiably be characterized as a major precipitating factor of Episode II.

This raises the larger issue of how independent the Reserve Bank of India is and has been in respect of the range of monetary policy instruments nominally within its control. As long as the central bank is subject to informal channels of direction from the executive arm of the government of the day, the autonomy of monetary policy is eroded at its very core. This is the central issue of concern. The RBI was clearly powerless to contain the surge at source through instruments that were well within its nominal control. Its inability to exercise those instruments remains the most serious erosion of autonomy, rather than the erosion of autonomy consequent upon an attempt to maintain currency stability in the face of a surge.

Finally, the composition of the current account surge shows that it was the result not so much of a merchandise turnaround as a surge in exports of services. Invisibles are a well-known channel for returning flight capital. It is entirely possible that the surge in exports of services could have occurred, in part if not entirely, in response to a fear of currency appreciation consequent upon the greater permissiveness toward banking capital inflows.

General Discussion

Several discussants pointed to the need to better understand the factors behind the change in the net flows of banking capital. Could the reserve bank control those flows? Some also doubted that banking capital should be viewed as more controllable than other types of capital flows. Sanjeev Sandal stressed the importance of distinguishing between permanent and transitory inflows. Allowing the exchange rate to appreciate would be more desirable if an inflow was believed to be permanent.

Rajnish Mehra pointed to the importance of determining why portfolio capital was flowing into India. Was the Indian equity market undervalued? If the exchange rate is fixed, foreign capital will continue to flow in until there is a perception that the costs to the central bank of maintaining the rate are excessive. At that point, there will be a large and sudden outflow. Vijay Joshi suggested a tax on capital inflows as an alternative to a more flexible exchange rate.

Kenneth Kletzer argued that policymakers should focus on the desired combination of fiscal and monetary policies, not the exchange rate. In the face of a partial liberalization of the capital account, monetary policy must chose between the interest rate or the exchange rate. Kletzer believed that India's continued focus on a fixed exchange rate would come at the cost of considerable interest rate volatility.

Ila Patnaik questioned the emphasis on capital inflows, since she believed that the pressure on the exchange rate resulted from a surplus in the current account. The capital inflows began only after a shift in exchange rate expectations that made it attractive to bet on rupee appreciation. She chose not to discuss in her paper what the exchange rate regime should be but whether it was still possible both to pursue an autonomous domestic monetary policy and to control the exchange rate.

References

Calvo, Guillermo A., and Carmen M. Reinhart. 2002. "Fear of Floating." *Quarterly Journal of Economics* 117 (2): 379–408.

Chinn, Menzie D., and Jeffery A. Frankel. 1994. "More Survey Data on Exchange Rate Expectations: More Currencies, More Horizons, More Tests." Technical Report 312. University of California, Santa Cruz.

Eichengreen, Barry, and Jeffrey Sachs.1985. "Exchange Rates and Economic Recovery in the 1930s," *Journal of Economic History* 49: 925–45.

Frankel, Jeffrey A., and Chudozie Okongwu. 1996. "Liberalised Portfolio Capital Inflows in Emerging Markets: Sterilisation, Expectations, and the Incompleteness of Interest Rate Convergence." *International Journal of Finance and Economics* 1(1): 1–23.

Frankel, Jeffrey A., and Shang-Jin Wei. 1994. "Yen Bloc or Dollar Bloc? Exchange Rate Policies of the East Asian Economies." In *Macroeconomic Linkage: Savings, Exchange Rates and Capital Flows*, edited by T. Ito and A. Krueger. University of Chicago Press.

Joshi, Vijay. 2003. "India and the Impossible Trinity." *World Economy* 26(4): 555–83.

Mundell, Robert. 1961. "The International Disequilibrium System." *Kyklos* 14: 154–72.

Patnaik, Ila. 2003. "India's Policy Stance on Reserves and the Currency." Technical report. ICRIER Working Paper 108.

Patnaik, Ila, and Deepa Vasudevan. 2000. "Trade Misinvoicing and Capital Flight from India." *Journal of International Economic Studies* 14: 99–108.

Pattanaik, Sitikantha, and Satyananda Sahoo. 2001. "The Effectiveness of Intervention in India: An Empirical Assessment." *Reserve Bank of India Occasional Papers* 22(1–3): 1–24.

Reinhart, Carmen M., and Kenneth S. Rogoff. 2002. "The Modern History of Exchange Rate Arrangements: A Reinterpretation." Technical Report 8963. Cambridge, Mass.: National Bureau of Economic Research.

Reinhart, Carmen, and Vincent R. Reinhart. 1999. "On the Use of Reserve Requirements to Deal with the Capital Flow Problem." *International Journal of Finance and Economics* 4(1): 27–54.

Schadler, Susan, Maria Carkovic, Adam Bennett, and Robert Kahn. 1993. "Recent Experiences with Surges in Capital Inflows." Occasional Paper 108. Washington: International Monetary Fund.

KENNETH M. KLETZER
University of California, Santa Cruz

Liberalizing Capital Flows in India: Financial Repression, Macroeconomic Policy, and Gradual Reforms

After decades of resistance to international economic integration, India has recently made significant progress in liberalizing trade and access to foreign investment, beginning in 1993. These policy changes reflect widespread concern that India's past inward orientation inhibited economic growth, especially in comparison with the developing countries of East Asia. The acceptance of economic liberalization and reform has allowed the relaxation of restrictions on foreign direct investment and inward portfolio capital flows. India retains tight controls on outward portfolio capital flows, restricting the access of residents to foreign capital markets and domestic markets in foreign currency–denominated securities. The relaxation of these controls and further liberalization of the capital account remain controversial policy issues for India.

The round of economic reforms in response to the balance-of-payments crisis in 1991 led to the publication of the Report of the Committee on Capital Account Convertibility (the Tarapore Report) in 1997.[1] This report, published by India's central bank, the Reserve Bank of India, outlined a plan for achieving full capital account convertibility. Ironically, the Tarapore Report appeared on the eve of the East Asian financial crises. It is not surprising that the absence of contagion effects on the Indian economy during these crises was taken as affirmation of the wisdom of India's controls on outward capital flows. Although capital account convertibility in developing countries became more controversial in the wake of the Asian crises, the liberalization of inward capital flows to the Indian economy has continued in the last few

1. Tarapore (1997).

years, and the prospects for further capital account liberalization in South Asia appear to be improving again.

The strong theoretical case for international capital market integration for developing countries has received increasing scrutiny in empirical research. Empirical studies support the view that financial crises in recently liberalized economies are mainly to blame for the ambiguous net gains from capital account convertibility in emerging market economies. They also reveal that domestic capital market development, together with prudent regulation and improved quality of governance in the public and the private sectors, raises the potential benefits from international financial integration and reduces the incidence and severity of crises. Crises in developing countries over the last two decades have repeatedly revealed that the transition from financial repression to financial liberalization often leads to a crash in an inadequately regulated financial system.[2] The financial crises of East Asia emphasized the important role of poor regulation and supervision of domestic financial activity and of public sector guarantees of banking sector liabilities in engendering crises in recently liberalized economies.[3] Crises elsewhere, notably in Latin America, attest to the importance of macroeconomic imbalances in provoking capital account crises that reverse economic growth.

A critical issue in the debate over capital account convertibility for India is this vulnerability of a previously financially repressed economy to capital account crisis after financial integration. Two related issues are, first, what policy reforms need to be undertaken before liberalizing controls on outward capital flows, and, second, what policy measures might protect an open Indian financial system from crisis. This paper considers the challenges to capital account liberalization for India and the vulnerability of the Indian economy to capital account and financial crises as it liberalizes. The level and growth of public sector debt and the state of the domestic banking sector are central issues. Many papers have focused on the need for fiscal reform and the growth of public debt in India, and others have surveyed in detail the challenges for banking reform.[4] The theme of this paper is how macroeconomic policy and the legacy of financial repression in the Indian

---

2. This observation by Díaz-Alejandro (1985) was particularly prescient for the 1990s.

3. Indeed, the banking crisis that began in the 1990s in one of the world's most advanced economies, Japan, attests to the impact that weak prudential regulation and supervision can have on any economy with a bank-centered financial sector (see Dekle and Kletzer, 2003).

4. Recent detailed analyses of fiscal policy in India include Pinto and Zahir (2003) and Singh and Srinivasan (2004). Bhattacharya and Patel (2004) provide a detailed analysis of financial sector reform and banking in India.

economy interact, and why they matter for sequencing economic reforms and for India's financial integration with the world economy.[5]

The first section of this paper places the international financial integration of the Indian economy in perspective by briefly reviewing the theoretical and recent empirical literature on the benefits of capital account liberalization for developing countries. The second section gives an interpretive overview of lessons learned from recent crises and the literature on capital account crises, to frame the discussion of the vulnerabilities of the Indian economy to future crises. The third section discusses India's recent liberalization of inward capital flows and the impact of these reforms. The fourth section, which is the core of the paper, discusses the vulnerabilities of the Indian economy to financial and balance-of-payments crises and the importance of the legacy of financial repression. The fifth section summarizes the risks for capital account convertibility, and the sixth discusses the appropriate policy sequence for liberalization. The last section concludes by arguing that India is in a good position to undertake further liberalization, and that efforts to meet the as-yet-unmet preconditions for capital account convertibility in India are desirable financial and macroeconomic policy reforms in their own right.

The Gains from International Financial Integration

The basic theoretical argument for the liberalization of capital flows is well known. Just as there are gains from contemporaneous trade in goods and services, so, too, should there be gains from trade in commodities across time. In neoclassical growth models, capital flows from relatively capital-abundant countries to a developing country allow higher rates of investment and economic growth in the latter, without a greater sacrifice of current consumption. Capital inflows allow the recipient country to invest and consume more than it produces when the marginal productivity of capital within its borders is higher than in the capital-rich regions of the world. Comparative advantage implies that capital-poor regions should borrow and that they should repay their debts only after their capital stock and output per capita have converged toward those in the advanced economies. By reallocating savings and resources toward the most productive investment opportunities, capital flows should result in welfare gains for both borrowers and lenders.

---

5. Roubini and Hemming (2004) also discuss the crisis vulnerability of the Indian economy, concentrating on comparisons with recent crisis economies.

The theoretical literature is not conclusive about the magnitude of the gains from this convergence of factor abundance ratios. Robert Lucas argues that neoclassical growth models imply larger international capital flows and higher rates of convergence of GDP per capita than are observed.[6] Pierre-Olivier Gourinchas and Olivier Jeanne, however, calibrate a simple neoclassical growth model and find welfare gains from free international capital mobility of between 1 and 2 percent of GDP for capital-poor countries.[7] This estimate is approximately the same as that for the benefits of eliminating economic fluctuations in developing countries. Convergent growth models that assume away domestic financial market imperfections might be expected to underestimate the impact of financial market integration.

Recent empirical research on economic growth finds that factor productivity differences dominate differences in factor abundance as a source of variation in growth rates of income per capita across countries.[8] Percentage differences in total factor productivity between advanced industrialized countries and developing countries such as India substantially exceed percentage differences in capital stocks. This empirical evidence suggests that the importance of liberalization for growth may well rest on the relationship between international financial integration and productivity growth. Countries that are financially integrated do attract more foreign direct investment, which can contribute to productivity growth through technology transfer and through spillovers of know-how from foreign-owned to other domestic firms. Interactions between financial integration and factor productivity could be more important than increasing net capital inflows.

Financial integration can raise welfare and accelerate growth by allowing the sharing of risk between savers and investors across borders. Access to international financial markets allows domestic residents to diversify their investment risks, possibly increasing their saving rates, and gives diversified foreign investors access to risky investment projects with high expected returns. Maurice Obstfeld develops an endogenous growth model with consumption risk that predicts recurrent gains from full international financial integration for developing countries of between 0.5 and 5.3 percent of GDP.[9] Eswar Prasad and coauthors survey studies of the gains from international risk diversification and estimate the gains separately for more and less financially integrated economies.[10] The estimated gains for the former (which today include India) exceed 2.5 percent of GDP, and those for the latter are about

---

6. Lucas (1990).
7. Gourinchas and Jeanne (2003).
8. For example, Hall and Jones (1999).
9. Obstfeld (1994).
10. Prasad and others (2003).

6 percent of GDP. These theoretical gains rely on financial integration reducing consumption volatility while allowing output volatility to rise. National consumption volatility typically exceeds output volatility. For India the volatilities of consumption growth and output growth were 5 percent and 3 percent, respectively, between 1960 and 1999, and the ratio of consumption growth volatility to output growth volatility rose from the 1980s to the 1990s.[11] Ayhan Kose and coauthors show that, contrary to the theoretical models, financial openness (as measured by capital flows) raises this ratio, whereas trade openness lowers it, for a large sample of developing countries.[12]

In recent years equity market reform in India has opened foreign access to investment in domestic stocks and given domestic firms access to foreign stock markets. Cross-country empirical studies find positive but small effects of international equity market liberalization on growth of income per capita. These studies also show that equity market liberalization reduces the volatility of both production and consumption.[13]

Capital account liberalization may also provide a means for forcing an end to financially repressive policies. The ability of financial resources to move across borders in response to current or anticipated future taxation of capital earnings or unsustainable fiscal or financial policies may impose discipline on public authorities, enhancing domestic financial intermediation and investment. The adverse impact of raising effective rates of taxation on financial intermediation and on the earnings of capital can be much greater in an open economy than in a financially closed economy. Access of domestic savers to international capital markets also limits the capacity of the public sector to borrow domestically at low rates of interest. International financial integration thus enhances the incentives for tax reform and deficit reduction.

Liberalization and the Risk of Crisis

The capital account crises in emerging market economies over the last decade have raised doubts about the net benefits of capital account liberalization for developing countries. In several cases the liberalization of financially repressed economies led to rapid capital inflows followed by sudden

11. From Kose, Prasad, and Terrones (2003).
12. Kose, Prasad, and Terrones (2003).
13. Bekaert, Harvey, and Lundblad (2002) and Henry (2003) find that liberalizing foreign equity investment raises growth of income per capita by between 1 and 2 percentage points a year over a five-year horizon. Bekaert, Harvey, and Lundblad also find that capital account liberalization raises consumption volatility and output volatility in emerging market economies.

reversals and financial crises. Such crises are costly for economic growth. However, in spite of the crises of 1997–98, compound growth rates of GDP per capita in most of the liberalized economies of East Asia, including South Korea, Malaysia, and Thailand, have exceeded that in India since India began its gradual reforms in the mid-1980s.[14] The experience with capital account liberalization indicates that its benefits depend upon the vulnerability of the recently liberalized economy to financial crisis. The vulnerability of India to capital account crisis following further liberalization is a central concern of this paper.

The debate on the empirical effects of capital account liberalization on economic growth is not very conclusive. How one constructs indicators of capital account openness can significantly affect the results, raising doubts about evidence that capital account liberalization fails to promote economic growth. Some provisional conclusions do emerge, however. Opening the capital account under conditions of significant macroeconomic imbalance reduces the net gains and raises the prospects of subsequent crisis. Countries tend to benefit from liberalization when they are better able to absorb capital inflows by virtue of having higher levels of human capital, more developed domestic financial markets, and greater transparency in financial and corporate governance and regulation. Measures of the prevalence of corruption also have a significant relationship with the benefits of openness. For example, greater transparency in governance and control of corruption in developing countries are associated with higher levels of inward foreign direct investment and larger growth benefits from that investment.[15]

Several causes of crises in emerging markets have been identified. The first is that fiscal and external imbalances, and in particular unsustainable fiscal policies, frequently lead to a rapid currency depreciation, which then precipitates a financial crisis. Under a pegged exchange rate regime, if monetization of public sector budget deficits occurs to a degree that is inconsistent with the pegged rate of depreciation, sooner or later a sudden outflow of international reserves will force abandonment of the regime. If unsustainable deficits and public debt lead market participants to expect them to be met by future monetization, it can lead to the collapse of a currency peg before the required monetary expansion

---

14. This statement is verified by data in Maddison (2003) and elsewhere.

15. These conclusions are drawn from Prasad and others (2003), who survey the cross-country evidence on capital account liberalization. Rodrik (1998) initiated the current debate by finding an absence of benefits from financial openness. Arteta, Eichengreen, and Wyplosz (2001) discuss the importance of how one measures capital account openness.

or fiscal reform begins. Anticipated future monetization of unsustainable government debt can also induce capital flow reversals and rapid reserve losses under a managed float when the central bank intervenes to resist depreciation.

Another aspect of financial crises in emerging market economies is the occurrence of banking crises. Although the association between banking and currency crises has received much attention because of the frequency with which they occur together, banking crises often follow financial liberalization without a currency crisis and are exacerbated by access to foreign capital inflows.[16] The deterioration of the banking system in a recently liberalized economy typically results from the combination of inadequate prudential regulation, supervision, and enforcement with an increase in the potential volatility of bank deposits. Not only are emerging market financial crises that involve banking crises costly in terms of economic growth, but costly banking crises following financial liberalization are not confined to developing countries or to pegged exchange rate regimes. The Japanese banking crisis that began in the 1990s was central to Japan's poor economic performance over the last decade, and regulatory forbearance is largely responsible for that country's banking sector problems.[17]

The fiscal impact of a banking crisis can contribute to a financial crisis. Contingent liabilities of the public sector are seldom counted in measures of the outstanding stock of public debt. Prominent among these liabilities in emerging market economies are public guarantees, explicit or implicit, on deposits in domestic banks and other financial intermediaries. In the East Asian crisis countries, deposits that had not been subject to deposit insurance or other explicit guarantees (for example, household deposits in finance companies in Thailand) were guaranteed by the government after the fact.[18] These contingent liabilities can be realized suddenly in the event of a crisis, leading to a sudden increase in public debt, which then justifies the expectation of future monetization. Further, the possibility that the government will bail out depositors creates a moral hazard in banking, as banks lose their incentive to protect against those losses that will be correlated

16. Kaminsky and Reinhart (1999) show that twin crises have larger effects on output on average than do banking or currency crises alone and that banking crises often precede macroeconomic crises.

17. Dekle and Kletzer (2003) discuss this argument and present a model for how a banking crisis can evolve without a fixed exchange rate. Bhattacharya and Patel (2002) propose an extension of Dekle and Kletzer's (2002) moral hazard model of endogenous banking crises under exchange rate pegs to India.

18. See Dekle and Kletzer (2002) for a survey.

with losses in the rest of the banking system. Under a pegged exchange rate, this extends to incentives to hedge against foreign currency risk, so that the banking system will choose to carry foreign currency–denominated liabilities against assets denominated in domestic currency.

Weak financial sector regulation and regulatory forbearance allow banks to accumulate net contingent claims against the government under deposit insurance schemes. Since experience shows that the forswearing of public sector bailouts of the domestic financial system is not credible, regulation of the financial system is necessary to ensure against the accumulation of off-budget contingent liabilities that become on-budget liabilities in the event of a crisis. The reduction or elimination of capital account restrictions expands the resource base from which domestic banks can draw in generating implicit contingent claims against the government. The relationship in emerging market economies between financial crises and poor financial regulation and prudential supervision implies the observation that better governance will result in lower macroeconomic volatility under an open capital account.

One of the major roles of financial intermediation is to transform short-maturity deposits into long-maturity investments. Banking necessarily involves the management of maturity risk, and a major reason for bank regulation is to ensure that this risk is adequately hedged. The problem of maturity mismatch also arises for other types of international capital flows to developing countries. Lending at short maturities arises endogenously in simple theoretical models in the presence of investment gestation lags. With such lags, a reversal of short-term lending can lead to a liquidity crisis even if the country could repay its debt in full if the reversal had not occurred. In such cases long-maturity loans are welfare improving, but short-maturity lending allows creditors to exit before the country is forced to restructure its debt. With short-term debt in the market, long-maturity debt becomes risky, and lenders can demand a large risk premium, leading debtors to borrow at short maturities.[19] Under strict capital controls, a capital account reversal is impossible, and so there is no gain from shortening maturities. The implication is that debt maturities are endogenous to capital account liberalization. This point extends to public sector borrowing with policy uncertainty. Capital account liberalization may shorten the maturity of government debt. Similarly, developing country governments face difficulty in issuing international debt denominated in domestic currency, if they can do it at all.

---

19. Rodrik and Velasco (2000) present a simple model demonstrating this.

The volatility of capital flows to emerging markets motivates the widespread view that foreign direct investment is a more desirable form of capital inflow. Direct investment generates equity claims in firms that match the maturity of the investment and are denominated in the same currency as the firm's sales and expenses. Foreign direct investment flows are less vulnerable to sudden reversals, and they bring with them the potential growth benefits associated with technology transfer. Foreign direct investors, however, can hedge against their domestic currency assets in the foreign exchange market, and, under a fully liberalized capital account, they can repatriate their earnings and liquidate investments into foreign currency if they anticipate a depreciation. Portfolio borrowing by domestic corporations and foreign direct investment are fungible to a significant extent. In the case of India, repatriation and liquidation of domestic investments into foreign currency by nonresidents are now unrestricted, so that reversals are possible.

One aspect of financial crises in emerging market economies has been a tendency to peg the exchange rate. Banking crises and fiscal crises can occur under floating exchange rates, but exchange rate pegs can greatly exacerbate such crises by diminishing the incentives of banks and corporations to hedge their foreign currency risk. The risk of an eventual large devaluation rather than of daily exchange rate fluctuations should also affect the incentives of foreign creditors to hedge risk and the maturity of the assets they acquire. There has been a strong tendency in India to resist exchange rate movements, just as Guillermo Calvo and Carmen Reinhart have observed in many other emerging market economies.[20] A managed float removes the implicit guarantees of a fixed exchange rate regime, but resistance to fluctuations can still create incentives, in countries with integrated capital markets, to take on currency risk that creates contingent liabilities for the government.

Capital account liberalization allows rapid reversals of foreign capital inflows that force the contraction of domestic consumption or investment, or both. The recent experience of crises in emerging market economies implies that sustainable fiscal policies, financial reform and regulatory improvement, and flexible exchange rate regimes reduce the likelihood of capital account crisis. Each of these reduces the incentives of foreign creditors and domestic residents to withdraw credit suddenly from an emerging market economy and reduces the potential exposure of the government to unhedged risk.

---

20. Calvo and Reinhart (2000).

Economic Reform in India and Capital Inflows

After independence, India had a comparatively unrestricted financial system until the 1960s, when the government began to impose controls for the
purpose of directing credit toward development programs. Over the 1960s,
interest rate restrictions and liquidity requirements were adopted and progressively tightened. The government established the state banks and by
the end of the decade had nationalized the largest commercial banks, giving authorities broader control over the allocation of credit across sectors
and enterprises. Through the 1970s and into the 1980s, directed credit took
a rising share of domestic lending, and interest rate subsidies for targeted
industries became commonplace. With the start of economic reforms in
1985, the government began to reduce financial controls by partly deregulating bank deposit rates. In 1988 these controls were reinstated, and the
government began to relax ceilings on lending rates of interest. Progressive
relaxation of restrictions on both bank deposit and lending rates of interest
and the reduction of directed lending had begun by 1990. The gradual
reduction in interest rate controls and directed lending proceeded throughout the 1990s.[21]

Until reforms began in the late 1980s, international capital inflows and
outflows were restricted by administrative controls or outright prohibition
on the purchase of foreign assets by residents, direct investment by foreigners, and private external borrowing. After India encountered balance-
of-payments difficulties in 1991, the authorities began to gradually relax
restrictions on inward capital flows and on currency convertibility for current account transactions. The rupee was made fully convertible for current
account transactions in August 1994, when the government agreed to the
obligations of Article VIII of the Articles of Agreement of the International
Monetary Fund. Trade liberalization also proceeded during the 1990s, with
tariff rates reduced substantially.

Over the last several years, restrictions on foreign direct investment,
portfolio borrowing, and foreign portfolio equity ownership have been
relaxed. This marked a significant turnaround from banning foreign investment and ownership to actively seeking it (at least in the case of direct
investment). Restrictions on the share of foreign ownership in enterprises

21. Demetriades and Luintel (1996, 1997) estimate the impact of banking controls on
economic growth in India and conclude that they had a negative effect. Their index of financial repression for India based on quantitative restrictions on financial intermediation
displays an upward trend from 1969 through 1984, followed by a decreasing trend beginning in 1988.

have been removed in most sectors, and the upper bounds for automatic approval of direct and portfolio investments have been progressively raised. The procedures for investments over these thresholds have also been simplified and clarified in an effort to reduce delays and arbitrary rulings. Foreign investment income is fully convertible to foreign currency for repatriation. External commercial borrowing has been relaxed but is regulated with respect to maturities and interest rate spreads.[22]

Effective restrictions remain on residents' acquisition of foreign financial assets and on currency convertibility for capital account transactions. Recently, these restrictions have been slightly eased to allow domestic residents to invest in foreign equities. It is also apparent that some domestic investment, notably in equity, by domestic residents is intermediated through Mauritius to take advantage of favorable tax treatment under India's reciprocal tax agreement with that country. Direct deposits and equity and bond holdings by nonresident Indians are subject to favorable treatment but remain small relative to the size of the financial sector.

The imposition of controls on cross-border financial transactions in the 1960s paralleled deep government intervention in domestic financial intermediation. As in other countries, the initial motivation for financial controls was to direct savings toward investment in certain targeted sectors as part of a development plan. State ownership of intermediaries, interest rate restrictions, foreign exchange controls, and directed credit schemes were all part of a policy of financial repression. The government also required, and continues to require, that banks hold a large share of their assets in public debt instruments. These instruments paid below-market rates of interest, imposing an implicit tax on financial intermediation and providing a significant source of revenue for the government. Indeed, the role of financially repressive policies evolved over the decades, from one of addressing development objectives to one of fiscal necessity, as it has in a number of other developing countries.[23] As analyzed below, liberalization has brought about a decrease in the fiscal revenue generated by financial repression.

Policies of financial repression impose an implicit tax on saving and investment, one that can vary widely by source and activity. Such policies can significantly distort and discourage capital accumulation and slow economic growth.[24] Capital controls distort different financial activities to

22. The Reserve Bank of India describes the restrictions on direct investment, portfolio investment, and bank borrowing in detail in its *Annual Report, 2002–03*, and *Report on Currency and Finance, 2002–03*.

23. This observation is documented by Fry (1988, 1997) and Giovannini and de Melo (1993), among others.

different degrees when they essentially eliminate private international financial transactions, as they did in India in the 1970s and 1980s. The selective imposition and partial relaxation of controls (the current situation in India) also distorts financial activities in myriad ways, which may not be recognized or easily quantified. Because the differences in rates of return to different saving and investment vehicles can have large effects on the size of financial flows, the microeconomics of capital controls can have macroeconomic impacts.

One of the focal points of inward capital account liberalization in India has been, as already noted, the encouragement of foreign direct investment. Total flows of foreign direct investment into India increased sixty-fold in dollar terms from 1990–91 to 2001–02, to over $6 billion, and inward portfolio investment was $2 billion in 2001–02. However, foreign direct investment inflows to India remained less than 6 percent of total foreign direct investment entering the developing countries of Asia in 2001.[25] The high growth rate of direct investment inflows is unsurprising given that it started from nothing in the late 1980s.

Comparisons with foreign direct investment in China are frequent in official reports and in the Indian press—evidence of concern that foreign direct investment is not higher. In 2001 foreign direct investment inflows were equivalent to 33.2 percent of GDP for China and 5.6 percent of GDP for India; flows per capita were four times greater for China than for India, and as a share of gross capital formation they were half as great in India as in China.[26] The proper concern may be that, although foreign direct investment is rising rapidly in India and the share of growth in the capital stock attributable to foreign investment is rising, total investment as a share of GDP remains much lower in India than in China. Impediments to investment and disincentives to save, along with remaining restrictions on access to foreign capital, might explain lower rates of foreign direct investment. Shang-Jin Wei argues that a lack of transparency in governance and control of corruption in China and India inhibits inward foreign direct investment to both countries.[27] Along with red tape, widely varying taxes and regulatory policies in India and across the states of India may inhibit foreign direct investment. Further, gradualism itself, by creating uncertainty about the timing and nature of future reforms, could make direct investment

24. There is a copious literature on this topic, which is surveyed by Fry (1988, 1997).

25. Data are from Reserve Bank of India, *Report on Currency and Finance, 2002–03*, tables 6.6 and 6.4.

26. Reserve Bank of India, *Report on Currency and Finance, 2002–03*, chapter 6.

27. Wei (1999).

riskier. The importance of fiscal and regulatory distortions is readily evidenced by the dominance of capital inflows from Mauritius in total inflows, alluded to above. Foreign direct investment inflows from Mauritius were three times as great as flows from the second largest contributor, the United States. Inhibition of direct investment by European, East Asian, and North American corporations is unlikely to raise capital inflows and technology transfer.

Vulnerabilities of the Indian Economy to Crisis

Three primary challenges for the success of capital account liberalization in India can be identified. The first is the high and rising ratio of outstanding public debt to GDP despite recent high growth rates of GDP. The second is the uncertain capacity of the domestic financial system to absorb foreign capital inflows. The third is the potential vulnerability of the financial sector to capital account crisis as capital outflows are liberalized. All three challenges have a common theme: the legacy of financial repression and its role in fiscal and financial policy in India. Recent economic reforms in the presence of financial repression provide the initial conditions for further liberalization and have implications for the potential vulnerabilities of the economy to capital account crisis.

Fiscal Sustainability

India's large outstanding public sector debt and large primary deficits of the central and state governments have led to frequent calls for fiscal reform to facilitate deficit reduction. Compared with those of other emerging market economies, India's external sovereign debt is low in proportion to GDP. However, domestic public debt is high, so that the total outstanding public debt exceeds 80 percent of GDP. The combined deficits of the central and state governments are about 10 percent of GDP, and the combined primary deficit, which excludes interest payments, averaged 3.5 percent of GDP from 1997 through 2002. Table 1 shows the combined central and state debt and deficit ratios since the early 1990s. The short-lived fiscal retrenchment during the middle of the 1990s and the rising deficits of the last several years are both apparent.

The pattern of public debt accumulation for India suggests that the current financing path of public expenditure may not be sustainable over a long horizon. Indeed, this possibility has been noted frequently by others.[28] For

TABLE 1. Consolidated Debt and Deficits of Central and State Governments
Percent of GDP

Fiscal year	Public debt	Gross deficit	Primary deficit	Interest payments
1990–91	64.0	9.8	5.2	4.6
1991–92	62.9	7.3	2.4	4.9
1992–93	62.5	7.2	2.2	5.0
1993–94	64.6	8.5	3.4	5.2
1994–95	62.4	7.4	2.0	5.4
1995–96	60.3	6.8	1.6	5.2
1996–97	58.5	6.6	1.3	5.3
1997–98	60.3	7.5	2.2	5.3
1998–99	61.3	9.3	3.8	5.5
1999–2000	64.0	9.8	4.0	5.9
2000–01	67.0	9.7	3.8	6.0
2001–02	73.0	10.6	4.1	6.4
2002–03	77.5	9.8	3.2	6.8

Sources: Reserve Bank of India, *Handbook of Statistics on the Indian Economy, 2002*; and Reserve Bank of India, *Bulletin, June 2004*.

example, Montek Ahluwalia points out that the growth of public debt in India has equaled or exceeded that in Russia, Turkey, and Argentina before those countries' recent crises.[29] Willem Buiter and Urjit Patel formally tested and rejected the hypothesis that India's public debt was sustainable over the earlier period of rising public sector deficits that parallels the current increase.[30] However, the recent high growth rates of real GDP and low international real rates of interest can change even back-of-the-envelope calculations. Nouriel Roubini and Richard Hemming argue that the current level of public debt is sustainable and will continue to rise toward a steady state.[31] However, their conclusion is based on the assumption that the international macroeconomic environment of the past few years is a good approximation of the long-run environment for fiscal policy sustainability—an assumption that is probably inappropriate.

The sustainability of public debt is typically assessed by a simple calculation of the dynamics of debt using recent growth rates, interest rates, and primary public sector balances. The standard calculation uses the public sector flow budget identity, which equates the change in the debt-to-GDP ratio to the sum of the debt-to-GDP ratio, multiplied by the difference between the real interest on public debt and the growth rate of real GDP, and the pri-

28. Recent examples include Pinto and Zahir (2003), Roubini and Hemming (2004), and Srinivasan (2002).
29. Ahluwalia (2002).
30. Buiter and Patel (1997).
31. Roubini and Hemming (2004).

TABLE 2. **Real Interest Rates and Interest Payments on Government Debt**
Percent

Fiscal year	Weighted-average real interest rate[a]	Ratio of interest payments to debt		Real annual GDP growth
		Deflated by wholesale price index	Deflated by GDP deflator	
1990–91	1.1	−3.2	n.a.	6.0
1991–92	−1.9	−5.9	n.a.	2.1
1992–93	2.4	−2.0	1.4	4.2
1993–94	4.2	−0.4	2.2	5.0
1994–95	−0.6	−3.9	−1.1	6.8
1995–96	5.7	0.5	1.8	7.6
1996–97	9.1	4.5	−2.4	7.5
1997–98	7.6	4.4	2.2	5.0
1998–99	6.0	3.1	1.5	5.8
1999–2000	8.5	6.0	4.1	6.7
2000–01	3.8	1.8	2.9	5.4
2001–02	5.8	5.2	5.2	4.0
2002–03	n.a.	4.3	6.2	4.7

Sources: Reserve Bank of India, *Handbook of Statistics on the Indian Economy, 2002*; and International Monetary Fund, *World Economic Outlook*, 2004.
a. Weighted average of annual interest rates on central government debt, deflated by the wholesale price index.

mary surplus of the public sector (as a proportion of GDP). Table 2 reports real interest rates on domestic public debt in India and real GDP growth. The first column reports average real interest rates for internal government debt, calculated as the difference between the weighted-average nominal interest rate for central government securities and the wholesale price inflation rate.[32] These interest rates are representative of other indices of interest rates on central and state public debt reported by the central bank. The second column reports a similar calculation using the ratio of interest payments to outstanding domestic public debt. The third column repeats this calculation using data from the IMF *World Economic Outlook* database, also used by Roubini and Hemming. This column, therefore, reports the real interest rate calculated using the GDP deflator. The fourth column reports the real GDP growth rate calculated from the same source.

The current general government debt of about 82 percent of GDP and the primary deficit of about 3.6 percent of GDP are sustainable only if the growth rate of real GDP exceeds the real interest rate on government debt

32. The calculations in this column are reported by Mohan (2002) and use data from Reserve Bank of India, *Handbook of Statistics on the Indian Economy, 2002*.

by 4.4 percent. This is clearly not the case. For the calculated real rates of interest reported in the first column of table 2, the growth-adjusted interest factor (the real interest rate minus the real growth rate) averages 0.95 percent for the fiscal years 1997–98 through 2000–01. This implies that the debt-to-GDP ratio would remain constant if the primary balance improved from a deficit of 3.6 percent of GDP to a surplus of almost 0.8 percent of GDP. The fiscal gap, which is the amount by which the primary surplus must rise to keep the debt-to-GDP ratio constant, equals 4.4 percent of GDP using recent weighted averages of interest rates on central government debt. This standard calculation leaves out seignorage revenue that accrues to the government. India's monetary base grew at an average annual rate of 10 percent from 1997 through 2002. Seignorage revenue as a fraction of GDP during this period averaged about 1.4 percent (see table 4 below for data and sources). This revenue—the revenue realized from expansion of the monetary base to meet growth and modest inflation—should be added to the primary surplus of the consolidated public sector. This reduces the estimate of the fiscal gap to about 3 percent, and the implied growth rate of the public debt-to-GDP ratio equals 3.6 percent a year. Using these interest rates, current fiscal and monetary policies are not sustainable.

The alternative of using the ratio of interest payments to outstanding debt and deflating yields an estimate of the real rate of interest that is 1.9 percentage points lower than the average growth rate over the period from 1997 through 2003. This implies that a debt-to-GDP ratio of 82 percent is sustainable if the primary balance improves by 2 percent of GDP to a deficit of 1.6 percent. When seignorage revenue is again subtracted, these interest rate estimates imply that an improvement in the primary surplus by 0.6 percent of GDP is needed to stabilize the debt-to-GDP ratio at 82 percent. The excess of the growth rate over the interest rate also implies that the debt-to-GDP ratio will continue to rise until it reaches 116 percent of GDP.[33]

A simple lesson from the public sector budget identity is that a positive debt-to-GDP ratio and a positive primary deficit are sustainable only if the long-run real rate of interest on government debt is less than the real growth rate of the economy. This condition will hold in a dynamically efficient economy only if the interest rate on government debt is less than the opportunity interest rate, adjusted for risk. In this case the government imposes an implicit tax on its creditors. The difference between the opportunity

---

33. Roubini and Hemming (2004) use the negative growth-adjusted interest rate term and calculate debt sustainability for several standard scenarios for primary deficits and GDP growth.

interest rate and the public sector borrowing rate, multiplied by the outstanding public debt, equals the revenue collected through this implicit tax. Therefore, assessing long-run sustainability using an approximation of the long-run real interest rate that is less than the long-run growth rate of the real economy means that a portion of tax revenue is counted in the interest on government debt and not in the primary surplus. Such implicit revenue is approximated below.

The two calculations clearly indicate that the choice of the long-run real rate of interest, even if the recent rapid growth of the Indian economy is expected to continue, is critical and prone to error. It is not particularly realistic to assume as permanent at least two characteristics of the current interest rates paid on government debt in India: first, global real rates of interest are at historically very low levels, and second, India enjoys concessional terms on a significant share of its foreign public debt.[34] Excluding interest on foreign debt from these calculations and using yields on public debt issued domestically may give a better estimate of future public debt sustainability than those implied by using aggregate data. An important characteristic of countries suffering repeated macroeconomic crises is the volatility of fiscal policy. The primary balances for India shown in table 1 do not display very much historical volatility, but the rising trend of the primary deficit as a share of GDP makes a sufficient case for fiscal adjustment.

Moreover, the budget balances for the combined central and state governments do not give a complete accounting of public sector liabilities. In addition to unfunded pension liabilities and various contingent liabilities, the government guarantees debt issued by unprofitable public enterprises. The largest of these losses are those of the State Electricity Boards. Inclusion of these ongoing additions to public sector liabilities increases the consolidated deficit by between 1.0 and 1.5 percent of GDP.[35] Additional explicit debt guarantees include those on borrowing through special-purpose vehicles for irrigation projects, and lending by banks and other nonbank financial institutions under state guarantees. The total contingent guarantees of the state and central governments are estimated to amount to 11.5 percent of GDP for 2002–03.[36] Brian Pinto and Farah Zahir report that pension liabilities for both the central and state governments are growing at

---

34. Reynolds (2001) also uses a simple growth model to argue that India took advantage of low real interest rates to sustain the growth of public debt after 1996.

35. This estimate is from Pinto and Zahir (2003) based on data from the Planning Commission.

36. Reserve Bank of India, *Annual Report, 2002–03*, table 4.16.

TABLE 3. Gross Private Capital Formation
Percent of GDP

Year	Total	Private
1991	27.8	14.1
1992	24.2	13.9
1993	23.4	15.0
1994	22.8	15.6
1995	21.3	16.7
1996	20.6	18.3
1997	18.8	17.7
1998	17.2	16.6
1999	16.4	16.5
2000	15.9	17.0
2001	15.2	17.2
2002	15.0	17.3
2003	14.5	17.9

Source: International Monetary Fund, *World Economic Outlook*, 2004.

approximately 20 percent a year, although current pension expenditure is only about 2 percent of GDP.[37] The implicit and explicit deposit insurance guarantees of the public sector can be estimated by the net nonperforming assets of the banking sector after loan-loss provisions are subtracted, and are less than 2 percent of GDP.[38]

The large public debt and large public sector budget deficits, in the presence of tight restrictions on international capital outflows from the private sector, suggest that domestic capital formation is being crowded out. Table 3 reports the ratios of gross private capital formation and of total (private and public) gross capital formation to GDP for India since 1990. The table shows that private capital formation has increased modestly, although public investment has contracted substantially. The decrease in public investment has a counterpart in the increase in the share of interest payments in public expenditure. Because inward foreign investment rose as restrictions on financial inflows were relaxed over the past several years, the very slight increase in the share of private capital formation in GDP may reflect increasing crowding out by public sector borrowing on top of the decline in the share of public infrastructure spending.

37. Pinto and Zahir (2003).
38. Data from Reserve Bank of India, *Report on Trend and Progress of Banking in India, 2002–03*.

Fiscal Consequences of Gradual Reforms

As part of its financial sector reforms over the past decade, the government has progressively relaxed interest rate ceilings, reduced the requirements of commercial banks to invest in government debt, and actively encouraged a domestic market in government debt instruments. These reforms have been part of the progressive reversal of the financially repressive policies adopted during the 1960s.

By the 1980s financial repression had become an important means of financing public expenditure in India. The imposition of reserve requirements on commercial banks has played an important role in raising public resources by implicitly taxing domestic financial intermediation. The cash reserve ratio and the statutory liquidity ratio impose minimum levels for holdings of cash assets and public sector interest-bearing debt, respectively, as proportions of deposits in scheduled commercial banks. These ratios have varied significantly over time, revealing their use as active measures of monetary and fiscal policymaking, and both have been reduced in recent years (figure 1). Interest rate restrictions were also substantially reduced in the 1990s, and government debt now trades on the domestic financial market. These policy reforms imply that the implicit rate of taxation on financial intermediation has eased since 1993. Although the statutory liquidity ratio was set at 25 percent of deposits, the scheduled commercial banks held over 40 percent of their deposits in approved public sector securities at the end of 2003. Together, the scheduled commercial banks held over 60 percent of the consolidated central and state government debt at the end of 2002. Additional amounts are held by nonbank financial intermediaries and by the Life Insurance Corporation of India, which alone held an additional 20 percent of government debt, equal to more than 70 percent of its assets, at the end of 2002. Two institutions, the State Bank of India and the Life Insurance Corporation of India, together held 52 percent of government debt in 2003.[39] These holdings indicate a significant preemption of private sector loan resources by the government.

Policies of financial repression allow governments to finance public sector budget deficits through domestic credit creation at lower rates of inflation than would be possible in a financially liberalized economy. Even in the absence of interest rate ceilings and the presence of market-determined yields on primary issues of government debt, capital controls

---

39. Data reported in this paragraph are from the Reserve Bank of India, *Report on Trend and Progress of Banking in India, 2002–03;* and *Handbook of Statistics on the Indian Economy, 2002.*

FIGURE 1. Cash Reserve Ratio and Statutory Liquidity Ratio, 1980–2003

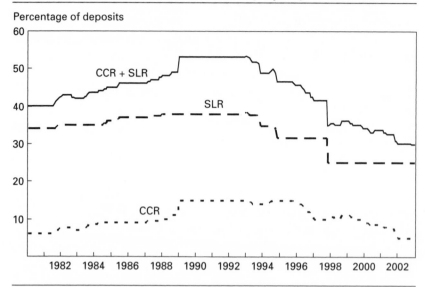

Percentage of deposits

Source: Data from Reserve Bank of India, *Handbook of Statistics on the Indian Economy, 2002,* table 41.

provide the public sector with a captive capital market and allow the government to pay interest rates on its debt that are below the opportunity rate. The fact that banks and other financial institutions hold more public debt than required by statute should not be taken as evidence that financial repression no longer plays a role in public finance. The commercial banking sector is dominated by government-owned banks (which hold about 80 percent of deposits), and regulations mandate holdings by other financial entities. The Reserve Bank of India reports that real rates of interest for fiscal years 1996–97 through 2001–02 averaged 6.8 percent for the central government, 12.5 percent for other borrowers, and 1.9 percent for depositors.[40] Although positive real rates of interest on public sector borrowing reveal the effects of financial liberalization, the high real rates of interest facing large corporate investors and the significant interest rate differential favoring government debt imply that intermediation remains hampered.

There has, however, been a decline in the collection of implicit government revenue from financial repression. Table 4 reports calculations of public sector revenue from domestic public borrowing through financial

40. Mohan (2002).

TABLE 4.   **Estimated Public Sector Revenue from Financial Repression**
Percent of GDP

| Year | Implicit interest subsidy | | Seignorage |
	On consolidated public debt	On central government debt	
1980	2.60	2.28	2.00
1981	8.36	7.18	0.92
1982	4.57	4.04	1.12
1983	6.99	6.14	2.68
1984	13.98	12.24	2.53
1985	2.16	1.91	1.06
1986	7.42	6.60	2.13
1987	0.90	0.81	2.45
1988	10.69	9.53	2.25
1989	10.27	9.13	3.01
1990	6.45	5.71	1.79
1991	27.50	24.22	1.79
1992	0.82	0.72	1.51
1993	11.87	10.44	3.25
1994	−0.80	−0.70	3.02
1995	7.25	6.31	2.12
1996	0.29	0.25	0.40
1997	5.04	4.36	1.74
1998	4.32	3.69	1.89
1999	−0.71	−0.59	1.10
2000	2.88	2.40	1.08
2001	−0.39	−0.33	1.51
2002	−3.18	−2.66	1.31

Sources: Author's calculations using data from International Monetary Fund, *International Financial Statistics*, 2004; World Bank, *Global Development Finance*, 2003; Reserve Bank of India, *Handbook of Statistics on the Indian Economy, 2002*; and Reserve Bank of India, *Annual Report*, 2002–03.

repression in India for the period 1980–2002, after estimating the interest subsidy realized by the government on its borrowings on domestic financial markets. This subsidy decreased significantly after 1991, leading to the decline in revenue from financial repression shown in the table.[41] The implicit subsidy is calculated by estimating the difference between the average interest rate for government debt issued in India in rupees and the average opportunity interest rate for government borrowing from abroad. The opportunity interest rate is estimated by first dividing external interest payments on nonconcessional long-term debt by the sum of nonconcessional long-term debt and new disbursements. This gives the opportunity interest

41. The estimates revise and update those made by Kletzer and Kohli (2001). The methodology is adapted from Giovannini and de Melo (1993).

rate for government borrowing in dollar terms. Actual rupee depreciation (from end of year to end of year) is used to convert this average dollar interest rate to a rupee-equivalent rate under the assumption that uncovered interest parity holds ex post. The interest rate on domestic government debt is calculated by dividing current-year interest payments by current-year outstanding government debt. The estimated interest rate differential is then multiplied by the ratio of consolidated central and state government debt to GDP and by the ratio of central government debt alone to GDP to obtain the numbers in the first and second columns, respectively, of table 4.

Revenue from financial repression also includes the inflation tax and a portion of traditional seignorage revenue. The real capital losses to the holders of government bonds due to inflation are included in the estimates of the real interest subsidy for public debt issued in rupees, shown in the first two columns of table 4. This includes the anticipated inflation tax, to the extent that interest rates are controlled, as well as the unanticipated inflation tax. The impact of the inflation tax is illustrated by the effect of the depreciation of the rupee in July 1991 on revenue from financial repression. Seignorage revenue is reported in the last column of table 4. This is calculated as the change in reserve money as a ratio to GDP. Seignorage revenue, however, includes revenue from the growth of output and financial deepening along with revenue generated by the imposition of reserve requirements on the banking system.

The estimates reveal an important trend. Revenue from financial repression clearly fell with the advancement of financial reform beginning in 1993. Average revenue from the implicit subsidy to the government for 1980–93 was about 8.2 percent of GDP. Average revenue from the estimated interest differential fell to 1.6 percent of GDP for 1994–2002. These calculations, however, cannot account for any missing currency risk premium. Another way to look at the interest differential between the external opportunity cost and the domestic cost of public borrowing is to compare international interest rates with rates on government-guaranteed bond issues, such as the Resurgent India Bonds issued by the State Bank of India in 1998 to attract capital inflows from nonresident Indian investors. The interest spread on the dollar-denominated portion of these bonds over five-year treasuries was 2.49 percentage points, despite a reported lower spread over the London interbank offered rate (LIBOR) for comparable bonds issued by similarly rated emerging market countries.[42]

---

42. Reserve Bank of India, *Report on Currency and Finance, 2002–03*, p. 170.

Seignorage revenue has also declined in recent years; the average over the entire period was slightly less than 2 percent of GDP, but it was only 1.4 percent of GDP over the period from 1997 through 2002. These declines coincided with a fall in actual inflation, but they also suggest a decline in repressed inflation as financial restrictions were relaxed. The decrease in public sector revenue from financial repression is large and indicates significant progress in financial policy reform.

The decline in revenue from financial repression followed financial sector reforms that have come in advance of (as yet unaccomplished) fiscal reforms needed to broaden the tax base, improve tax compliance, and reduce tax distortions. The significant reduction in revenue from the taxation of financial intermediation, a highly distortionary source of revenue, without replacement through less distortionary taxation has contributed significantly to the growth of the general government budget deficit and the rise in the public debt-to-GDP ratio. The rise in domestic borrowing by the government (perhaps coupled with incentives for banks to invest in government securities), however, continues to contribute to the repression of financial intermediation and capital formation. Completing the task of reducing financial repression will require fiscal reform, because the substantial holding of government debt by financial intermediaries not only crowds out private investment, but also inhibits the efficient matching of saving with investment. The capacity of banks to evaluate and monitor borrowers, diversify investment risk, and diversify maturity structure risk between assets and liabilities is underutilized when bank assets are dominated by public debt. The creation of a public debt market in India has been insufficient, simply because the participants in this market are overwhelmingly state-owned financial intermediaries.

Financial repression is important for the growth of public debt in India because capital controls allow the government to avoid monetizing its deficits by borrowing in a closed capital market. Liberalization of the capital account would reduce the capacity of the government to preempt domestic financial savings and realize a real interest rate below its opportunity interest rate. This could worsen the public debt problem by raising the real interest rate on public debt as the government relaxes its hold on a captive domestic institutional market for that debt. India's increasing public debt-to-GDP ratio must eventually lead either to fiscal reform to close the fiscal gap, or to monetization of public sector budget deficits, or a combination of the two. Liberalization of international financial transactions will raise pressure for inflationary monetary growth and make the need for fiscal reform more urgent.

Vulnerabilities of the Financial System

The legacy of financial repression hampers domestic financial intermediation and raises the vulnerability of the banking system to crisis as international financial integration increases. Policies of financial repression have included the preemption of assets by government borrowing, interest rate controls, and directed lending to priority sectors. The scheduled commercial banks, which dominate financial intermediation in India, hold a large share of their assets in public sector debt, as already noted, and in loans made to government-mandated priority sectors. At the end of March 2003, gross nonperforming assets of the commercial banks equaled 9.5 percent of bank advances, according to the Reserve Bank of India. Nonperforming assets exceeded banks' provisions against losses on those assets by 4.5 percent of bank advances. Directed credit to priority sectors accounted for about 31 percent of commercial banks' assets, but about 40 percent of their nonperforming assets.[43] In addition to the concentration of government debt in the assets of banks and nonbank financial intermediaries, directed credit leaves the financial system of India with limited resources for investment in growing industries.

Nonperforming assets of the banking system net of loan-loss provisions are not large in proportion to GDP (about 2 percent) compared with those of the post-crisis countries of East Asia, but neither are these a modest share of bank assets net of government debt. Further, Saugata Bhattacharya and Patel argue that the official estimates may undercount the actual share of nonperforming assets on bank balance sheets by as much as half.[44] In addition, regulatory forbearance and state ownership of the banking sector could imply hidden contingent liabilities for the public sector. Regulatory forbearance may also be an important problem, whose potential impact is masked by the large share of assets held in government debt by the banks and required to be held by other financial intermediaries.

The experience with capital account liberalization elsewhere suggests that opening domestic financial markets to international capital flows exacerbates imprudent banking practices under weak regulation or regulatory forbearance. Nonperforming assets are a burden to financial intermediation as well as an indicator of how crisis-prone the banking sector might be. The share of net nonperforming assets in the financial sector could rise significantly with international financial integration and rapid growth in domestic

43. Numbers given are for March 2003 and are reported in Reserve Bank of India, *Report on Trend and Progress of Banking in India, 2002–03.*
44. Bhattacharya and Patel (2004).

financial intermediation. However, as Bhattacharya and Patel point out, the nonperforming assets of the Indian commercial banks are concentrated in industry, infrastructure projects, and priority sectors rather than in loans for real estate and equity purchases as in the crisis countries of East Asia.[45] Corporate governance and transparency as well as prudential regulatory enforcement will be important for maintaining financial sector stability and avoiding the rapid growth of contingent liabilities that followed financial liberalization in East Asia. Bhattacharya and Patel apply the model of Robert Dekle and Kenneth Kletzer for the East Asian crisis and noncrisis economies to the Indian economy and argue that financial regulatory forbearance is a similar source of concern in India.[46]

The predominance of state-owned banking and the holding of government debt by these banks in excess of statutory requirements not only suggest that the public sector is a preferred borrower. They also imply that regulatory efforts and procedures may be adapted to the situation in which the government as shareholder is liable for losses. They could be poorly suited to regulating new private banks and nonbank financial intermediaries that borrow in an integrated capital market and whose shareholders face limited liability. Further, there is no reason to expect that the short-term external debt exposure of the Indian economy will remain at its current very low level. Financial liberalization and the integration of emerging market economies with private international financial markets tend to increase the short-term debt exposure of the financial system and the public sector. The capacity of Indian governments to borrow domestically at medium to long maturities and the very low levels of short-term external indebtedness may be viewed as outcomes of financial repression and a holdover from the preliberalization environment. The level of public indebtedness, its rate of increase or decrease, and the potential for growing contingent liabilities with capital inflows may be better indicators of the vulnerability of a postliberalization economy to financial crisis.

Because India's banks hold over 40 percent of their assets in public sector liabilities, treasury transactions are a primary activity of bankers and, in recent years, have generated the bulk of bank profits. The long maturities and fixed nominal interest rates on government securities make these risky assets for banks to hold in the presence of interest rate volatility. The recent declines in interest rates generated capital gains on government securities held by the commercial banks and by other financial institutions

45. Bhattacharya and Patel (2002).
46. Bhattacharya and Patel (2002); Dekle and Kletzer (2002).

(for example, in insurance). Prudent banking practices require that banks hedge against their holdings of fixed-interest-rate public debt either by issuing deposit liabilities with inflexible interest rates or by trading in interest-based derivatives. The liberalization of rates on many deposits and their large holdings of government debt expose the banks to interest rate risk that must be hedged. Ila Patnaik and Ajay Shah analyze a sample of bank balance sheets and find the extent of unhedged interest rate exposure in the Indian banking system to be substantial.[47] They conclude that the banking system is exposed to significant interest rate risk. Unhedged interest rate exposure of financial intermediaries implies the need for improved regulatory oversight and prudential regulation as the financial system is further liberalized and opened to entry.

An overview of the literature on the costs and benefits of capital account liberalization reveals that general measures of governance and regulatory institutions in domestic finance are significantly associated with positive gains from liberalization.[48] Financial sector reform should address the inheritance of nonperforming assets from directed credit programs in the state-owned banks and the roles of prudential regulation and enforcement in providing incentives to manage risk as the banking system is opened to competition.

External Vulnerabilities

India's external debt-to-GDP ratio was 20 percent in 2003, 40 percent of which consisted of government borrowing from official creditors primarily on concessional terms (37 percent of gross external debt carried concessional terms). External commercial borrowing accounted for 21 percent of gross external debt in 2003. The government of India has not issued sovereign bonds on international markets, although corporate sector bond and bank borrowing has increased as restrictions have been relaxed. India is rated a speculative grade borrower, with ratings of BB and Ba2 by Standard and Poor's and Moody's, respectively. Compared with other emerging market economies with similar bond ratings, India has a low ratio of external debt to GDP but a high ratio of public debt to GDP, as shown along with several other indicators by Roubini and Hemming.[49] Importantly, the average maturity of India's external debt is about nine years, and the average share of short-term debt in total external debt was only 4.6 percent from

---

47. Patnaik and Shah (2004).
48. See Prasad and others (2003) for a thorough survey.
49. Roubini and Hemming (2004).

1997 through 2002, consisting of trade-related credits and deposits of non-resident Indians.[50]

The Indian economy appears to be far from vulnerable to a capital account crisis. The outstanding debt of the public sector is primarily held by domestic residents and is denominated in domestic currency. The outstanding foreign currency–denominated liabilities of the economy are small in proportion to GDP, and the external debt of 20 percent of GDP is well below the 30 percent threshold for potential debt problems in emerging market economies observed by Reinhart, Kenneth Rogoff, and Miguel Savastano.[51] Further, the share of short-term debt in total external debt in the mid-1990s in the East Asian economies that suffered crises in 1997–98 ranged between 20 and 50 percent, far higher than India's small share.

The external position of the Indian economy suggests a favorable environment for relaxing capital controls further and moving forward with capital account convertibility. The stock of international reserves has risen rapidly over the past several years, to 17.6 percent of GDP ($113 billion) at the end of March 2004.[52] This stock of reserves rose during a period in which the current account was mostly in (small) deficit, although the current account balance recently became positive. (Table 5 reports the accumulation of reserves and foreign debt and the short-term debt exposure of India over the 1990s.) That implies that reserves were accumulated through foreign capital inflows and do not represent a net accumulation of foreign assets by the economy. This is not particularly relevant to the question of India's crisis vulnerability, although it does raise questions about whether the capital inflows are being put to best use. The international liquidity position of the central bank is strong by standard measures: reserves cover at least nine months of imports and are about twenty times the country's short-term external indebtedness. Indeed, liquid international reserves are being accumulated against longer-maturity liabilities of the domestic corporate and financial sectors. The Reserve Bank of India's 2002–03 *Report on Currency and Finance* contains a thorough analysis and international comparison of liquidity measures for the Indian economy.

The large accumulation of reserves by the Reserve Bank of India provides insurance against rapid capital outflows, but at the cost of forgone interest earnings. Assets held by the central bank are offset by government debt held by the public. The difference in opportunity interest rates (not

50. Figures are from Reserve Bank of India, *Annual Report, 2002–03, Report on Currency and Finance, 2002–03*, and *Handbook of Statistics on the Indian Economy, 2002*.
51. Reinhart, Rogoff, and Savastano (2003).
52. Reserve Bank of India, *Bulletin*, June 2004.

TABLE 5. Reserves, External Debt, and Current Account Balance
Percent of GDP

Fiscal year	International reserves	Foreign debt Total	Foreign debt Short term	Current account balance
1990–91	2.1	26.8	2.7	−3.2
1991–92	3.2	28.7	3.0	−0.4
1992–93	4.5	38.7	3.2	−1.8
1993–94	8.0	37.5	2.7	−0.4
1994–95	9.2	33.8	1.3	−1.1
1995–96	6.7	30.8	1.3	−1.7
1996–97	7.6	27	1.4	−1.2
1997–98	7.7	24.5	1.8	−1.4
1998–99	8.4	24.3	1.3	−1.0
1999–2000	9.3	23.6	1.0	−1.1
2000–01	9.5	22.1	0.9	−0.6
2001–02	12.0	22.4	0.8	0.3
2002–03	16.0	20.9	0.6	0.7

Sources: Reserve Bank of India, *Handbook of Statistics on the Indian Economy, 2002*; and Reserve Bank of India, *Bulletin*, June 2004.

necessarily the distorted market rates under capital controls) between domestic public debt and foreign treasuries represents a quasi-fiscal cost of sterilizing capital inflows. This difference adds to the consolidated public sector deficit, and hence to depreciation pressure if markets anticipate a future monetization of government liabilities. Large reserve holdings can be more costly than beneficial and thereby induce a depreciation. Kletzer and Ashoka Mody discuss these offsetting risks and the use of reserves as a self-protection mechanism against crises.[53]

A modest note of caution may be all that is needed, but full liberalization of the capital account should be expected to change the maturity structure of external debt and perhaps its currency composition. Currently India's debt is dominated by government borrowing from private sources, and capital inflows to private domestic capital markets are small and subject to continued restrictions. It would seem imprudent to assume that the average maturity of new publicly guaranteed and nonguaranteed borrowing by domestic financial markets will not decline as capital markets become more integrated and entry into India's domestic financial markets increases. Managing the foreign currency and maturity exposures of a liberalized banking system that is likely to enjoy the explicit and implicit guarantees of the public sector seen in other emerging market economies will be an emerging policy challenge for capital account liberalization.

53. Kletzer and Mody (2000).

Exchange Rate Management and Financial Repression

Capital controls allow policymakers to manage the nominal exchange rate and influence domestic rates of interest as independent objectives of monetary policy. When the capital account is liberalized, the government can no longer use monetary policy to target interest rates and resist exchange rate movements indefinitely. The tendency for authorities in emerging market economies to manage exchange rate movements even in the absence of a formal peg is well documented, and currency crises were central to many recent financial crises in emerging markets.

The behavior of the nominal exchange rate during the last decade under a managed float may be an indicator of the importance of limiting exchange rate movements in India. After the 17.4 percent devaluation of the rupee in July 1991, the rupee was again pegged to the dollar until March 1993, when it was devalued another 19.2 percent. The formal exchange rate regime was then changed to a managed float. However, the rupee was virtually unchanged against the dollar until August 1995, suggesting a de facto peg. From late 1995 to early 2003, the rupee depreciated at an annual average rate of 2.5 percent, although the growth rate of the monetary base exceeded the rate of real GDP growth by about 7 percent annually. The standard deviation of monthly percentage changes in the rupee-dollar exchange rate from August 1995 to the end of 2003 was 1.33. This is comparable to the standard deviation for Malaysia from 1990 to the onset of the Thai currency crisis in 1997, and it is almost twice the average for the East Asian crisis countries excluding the Philippines.

The Reserve Bank of India has intervened in the foreign currency market in a number of ways. Although short-term fluctuations are reduced through forward intervention (reported monthly as changes in net foreign sales of foreign exchange), it can be argued that the government implicitly pursues sterilized intervention. As argued and formally modeled by Kletzer and Renu Kohli,[54] some of the means of financial repression also allow the central bank to influence the movement of the exchange rate. The cash reserve and statutory liquidity ratios were managed actively over the 1990s, changing private sector holdings of outstanding public debt. Bank credit to the government is surprisingly closely correlated with changes in official reserves in the second half of the 1990s. During that period official foreign reserves grew rapidly, along with commercial bank credit to the public sector. The correlation between monthly increases in commercial bank credit to the government and reserve inflows over the entire period from August

54. Kletzer and Kohli (2001).

1995 to October 2003 is 0.40.[55] This suggests that increases in the holdings of public debt by the financial sector have partly sterilized capital inflows. Patnaik tests this sterilization hypothesis and finds that changes in international reserves and holdings of government debt by the commercial banks do indeed move together.[56] These results imply that the accumulation of reserves is a by-product of the sterilization of capital inflows to manage the exchange rate. The willingness of state-owned banks to hold government debt in excess of the statutory liquidity ratio appears to play an important role in exchange rate management in India.

Past exchange rate management in India displayed a resistance to currency depreciation consistent with the experience of many other emerging market economies, especially in East Asia. The adoption of a floating exchange rate, albeit one that is managed relatively tightly, reduces a country's vulnerability to crisis. The government can resist exchange rate movements while offering no guarantee of exchange parity as under a pegged exchange rate (or crawling peg or narrow target zone). The uncertainty thereby induced, especially for short-term rates of change in the exchange rate, could lead to private sector hedging against currency risk. A possible source of concern is the revealed tendency of the government to lean against exchange rate movements that could result in sudden losses of reserves and capital account reversals under an open capital account.

The Risks of Capital Account Convertibility for India

Capital controls are instrumental to financial repression in India in that they separate domestic financial intermediation from international financial markets and capture domestic savings for the financing of public sector budget deficits. The preemption of domestic financial resources for public finance interferes with the mobilization of savings toward domestic capital accumulation and reduces the incentives for banks to facilitate investment and innovation. Directed lending, interest rate restrictions, and various restraints on lending have left India's commercial banks with a burden of nonperforming assets and the public sector with unrealized contingent liabilities with uncertain risks. Capital controls and various approval procedures themselves impose widely varying implied rates of taxation on different

55. Data for this calculation are from International Monetary Fund, *International Financial Statistics* (January 2003), where deposit bank credit to the government is converted to dollars using contemporaneous exchange rates.
56. Patnaik (2003).

activities, distorting the allocation of resources and weakening incentives to save and invest. The distortionary impact of capital controls on investment and saving gives a sufficient reason for reducing and eliminating impediments to capital flows. The risk of crisis in emerging market economies also gives a sufficient reason for preparing to manage an open capital account.

The vulnerability of the Indian economy to crisis, with or without further relaxation of capital controls, rests on the impact of financial repression on domestic financial markets and fiscal policy. The two are linked. The high level of government indebtedness is sustained through borrowing on closed domestic financial markets. High levels of government debt impede the mobilization of household and enterprise savings for capital accumulation and leave bank balance sheets dominated by public debt instruments. When state-owned banks, hampered by lending to the government and high transactions costs, are exposed to international competition, the result could well be to increase the cost of contingent public liabilities in the financial sector. The deposit base of the banks could easily shrink as savings seek higher returns from more efficient intermediaries. This in turn could reduce the capacity of the government to borrow domestically at long maturities in domestic currency. Together, the liabilities of the government could rise even as its need to borrow internationally or monetize its debt increases.

The elimination of controls on outward capital flows could easily lead to rising capital inflows and entry in the financial sector. At the same time, the capacity of the government to borrow on domestic financial markets on favorable terms should contract. The current favorable terms for public sector borrowing from the commercial banks and other financial institutions include long maturities, large negative interest spreads compared with those on private lending, rupee denomination, and, perhaps, underpriced risk premiums over international rates of interest in major currencies. One consequence of rising real rates of interest for government debt arises from the long average maturity of public debt held by the commercial banks. The exposure to interest rate risk observed by Patnaik and Shah implies that financial opening could lead to net capital losses for the banks as interest rates rise on both deposits and public debt.[57] These losses could ultimately become a liability for the government. Liberalization could raise this risk by increasing competition for deposits and eliminating low and fixed interest rates on the liability side of bank balance sheets, or it could induce banks to hedge more on deeper markets.

---

57. Patnaik and Shah (2004).

Capital account convertibility would expose the public sector to international terms on its large debt and significant annual financing requirements. India's public debt burden, underestimated at 82 percent of GDP because of excluded losses of state-owned enterprise and contingent liabilities, is greater than in most countries that have suffered financial crises after liberalization.[58] However, the long maturity structure of India's rupee-denominated public debt means that a sudden crisis cannot materialize. The existing debt and fiscal policies are important to the extent that ongoing deficits need to be financed and existing public debt that is coming due needs to be refinanced. Therefore, the capacity of the government to raise tax revenue for deficit reduction, reduce electricity board losses and other off-budget liabilities, and avoid large contingent losses in the banking sector will determine the impact of the public debt burden on macroeconomic stability following capital account liberalization. Given the maturity structure of its rupee-denominated debt, the government may have the incentive to inflate that debt away. However, most Indian government debt is held by institutions that either are publicly owned or enjoy guarantees. Thus the government has little to gain—and much to lose in reputational capital in international and domestic financial markets—from unanticipated inflation.

Domestic financial intermediaries suffer from their role as the primary creditors of the public sector and from the incentive structure in state-owned banking. Ending capital controls will not eliminate the burden of financial repression without a reduction in the lending requirement imposed on the banking system by the government. Fiscal reforms are necessary to improve the stability of the banking system following a significant reduction in capital controls. The elimination of capital controls may also be necessary to improve financial intermediation, possibly through both entry and exit of intermediaries, by forcing a solution to the public sector finance problem.

Prudential regulation and enforcement are important for a stable financial environment. Capital controls can be forgiving of regulatory forbearance, because the losses of the banking sector must accumulate through flows from domestic savings to domestic investment. Two-way international transactions allow cross-border stock shifts, which can rapidly change financial sector balance sheets. Liquidity runs in a closed capital market are easier to contain than runs by foreign depositors. However, many countries

---

58. This comparison is made by several authors, most recently by Roubini and Hemming (2004), including publications of the Reserve Bank of India, such as the *Report on Currency and Finance, 2002–03.*

have managed to regulate open financial sectors successfully, and international standards provide reasonable guidelines for doing so. Detailed financial restrictions may inhibit financial instability at the cost of capital accumulation, but sound regulatory institutions and transparency in financial sector corporate governance (and corporate governance in general) can provide similar stability and a more efficient allocation of capital.

Sequencing Liberalization and Reform in India

The rapid liberalization of a financially repressed economy often leads to large capital inflows and rapid expansion of domestic financial markets, followed by a capital account crisis and economic contraction. The "Washington consensus" prescription for the sequencing of economic liberalization and international integration puts capital account convertibility last, after liberalizing trade, other current account transactions, and domestic financial markets. This prescription, however, is frequently observed in the breach.[59] The domestic political economy of reform is the first explanation that comes to mind. It may be difficult to form a coalition to support each step in a gradual reform, whereas the sudden expansion of opportunities for financial transactions creates market support. The elimination of capital controls exposes domestic capital markets and macroeconomic policies to the discipline of international capital markets, starting a race between financial reform and crash.

Indian policy is following a determinedly gradual path toward economic liberalization and international integration. Following the liberalization of transactions on the current account, restrictions on capital inflows have been relaxed steadily, with an emphasis on encouraging long-term investment and lending. The relaxation of interest rate regulation and similar controls on domestic financial intermediation has partly reduced the impact of financial repression on domestic finance and is complemented by reforms in the equity market and development of a public debt market. The relaxation of restrictions on portfolio capital inflows has been notable for its gradualism. Ceilings on interest rate spreads, which differ by debt maturity, are imposed to discourage short-term and volatile foreign portfolio inflows, and restrictions on equity flows have been relaxed substantially. Liberalization of capital inflows has followed a pattern of gradually raising quantitative restrictions on inflows and increasing the size of flows that are automatically

59. Williamson and Maher (1998) discuss the record of putting capital account liberalization last versus first.

approved. The gradual relaxation of restrictions on capital outflows would logically follow, and restrictions that discourage short-term inflows are part of the current policy agenda.

The size of the public debt and of the combined state and central government deficits is cause for concern, as is the interaction between public debt and domestic financial intermediation. Proper sequencing alone cannot ensure the smooth integration of the Indian economy with international financial markets. Although India's external debt is well within the range among countries with sustainable foreign debt, the public debt-to-GDP ratio and the primary deficits of the public sector are very high, and fiscal reform is needed to ensure that the debt is sustainable. The macroeconomic crisis of 1991 played out slowly, with an essentially closed capital account. Reserves would have had to be very low relative to GDP for any sudden reversal of deposits by nonresident Indians (which were a small share of total deposits) to provoke a balance-of-payments crisis. With an open capital account, the potential outflow of funds from domestic capital markets would be many times greater, because domestic residents could withdraw from domestic banks and from the bond and equity markets along with foreign investors. Any tendency to resist currency depreciation could raise the probability of a capital account reversal, although debt sustainability still matters for macroeconomic performance and growth under a pure float.

Capital controls mean that the government borrows on a captive domestic financial market regardless of any financial reforms that have been implemented. The real interest rate paid on government debt must be lower than it would be if domestic households had access to international financial markets. Partial liberalization appears to contribute to the primary deficit of the public sector, and full liberalization could drive the financing costs of public debt higher. Large public sector deficits do not simply substitute for domestic investment as a destination for domestic and foreign savings in the Indian economy; they appear to raise the cost of domestic financial intermediation and retard financial deepening as well.

International financial integration typically leads to both inward and outward gross capital flows. Gross capital flows, indeed, are much larger internationally than net flows. With capital account liberalization, India could well experience a large outflow of domestic savings from high-cost domestic financial intermediaries to international capital markets. As experience elsewhere has shown, these gross outflows could be offset by lending and direct investment from abroad at lower intermediation costs. Taking advantage of foreign financial markets can be beneficial to the extent that higher-income countries have comparative advantage in financial intermediation, but tax distortions can also induce capital flight and offshore intermediation. The end result of high domestic public debt and deficits under capital account convertibility is likely to be an exodus of domestic savings, a contraction of domestic financial intermediation, and a fiscal crisis accompanied by rising inflation.

As argued above, high levels of public debt interact with capital controls in India. Reducing financial repression increases the urgency of already desirable fiscal reforms. Prospective international financial integration increases the need for fiscal reform and containing public debt expansion. The priority in the approach to capital account convertibility should be fiscal reform and reduction of the combined deficits of the central and state governments. Fiscal reform not only is needed for fiscal sustainability, to avoid macroeconomic crisis, but is conducive to financial reform and deepening as well.

With the exception of the public finances, the initial conditions for capital account convertibility in India are fairly strong. The very low exposure to short-maturity foreign debt, the low overall foreign debt, the large stock of foreign reserves, and a flexible exchange rate place the Indian economy in a favorable position compared with other, similar countries. One should expect that the average maturities of foreign and public debt will fall with international financial integration, but a prospective rise in short-term debt does not justify capital controls. The stock of foreign reserves is several times current external short-term debt. Liberalization and further opening of the banking system will require regulatory improvement, but the present level of nonperforming assets of the banking system is not excessive in comparison with other emerging markets.

The process of opening the Indian economy to foreign capital inflows is not complete, and making India more attractive to foreign direct investment will require more than the relaxation of constraints on inflows and foreign ownership. Domestic policy distortions and regulatory uncertainty can inhibit investment inflows, perhaps significantly. Opening the capital account to outflows could also enhance foreign direct investment. To the extent that profitable investment uses the transfer of foreign technologies and skills, domestic savings that flow abroad might be seen as financing foreign investment in general equilibrium. Domestic savings that go to foreign equity markets could find their way back in investments that transfer technologies, and that may make foreign investors feel more secure against the risk of adverse policy changes in an internationally integrated domestic financial market.

Conclusion

Capital controls play a central role in financial repression in India. They provide the government with the opportunity to sustain high levels of domestic debt by limiting competition for domestic financial savings. A closed capital account facilitated the taxation of financial intermediation and hence reduced incentives for tax reform to enhance revenue and promote efficiency in domestic investment. A large public debt and repression of domestic financial intermediation are mutually reinforcing. India's public debt burden poses a risk for capital account liberalization, creating a barrier to financial liberalization. Continued controls on international financial outflows reduce the incentives for deficit reduction.

The gradual liberalization of capital controls and the reform of the financial sector in India are having an effect. Financial sector reform has already reduced the impact of public debt on financial intermediation. Reduced taxation of financial intermediation contributes to public sector deficits and is beginning to break the link between public finance and financial repression and raise political pressure for deficit reduction. The relaxation of inward capital controls has been successful in the sense that capital inflows are rising and gradual liberalization appears to be becoming the status quo.

Although fiscal imbalances pose a risk for capital account liberalization, a capital account crisis in India, if one occurred, might play out slowly given the long maturity structure of the large share of the public debt denominated in domestic currency and issued at fixed interest rates, and given the current low proportion of foreign currency debt and of short-maturity foreign debt. Financial integration does pose two fiscal challenges. The first stems from the borrowing requirement of the government, consisting of the primary deficit and the existing public debt coming due, which would need to be financed on international terms under an open capital account. The second is that the banking system holds the overwhelming majority of the public debt, and with international financial integration, this debt becomes a risky asset for the banks to hold. Any gain to the government from currency depreciation or rising interest spreads on public debt would be negated by losses by the banks. These holdings thus pose a threat to the banking system, and a capital account crisis could begin with exit by domestic depositors. In this case deposit insurance could reduce the exposure of the banking system to crisis. Limiting the contingent liability of the government created by deposit insurance so that it just offsets the capital gains to the public sector will require institutional reform to ensure successful prudential regulation.

The potential benefits for India from completing capital account liberalization could be significant. India has much to gain from foreign direct investment and access to foreign savings for domestic investment. The liberalization of capital inflows is not complete. Debt reduction may not be necessary before India proceeds with the elimination of outward capital controls, but fiscal reform to achieve deficit reduction probably is. The vulnerability of the banking sector to crisis implies that institutional reform, both fiscal and prudential, is needed.

Comments and Discussion

Stanley Fischer: Ken Kletzer's paper does an excellent job both in summarizing the literature and in applying its lessons to India. Ken starts with a general discussion of the costs and benefits of capital account liberalization and then discusses the Indian case. Let me follow that order.

It has been very hard to show major benefits of capital account liberalization, either in cross-country regressions or in calibration exercises using growth models. But it is generally difficult to produce robust results using cross-country regressions and even more difficult to produce big costs as a result of distortions in calibration exercises. It is not clear what to make of these difficulties. Ken says that the benefits of capital account liberalization are approximately equivalent to—and in some cases larger than—the benefits of eliminating trade cycle fluctuations, as calculated by Lucas. However, Lucas's calculations implied that the trade cycle really did not matter. In my view, these results, rather than telling us something about the world, suggest that there is something wrong with this way of approaching the issue.

There is another way of thinking about policy choices, namely revealed preference. It is amazing that, despite the devastation of the 1997 crisis, despite everything that academic economists have said, no one—and I mean no country—has withdrawn from the international financial system as a result. No country, not even Malaysia, imposed controls of major magnitude for any length of time. Malaysia reformulated its controls within a year and has gradually been easing back into the system.

My views have also been influenced by discussions with some Latin American finance ministers during the crises of the 1990s. When I asked whether they wanted to impose capital controls, their answer was that they had tried that in the 1980s and they were not going to do it again. They said that capital controls were inefficient and bred corruption and that it took a long time to recover from their imposition. Those conversations are not hard evidence, but they made a big impression on me.

It seems to be generally accepted that the Malaysian imposition of controls was successful. I do not know how that can be established. Those controls were imposed almost exactly at the moment that exchange rates in all the crisis countries were at their most depreciated levels. Malaysia pegged its exchange rate at that depreciated level, which made the currency increasingly undervalued relative to those of its neighbors, all of whose currencies appreciated subsequently. Capital did stop flowing out of Malaysia following the imposition of the controls, but that happened also in the other Asian crisis countries. So, I do not think the Malaysian experience shows a whole lot about the efficacy of capital controls.

I was surprised by one successful aspect of Malaysian controls. When the controls were imposed, I expected that they would be used to slow the process of financial reconstruction and the reform of the banking system. But the Malaysian authorities did not do that. Their banking system reforms were as rapid following the imposition of controls as those anywhere else. So the political economy suspicion that I had was not right.

Some changes—two in fact—did take place as a result of the 1997 crisis. The first was the general move toward flexible exchange rates. All the crisis countries had pegged their currencies, formally or informally, before the crisis. By "pegged," I mean that it was presumed by market participants that the exchange rate would be stable. That presumption played a major role in the behavior of the actors in the economy leading up to the crisis. Subsequently all the crisis countries except Malaysia allowed their exchange rates to become more flexible.

The second development is that although there has been no fundamental change in emerging market countries' desire to integrate into the global financial system, there has been a greater willingness to find ways of breaking the link between the domestic and foreign interest rates, or onshore and offshore interest rates. This has long been done by Singapore, which discouraged the use of its currency in international transactions and discouraged economic agents from taking positions in the currency.

There are a variety of ways of doing that, all of which build on the fact that if you are going to hedge yourself against exchange rate changes, at some point you need to have access to the domestic banking system to purchase the local currency. The authorities can impose controls to make that very difficult, without interfering with other transactions in the currency. Such changes have been imposed in Thailand and to some extent in Indonesia, the latter not very successfully.

Returning now to India: Ken presents the standard view, which is that capital flows should be liberalized only when the financial systems and policies are sufficiently strong. That view draws on both theory and bitter experience, and by and large it is valid. The most relevant macro weakness in India is the large and growing public debt. That problem needs to be fixed in any case.

It is sometimes argued that delaying capital account liberalization until the preconditions are in place only delays action on the preconditions. The suggestion is that by setting a schedule for capital account liberalization, the authorities would force themselves to fix the financial and fiscal systems. Well, that is a very delicate and dangerous argument. Think for instance about Mexican *tesebonos*. They were introduced to persuade potential investors that Mexico would not devalue, because the costs of doing so would be extremely high. The threat was very credible, and ex post the costs were extremely high. The problem with policy choices that suggest that something will be done because the costs of failure are high is that sometimes failures will occur, and the price will have to be paid.

It would be much better if India's fiscal and debt problems were put on a road to solution soon. So far the problem has not been attacked. That is the major disappointment of Indian macro policy in the last decade. Dealing with the fiscal problem is also a structural issue, one that will require a change in relations between the center and states, because as is well known, at least half of the general government deficit is due to state governments.

Turning to the banking system: the Indian banking system is in better shape than the financial systems of the East Asian countries were on the eve of their crisis. Ken states that the NPA ratio is around 6 percent, which would not be a cause of major distress if the capital account were opened. But it must be recognized that a crisis that put the banking system under stress could increase the NPA ratio significantly. Looking at other vulnerability indicators, India's short-term external debt ratio is very low. Further, Indian financial regulators are fully aware of the banking system difficulties in the Asian and other crises, and they should be able to maintain strong precautionary control over the system.

There is one other key difference between India and the Asian crisis countries: the exchange rate regime. The Indian exchange rate is flexible. The importance of that in terms of the likelihood of suffering a financial crisis—and in terms of the cost of a crisis were one to occur—cannot be overestimated. The Brazilian crisis in 2002 illustrates the benefits of having a flexible exchange rate. It is simply inconceivable that Brazil could have avoided a massive financial crisis if it had had a pegged exchange rate in 2002.

The key is flexibility of the exchange rate, rather than free floating. That means that in a crisis the authorities could both allow the exchange rate to depreciate and intervene to moderate the extent of the depreciation. That must be why the authorities are holding such large reserves. I do not believe that in a crisis managing the exchange rate is necessarily undesirable, provided that it is possible. But there is a cardinal sin that has to be avoided, which is to target a fixed exchange rate or a narrow range of rates. If a country with free capital flows tries to do that in a crisis, it will fail and pay a high price.

There is one other reason why exchange rate flexibility matters: market participants are less likely to borrow short abroad when they know that the exchange rate is flexible. Further, once the exchange rate is flexible, hedging instruments are likely to appear. Both those developments took place in Mexico following its shift to exchange rate flexibility: Mexico's short-term debt ratio is now very low, and short- and long-term foreign exchange hedges are available in the market.

So, India should continue opening up the capital account. Doing so will bring increasing benefits over the course of time. I believe India's gradualist approach has put it on the right track. But it really is important to reduce the fiscal deficit.

Surjit S. Bhalla: The effect of capital account liberalization on growth is a much-debated subject, and Kletzer provides a very useful summary of the issues, bringing out the complexity of the Indian financial sector and the diversity of its experience. Kletzer's application to the Indian experience will serve as a reference point for other scholars.

Only on two issues does my perspective differ from the author's, but both of my disagreements serve to strengthen Kletzer's overall conclusion. The first pertains to the examination of the effect of capital account liberalization (CAL) on economic growth and so forth. Here, it would be useful to analyze the effects of CAL on growth *subject to the nature of the currency regime*. It matters whether the exchange rate is fixed, pegged, a managed float, or even a currency board. Several of the currency crises have resulted not from the fiscal deficit, and not even from CAL, but from the overvaluation of the exchange rate. Malaysia, Korea, and Indonesia had all opened up to the world, had more CAL than most, and were not crisis prone. Indeed, most if not all of these countries were running a fiscal surplus and a managed float at the time of the financial crisis in 1997.

Thailand was a different story: its exchange rate was pegged at 25 baht to the dollar, and its fiscal house was in order—fiscal surpluses above 2 percent of GDP the last five years and an average of 2.7 percent of GDP for nine years prior to the crisis year of 1997! What differentiated Thailand from the other East Asian countries was its imbalance on the current account—around 5 percent of GDP. It is plausible that if the Thai authorities had allowed even a minimal fluctuation of the exchange rate (as was done by the East Asian crisis countries just mentioned), then some part of the imbalance would have been corrected before 1997, and (possibly) a crisis averted. In other words, it was not necessarily CAL or the banking sector—rather, it was an overvalued exchange rate. Thus it is useful to take the exchange rate and the valuation of the currency into account in analyzing CAL. If this is done, my expectation would be that the results would be even stronger regarding the benefits of CAL.

The second point pertains to financial repression. In most countries, financial repression is correctly defined as too low real interest rates. In India, financial repression has occurred through too *high* real interest rates. In regard to the high fiscal deficit, it is noteworthy that the consolidated fiscal deficit for India has ranged between 8 and 10 percent for twenty-four years (since 1980). The states' share of this deficit, however, has shown a significant trend increase—from about 30 percent of the total in the early 1990s to about 60 percent today. The story of how the states finance this deficit is one of financial repression—and nontransparent nongovernance.

The accompanying table 5 shows the interest rates given to depositors in "small savings"—a political misnomer for what can otherwise be termed (Ponzi) "scam savings." Note the large increase in the states' fiscal deficit and the collection of small savings (and prior to the Pay Commission–induced increase in 1999). Also note the increase in the real rate of interest given to such savings after 1995, which occurred because the government kept the nominal rate fixed as inflation fell. This easy source of financing of state deficits (through collections based on high rates of return to deposits) means that financial repression continues unabated. The seeds of a future financial crisis are being sown not through financial repression of the traditional type, nor through banking "problems," nor even through CAL. If a crisis occurs it will be because the government willfully pursued a "lazy" fiscal policy, one without any checks on state-level expenditures.

TABLE 5. Financial Repression, Indian Style: The High Cost of Government Borrowing
Percent, unless otherwise indicated

		Interest rates				Small savings deposits (rupees, billions)	Gross fiscal deficit of states (rupees, billions)	Small savings share of GFD[a]
Year	Inflation	Government securities	Small savings	Government securities real rate	Small savings real rate			
1990	9.8	11.4	10.3	1.6	0.5	189	188	75
1991	12.9	11.8	9.9	-1.1	-3.0	186	189	74
1992	9.6	12.5	10.2	2.9	0.6	194	209	70
1993	8.0	12.6	10.6	4.6	2.6	273	206	99
1994	11.8	11.9	11.0	0.1	-0.8	375	277	101
1995	7.8	13.4	10.8	5.6	3.0	366	314	87
1996	4.5	13.7	10.9	9.2	6.4	380	373	76
1997	4.3	12.0	11.2	7.7	6.9	518	442	88
1998	5.8	11.9	11.2	6.1	5.4	621	743	63
1999	3.2	11.8	10.6	8.6	7.4	754	915	62
2000	6.9	11.0	9.9	4.1	3.0	885	895	74
2001	3.5	8.8	8.4	5.3	4.9	904	960	94
2002	3.4	6.5	8.0	3.1	4.6	1,167	1,166	100
2003	5.3	5.3	7.9	0.0	2.6	1,243	1,162	107

Source: Government securities and small savings data are from *RBI Handbook of Statistics on State Government Finances*, various years, and *Reserve Bank of India Bulletin*, various years.
a. Before 2001 the small savings share of GFD was multiplied by .75 because 75 percent of the deposits went to the states and 25 percent to the central government.

General Discussion

Abhijit Banerjee said that the models that he finds most illuminating are those characterized by multiple equilibriums in which just the belief that the banking sector in a country may be fragile can shift the equilibrium radically. These models explain why crises may visit even a country like Korea, which is the most worrying aspect of capital account convertibility.

Expressing agreement with Banerjee, Montek Singh Ahluwalia noted that the real cost of a crisis is not just the short-term fall in incomes. In India, the likelihood of major reversal of economic reforms in the event of a crisis is very high. In any case, Ahluwalia saw absolutely no chance of any rapid movement to capital account convertibility in India; therefore he felt that the most useful approach would be to suggest what steps the Reserve Bank of India could be taking toward a staged opening up of the capital account. What warning signals should the RBI be watching for? What supplementary instruments should it begin to build into the system? For example, India lacks the hedging instruments necessary to support the opening up it already has achieved. The other important point is to avoid balance sheet mismatches, especially in the context of gradual opening up. Ahluwalia said that he was not aware that this was happening in the public sector banks but that the private sector banks were probably using good practices and would not run into that problem. However, currency mismatches may well be happening in the corporate sector. Were banks sufficiently aware that this might be happening? Were they doing something about it?

John Williamson made two points. First, to about 99 percent of the world, "capital account convertibility" means that somebody who has capital is entitled to switch in or out of any of the currencies, irrespective of the exchange rate regime. He noted two exceptions to this definition, however: Argentina, where convertibility means a fixed exchange rate, and Surjit Bhalla, who thinks convertibility means a floating exchange rate. The second point Williamson made was that Ken had identified out precisely the difficulties and dangers that come with capital account convertibility, but he had also cited many papers that mentioned gains from financial liberalization. Williamson acknowledged that there are all sorts of gains from financial liberalization; for instance, few would argue that the United Kingdom should go back on capital account convertibility. But Europe had taken thirty years to get to full convertibility. India should be thinking of the European experience. Williamson noted that he had made this point as far back as twenty-three years ago, so there had been a lot of earlier thinking on this subject.

Urjit Patel said that we must widen the definition of "nonperforming assets" (NPAs). In particular, we must bring important financial institutions such as the Life Insurance Corporation and Employee Provident Fund Organization into the calculation. He noted that the conventional estimates of NPAs typically understate the problem; a good rule of thumb once used at the IMF was to double the estimate you actually obtained. Echoing Bhalla, Patel advocated a wider definition of "public sector borrowing requirement" (PSBR) to get a better handle on the crowding out of private-sector investment. He noted that a passable PSBR measure is actually reported in the *Economic Survey*. It includes the borrowings of the State Electricity Boards (SEBs) and Public Sector Units (PSUs) and places the PSBR at 11.5 to 12 percent.

Responding to Fischer's assertion that crises had actually led the affected countries to undertake greater liberalization and reform, Arvind Panagariya said that this had not been the case in Mexico. According to his Maryland colleague Enrique Mendoza, who comes from Mexico, after the 1994 crisis reforms in Mexico came to a virtual standstill. Panagariya also noted that contrary to the view expressed by Ahluwalia, India has been moving toward capital account liberalization. Direct foreign and portfolio investment have been open for some time. Firms also are allowed to borrow abroad, subject to maturity restrictions, and resident Indians have been allowed to hold foreign currency accounts. If banks are permitted to use the resulting deposits to lend onshore in rupees, there could readily be a currency mismatch. Panagariya put forward a question for all present: "T. N. Srinivasan has said recently that India should aim to achieve full convertibility in five years' time; is it possible to outline a set of steps and the associated timeline to achieve this objective?"

Responding to Panagariya's comments, Ahluwalia said that he would dismiss the moves toward liberalization, which occurred because India had an excess of foreign exchange reserves. One should not read from the liberalization today that this opening would not get reversed if foreign exchange reserves became scarce. Ahluwalia argued that that was not liberalization. Liberalization means that when foreign exchange reserves are scarce, one still lets the rupee fall to the level where it will become undervalued and investors still will return to it. Ahluwalia saw no intellectual support for that kind of approach in India. What one has observed is that because there is a lot of money lying around, some windows have been opened, which is good. But from this one should not conclude that India is going to an open capital account in five years.

Ila Patnaik returned to the subject of hedging, nothing that the RBI now allows some agents with direct exposure to hedge. But many agents—for example, households that are now allowed to hold foreign currency deposits—are not permitted to hedge. Today, when the RBI is keeping the rupee's volatility low, they are actually providing a public good. Those not permitted to hedge can still feel safe. But if the rupee's volatility goes up, there is no justification for the policy of denying access to hedging to any agents who feel the need. It takes time to build hedging institutions and instruments, and it is time to start thinking about them.

Kenneth Kletzer began his response by agreeing with the comment by Fischer that his paper was particularly cautionary but suggested that it is a reasonable approach. Regarding the exchange rate, he noted that there has been a strong tendency to resist its movement, though the current exchange rate regime is not what one must consider when thinking of capital account convertibility. On the banking system, Kletzer expressed agreement with Fischer that in comparison with other countries the unprovisioned nonperforming assets in the banking system in India were quite small. And they were certainly small compared with the resources available to the RBI to recapitalize them.

Kletzer defended the literature regarding the net gains from international capital mobility and international financial integration. He noted that the revealed preference of the countries—meaning the choices that countries are actually making—was one way to address the issue of whether capital account convertibility is desirable, as suggested by Fischer. However, he expressed discomfort with claiming larger gains without first looking for better ways to do the calibration exercises and cross-country regressions. The research studies and the puzzles therein relating to low gains from capital account convertibility are there, and we cannot ignore them. The fact that the gains from convertibility as measured by the existing studies are small is disturbing because it certainly runs counter to theory and is counterintuitive given the enthusiasm for liberalization that one currently sees in the world.

Moving forward, Kletzer noted that a key issue he would like to consider in his revision is identifying the danger signals as India opens up its capital account. On the question of how deficits are managed, he thought that liberalization had certainly contributed toward increasing the difficulties of the government in financing itself. Tariff liberalization had caused the loss of customs revenues. The same thing is going to happen with capital account liberalization in relation to the captive capital market for government borrowing. One can take the view that opening up the economy and a little bit of financial discipline will do the government some good. The other view, of course, is that the risk of crisis may be very bad for reform.

References

Ahluwalia, Montek S. 2002. "India's Vulnerability to External Crisis: An Assessment." In *Macroeconomics and Monetary Policy: Issues for Reforming the Economy*, edited by Montek Ahluwalia, S. S. Tarapore, and Y. V. Reddy. New Delhi: Oxford University Press.

Arteta, Carlos, Barry Eichengreen, and Charles Wyplosz. 2001. "On the Growth Effects of Capital Account Liberalization." Working paper 8414. Cambridge, Mass.: National Bureau of Economic Research.

Bekaert, Geert, Campbell Harvey, and Christian Lundblad. 2002. "Growth Volatility and Equity Market Liberalization." Working paper. Duke University.

Bhattacharya, Saugata, and Urjit Patel. 2002. "Financial Intermediation in India: A Case of Aggravated Moral Hazard." Working Paper 145. Stanford Center for International Development (July).

———. 2004. "Reform Strategies in the Indian Financial Sector." Working Paper 208. Stanford Center for International Development (February).

Buiter, Willem, and Urjit Patel. 1997. "Solvency and Fiscal Correction in India: An Analytical Discussion." In *Public Finance: Policy Issues for India*, edited by S. Mundle. New Delhi: Oxford University Press.

Calvo, Guillermo, and Carmen Reinhart. 2000. "Fear of Floating." Working Paper 7993. Cambridge, Mass.: National Bureau of Economic Research (November).

Dekle, Robert, and Kenneth Kletzer. 2002. "Domestic Bank Regulation and Financial Crises: Theory and Empirical Evidence from East Asia." In *Preventing Currency Crises in Emerging Markets*, edited by Sebastian Edwards and Jeffrey Frankel. University of Chicago Press.

———. 2003. "The Japanese Banking Crisis and Economic Growth: Theoretical and Empirical Implications of Deposit Guarantees and Weak Financial Regulation." *Journal of the Japanese and International Economies* 17: 305–35.

Demetriades, Panicos O., and Kul B. Luintel. 1996. "Financial Development, Economic Growth and Banking Sector Controls: Evidence from India." *Economic Journal* 106: 359–74.

———. 1997. "The Direct Costs of Financial Repression: Evidence from India." *Review of Economics and Statistics* 74: 311–20.

Díaz-Alejandro, Carlos. 1985. "Good-bye Financial Repression, Hello Financial Crash." *Journal of Development Economics* 19: 1–24.

Fry, Maxwell. 1988. *Money, Interest and Banking in Economic Development.* Johns Hopkins University Press.

———. 1997. *Emancipating the Banking System and Developing Markets for Government Debt.* London: Routledge.

Giovannini, Alberto, and Martha de Melo. 1993. "Government Revenue from Financial Repression." *American Economic Review* 83: 953–63.

Gourinchas, Pierre-Olivier, and Olivier Jeanne. 2003. "The Elusive Gains from International Financial Integration." Working Paper 9684. Cambridge, Mass.: National Bureau of Economic Research.

Hall, Robert, and Charles Jones. 1999. "Why Do Some Countries Produce So Much More Output per Worker than Others?" *Quarterly Journal of Economics* 114: 83–116.

Henry, Peter B. 2003. "Capital Account Liberalization, The Cost of Capital, and Economic Growth." *American Economic Review, Papers and Proceedings* 93 (2, May): 91–96.

Kaminsky, Graciela, and Carmen Reinhart. 1999. "The Twin Crises: The Causes of Banking and Balance-of-Payments Problems." *American Economic Review* 89 (3): 473–500.

Kletzer, Kenneth, and Renu Kohli. 2001. "Financial Repression and Exchange Rate Management in Developing Countries: Theory and Empirical Evidence for India." Working Paper 01/103. Washington: International Monetary Fund.

Kletzer, Kenneth, and Ashoka Mody. 2000. "Will Self-Protection Policies Safeguard Emerging Markets from Crises?" In *Managing Financial and Corporate Distress: Lessons from Asia*, edited by C. Adams, Robert Litan, and M. Pomerleano. Brookings.

Kose, Ayhan, Eswar Prasad, and Marco Terrones. 2003. "Financial Integration and Macroeconomic Volatility." International Monetary Fund *Staff Papers* 50 (special issue): 119–42.

Lucas, Robert E., Jr. 1990. "Why Doesn't Capital Flow from Rich to Poor Countries?" *American Economic Review, Papers and Proceedings* 80 (2, May): 92–96.

Maddison, Angus. 2003. *World Economy: Historical Statistics*. Paris: Organization for Economic Cooperation and Development.

Mohan, Rakesh. 2002. "Transforming Indian Banking: In Search of a Better Tomorrow." Speech given December 29. Mumbai, India: Reserve Bank of India.

Obstfeld, Maurice. 1994. "Risk-taking, Global Diversification and Growth." *American Economic Review* 85: 1310–29.

Patnaik, Ila. 2003. "The Consequences of Currency Intervention in India." Working Paper 114. New Delhi: Indian Council for Research on International Economic Relations (October).

Patnaik, Ila, and Ajay Shah. 2004. "Interest Rate Volatility and Risk in Indian Banking." Working Paper 04/17. Washington: International Monetary Fund (January).

Pinto, Brian, and Farah Zahir. 2003. "India: Why Fiscal Adjustment Now." World Bank (December).

Prasad, Eswar, Kenneth Rogoff, Shang-Jin Wei, and Ayhan Kose. 2003. "Effects of Financial Globalization on Developing Countries: Some Empirical Evidence." Occasional Paper. Washington: International Monetary Fund.

Reinhart, Carmen, Kenneth Rogoff, and Miguel Savastano. 2003. "Debt Intolerance." *BPEA*, no. 1: 1–74.

Reynolds, Patricia 2001. "Fiscal Adjustment and Growth Prospects in India." In *India at the Crossroads: Sustaining Growth and Reducing Poverty*, edited by T. Callen, P. Reynolds, and C. Towe. Washington: International Monetary Fund.

Rodrik, Dani. 1998. "Who Needs Capital-Account Convertibility?" Essays in International Finance 207. Princeton University.

Rodrik, Dani, and Andres Velasco. 2000. "Short-Term Capital Flows." In *Annual World Bank Conference on Development Economics, 1999.* Washington: World Bank.

Roubini, Nouriel, and Richard Hemming. 2004. "A Balance Sheet Crisis for India?" Paper presented at a conference sponsored by the National Institute for Public Finance and Policy and the International Monetary Fund, April.

Singh, N., and T. N. Srinivasan. 2004. "Fiscal Policy in India: Lessons and Priorities." Working Paper 207. Stanford Center for International Development (February).

Srinivasan, T. N. 2002. "India's Fiscal Situation: Is a Crisis Ahead?" In *Economic Policy Reforms and the Indian Economy,* edited by Anne O. Krueger. University of Chicago Press.

Tarapore, S. S. 1997. *Report of the Committee on Capital Account Convertibility.* Mumbai: Reserve Bank of India.

Wei, Shang-Jin. 1999. "Can China and India Double Their Inward Foreign Direct Investment?" Paper presented at a conference sponsored by the National Bureau of Economic Research and the National Council for Applied Economic Research.

Williamson, John, and Maria Maher. 1998. "A Survey of Financial Liberalization." Essays in International Finance 211. International Finance Section, Princeton University.

ABHIJIT V. BANERJEE
Massachusetts Institute of Technology

SHAWN COLE
Massachusetts Institute of Technology

ESTHER DUFLO
Massachusetts Institute of Technology

Banking Reform in India

Measured by share of deposits, 83 percent of the banking business in India is in the hands of state or nationalized banks, banks owned by the government in some increasingly less clear-cut way. Moreover, even non-nationalized banks are subject to extensive regulations on whom they can lend to, in addition to the more standard prudential regulations.

Government control over banks has always had its fans, ranging from Lenin to Gerschenkron. Although some advocates have emphasized the political importance of public control over banking, most arguments for nationalizing banks are based on the premise that profit-maximizing lenders do not necessarily deliver credit where the social returns are highest. The Indian government, when nationalizing all the larger Indian banks in 1969, argued that banking was "inspired by a larger social purpose" and must "subserve national priorities and objectives such as rapid growth in agriculture, small industry and exports."[1]

A body of direct and indirect evidence now shows that credit markets in developing countries often fail to deliver credit where its social product might be the highest, and both agriculture and small industry are often mentioned as sectors that do not get their fair share of credit.[2] If nationalization

We thank the Reserve Bank of India, in particular Y. V. Reddy, R. B. Barman, and Abhiman Das, for generous assistance with technical and substantive issues. We also thank Abhiman Das for performing calculations that involved proprietary RBI data and Saibal Ghosh and Petia Topalova for helpful comments. We are grateful to the staff of the public sector bank we study for allowing us access to their data. We gratefully acknowledge financial support from the Alfred P. Sloan Foundation.

1. From the "Bank Company Acquisition Act of 1969." Quoted by Burgess and Pande (2003).

2. See Banerjee (2003) for a review of the evidence.

succeeds in pushing credit into these sectors, as the Indian government claimed it would, it could indeed raise both equity and efficiency.

The cross-country evidence on the impact of bank nationalization, however, is not encouraging. For example, Rafael La Porta and colleagues find in a cross-country setting that government ownership of banks is negatively correlated with both financial development and economic growth.[3] They interpret this as support for their view that the potential benefits of public ownership of banks, and public control over banks more generally, are swamped by the costs that come from the agency problems it creates—problems such as cronyism, which leads to the deliberate misallocation of capital; bureaucratic lethargy, which leads to less deliberate but perhaps equally costly errors in the allocation of capital; and inefficiency in mobilizing savings and transforming them into credit.

Interpreting this type of cross-country analysis is never easy, especially in the case of something like bank nationalization, which is typically part of a package of other policies. Microeconomic studies of the effect of bank nationalization are rare. One exception is Atif Mian's examination of the 1991 privatization of a large public bank in Pakistan.[4] He finds that the privatized bank did a better job both at choosing profitable clients and monitoring existing clients than the commercial banks that remained public. Studying a liberalization episode in France, Marianne Bertrand and colleagues find that after deregulation banks responded more to profitability when making lending decisions, and that borrowing firms were more likely to exit or restructure following a negative shock.[5]

In a 2003 paper we used micro data from a nationalized bank to evaluate the effectiveness of the Indian banking system in delivering credit.[6] Our conclusion was that the Indian financial system is characterized by underlending in the sense that many firms could earn large profits if they were given access to credit at the current market prices.

This paper builds on previous work of our own and of others to assess the role of the Indian government in the banking sector. We begin by providing a brief history of banking in India. Next we investigate the quality of intermediation. We first present evidence of substantial under-lending in India. To understand what role public ownership of banks may play in underlending, we identify differences between public and private banks in the sectoral allocation of credit. In particular, we focus on whether being

3. La Porta, Lopez-de-Silanes, and Shleifer (2002).
4. Mian (2000).
5. Bertrand, Schoar, and Thesmar (2003).
6. Banerjee, Cole, and Duflo (2003).

nationalized has made these banks more responsive to what the Indian government wants them to do. We report results, based on work by Shawn Cole, showing that on many of the declared objectives of "social banking," with the exception of agricultural lending, the private banks were no less responsive than the comparable nationalized banks.[7] And we compare the performance of public and private banks as financial intermediaries and conclude that the public banks have been less aggressive than private banks in lending, in attracting deposits, and in setting up branches, at least since 1990.

To understand under-lending, we dig deeper into the lending processes of nationalized banks and find that official lending policy is very rigid. Moreover, loan officers do not appear to use what little flexibility they have. Bankers in the public sector appear to have a preference for what we may call passive lending. To understand why, we examine the incentives and constraints faced by public loan officers. We focus on whether vigilance activity impedes lending and whether public sector banks prefer to lend to the government, rather than private firms.

Next we compare the performance of public and private banking in two other areas. First, we examine how nationalization of banks has affected the availability of bank branches in rural areas and find that, if anything, nationalization appears to have *inhibited* the growth of rural branches. Second, we address the sensitive issue of nonperforming assets and bailouts. While the data set we have now is rather sparse, it appears that the bailouts of the public banks have proved more expensive for the government, but once we control for differences in size between the public and private banks, this conclusion is less clear-cut.

We conclude with a short discussion of the implications of these results for the future of banking reform.

Background

India has a long history of both public and private banking. Modern banking in India began in the eighteenth century, with the founding of the English Agency House in Calcutta and Bombay. In the first half of the nineteenth century, three presidency banks were founded. After the 1860 introduction of limited liability, private banks began to appear, and foreign banks entered the market. The beginning of the twentieth century saw the

---

7. Cole (2004).

introduction of joint stock banks. In 1935 the presidency banks were merged to form the Imperial Bank of India, subsequently renamed the State Bank of India. That same year, India's central bank, the Reserve Bank of India (RBI), began operation. Following independence, the RBI was given broad regulatory authority over commercial banks in India. In 1959 the State Bank of India acquired the state-owned banks of eight former princely states. Thus, by July 1969, approximately 31 percent of scheduled bank branches throughout India were government-controlled as part of the State Bank of India.

India's postwar development strategy was in many ways a socialist one, and the government felt that banks in private hands did not lend enough to those who needed it most. In July 1969, the government nationalized all banks whose nationwide deposits were greater than Rs. 500 million, nationalizing 54 percent more of the branches in India and bringing the total share of branches under government control to 84 percent.

Prakesh Tandon, a former chairman of the Punjab National Bank (nationalized in 1969) describes the rationale for nationalization as follows:

> Many bank failures and crises over two centuries, and the damage they did under "laissez faire" conditions; the needs of planned growth and equitable distribution of credit, which in privately owned banks was concentrated mainly on the controlling industrial houses and influential borrowers; the needs of growing small-scale industry and farming regarding finance, equipment and inputs; from all these there emerged an inexorable demand for banking legislation, some government control and a central banking authority, adding up, in the final analysis, to social control and nationalization.[8]

After nationalization, the Indian banking sector expanded in breadth and scope at a rate perhaps unmatched by any other country. Indian banking has been remarkably successful at achieving mass participation. Since the 1969 nationalizations, more than 58,000 bank branches have opened in India. As of March 2003, these new branches had mobilized more than Rs. 9 trillion in deposits, the overwhelming majority of deposits in Indian banks.[9] This rapid expansion is attributable to a policy requiring banks to open four branches in unbanked locations for every branch opened in banked locations.

Between 1969 and 1980, private branches grew more quickly in number than public banks, and on April 1, 1980, they accounted for approximately 17.5 percent of bank branches in India. In April 1980, the government undertook a second round of nationalization, placing under its control the

8. Tandon (1989, p. 198).
9. Reserve Bank of India, *Statistical Tables Relating to Banks in India* (2003).

six private banks whose nationwide deposits were above Rs. 2 billion, or a further 8 percent of bank branches, leaving approximately 10 percent of bank branches in private hands. That share stayed fairly constant between 1980 and 2000.

Nationalized banks remained corporate entities, retaining most of their staff, with the exception of the boards of directors, who were replaced by appointees of the central government. The political appointments included representatives from the government, industry, and agriculture, as well as the public. (Equity holders in the national bank were reimbursed at approximately par.)

Since 1980, there has been no further nationalization, and indeed the trend appears to be reversing itself, as nationalized banks are issuing shares to the public in what amounts to a step toward privatization. The considerable accomplishments of the Indian banking sector notwithstanding, advocates for privatization argue that privatization will lead to several substantial improvements.

Recently, the Indian banking sector has witnessed the introduction of several "new private banks," either newly founded or created by existing financial institutions. The new private banks have grown quickly in the past few years, and one is now the nation's second largest bank. India has also seen the entry of more than two dozen foreign banks since the commencement of financial reforms in 1991. Although we believe both these types of banks deserve study, our focus here is on the older private sector and on nationalized banks, because they represent the overwhelming majority of banking activity in India.

The Indian banking sector has historically suffered from high intermediation costs, in no small part because of the staffing at public sector banks. As of March 2002, nationalized banks had 1.17 crore of deposits per employee, as against 2.05 crore per employee for private sector banks. As with other government-run enterprises, corruption is a problem for public sector banks. In 1999, 1,916 cases of possible corruption attracted attention from the Central Vigilance Commission. Although not all these cases represent crimes, the investigations themselves may have a harmful effect if bank officers fear that approving any risky loan will inevitably lead to scrutiny. Advocates for privatization also criticize public sector banking as unresponsive to credit needs.

In the rest of the paper, we use recent evidence on banking in India to shed light on the relative costs and benefits of nationalized banks. Throughout this exercise, it is important to bear in mind that the Indian banking sector is going through something like a transformation. Thus, evaluating its performance using historical data requires caution. Nevertheless, data from the past are all we have, and change is not so rapid as to invalidate the lessons learned.

Quality of Intermediation

In this section, we carefully examine how credit is allocated in India. We focus initially on small-scale industries (SSI), because small firms typically turn to banks for external financing and because providing credit to this sector is an important objective of Indian banking policy. Finding that small firms are indeed constrained, we then ask how bank nationalization has affected the flow of credit to small-scale industry and other sectors. Finally, we take a longer view of financial development, comparing how quickly public sector banks grew compared with their private counterparts.

The Problem of Under-Lending

A firm is getting too little credit if the marginal product of its capital is higher than the rate of interest it is paying on its marginal rupee of borrowing. A firm's inability to raise enough capital is a problem involving not merely its own bank but the market as a whole. Under-lending therefore is a characteristic of the entire financial system. Although we focus in this paper on the clients of a single public sector bank, if these firms are getting too little credit from that bank, they should in theory have the option of going elsewhere for more credit. If they do not or cannot exercise this option, the market cannot be doing what, in its idealized form, we would have expected it to do.

We know, however, that the Indian financial system does not function as the ideal credit market might. Most small or medium firms have a relationship with one bank, which they have built up over some time. They cannot expect to walk into another bank and get as much credit as they want. For that reason, their ability to finance investments they need to make does depend on the willingness of that one bank to finance them. In this sense the results we report below might very well reflect the specificities of the public sector banks, or even the one bank that was kind enough to share its data with us, though given that it is seen as one of the best public sector banks, it seems unlikely that we would find much better results in other banks in its category. On the other hand, we do not have comparable data from any private bank and therefore cannot tell whether under-lending is as much of a problem for private banks. We will, however, later report some results on the relative performance of public and private banks in terms of overall credit delivery.

Our identification of credit-constrained firms is based on the following simple observation: if a firm that is *not* credit constrained is offered extra credit at a rate below what it is paying on the market, then the best way to use the new loan must be to pay down the firm's current market borrowing, rather than to invest more. Because any additional investment by a firm that is not credit constrained will drive the marginal product of capital below what the firm is paying on its market borrowing, it follows that such a firm will expand its investment in response to the availability of additional subsidized credit only if it has no more market borrowing. By contrast, a firm that is credit constrained will always expand its investment to some extent.

A corollary to this prediction is that for unconstrained firms, growth in revenue should be slower than the growth in subsidized credit. This is a direct consequence of the fact that firms are substituting subsidized credit for market borrowing. Therefore, if these growth rates are the same, the firm must be credit constrained. Of course, revenue could increase more slowly than credit even for nonconstrained firms, if the firm faces declining marginal returns to capital.

These predictions are more robust than the traditional way of measuring credit constraints as the excess sensitivity of investment to cash flow.[10] Our approach inscribes itself in a literature that tries to identify specific shocks to wealth in order to identify credit constraints.[11]

In an earlier paper, two of us (Banerjee and Duflo) tested these predictions by taking advantage of a recent change in the "priority sector" rules: all banks in India are required to lend at least 40 percent of their net credit to the priority sector, which includes small-scale industry, at an interest rate no more than 4 percentage points above their prime lending rate.[12] Banks that do not satisfy the priority sector target are required to lend money to specific government agencies at low rates of interest. In January 1998, eligibility for inclusion in the small-scale industry category was expanded, and the limit on a firm's total investment in plants and machinery was raised from Rs. 6.5 million to Rs. 30 million. Our empirical strategy focuses on the firms that became newly eligible for credit in this period;

---

10. See Bernanke and Gertler (1989), Fazzari, Hubbard, and Petersen (1998), and the criticism in Kaplan and Zingales (2000).

11. See, inter alia, Blanchflower and Oswald (1998), Lamont (1997).

12. Banerjee and Duflo (2003).

we use firms that were already eligible as a control. The results from our analysis are reported briefly below.

Data: Our data are from one of the better-performing Indian public sector banks. The bank's loan folders report on profit, sales, credit lines and utilization, and interest rates, as well as all numbers that the banker was required to calculate (for example, his projection of the bank's future turnover and his calculation of the bank's credit needs) in order to determine the amount to be lent. We record these and will use them in the analysis described in the next section. We have data on 253 firms (including 93 newly eligible firms); for 175 of these firms, the data are available for the entire 1997 to 1999 period.

Specification: Through much of this section we will estimate an equation of the form

$$(1) \qquad y_{it} - y_{it-1} = \alpha_y BIG_i + \beta_y POST_t - \gamma_y BIG * POST_t + \varepsilon_{yit},$$

with y taking the role of the various outcomes of interest (credit, revenue, profits, and so forth) and the dummy *POST* representing the post-January 1998 period. We are in effect comparing how the outcomes change for the big firms after 1998 with how they change for the small firms. Because y is always a growth rate, this is, in effect, a triple difference. We can allow small firms and big firms to have different rates of growth, and the rate of growth to differ from year to year, but we assume that there would have been no differential changes in the rate of growth of small and large firms in 1998 absent the change in the priority sector regulation.

Using, respectively, the log of the credit limit and the log of next year's sales (or profit) in place of y in equation 1, we obtain the first stage and the reduced form of a regression of sales on credit, using the interaction *POST * BIG* as an instrument for credit. We will present the corresponding instrumental variable regressions.

Results: The change in the regulation certainly had an impact on who got priority sector credit. The credit limit granted to firms below Rs. 6.5 million in plant and machinery (henceforth, small firms) grew by 11.1 percent during 1997, while that granted to firms between Rs.6.5 million and Rs. 30 million (henceforth, big firms) grew by 5.4 percent. In 1998, after the change in rules, small firms had 7.6 percent growth while the big firms had 11.3 percent growth. In 1999, both big and small firms had about the same growth, suggesting they had reached the new status quo.

This is confirmed when we estimate equation 1 using bank credit as the outcome. The result is presented in column 2 of table 1 for the entire sample of firms. The coefficient of the interaction term *POST * BIG* is 0.095,

TABLE 1. Regressions Estimating the Effect of the 1998 Reform
of Bank Regulation on Changes in Bank Credit to Firms[a]

	Sample and dependent variable[b]				
	Whole sample		Sample with change in credit limit		
Independent variable	Dummy for any change in limit	Change in bank lending to firm	Change in bank lending to firm	Change in interest rate to firm	Change in firm utilization of credit limit
POST[c]	0.000	−0.034	−0.115	−0.007	−0.030
	(0.05)	(0.026)	(0.074)	(0.015)	(0.336)
BIG[d]	−0.043	−0.059	−0.218	−0.002	0.257
	(0.052)	(0.028)	(0.088)	(0.014)	(0.362)
POST * BIG	−0.022	0.095	0.271	0.009	−0.128
	(0.087)	(0.033)	(0.102)	(0.02)	(0.458)
No. of observations	487	487	155	141	44

Source: Authors' regressions using data on client firms of a public sector bank in India.

a. Each column reports regression coefficients for a single regression using ordinary least squares. Standard errors, corrected for heteroskedasticity and for clustering at the sectoral level, are in parentheses.

b. All dependent variables (except in the first column) are calculated as differences in logarithms (for example, the logarithm of lending in the current period minus the logarithm of lending in the previous period).

c. Dummy variable taking a value of 1 when the year is 1998 or later, following the change in regulation on lending to the priority sector.

d. Dummy variable taking a value of 1 when the firm has plant and machinery valued at more than Rs. 6.5 million.

with a standard error of 0.033. Column 1 estimates the probability that a firm's credit limit was changed: the coefficient on *POST * BIG* is close to zero and insignificant, suggesting that the reform did not affect *which* firm's limits were changed. This corresponds to the general observations that whether a firm's file is brought out for a change in limit responds not to the needs of the firm, but to internal dynamics of the bank. We use this fact to partition the sample into two groups on the basis of whether there was a change in the credit limit: we use the sample where there was no change in limit as a "placebo" group, where we can test our identification assumption. Finally, column 3 gives the estimated impact of the reform on loan size for firms whose limit was changed: the coefficient of the interaction *POST * BIG* is 0.27, with a standard error of 0.10.

This increase in credit was not accompanied by a change in the rate of interest (column 4). It did not lead to reduction in the rate of utilization of the limits by the big firms (column 5): the ratio of total turnover (the sum of all debts incurred during the year) to credit limit is not associated with the interaction *POST * BIG*. The additional credit limit thus resulted in an increase in bank credit utilization by the firms.

TABLE 2. Regressions Estimating the Effect of Priority Sector Reform on Firm Sales, Sales-to-Loans Ratios, and Profits[a]

	Dependent variable and sample		
	Change in firm sales[b]		
Regression	Complete sample	Sample without credit substitution	Change in firm profits[b]
Reduced-form estimates			
Sample with change in credit limit			
Coefficient on POST * BIG	0.194	0.168	0.538
Standard error	(0.106)	(0.118)	(0.281)
No. of observations	152	136	141
Sample with no change in credit limit			
Coefficient on POST * BIG	0.007	0.022	0.280
Standard error	(0.074)	(0.081)	(0.473)
No. of observations	301	285	250
Whole sample			
Coefficient on POST * BIG	0.071	0.071	0.316
Standard error	(0.068)	(0.069)	(0.368)
No. of observations	453	421	391
Instrumental variables estimates			
Sample with change in credit limit			
Estimate for change in lending[c]	0.75		1.79
Standard error	(0.37)		(0.94)
No. of observations	152		141

Source: Authors' regressions using data on client firms of a public sector bank in India.

a. Dummy variables POST and BIG are defined as in table 1. Standard errors, corrected for heteroskedasticity and for clustering at the sectoral level, are in parentheses.

b. Changes in sales and in profits are calculated as differences in logarithms from the previous to the current period.

c. Calculated as the difference in logarithms from the previous to the current period.

Table 2 presents the impact of this increase in credit on sales and profits. The coefficient of the interaction POST * BIG in the sales equation in the sample where the limit was increased is 0.19, with a standard error of 0.11 (column 1). By contrast, in the sample where there was no increase in limit, the interaction POST * BIG is close to zero (0.007) and insignificant (column 1, line 2), which suggests that the sales result is not driven by a failure of the identification assumption. The coefficient of the interaction POST * BIG is 0.27 in the credit regression and 0.19 in the sales regression: thus, sales increased almost as fast as loans in response to the reform. This is an indication that there was little or no substitution of bank credit for nonbank credit as a result of the reform and thus that firms are credit constrained.

Additional evidence is provided in column 2. We restrict the sample to firms that have a positive amount of borrowing from the market both before and after the reform and thus have not completely substituted bank borrowing for market borrowing. In this sample as well, we obtain a positive and significant effect of the interaction *POST * BIG*, indicating that these firms must be credit constrained.

In column 3, we present the effect of the reform on profit. Because our dependent variable is the logarithm of profit, we can estimate the impact only on firms whose profits were positive. The effect is even bigger than that on sales: 0.54, with a standard error of 0.28. Here again, we see no effect of the interaction *POST * BIG* in the sample without a change in limit (line 2), which lends support to our identification assumption.

The large effect on profit is not sufficient to establish the presence of credit constraints: even unconstrained firms should see profits increase when they gain access to subsidized credit, because they would substitute cheaper capital for more expensive capital. However, if firms were not expanding, we should not expect to see sales (column 1) or costs (not reported) expand as well.

The instrumental variable (IV) estimate of the effect of loans on sales and profit implied by the reduced form and first stage estimates in columns 1 and 3 are presented in the bottom panel of table 2. Note that the coefficient in column 1 is a lower bound of the effect of working capital on sales, because the reform should have led to some substitution of bank credit for market credit. The IV coefficient is 0.75, with a standard error of 0.37. The effect of working capital on sales is very close to 1, a result that would imply that there cannot be an equilibrium without credit constraint.

The IV estimate of the impact of bank credit on profit is 1.79, though again the sample is limited to firms with positive profits. The estimate is substantially greater than 1, which suggests that the technology has a strong fixed-cost component. However, these coefficients also allow us to estimate the effect of credit expansion on profits.

We can use this estimate to get a sense of the average increase in profit caused by every rupee in loan. The average loan is Rs. 86,800. Therefore an increase of Rs. 1,000 in the loan corresponds to a 1.15 percent increase in loans. Taking 1.79 as the estimate of the effect of the log increase in loan on log increase in profit, an increase of Rs. 1,000 in lending causes a 2 percent increase in profit. At the mean profit (which is Rs. 36,700), this would correspond to an increase in profit of Rs. 756.[13]

13. This estimate may be affected by the fact that the firms with negative profits are dropped from the sample. We have also computed the estimate of the marginal product of capital using data on sales and cost instead of using profits directly. We found that an increase of Rs. 1,000 in the loans leads to an increase of Rs. 730 in profits.

A last piece of important evidence is whether big firms become more likely to default than small firms after the reform: the increase in profits (and sales) may otherwise reflect more risky strategies pursued by the large firms. To answer this question, we collected additional data on the firms based in the Mumbai region (138 firms, a bit over half the sample). In particular, we collected data on whether any of these firms' loans had become nonperforming assets (NPA) in 1999, 2000, or 2001, or were NPA before 1999. The number of NPAs is disturbingly large (consistent with the high rate of NPAs in Indian banks), but large and small firms are equally likely to have a non-performing loan: 7.7 percent of the big firms and 7.29 percent of the small firms (who were not already NPA) defaulted on their loans in 2000 or 2001. Among the firms in Mumbai, 2.5 percent of the large firms and 5.96 percent of the small firms had defaulted between 1996 and 1998. The fraction of firms that had defaulted thus increased a little bit more for large firms, but the difference is small and not significant. The increase in credit did not cause an unusually large number of big firms to default.

Default rate and the higher cost of lending to the firms in the priority sector are not sufficient to narrow significantly the gap between our estimate of the rate of returns to capital and the interest rate. Using these estimates and our previous estimates of the cost of lending to small firms (from previous work[14]), we compute that the interest rate banks should charge to these firms is close to 22 percent rather than the 16 percent they are charging on average. This means that the gap between the social marginal product of capital and the interest rate paid by firms is at least 66 percent. These results provide clear evidence of very substantial underlending: some firms clearly can absorb much more capital at high rates of return. Moreover, the firms in our sample are by Indian standards quite substantial: these are not the very small firms at the margins of the economy, where, even if the marginal product is high, the scope for expansion may be quite limited.

These data do not tell us anything directly about the efficiency of allocation of capital across firms. However, the IV estimate of the effect of loans on profit is strongly positive, while the OLS estimate is not different from zero. In other words, firms that have higher growth in loans do not generate faster growth in profits, suggesting that normally banks do not target loan enhancements to the most profitable firms. This is consistent with

---

14. Banerjee and Duflo (2001).

evidence reported in A. Das-Gupta,[15] that the interest rate paid by firms and by implication the marginal product of capital varies enormously within the same sub-economy.[16] It is also consistent with the more direct evidence in Banerjee and Kaivan Munshi showing substantial variation in the productivity of capital in the knitted garment industry in Tirupur.[17] Furthermore, although we have no direct data on this point, bankers' lore suggests that the firms that have relatively easy access to credit tend to be the bigger and longer established firms.

The under-provision of credit to small-scale industry was one of the key reasons cited for nationalization in 1969: thus, it might in fact be the case that although the public sector banks provide relatively little credit to small-scale industry firms, private banks are even worse. In the next subsection we examine the effect of bank ownership on bank allocation of credit.

Bank Ownership and Sectoral Allocation of Credit

As noted, an important rationale for Indian bank nationalizations was to direct credit toward sectors the government thought were underserved, including small-scale industry, as well as agriculture and backward areas. Ownership was not the only means of directing credit: the Reserve Bank of India issued guidelines in 1974 requiring both public and private sector banks to provide at least one-third of their aggregate advances to the priority sector by March 1979. In 1980, the RBI announced that this quota would increase to 40 percent by March 1985. It also specified sub-targets for lending to agriculture and weaker sectors within the priority sector. In this section we focus on how ownership affected credit allocation in this situation with both public and private banks facing the same regulation.

Comparing nationalized and private banks is never easy: banks that fail are often merged with healthy nationalized banks, which makes the comparison of nationalized banks and non-nationalized banks close to meaningless. The Indian nationalization experience of 1980 represents a unique chance to learn about the relationship between bank ownership and bank lending behavior. The 1980 nationalization took place according to a strict policy rule: all private banks whose deposits were above a certain cutoff were nationalized.[18] Both the banks that were nationalized under this rule

15. Das-Gupta (1989).
16. Banerjee (2003) summarizes this evidence.
17. Banerjee and Munshi (2004).
18. Although the 1969 nationalization was larger and also induced a discontinuity, we do not use it because many of the banks just below the cut-off in 1969 were nationalized in 1980.

and those that were not continued to operate in the same environment and face the same regulations. Therefore they ought to be directly comparable.

Banks nationalized in 1980, however, are larger than the banks that remained private. If size influences bank behavior, it would be incorrect to attribute all differences between nationalized and private sector banks to nationalization. In this section, based on work by Cole, we adopt an approach in the spirit of regression discontinuity design and compare banks just above the 1980 cutoff with those just below it, while controlling for bank size in 1980.[19] The idea behind this comparison is that the relationship between size and behavior should not change dramatically around the cutoff, unless nationalization itself causes changes in bank behavior. This will allow for credible causal inference on the role of bank ownership on bank behavior.

To get a sense of the magnitude of lending differences among bank types, we first divide the banks into five groups, based on their size in 1980: State Bank of India and its affiliates, large nationalized banks (nationalized in 1969), "marginal" nationalized banks (nationalized in 1980), "marginal" private banks (relatively large, but just too small to be nationalized in 1980), and small private banks. Because the geographic districts in which banks are located vary (soil quality, rural population, and so forth) and face different economic shocks, we focus here on comparing differential bank behavior within each district. Our outcomes of interest include average loan size, residual interest rate, and share of bank lending to the following areas: agriculture, rural credit, small-scale industry, government credit, and "trade, transport, and finance."[20] The unconditional, India-wide means of these variables are given in column 1 of table 3. To estimate bank-group effects, we regress credit outcome variables for each bank group g in district d on D district dummy variables and $BG_1, \ldots, BG_G$ bank group dummy variables. The State Bank of India group is the omitted category. Specifically, we estimate:

$$(2) \qquad y_{b,d,t} = \sum_{i=1}^{G} \gamma_i BG_i + \sum_{i=1}^{G} \delta_i \, \text{District}_i + \varepsilon_{b,d,t}.$$

The estimated bank group effects, $\hat{\gamma}_1, \ldots, \hat{\gamma}_G$, give the deviation in average share of credit of each bank from the average share of credit of the State Bank

19. Cole (2004).

20. The residual interest rate is obtained by regressing the interest rate on a wide range of control variables: an indicator variable for small scale industry, borrower occupation dummies (at the three-digit level), district fixed effects, size of loan, an indicator for whether the borrower is from the public or private sector, and dummies indicating whether the loan is given in a rural, urban, semi-urban, or urban area.

**TABLE 3. Regressions Estimating Differences in Loan Size and
Sectoral Lending by Type of Bank**

		Estimated bank group effects[a]				
Measure	Uncon-ditional mean	Large nation-alized banks	Marginal nation-alized banks	Marginal private sector banks	Small private sector banks	Test of differ-ence[b]
Average loan size (thousands of rupees)[c]	48.32	−6.43	8.35	35.31	58.50	13.94
		(1.27)	(2.68)	(7.37)	(9.21)	(0.00)
Sectoral share of total lending[d]						
Agriculture	0.11	0.00	−0.08	−0.13	−0.17	23.65
		(0.01)	(0.01)	(0.01)	(0.01)	(0.00)
Small-scale industry	0.09	−0.02	−0.02	−0.04	−0.02	8.35
		(0.00)	(0.01)	(0.01)	(0.01)	(0.00)
Rural areas	0.12	0.08	−0.03	−0.07	−0.12	4.38
		(0.01)	(0.01)	(0.01)	(0.01)	(0.04)
Government enterprises	0.03	-0.01	−0.02	−0.02	−0.03	3.70
		(0.00)	(0.00)	(0.00)	(0.00)	(0.05)
Trade, transport, and finance	0.21	0.01	0.07	0.13	0.13	36.70
		(0.00)	(0.01)	(0.01)	(0.01)	(0.00)

Source: Authors' calculations using credit data from Reserve Bank of India, *Basic Statistical Returns*, 1992, 1993, 1999, and 2000.

a. Banks are divided into groups based on their status in 1980. "Large nationalized banks" comprises those banks that were nationalized in 1969; "Marginal nationalized banks" comprises those that were nationalized in 1980; "Marginal private sector banks" comprises the nine largest banks in 1980 that were not nationalized; "Small private sector banks" comprises the remainder of private sector banks in 1980.

b. F-statistics and (in parentheses) p values for the test of the hypothesis that the estimates for the "Marginal nationalized banks" and the "Marginal private sector banks" are the same.

c. The first column represents the unconditional average size of all bank loans in India issued over the time period; the second through the fifth columns report estimates of the average loan size by each bank group, after controlling for the district in which the loan was issued. Standard errors are in parentheses.

d. The first column reports the unconditional mean share of all bank credit to the indicated sector; the second through the fifth columns report the estimated deviation in the share lent by each bank group from the share lent by the State Bank of India group, after controlling for the district in which the loan was issued. Standard errors are in parentheses.

Group of India, after controlling for differences across districts. These coefficients are presented in table 3. (We use data from 1992, 1993, 1999, and 2000.) For example, compared with the average loan size of the State Bank of India, nationalized banks gave slightly smaller loans (an average of Rs. 6,430 lower), while marginal nationalized banks gave slightly larger loans (the average was Rs. 8,350 greater), marginal private banks gave much larger loans (Rs. 35,310 more), and small private banks gave loans much larger on average (Rs. 58,500 more). These results appear to confirm conventional wisdom that nationalized and public banks give smaller loans than private banks.

The most informative comparison is between what we called the "marginal" nationalized and the "marginal" private bank, which were similar in size, but with the former nationalized and the latter not. Many of the differences between the marginal nationalized and the marginal private banks are large: the marginal private banks gave 5 percentage points less credit to agriculture than the marginal nationalized banks: given that the all-India share of credit to agriculture is 11 percent, this difference is substantial. The results also suggest that nationalization led to more credit to small-scale industry (an increase of 2 percentage points relative to the private banks; India-wide small-scale industry receives 9 percent of total credit), 4 percentage points more credit to rural areas (compared with a national average of 12 percent), and slightly more to government enterprises (0.7 percent more; the India-wide figure is 3 percent.). These increases come at the expense of credit to trade, transport, and finance (nationalized banks gave 6 percent points less, compared with the national average share of 21 percent). The final column in table 3 gives the results of an F-test of the hypothesis $\gamma_{\text{Marginal Private}} = \gamma_{\text{Marginal Nationalized}}$. The rural and government lending differences are significant at the 5 percent level, while all others are significant at the 1 percent level.

Although this finding suggests that private and public banks behave differently, the values in the table vary not only between marginal private and marginal nationalized banks, but across other bank groups as well. Thus, from this data alone, we cannot rule out the possibility that the difference in lending behavior is attributable to bank size, rather than ownership.

To obtain an accurate measure of the impact of nationalization, we examine lending behavior at the individual bank level, adopting a full-fledged regression-discontinuity approach. We first estimate bank effects analogous to the group effects estimated in equation 2, by replacing the bank group dummy indicators with individual bank dummy indicators, to obtain coefficients $\hat{\beta}_1, \ldots \hat{\beta}_B$. These coefficients tell us to what extent bank b behaves differently from other banks, after controlling for the characteristics of the districts in which each bank operates. We then regress the individual indicators $\hat{\beta}_b$ on log deposits of the bank in 1980 ($size_b$), an indicator variable (NAT_b) which takes the value of 1 when the size was larger than the cutoff and the bank therefore nationalized, and an interaction term ($NAT_b * size_b$). This specification thus allows for a break at the nationalization cutoff value, as well as differential slopes for banks below and above the cutoff:

$$(3) \qquad \hat{\beta}_b = \alpha + \delta_1 SIZE_i + \gamma_1 NAT_i + \delta_2 (NAT_b * SIZE_b) + \varepsilon_i .$$

Figure 1 presents the average share each bank provides to small-scale industry, "trade, transport, and finance," agriculture, and in rural areas.

FIGURE 1.   **Effects of Nationalization and Trade Credit**[a]

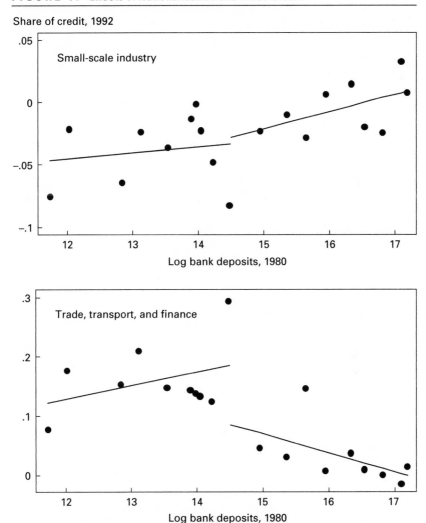

Source: Authors calculations, based on data from the Reserve Bank of India.

a. Each dot represents the average share of credit of two or three banks provided to the sector indicated in the title. The banks are ordered according to the log size of deposits in 1980, which is graphed along the x-axis. The left line gives the fitted relationship for the banks that were not nationalized, while the line on the right gives the fitted relationship for nationalized banks. The distance between the lines at 14.5 is the implied causal impact of nationalization. The sample includes 42 banks, which were aggregated into 19 groups to avoid disclosing any bank-specific information.

FIGURE 1. (*continued*)

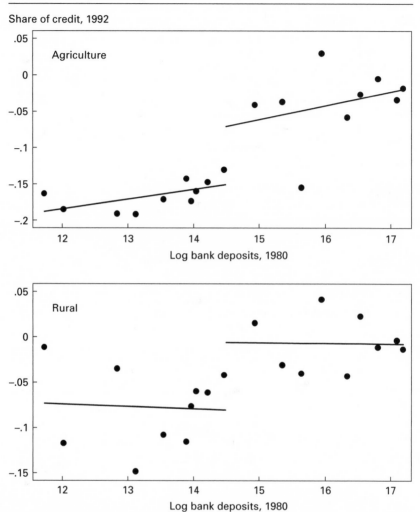

Share of credit, 1992

In the figure, banks are ordered by the size of their deposits in 1980, so that banks below the cutoff of 14.5 are private, while banks above were nationalized in 1980.[21] The left line gives the relationship $\hat{\alpha} + \hat{\delta}_1 * SIZE_i$, while the right line gives the relationship $\hat{\alpha} + \hat{\gamma}_1 + (\hat{\delta}_1 + \hat{\delta}_2) * SIZE_i$. Contrary to

21. To avoid disclosing bank-specific data, we have grouped banks with similar deposit size in 1980 into pairs or groups of three. Thus, although our sample includes forty-two banks that were private or nationalized in 1980, there are only nineteen points on the graph. The statistical analysis presented in table 4 provides estimates based on individual bank-level data.

the results obtained by simple comparison of means, there does not appear to be any significant difference in lending to small-scale industry between public and private banks of similar size. That is, we cannot reject the hypothesis that nationalization had no effect on credit to small-scale industry. On the other hand, nationalization appears to have lowered the amount of credit banks provide to trade, transport, and finance.

Nationalization appears to have had a large effect on credit to agriculture, as indicated in that panel. There is a relationship between size in 1980 and lending to agriculture in 1992: larger banks lend more to agriculture. However, there is a visible break in the relationship at the nationalization cutoff: banks just above the cutoff lend substantially more to agriculture than banks just below, even after accounting for the effect of size. The analogous graph for rural credit is also presented.

Table 4 provides estimates of the size of the discontinuity, $\hat{\gamma}_1 + \hat{\delta}_2 * 14.5$, estimated on data from 1992 and 2000 separately. For example, for agriculture in 1992, the estimated break is .082, with a standard error of .030: the difference between nationalized and private banks is quite significant, both economically and statistically.

The point estimates of the structural break confirm some of the differences described above but suggest that others are merely functions of bank size. In particular, as measured by credit in 1992, nationalization had a causal effect on agricultural credit and rural credit, increasing each by about 8 percentage points. These numbers are large, given that the set of all banks lent only 11 percent of credit to agriculture and 12 percent to rural areas. These results are significant at the 1 percent level. Nationalization appears to have had no effect on the amount of credit banks lend to small-scale industry, but caused a 9 percentage point decrease in the credit banks issued to trade, transport, and finance. Not surprisingly, we see that nationalized banks lend more to government-owned enterprises; the 2 percentage point difference is particularly large in light of the fact that credit to government borrowers represents only 2 percent of bank credit. Public sector banks appear to lend at slightly lower interest rates, though the point estimate, 70 basis points, is not statistically significant. We also attempted to measure whether public sector banks gave more credit to industries that had been identified for support in various five-year plans after 1980, but found no evidence that these industries were favored.

The differences between the nationalized and private banks seem to have decreased over time: in the 2000 data, the point estimate on agricultural lending drops from 8 to 5 points, on rural lending from 7 to 3 points, and on trade, transport, and finance from −11 to −6 points.

TABLE 4. Point Estimates of the Effect of Bank Nationalization on Average Loan Size, Sectoral Lending, and Interest Rates

Measure	Estimate of discontinuity[a]	
	1992	*2000*
Average loan size	−24.753	−143.867
	(10.332)	(69.784)
Share of total lending		
Agriculture	0.082	0.031
	(0.030)	(0.021)
Rural areas	0.073	0.021
	(0.027)	(0.023)
Small-scale industry	0.009	0.020
	(0.017)	(0.026)
Trade, transport, and finance	−0.073	−0.037
	(0.040)	(0.031)
Government enterprises[b]	0.020	
	(0.011)	
Interest rate (residual[c])	−0.007	−0.007
	(0.008)	(0.006)

Sources: Authors' calculations using data from Reserve Bank of India, *Basic Statistical Returns*, 1992 and 2000.

a. Calculated by estimating the relationship between bank lending behavior and bank size according to the following equation:

$$\beta_i = \alpha + \delta_i SIZE_i + \gamma_1 NAT_i + \delta_2 NAT * SIZE + \varepsilon_{ir}$$

where $SIZE_i$ is the logarithm of deposits of bank i in 1980 and NAT_i is a dummy variable taking the value of 1 if the bank was above the threshold for nationalization in 1980, and then evaluating the fitted regression equations for marginal nationalized and marginal private sector banks (as defined in table 3) at the threshold for nationalization (14.5, in logarithms) and subtracting. Standard errors are in parentheses.

b. Data on lending to government in 2000 were not available.

c. Estimated residual from a regression of the interest rate on a range of loan characteristic variables and district fixed effects. See the notes to the text for a list of all controls.

In sum, bank ownership does seem to have had a limited impact on the government's ability to direct credit to specific sectors. Through the early 1990s, the credit environment in India was very tightly regulated. The government set interest rates and required both public and private banks to issue 40 percent of credit to the priority sector and to meet specific subtargets within the priority sector. Nevertheless, banks controlled by the government provided substantially more credit to agriculture, rural areas, and the government, at the expense of credit to trade, transport, and finance. Surprisingly, there was no effect on credit to small-scale industry. Lending differences shrunk over the 1990s and in 2000 to about half what they were in the early 1990s. This might reflect either the increasing dynamism of the private sector banks in the liberalized environment of the 1990s or the loosening grip of the government on the nationalized banks.

Bank Ownership and Speed of Financial Development

To determine whether public ownership of banks inhibits financial intermediation, we again compare banks just above and just below the 1980 nationalization cutoff, using data from the Reserve Bank of India, for the period 1969 to 2000. We include the six banks above, which were nationalized, and the nine largest below, which were not.[22] Because we have data from both before and after the 1980 nationalization, we adopt a difference-in-differences approach. Specifically, we regress the annual change in bank deposits, credit, and number of bank branches on a dummy for post-nationalization (POST$_t$ = 1 if year $\in$ (1980 – 1991)) and a dummy for post-nationalization in a liberalized environment (NINETIES$_t$ = 1 if year $\in$ (1992 – 2000)). We break the post-nationalization analysis up into two periods (1980–91 and 1991–2000) because the former period was characterized by continued financial repression, while substantial liberalization measures were implemented in the beginning of the 1990s. Public and private banks could well behave differently before and after liberalization. Because larger banks may grow at different rates than small banks, we include bank fixed effects (β_i). We thus regress:

$$(4) \quad \ln (y_{b,t}/y_{b,t-1}) = \beta_i + \theta_1 POST_t + \theta_2 * NINETIES_t + \gamma_1 (POST_t * NAT_b) + \gamma_2 (NINETIES_t * NAT_b) + \varepsilon_{b,t}$$

The parameters of interest are γ_1 and γ_2, which capture the differential behavior of nationalized banks after the nationalization. Standard errors are adjusted for auto-correlation within each bank.

Table 5 presents the results for growth in credit, deposits, and bank branches. The results suggest that although the overall rate of growth in deposits and credit slowed substantially during 1980–90 relative to 1969–79, there was no differential effect for nationalized and private banks. In the nineties, deposit and credit growth slowed further still. In this liberalized environment, deposits and credit of the nationalized banks slowed more than those of the private banks: deposits grew 7.3 percent more slowly, while credit grew 8.8 percent more slowly. These results are significant at the 10 percent and 5 percent level, respectively.

22. In 1985, the Lakshmi Commercial Bank was merged with Canara Bank, a large public sector bank, because of financial weakness. In 1993, the New Bank of India (nationalized in 1980) was merged with the Punjab National Bank. Because both the Canara and Punjab National banks were nationalized in 1969, they are not in our sample.

TABLE 5. Regressions Estimating the Effect of Nationalization on Growth of Deposits, Credit, and Number of Branches[a]

	Dependent variable			
	Log real growth of		Log growth rate of	
Independent variable	Deposits	Credit	No. of branches	No. of rural branches
POST	−0.085	−0.078	−0.114	−0.181
	(0.014)	(0.015)	(0.017)	(0.024)
POST * NATIONALIZATION	−0.026	−0.012	−0.044	−0.066
	(0.033)	(0.036)	(0.033)	(0.031)
NINETIES	−0.040	−0.027	−0.122	−0.219
	(0.014)	(0.017)	(0.018)	(0.022)
NINETIES * NATIONALIZATION	−0.073	−0.088	−0.053	−0.086
	(0.039)	(0.041)	(0.034)	(0.028)
R^2	.15	.11	.48	.31
No. of observations	440	440	420	434
No. of clusters	15	15	14	14

Source: Authors' calculations from data in Reserve Bank of India, *Statistical Tables Relating to Banks in India*, 1970–2000, and *Directory of Commercial Banks in India*, 2000.

a. The sample includes the six banks just above and the nine just below the cutoff for nationalization in 1980. Branch data were not available for the Lakshmi Commercial Bank, which failed in 1985 and was merged with Canara Bank, a large bank nationalized in 1969, which is not in the sample. Underlying data for deposits and credit are in rupees adjusted for inflation, and data for branches are annual growth rates (all in logarithms). The variable POST takes a value of 1 when the year is from 1980 to 1991 inclusive; NINETIES takes the value of 1 when the year is from 1992 to 2000 inclusive; NATIONALIZATION takes the value of 1 if the bank was nationalized in 1980. All regressions include bank fixed effects. Standard errors, adjusted for serial correlation, are in parentheses.

The growth rate in bank branches generally tracked credit and deposits, though the decline after 1980 was more severe. While the growth rates for nationalized banks were slightly lower in both periods, the differences are not statistically significant.

To answer the question of whether there was a significant difference between public and private banks before nationalization, we reestimate equation 4, replacing the bank fixed effects with a nationalization dummy, and a control function $(K_{b,80}) = \pi_1 K_{b,80} + \pi_2 K_{b,80}^2$, which controls for the effect of 1980 log deposits of each bank in 1980 (denoted $K_{b,80}$). (These results are not reported but are available from the authors.) The control function allows bank growth to depend on bank size, while the nationalization dummy will pick up any differences between the nationalized and non-nationalized banks that are not related to size. The estimates suggest that credit, deposits, and number of branches grew at the same speed between 1969 and 1979 for banks that were going to be nationalized in 1980 and those that were not. The coefficients on the interaction terms ($POST_t * NAT_b$) and ($NINETIES_t * NAT_b$) remain negative and are virtually unchanged from the specification we present in table 5. Thus, it is only *after* the 1980 nationalization that banks nationalized in 1980 started to grow more slowly. These results provide some evidence that nationalization hindered the spread of intermediation in the 1990s, but not earlier.

Constraints on Public Sector Lending

Having established that small-scale firms in India are credit constrained, and that, if anything, bank nationalization exacerbated these constraints, we now attempt to determine *why* public sector banks appear so reluctant to lend. We first look at the rules public sector banks use to allocate credit, and then examine how the incentives for loan officers affect lending decisions.

Lending Policy

We begin by examining the official rules used by public sector banks to allocate credit. We find the rules surprisingly conservative. Because theory and praxis often differ, we then examine actual lending decisions and find that the conservative character of the rules is exacerbated by conservative deviations from the rules.

OFFICIAL LENDING POLICIES. Although public sector banks in India are nominally independent entities, they are subject to intense regulation by the Reserve Bank of India (RBI). Among the rules is one that limits how much a bank can lend to individual borrowers—the so-called "maximum permissible bank finance." Until 1997, the rule was based on the working capital gap, defined as the difference between the current assets of the firm and its total current liabilities excluding bank finance (other current liabilities). The presumption is that the current assets are illiquid in the very short run and therefore the firm needs to finance them. Trade credit is one source of finance, and what the firm cannot finance in this way constitutes the working capital gap.

Firms were supposed to cover a part of this financing need, corresponding to no less than 25 percent of the current assets, from equity. The maximum permissible bank finance under this method was thus:

(5) $0.75 * CURRENT\ ASSETS - OTHER\ CURRENT\ LIABILITIES$

The sum of all loans from the banking system was supposed not to exceed this amount.[23]

This definition of the maximum permissible bank finance applied to loans greater than Rs. 20 million. For loans less than Rs.20 million, banks were supposed to calculate the limit based on the projected turnover of the firm. Projected turnover was to be determined by a loan officer in consultation with the client. The firm's financing need was estimated to be 25 percent of the projected turnover, and the bank was allowed to finance up to 80 percent of what the firm needs, that is, up to 20 percent of the firm's projected turnover. The rest, amounting to at least 5 percent of the projected turnover, has again to be financed by long-term resources available to the firm.

In the middle of 1997, the RBI set up a committee, headed by P. R. Nayak, to make recommendations regarding the financing of small-scale industries. Following the committee's advice, the RBI decided to give each bank the flexibility to evolve its own lending policy, under the condition that it be made explicit. Moreover, they adopted the recommendation that the turnover rule be used to calculate the lending limit for all loans less than Rs. 40 million.

Given the freedom to choose the rule, different banks went for slightly different strategies. The bank we studied adopted a policy that was, in effect, a mix between the now recommended turnover-based rule and the older rule based on the firm's asset position. First the limit on turnover basis was calculated as:

$$(6) \quad \min(0.20 * \text{Projected turnover}, 0.25 * \text{Projected turnover} - \text{Available margin}).$$

The available margin here is the financing available to the firm from long-term sources (such as equity) and is calculated as *CURRENT ASSETS – CURRENT LIABILITIES* from the current balance sheet. In other words, the presumption is that the firm has somehow managed to finance this gap in the current period and therefore should be able to do so in the future. Therefore the bank needs to finance only the remaining amount. Note that if the firm had previously managed to get the bank to follow the turnover-based rule exactly, its available margin would be precisely 5 percent of turnover and the two amounts in equation 6 would be equal.

23. Thus, a particular bank had to deduct from this amount the credit limits offered by other banks. Following this rule implies that the current ratio will be more than 1.33, and the rule is often formulated as the requirement that the current ratio exceeds 1.33.

The rule did not stop here. For all loans less than Rs. 40 million (as all loans in our sample are), the loan officer was supposed to use both equation 6 and the older rule represented by equation 5. The largest permissible limit on the loan was the maximum of these two numbers.

Two comments about the nature of this rule are in order. First, this turnover-based approach to working capital finance is relatively standard even in the United States. However, the view in the United States is that working capital finance is essentially financing inventories and is therefore backed by the value of the inventories. In India, the inventories do not seem to provide adequate security, as evidenced by the high rates of default. In such cases it may be much more important to pay attention to profitability, because profitable companies are less likely to default. Second, in the United States the role of finding promising firms and promoting them is carried out largely by venture capitalists. In India the venture capital industry is still nascent and is not yet able to play the role that we expect of its U.S. equivalent. Therefore banks may have to be more proactive in promoting promising firms. Following a rule that puts no weight on profits may not be the way to favor the most promising firms: although the projected turnover calculation does favor faster-growing firms, the loan officer is not allowed to project a growth rate greater than 15 percent. This may be enough to meet the needs of a mature firm, but a small firm that is growing fast clearly needs much more than 15 percent. It is important that the rules encourage the loan officers to lend more to companies on the basis of promise.

ACTUAL LENDING POLICY. The lending policy statements give us the outside limits on what the banks can lend. Nothing in the policies stops them from lending less, though official documents always enjoin bankers to lend as much as possible.[24] It is also possible, given that it is not clear how these rules are enforced, that the banks sometimes exceed the limits— it is, for example, often alleged that loan officers in public sector banks give out irresponsibly large loans to their friends and business associates. It is not even clear how one would necessarily know that a banker had lent too much given that he is given the task of estimating expected turnover. In this subsection, based on work by Banerjee and Duflo, we therefore look at the actual practice of lending in our sample of loans.[25]

---

24. For example, a document prepared for the board meeting of the bank we studied reads "The busy season credit policy announced by the Reserve Bank of India stresses on increase in credit off-take by imparting further liquidity into the system and by rationalizing some of the existing guidelines. Banks have, therefore, to pay special attention to this aspect in the coming months and locate all potential/viable avenues so as to accelerate the path of credit expansion."

25. Banerjee and Duflo (2001).

TABLE 6. Actual Credit Limits Granted to Firms
Compared with Permissible Limits

	Limit actually granted versus limit on turnover basis		Limit actually granted versus limit officially permitted[a]		Limit actually granted versus previous limit granted[b]		Limit officially permitted versus limit previously permitted[c]	
	No. of firms	Percent of total	No. of firms	Percent of total	No. of firms	Percent of total	No. of firms	Percent of total
Smaller	255	62	542	78	22	4	153	35
Same	81	20	9	1	322	64	6	1
Larger	74	18	142	20	158	31	281	64

Source: Authors' calculations from account-level data from one large public sector bank in India during 1997–99.

a. Maximum officially permitted credit limit is the larger of the limit calculated by the turnover method or that calculated by the working capital gap method.

b. "Previous limit granted" is the amount offered to the same firm the year before.

c. "Limit previously permitted" is the value of the official limit for the firm in the previous year.

Data: Our data source is the same used in previous work by Banerjee and Duflo (and described in connection with equation 1).[26] Because we have data on current assets and other current liabilities, it is simple to calculate the limit according to the traditional, working capital gap–based method of lending (henceforth LWC). We can also calculate the limit on turnover basis (henceforth LTB). The maximum of LTB and LWC is, according to the rules, the real limit on how much the banker can lend to the firm.

Results: In table 6, we compare the actual limit granted with LTB, LWC. In 78 percent of the cases, the limit granted is smaller than the amount permitted. Most strikingly, in 64 percent of the cases for which we know the amount granted in the previous period, the amount granted is exactly equal to that granted in the previous period (it is smaller 4 percent of the time and goes up only in 31 percent of the cases). Given that that inflation rate was 5 percent or higher, the real amount of the loans therefore decreases between two adjacent years in a majority of the cases. To make matters worse, in 73 percent of these cases the firm's sales had increased, implying, one presumes, a greater demand for working capital. Further, this is the case even though according to the bank's own rules, the limit could have gone up in 64 percent of the cases (note that getting a higher limit is simply an option and does not cost the firm anything unless it uses the money). Finally, this tendency seems to become more pronounced over

26. Banerjee and Duflo (2003).

TABLE 7. **Regressions Explaining Actual Credit Limits and Interest Rates**[a]

| | Dependent variable | | | | |
| | Actual credit limit granted | | | Interest rate | |
Independent variable	(1)	(2)	(3)	(4)	(5)
Limit granted in previous year	0.757	0.540	0.455	−0.198	−0.260
	(0.04)	(0.059)	(0.084)	(0.108)	(0.124)
Previous interest rate				0.823	0.832
				(0.038)	(0.041)
Maximum limit under bank's internal rule[b]	0.256 (0.042)				
Limit on turnover basis as calculated by the bank		0.145 (0.036)		−0.019 (0.102)	
Limit on turnover basis as calculated by authors[c]			0.102 (0.025)		−0.025 (0.09)
Limit based on working capital gap		0.240 (0.046)	0.279 (0.061)	0.091 (0.083)	0.083 (0.084)
Ratio of profits to firm's assets		0.021 (0.017)	−0.001 (0.021)	−0.048 (0.043)	−0.036 (0.044)
Dummy variable for negative profits		−0.037 (0.115)	0.053 (0.129)	−0.045 (0.272)	−0.037 (0.266)
Ratio of tangible net worth to firm's debt		−0.104 (0.029)	−0.112 (0.032)	−0.064 (0.076)	−0.087 (0.07)
Assets		0.080 (0.056)	0.143 (0.065)	0.063 (0.104)	0.168 (0.118)
Interest paid as share of year-before granted limit			0.005 (0.037)		
Constant term	0.011 (0.079)	−0.009 (0.154)	−0.021 (0.195)	2.547 (0.749)	2.180 (0.843)
R^2	.952	.955	.962	.878	.881
No. of observations	298	241	145	198	194

Source: Authors' calculations from account-level data from one large public sector bank in India.
a. All data except interest rates and dummy variables are in logarithms. Standard errors, corrected for clustering at the account level, are in parentheses.
b. Higher of limit based on turnover as calculated by the bank or limit based on working capital gap.
c. Using bank's projection of turnover.

time: in 1997, the limit was equal to the previous granted limit 53 percent of the time. In 1999, it remained unchanged in 70 percent of the cases.

In table 7, we regress the limit granted on information that might be expected to play a role in its determination. Not surprisingly, given everything we have said, past loan is a very powerful predictor of today's loan. The R-squared of the regressions is also very high (over 95 percent). In column 1, we regress (log) current loan amount on (log) limit granted in the previous year and the (log) maximum limit according to the bank's internal rules. Note that the bank's rule never refers to past loan as a determinant of the loan amount to be given out. Yet the coefficient of past loan is 0.757, with a t statistic of 18 (a 1 percent increase in past loan is associated with a 0.756 percent increase in current loan, after controlling for the official rule). The maximum limit is also a significant determinant of loan amount, with a coefficient of 0.256. The standard deviation of these two variables is very close (1.50 and 1.499, respectively). These coefficients thus mean that a one standard deviation increase in the log of the previous granted limit increases the log of the granted limit by three times as much as a one standard deviation increase in the log of the maximum limit as calculated by the bank.

In column 2, we "unpack" the official limit: we include separately the bank's limit on turnover basis (LTB) and the limit based on the traditional method (LWC) and now include the logarithm of profits. As in the previous regression, past loan is the most powerful predictor of current loan. Both limits enter the regression. Neither the log of profit nor the dummy for negative profit enter the regression, as might have been expected given the nature of the rules.

In column 3 we include in addition a measure of the utilization by the client of the limit granted to him in the previous year: the ratio of interest earned by the bank to the account limit. This is clearly of direct interest to the bank, because it loses money when funds are committed, but not used. This information is routinely collected on each client. Yet this variable is uncorrelated with granted limit. We tried other measures of utilization of the limit (turnover on the account divided by granted limit, and maximum debt divided by granted limit), and none of these measures is significant.

In columns 4 and 5 we investigate the determinants of interest rates. Past interest rates seem to be the only significant determinant of today's interest rates. Past loans, LTB, and LWC do not enter the regression.

In sum, the actual policy followed by the bank seems to be characterized by systematic deviation from what the rules permit in the direction of inertia. To the extent that limits do change, what seems to matter is the size of the firm, as measured by its turnover and outlay, and not profitability or the utilization of the limit by the client.

It could be argued that inertia is rational: the past loan amount picks up all the information that the loan officer has accumulated about the firm that we do not observe. But this explanation does not fit well with the fact that the loan amount remains exactly the same—the past may be important, but, as noted, the firm's needs are changing, if only because of inflation.

There is also a simple test of this view. The weight on past loans represents the bank's experience with the firm: the fact that the weight is so high presumably reflects the fact that the past is very informative, suggesting a stable environment. But a stable environment necessarily implies that the bank knows a lot more about its old clients than it does about its newest clients. Therefore we should see the weight going up sharply with the age of the firm. Yet when we run the regressions predicting the loan amount separately for firms that have been the client of the bank for 5 years or more and for those who have been clients for less than 5 years, we find that banks do not put less weight on the past loans for recent clients than for old clients. If anything, when we include today's sales in the regression the bank seems to put more weight on past loans for recent clients than for old clients.[27] If there is a good reason for the inertia, it has to be something much more complicated.

It is also conceivable that it is rational to ignore profit information in lending if the projected turnover calculated by the bank and included in the calculation of LTB already takes into account any useful information contained in the profits. To examine this, we looked at whether current profitability has any role in predicting future profitability, delay in repayment, and default, once we control for the variables that seem to determine the level of lending—past loans, LTB, LWC. As reported in Banerjee and Duflo, current profit is a good predictor of future profit, and the variables that the bank uses are not: the only good predictor of future negative profit is current negative profit.[28] Negative profits, in turn, predict default, while past loans, LTB, and LWC do not.[29]

Conclusion: This subsection suggests an extremely simple prima facie explanation of why many firms in India seem to be starved of credit. The nationalized banks, or at least the one we study (but again, this is one of the best public banks), seem to be remarkably reluctant to make fresh lending decisions: in two-thirds of the cases, there is no change in the nominal loan amount from year to year. While the rules for lending are indeed fairly rigid, this inertia seems to go substantially beyond what the rules dictate. Moreover, the deviations from the rules do not seem to reflect informed judgments, but rather a desire to do as little as possible.

Moreover, when banks take a decision to make a fresh loan, the beneficiaries tend to be firms whose turnover is growing regardless of profitability. This indifference to profitability is entirely consistent with the rules that bankers work with: none of the many calculations that bankers are supposed to do before they decide on the loan amount pays even lip service to

27. See Banerjee and Duflo (2001, table 5).
28. Banerjee and Duflo (2001).
29. There is some question about whether we have the right measure of default.

the need to identify the most profitable borrowers. Yet current profits do a much better job of predicting future losses and therefore future defaults, than do the variables that seem to influence the lending decision. In other words, it seems plausible that a banker who made better use of profit information would do a better job at avoiding defaults. Moreover, he or she might do a better job of identifying the firms where the marginal product of capital is the highest. Lending based on turnover, by contrast, may skew the lending process toward firms that have been able to finance growth out of internal resources and therefore do not need the capital nearly as much.

What Causes Under-Lending?

Given that the rules for lending are quite rigid and largely indifferent to profitability, it is perhaps not surprising that there are opportunities for profitable investment that have not yet been exploited. What is surprising is that to the extent that there are deviations from the rules, they tend to be in the direction of lending less.

One plausible explanation is that the loan officers in these banks have no particular incentive to lend. As government employees on a more or less fixed salary and promotion schedule, their rewards are at best weakly tied to their success in making imaginative lending decisions. And failed loans, as discussed below, can lead to investigations by the Central Vigilance Commission, the body entrusted to investigate fraud in the public sector. Loan officers therefore have much to lose and little to gain from being aggressive in lending. Not taking any new decisions may dominate any other course of action, especially if there are attractive alternatives to lending, such as putting money in government bonds.

The next sub-section examines how the fear of prosecution discourages lending. The following sub-section asks whether the reluctance to lend is exacerbated when the rewards from putting money in government bonds become relatively more attractive.

INERTIA AND THE FEAR OF PROSECUTION. Because public sector banks are owned by the government, their employees are treated by law as public servants subject to government anti-corruption legislation. Bankers believe that it is easy to be charged with corruption and that the law states that any government functionary who takes a decision that results in direct financial gain to a third party is prima facie guilty of corruption and must prove her or his innocence.

The executive director of a large public sector bank was quoted saying "Fear of prosecution for corruption hangs over every loan officer's head like the sword of Damocles." The *Economic Times of India* has attributed slowdowns in lending directly to vigilance activity.[30] A working group on banking policy set up by the Reserve Bank of India, and chaired by M. S. Verma, noted:

> The [working group] observed that it has received representations from the managements and the unions of the banks complaining about the diffidence in taking credit decisions with which the banks are beset at present. This is due to investigations by outside agencies on the accountability of staff in respect of some of the NPA. The group also noticed a marked reluctance at various levels to take any credit decision.[31]

In response to criticism from bankers, economists, and others, the Central Vigilance Commission (CVC), the body entrusted to investigate potential cases of fraud in the public sector, introduced in 1999 a special chapter of the vigilance manual on vigilance in public sector banks. Although the new chapter was meant to reassure bankers, it may not have been entirely successful. The manual reads, for example, that although "every loss caused to the organization, either in pecuniary or non-pecuniary terms, need not necessarily become the subject matter of a vigilance inquiry . . . once a vigilance angle is evident, it becomes necessary to determine through an impartial investigation as to what went wrong and who is accountable for the same."[32]

Interviews with public sector bankers revealed widespread concern: the legal proceedings surrounding charges of corruption can drag on for years, leaving individuals charged with corruption in an uncertain state. Even if an individual is exonerated, he or she may have been relieved of duties, transferred, or passed over for promotion during the investigation. In theory, as well as practice, even one loan gone bad may be sufficient to start vigilance proceedings. The possible penalties stand in stark contrast to rewards. While banks are constantly urged by the Reserve Bank of India to lend as much as possible, there are neither explicit incentives for making good loans nor ways to penalize officers who make conservative decisions. In effect, bankers are accountable to more than one authority—the loan officer's boss is one, central vigilance may be another, and the press yet another. In such circumstances, it may be difficult to provide effective incentives.[33] If so, loan officers would prefer not to take new decisions.

30. "CVC Issues New Norms to Check Bank Frauds," *Hindustan Times* (1998), among others.
31. Quoted in Tannan (2001, p. 1579).
32. Government of India (2001, p. 5).
33. Dixit (1996) describes how the presence of multiple principles in bureaucracies may lead to inaction.

Simply renewing the loan without changing the amount is one easy way to avoid responsibility, especially if the original decision was someone else's (loan officers are frequently transferred). And when bankers do take a decision, making sure not to deviate enormously from the precedent is a way of covering themselves against charges of wrongdoing or worse.

Not surprisingly, the Central Vigilance Commission disputes the claim that there is a "fear psychosis" and to bolster its position released in 2000 a "critical analysis" of vigilance activity in public sector banks in 1999. The analysis reveals that in 1999 the commission received 1,916 references, 72 percent of which were credit-related, recommending punishment in the majority of cases. Their report states that "out of every 100 cases coming before it, the Commission would advise major penalty proceedings in 28 cases, minor penalty proceedings in 32 cases, and administrative warning/exoneration in 40 cases."[34] The author of the report, a CVC official, argued that this level of activity should not be enough to cause "fear psychoses": "These figures reveal that a person is not damned the moment his case is referred to the Commission. . . . These statistics appear to indicate a very fair and objective approach on the part of the Commission to the cases that were referred to it."[35]

The rest of this subsection, based on work by Cole, assesses the evidence for the fear psychosis.[36] The idea is simple: do bankers who are "close to" bankers who have been subject to CVC action slow down lending in the aftermath of that particular action?

Data: Monthly credit data, by bank, were provided by the RBI. Data on frauds are naturally difficult to come by. It is also the policy of the government of India to keep the data on vigilance activity confidential: although some statistics are published, they are too aggregated to be useful for econometric analysis. However, in 1998, in an effort to increase the penalty for fraud through stigma, the government authorized the CVC to publish the name, position, employing bank, and punishment of individual officers of government agencies charged with major frauds. This list consists of eighty-seven officials in public sector banks between 1992 and 2001. Although the nature of the fraud with which they are charged is not known, we do know that approximately 72 percent of frauds relate to illegal extension of credit, with the balance classified as kite-flying or "other."[37] Because our hypothesis is that vigilance decreases lending activity, the

34. Government of India (2000, p. 9).
35. Government of India (2000, p.10).
36. Cole (2002).
37. Government of India (2000).

inclusion of spurious non-credit-related vigilance activity should bias coefficients toward zero.

Empirical Analysis: The first approach is to use bank-level monthly lending data to estimate the effect of vigilance activity on lending, using the following equation,

$$(7) \qquad\qquad y_{it} = \alpha_i + \beta_t + \sum_{k=0}^{w} \gamma_k D_{i,t-k} + \varepsilon_{it}$$

where y_{it} is log credit extended by bank i in month t, α_i is a bank fixed effect, β_t is a month fixed effect, and $D_{i,t-k}$ is an indicator variable for whether vigilance activity was reported by the CVC for bank i in month t − k. Standard errors reported are adjusted for serial correlation and heteroskedasticity. The idea is to compare the bank affected by the vigilance activity with other public sector banks before and after the vigilance event. Which event window to use is not immediately clear: the appropriate start date would most likely be the month when it became known that vigilance proceedings were under way or perhaps the date bankers learned of the judgment. The data published by the CVC give only the date when the CVC provided advice on the case and the date on which action was taken. It is not clear how long it should take before an effect appears or how long one would expect this effect to last. We therefore let the data decide, by estimating models that allow effects ranging from one month to four years.

Table 8 presents estimation results from several similar specifications. Columns 1, 2, and 3 provide estimates for windows of one, twelve, and forty-eight months. There appears to be a clear effect of vigilance activity on lending decisions. Vigilance activity in a specific bank reduces credit supplied by all the branches of that bank by about 3-5 percent. This effect is estimated precisely and is significantly different from zero at the 5 percent level for contemporaneous effect (column 1) and at the 1 percent level for the joint parameters of zero to twenty-four months in columns 2 and 3. The effect is quite persistent, appearing in the data at its original level for up to eighteen months following the vigilance activity, finally becoming statistically indistinguishable from zero two years after the CVC decision or judgment.

This economic effect seems to be sizable for plausible values of the elasticity of gross domestic product with respect to money supply elasticity. For example, if the overall coefficient of 0.03 were accurate for a bank such as the State Bank of India, which provides approximately a quarter of the credit in the economy, decisions on whether to pursue vigilance cases could have measurable macroeconomic effects.

TABLE 8. Regressions Estimating Effect of Indicators of Vigilance Activity on Bank Credit[a]

Months before or after vigilance activity[b]	Regressions measuring effect of previous vigilance activity			Regressions measuring effect of future vigilance activity	
	(1)	(2)	(3)	(4)	(5)
Zero	−0.055	−0.040	−0.037	−0.042	−0.037
	(0.027)	(0.019)	(0.019)	(0.020)	(0.020)
Three		−0.039	−0.032	−0.035	−0.031
		(0.018)	(0.016)	(0.016)	(0.016)
Six		−0.031	−0.023	−0.029	−0.027
		(0.016)	(0.014)	(0.015)	(0.014)
Twelve		−0.036	−0.018	−0.018	−0.015
		(0.016)	(0.012)	(0.014)	(0.010)
Eighteen			−0.028		−0.006
			(0.013)		(0.010)
Twenty-four			−0.012		−0.001
			(0.013)		(0.011)
Thirty-six			−0.014		0.009
			(0.015)		(0.008)
Forty-eight			−0.022		0.022
			(0.028)		(0.015)
R^2	.98	.98	.98	.98	.98
No. of observations	2,997	2,997	2,997	2,997	2,997

Source: Authors' calculations using data from the Reserve Bank of India and the Central Vigilance Commission of India.

a. The dependent variable in all regressions is the logarithm of credit extended by an individual bank in a given month. Data are for twenty-seven public sector banks over 111 months. Standard errors, corrected for heteroskedasticity and serial correlation, are in parentheses.

b. Vigilance activity is defined as the CVC bringing charges against or punishing an officer of a bank. The independent variable of interest is a dummy variable that takes the value of 1 when vigilance activity occurred with respect to a particular bank the indicated number of months before (columns 1–3) or after (columns 4–5) the current month. The regression in column (1) includes a month dummy for the month contemporaneous with the vigilance activity only. In columns (2) and (4), month dummies are included for each of the twelve months before or after the vigilance activity, respectively, and in columns (3) and (5), month dummies are included for each of the forty-eight months before or after (only selected month coefficients are reported). All regressions also include bank and year fixed effects.

Columns 4 and 5 of table 8 present the same specification as in equation 7, but this time with dummies indicating whether a given bank-month is exactly *n* months before CVC vigilance activity.

Table 8 clearly indicates that banks reduced lending before the announced vigilance action, as well as after it. This is not surprising, as the formal vigilance activity usually follows a lengthy investigation. The CVC vigilance manual, introduced in 1999 to streamline the process of investigations, outlines a procedure that lists no binding time constraints, but suggests the entire process be completed within twenty months. Reassuringly, there is no discernable effect for vigilance activity farther out than one year ahead.

Conclusion: Evidence suggests that the fear of being investigated is reducing lending significantly: banks where someone is being investigated slow down lending relative to their own mean level of lending. This finding leaves open the question of whether this reaction is desirable; it is, after all, possible that the loans that are cut are those unlikely to be repaid. But the finding also raises the possibility that honest lenders are being discouraged by excessively stringent regulations.

LENDING TO THE GOVERNMENT AND THE EASY LIFE. Lending to the government is the natural alternative to lending to firms and offers the loan officers a secure vehicle for their money, with none of the legwork and headaches associated with lending to firms. The ideal way to measure how important high interest rates on government bonds might be in explaining under-lending would be to estimate the elasticity of bank lending to the private sector with respect to the interest rate on government securities or the spread between the interest rate on private loans and that on government securities. The problem is that the part of the variation that comes from changes in the rate paid by the government is the same for all banks and therefore is indistinguishable from any other time-varying effect on lending. The part that comes from the rates charged by the banks does vary by bank but cannot possibly be independent of demand conditions in the bank and other unobserved time-varying bank-specific factors. One cannot therefore hope to estimate the true elasticity of lending by regressing loans on the spread.

Our strategy is to focus on a more limited question: are banks more responsive to the central bank interest rates in slow-growing environments? We start by identifying the banks that are particularly likely to be heavily invested in the "easy life." These are banks that, for historical reasons, have most of their branches in the states that are currently growing more slowly than the rest. Our hypothesis is that these banks have a particularly strong reason to invest heavily in government securities, because in a slow-growing environment it is harder to identify really promising clients. They also probably have more "marginal" loans that they are willing to cut and reduce (or not increase) when the interest rate paid to government bonds increases. These banks therefore should be particularly responsive to changes in the interest rate paid by the government.

Data: The outcome we focus on is the ln(credit/deposit ratio) at the end of March of each year for twenty-five public sector and twenty private sector banks. Two minor public sector banks were excluded because of lack of data, and the new private sector banks were excluded for reasons of comparability. The data are from the Reserve Bank of India.

Data on the net state domestic product are from the Central Statistical Office. For our measure of interest rate spread, we subtract from the State Bank of India prime lending rate, the rate given as the weighted average of central government securities. Both interest rate measures are from the RBI, as is the price index used to deflate them.[38]

Specification: Two measures of growth are used. To measure the state growth rate $(growth_{it} = \ln(SDP_{it}) - \ln(SDP_{i,t-1}))$, we use a moving average of the real growth rates of the previous three years (e.g., $avgrowth_{it} = \sum_{t-3}^{t-1}(growth_{it})$. Bank environment growth is a weighted average of the growth rates in the states in which a bank operates:

$$ bkgrowth_{bit} = \sum_{i \in states} \omega_{bi} \, avgrowth_{bit} $$

where the weights ω_{bi} are the percentage of bank branches bank b had in state i in 1980: $\omega_{bi} = \dfrac{N_{bi}}{\sum_{s \in states} N_{bs}}$. Data on branch locations are from the of Directory Commercial Bank Offices in India.[39]

Results: We test this hypothesis with two pairs of linear regressions. First, we consider using the location of a bank's headquarters as an indicator of the growth environment in which a bank operates. Because the regulatory environment in India changed significantly beginning during 1991–92, we estimate our equations for the entire time period, 1985–2000, as well as the "post-reform period" of 1992–2000.

The results are reported in table 9. Columns 1 and 2 report the results using the growth environment of the state in which a bank is headquartered,

38. Data are from the 2001 edition of RBI, "Handbook of Statistics on the Indian Economy." We use the CPI-UNME, for Urban Non-Manual Employees.

39. Branch data are from Reserve Bank of India (2001). We have NSDP for all of the states in which bank headquarters are located. However, in constructing the index, NSDP for the following were not available: Jharkhand, Uttaranchal, Chandigrah, Dadra and Nagar Haveli, Chattisgarh, and Lakhsadeep. Rather than drop any bank that had a branch in one of these states, the ω_{bi} weights are constructed using only the set of branches for which GSP data are available. A second problem is that the growth data are not available for a few states for 1998 and 1999 (Nagaland, Sikkim, Andaman and Nicobar) or 1999 (Goa, Jammu & Kashmir). The two most logical ways of constructing indexes in the absence of these data, namely (i) not using those states when constructing state weights, and thus not using the growth information during 1985–97, and (ii) using one set of weights ω_{bi}^1 during 1985–97, which includes these states, and a second set ω_{bi}^2, which excludes these states in 1998 and 1999, produce essentially identical results. We choose the latter, because we feel Jammu and Kashmir and Goa warrant inclusion throughout 1985–98.

TABLE 9. Regressions Explaining Bank Credit with Spreads on Credit and Economic Growth by State[a]

	Growth measure[b]			
	Growth in net state domestic product in state where bank is headquartered		Weighted average of growth rates in states where bank operates[c]	
Independent variable	1992–2000	1985–2000	1992–2000	1985–2000
Growth rate	1.412	1.538	2.195	2.634
	(0.624)	(1.209)	(0.970)	(1.165)
Growth rate * (spread > 0)	−0.175	−0.137	−0.257	−0.219
(γ^+)	(0.110)	(0.119)	(0.104)	(0.103)
Growth rate * (spread < 0)	0.480	0.592	−0.079	0.473
(γ^-)	(0.521)	(0.405)	(0.791)	(0.562)
State fixed effects?	Yes	Yes	No	No
Bank fixed effects?	No	No	Yes	Yes
R^2	.46	.43	.71	.63
No. of observations	415	730	402	710

Source: Authors' regressions using data from the Reserve Bank of India.

a. The dependent variable in all regressions is the logarithm of the ratio of credit extended to deposits. Data are annual data for twenty-five public sector and twenty private sector banks. Standard errors, corrected for heteroskedasticity and serial correlation, are in parentheses. All regressions include year fixed effects.

b. In all regressions growth is measured as a moving average of real growth rates over the previous three years.

c. Fewer observations are available for these regressions because data on branch locations were unavailable for one bank.

with the first column representing the results for the entire period and the second, results for the post-reform era. Specifically, we estimate

$$(8) \quad \ln (CD_{bit}) = \alpha + \beta * avgrowth_{bit} + \gamma^+ (Spread_t * avgrowth_{bit}) * I_{Spread_t>0} \\ + \gamma^- (Spread_t * avgrowth_{bit}) * I_{Spread_t<0} + \theta_i + \delta_t + \varepsilon_{bit},$$

where $I_{Spread_t>0}$ (resp. $I_{Spread_t<0}$) are indicator variables for whether the spread is positive (resp. negative), θ_i is a state fixed effect, and δ_t is a year fixed effect. Avgrowth$_{bit}$ is the smoothed growth rate for the state where the headquarters of bank b are located. Standard errors are adjusted for serial correlation.

The regression controls for state and year fixed effects. While we see that the C/D is higher in states with more favorable growth rates, we are most interested in the coefficients γ^- and γ^+, which measure how banks in different growth environments differentially react to changes in the spread between the commercial lending rate and the rate on government securities.

Because a negative spread occurs only twice, and in a quite particular situation (in a perfectly flexible market, banks facing a negative spread should eliminate all credit from their portfolios), we allow a separate coefficient on ($Spread_t * avgrowth_{bit}$) when the spread is negative.

The negative and marginally statistically significant coefficient on γ^+ suggests that banks in high-growth environments substitute toward government securities (away from loans) *less* when the spread falls. We interpret this to mean that banks in low-growth states are more sensitive to government interest rates: because they face fewer attractive projects to finance, they are more likely to park money in government securities when government securities become more attractive. However, because the number of states where a bank is headquartered is relatively low, we have relatively low power once we account for serial correlation at the state level.

To achieve more precise estimates, we estimate the same equation, except that instead of measuring growth only in the states where commercial banks are headquartered, we use the synthetic index described above, which takes into account all the states where the bank is active. Columns 3 and 4 present results from:

$$(9) \quad \ln(CD_{bit}) = \alpha + \beta * bkgrowth_{bit} + \gamma^+ (Spread_t * bkgrowth_{bit}) * I_{Spread_t>0}$$
$$+ \gamma^- (Spread_t * bkgrowth_{bit}) * I_{Spread_t<0} + \theta_i + \psi_b + \delta_t + \varepsilon_{bit},$$

where $bkgrowth_{bit}$ is the growth index and ψ_b is a bank fixed effect. Column 3 represents the entire sample, while column 4 represents the post-reform period. The results in columns 3 and 4 are similar in sign to columns 1 and 2, and this time we may say with some confidence that they are statistically significant.

Conclusion: The evidence seems consistent with the view that banks are especially inclined toward the easy life in states where lending is hard. This suggests that the opportunity for lending to the government tends to hurt the firms that are relatively marginal from the point of view of the banks, such as firms in slow-growing states and smaller and less established firms.

Some Final Issues: Rural Branches, NPAs and Bailouts

We conclude our study by examining two final arguments given in favor of public ownership of banks: that public banks are more willing to expand into rural areas and that public banks are less likely to fail and therefore cost the government (or public) less than private banks.

Branch Expansion in Rural Areas

As mentioned in the introduction, in 1977 the government passed a regulation requiring both public and private banks to open four branches in unbanked locations for every branch they opened in banked locations. This regulation was repealed in 1990, though the Reserve Bank of India still maintained some authority of bank branch openings.

Robin Burgess and Rohini Pande have studied the impact of this regulation over the period 1977–90.[40] They find that a 1 percent increase in the number of rural banked locations, per capita, resulted in a 0.42 percent decline in poverty, and a 0.34 percent increase in total output.

Cole uses the empirical strategy described in the section on "Bank Ownership and Sectoral Allocation of Credit" to study the impact of bank nationalization on rural bank growth.[41] He shows that between 1980 and 2000 the growth rate of rural branches fell substantially, on the order of 20 percent. The nationalized banks in our sample fell even more sharply, with rural branch growth rates 6.6 percent and 8.6 percent slower than their private counterparts in the 1980s and 1990s. These results are reported in column 4 of table 5.

In summary, the regulation requiring the opening of rural banks may well have been beneficial, but, if anything, nationalization made banks slightly less responsive to the regulation.

Non-Performing Assets and Bailouts

Mounting nonperforming assets and resulting questions about the ability of the banks with high levels of NPA to honor their liabilities to their depositors have been important concerns in the 1990s.

Recent RBI figures suggest that public sector banks have substantially higher levels of nonperforming assets than do private banks. For example, for the year ending in March 2003, gross NPAs represented 4.6 percent of public sector banks' total assets, as against 4.3 percent of those of old private sector banks and 3.7 percent of those of new private sector banks. It is not clear, however, how well these numbers represent the true situation in these banks. There is some skepticism about the accuracy of reported NPA numbers: banks may engage in creative accounting or "evergreening," and the current classification norms mapping loan repayment delay to NPA do not yet meet international norms.

40. Burgess and Pande (2003).
41. Cole (2004).

An informative check, conducted by Petia Topalova, is to use data from corporate balance sheets to estimate the ability of firms to repay their loans.[42] Firms whose income (defined as earnings before interest, taxes, depreciation, and amortization) is less than their reported interest expense are either defaulting, are very close to default, or would be defaulting if their loans were not "evergreened." This share of "potential NPAs" has increased significantly in the past five years, while banks' reported level of NPAs has stayed fairly constant. Topalova also finds that banks are exposed to substantial interest rate risk: a 200 basis point increase in the rate of interest could result in a 4 percentage point increase in the share of NPAs in the banking system.

These high levels of NPAs raise obvious concerns about the stability of individual banks. But the government's policy so far has been to allay these concerns by simply taking over the uncovered liabilities of the failing banks, whether nationalized or private. Therefore we will measure the cost of the NPAs in terms of resources that have gone into bailing out these banks.

We are not aware of a systematic accounting of all bank failures in India since 1969. To calculate the cost of bank failures, we use data collected from annual issues of the RBI's *Statistical Tables Relating to Banks in India*, starting in 1969. Although the data are not comprehensive, we are optimistic that they can provide at least the correct order of magnitude.[43]

In 1969, we have deposits data for forty-five private sector banks. Between 1969 and 2000, we are able to identify twenty-one cases of bank failure, which resulted either in a bank's liquidation or its merger with a public sector bank. (An additional twenty banks were nationalized: fourteen in 1969, and six in 1980. We do not count these twenty nationalizations as failures.) The value of the deposits at the time the bank failed can be taken as an upper bound of the cost of a bank failure. Thus, we calculate the value (in Rs. 2000) of the deposits of these twenty-one banks.[44] The largest single failure was Laxhmi Commercial Bank, which merged with Canara Bank in 1985 and represents 18.5 percent of the share of real deposits

42. Topalova (2004).

43. For example, the data may not correctly account for the possibility that banks change their names or merge while healthy. We identify the failure of private sector banks by their disappearance from our data: in many cases, these failures can be confirmed by secondary sources, but it is possible (even likely) that we have missed some failures, or evaluated as bank failures some events that were not failures. We would welcome a more careful study of this issue.

44. For all price adjustments in this section, we use the consumer price index from the International Financial Statistics database of the International Monetary Fund.

of failed banks. The total value of deposits for banks that failed between 1969 and 2000 is approximately Rs. 45 billion, a substantial sum.[45]

The total cost of recapitalization is also unknown. We conduct a back-of-the-envelope exercise, using figures from the 1999–2000 issue of the RBI's *Report on Trends and Progress of Banking in India*.[46] These figures give the capital contribution of the central government to nationalized banks, as well as the amount of capital written down by the central government. While interpretation of the write-off is straightforward, the recapitalization funding requires a little work. Banks earned money from the recapitalization bonds. The recapitalization subscription will, at least in theory, be returned to the government (several public sector banks have already returned capital): thus, the true cost of recapitalization is best measured by the interest income forgone by the government. The 2000–01 *Report on Trends and Progress of Banking in India* reports the income from nationalized banks both as recorded on their books and after subtracting the income from recapitalization bonds. We take the difference between these two numbers as the implied subsidy from the government to the nationalized banks. To calculate this number for other years, we assume that the ratio of subsidized income (1,797 crore in 1998–99) to cumulative capital contributed by the central government (19,803 crore in 1998–99) was constant throughout the nineties, at approximately $1757/19,403 = 9$ percent. Taking the total reported capital investment in each year from 1992 to 2000 (again from the 2000–01 *Trends and Progress*) and adjusting for inflation gives an estimate of the subsidy from recapitalization of approximately 13,607 crore. Combined with 15,421 crore of written-down capital, this amounts to a recapitalization cost to the government of approximately Rs. 290 billion.

This number requires three important adjustments. First, some of the weakness from the nationalized banks' balance sheets may come from the assets of the failed private banks that were merged with the nationalized banks (this amount can be bounded above by the figure derived above, Rs. 45 billion—quite clearly, public sectors have many bad loans of their own). Second, and probably much more important, this represents the cost up to the year 2000. It is an open question how long it will take for the banks to return this capital to the government. Finally, it is also possible that the public sector banks will be unable to return all the capital subscribed by the government.

---

45. We stress again that this is an upper bound: although the banks that failed were insolvent, the banks had other assets, such as reserves, other performing loans, and real property, as well as deposit insurance, on which depositors were able to draw.

46. Reserve Bank of India (2001).

Thus the most favorable accounting for public sector banks (in which they wean themselves completely from recapitalization income starting in fiscal year 2004 and are absolved of the entire value of the Rs. 45 billion of the failed private banks) gives a total cost of recapitalization of public banks of approximately Rs. 300 billion.[47] A more realistic assessment might credit them for only half the value of the losses and assume that recapitalization bonds will be held for ten more years, until 2014. This would give an approximate bail-out cost of Rs. 540 billion.[48]

Comparing the figures requires attention to the relative size of the two bank groups. A rough estimate of the ratio of deposits of nationalized banks to private sector banks during 1969–2000 gives the following: during 1969–80, the ratio of deposits in nationalized banks to deposits in private banks was approximately 5 to 1; during 1980–93, the ratio was approximately 11-1; post liberalization, the ratio has been falling; in 2000 it stood at about 7.5 to 1.[49]

Thus, under the accounting most favorable to public sector banks, they squeak by as less costly to the government than private sector banks (the ratio of money spent bailing out public vs. private banks would be 6.67 to 1, less than the deposits ratio). However, using the estimate of Rs. 540 billion total cost gives a 12-1 ratio, which would imply that the public sector banks lost a greater portion of their deposits to bad loans.

The Future of Banking Reform

Where does this evidence, taken together, leave us? There are obvious problems with the Indian banking sector, ranging from under-lending to unsecured lending, which we have discussed at some length. There is now a greater awareness of these problems in the Indian government and a willingness to do something about them.

One policy option being discussed is privatization. The evidence from Cole, discussed above, suggests that privatization would lead to an infusion of dynamism into the banking sector. Private banks have been growing

47. Starting from the figure of Rs. 290 billion, we add the approximate subsidy for 2000–03, Rs. 60 billion, and subtract Rs. 45 billion of losses possibly imparted by the private sector banks.

48. We take the figure of Rs. 290 billion through 2000, subtract a Rs. 22.5 billion credit from the failed private sector banks, and add on a subsidy of 1950 crore a year for the next decade, giving us a final figure of Rs. 540 billion.

49. Reserve Bank of India figures. The ratio for 2000 excludes the new private sector banks.

faster than comparable public banks in terms of credit, deposits, and number of branches, including rural branches, though it should be noted that in our empirical analysis, the comparison group of private banks were the relatively small "old" private banks.[50] It is not clear that we can extrapolate from this how the State Bank of India, which is more than an order of magnitude greater in size than the largest "old" private sector banks, would change if it were privatized. The "new" private banks are bigger and in some ways would have been a better group to compare with. But while this group is also growing fast, it has been favored by regulators in some specific ways, which, combined with its relatively short track record, makes the comparison difficult.

Privatization will also free the loan officers from fear of the CVC and make them somewhat more willing to lend aggressively where the prospects are good, though, as will be discussed later, better regulation of public banks may also achieve similar goals.

Historically, a crucial difference between public and private sector banks has been their willingness to lend to the priority sector. The recent broadening of the definition of the priority sector has mechanically increased the share of credit from both public and private sector banks that qualify as priority sector lenders. The share of priority sector lending from public sector banks was 42.5 percent in 2003, up from 36.6 percent in 1995. Private sector lending has shown a similar increase from its 1995 level of 30 percent. In 2003 it may have surpassed for the first time ever public sector banks, with a share of net bank credit to the priority sector at 44.4 percent.[51]

Still, there are substantial differences between public and private sector banks. Most notable is the consistent failure of private sector banks to meet the agricultural lending sub-target, though they also lend substantially less in rural areas. Our evidence suggests that privatization will make it harder for the government to get the private banks to meet its goals. However, it is not clear that this reflects the greater sensitivity of the public banks to this particular social goal. It could also be that credit to agriculture, being particularly politically salient, is the one place where the nationalized banks are subject to political pressures to make imprudent loans.

Finally, one potential disadvantage of privatization comes from the risk of bank failure. In the past there have been cases where the owner of the private bank stripped its assets and declared it unable to honor its deposit

50. Cole (2004).
51. All numbers are from various issues of *Report on Trends and Progress of Banking in India.*

liabilities. The government is, understandably, reluctant to let banks fail, because one of the achievements of the past forty years has been to persuade people that their money is safe in the banks. Therefore, government has tended to take over the failed bank, with the resultant pressure on the fiscal deficit. Of course, this is in part a result of poor regulation—the regulator should be able to spot a private bank that is stripping its assets. Better enforced prudential regulations would considerably strengthen the case for privatization.

On the other hand, public banks have also been failing. The problem seems to be part corruption and part inertia and laziness on the part of the lenders. As we saw above, the cost of bailing out the public banks may well be larger (appropriately scaled) than the total losses incurred from every bank failure since 1969.

Once again the "newness" of the private banks poses a problem: So far none of them has defaulted, but because they are also new, they have not yet had to deal with the slow decline of once successful companies, which is one of the main sources of the accumulation of bad debt on the books of the public banks.

On balance, we feel the evidence argues, albeit quite tentatively, for privatizing the nationalized banks and tightening prudential regulations. On the other hand, we see no obvious case for abandoning the "social" aspect of banking. Indeed there is a natural complementarity between reinforcing the priority sector regulations (for example, by insisting that private banks lend more to agriculture) and privatization, because with a privatized banking sector it is less likely that the directed loans will get redirected based on political expediency.

However, there is no reason to expect miracles from the privatized banks. For a variety of reasons, including financial stability, the natural tendency of banks, public or private, the world over is toward consolidation and the formation of fewer, bigger banks. As banks become larger, they almost inevitably become more bureaucratic, because most lending decisions in big banks, by necessity, must be taken by people who have no direct financial stake in the loan. Being bureaucratic means limiting the amount of discretion the loan officers can exercise and using rules, rather than human judgment wherever possible, much as is currently done in Indian nationalized banks. Allen Berger and colleagues have argued in the context of the United States that this leads bigger banks to shy away from lending to the smaller firms.[52] Our presumption is that this consolidation

---

52. Berger and colleagues (2001).

and increased focus on lending to corporate and other larger firms is what will happen in India, with or without privatization, though in the short run the entry of a number of newly privatized banks should increase competition for clients, which ought to help the smaller firms.

In the end the key to banking reform may lie in the internal bureaucratic reform of banks, both private and public. In part this is already happening, as many of the newer private banks, such as HDFC Bank and ICICI Bank, try to reach beyond their traditional clients in the housing, consumer finance, and blue-chip sectors.

Such reforms will require a set of smaller step reforms, designed to affect the incentives of bankers in private and public banks. A first step would be to make lending rules more responsive to current profits and projections of future profits. This may be a way both to target better and to guard against potential NPAs, largely because poor profitability seems to be a good predictor of future default. It is clear, however, that choosing the right way to include profits in the lending decision will not be easy. On one side is the danger that unprofitable companies will default. On the other is the danger of pushing a company into default by cutting its access to credit exactly when it needs it the most, that is, right after a shock to demand or costs has pushed it into the red. Perhaps one way to balance these objectives would be to create three categories of firms. The first would be profitable to highly profitable firms. Within this category lending should respond to profitability, with more profitable firms getting a higher limit, even if they look similar on the other measures. The second category would be short-term marginally profitable to loss-making firms or once-profitable firms that have been hit recently by a temporary shock, such as an increase in the price of cotton because of crop failures. For these firms the existing rules for lending might work well. The third category would be long-term marginally profitable to loss-making firms or firms hit by a permanent shock, such as the removal of tariffs protecting firms in an industry in which the Chinese have a huge cost advantage. For these firms, there should be an attempt to discontinue lending, based on some clearly worked out exit strategy (it is important that the borrowers be offered enough of the pie that they feel that they will be better off by exiting without defaulting on the loans).

Of course, it is not always going to be easy to distinguish permanent and temporary shocks. In particular, what should we make of the firm that claims to have put in place strategies that help it survive the shock of Chinese competition, but that the strategy will work only in a couple of years? The best rule may be to use the information in profits and costs over several years and the experience of the industry as a whole.

One constraint on moving to a rule of this type is that it puts more weight on the judgment of the loan officer, who would now also have to judge whether a company's profitability (or the lack of it) is permanent or temporary. This increased discretion will obviously increase both the scope for corruption and the risk of being falsely accused of corruption. As we saw above, the data are consistent with the view that loan officers' fears of being falsely accused of corruption pushes them to avoid taking any decisions if they can help it. It would be difficult to achieve better targeting of loans without reforming the incentives of the loan officers.

Other steps can go some distance toward this goal, even within public banks. First, to avoid a climate of fear, there should be a clear separation between investigation of loans and investigations of loan officers. The loan should be investigated first (could the original sanction amount have made sense at the time it was given? were there obvious warning signs?), and a prima facie case that the failure of the loan could have been predicted must be made before the authorization to start investigating the officer is given. Ideally, until that point the loan officer should not know that there is an investigation. The authorization to investigate a loan officer should also be based on the most objective available measures of the lifetime performance of the loan officer across all the loans where he or she made decisions, and weight should be given both to successes and to failures. A loan officer with a good track record should be allowed some mistakes (even suspicious-looking mistakes) before he or she is open to investigation.

Banks should also create a separate division, staffed by bankers with high reputations, that is allowed to make a certain amount of high-risk loans. Officers posted to this division should be explicitly protected from investigation for loans made. Some extra effort will probably be needed to reach out more effectively to the smaller and less well-established firms not just on equity grounds, but also because these firms may have the highest returns on capital. A possible step in this direction would be to encourage established reputable firms in the corporate sector as well as multinationals to set up small specialized companies whose only job is to lend to smaller firms in a particular sector (and possibly in a particular location). These new companies would be the equivalent of the many finance companies that do extensive lending all over India, but with links to a much bigger corporate entity and therefore better creditworthiness. The banks would then lend to these entities at some rate that would be somewhat below the cost of capital (instead of doing priority sector lending), and these finance companies would then make loans to the firms in their domain, at a rate that is at most some fixed amount higher than their borrowing rates. Being small and connected to a particular industry, these finance companies could acquire detailed knowledge of the firms in the industry and would have an incentive to make loans that would appear adventurous to outsiders.

Finally, giving banks a stronger incentive to lend by cutting the interest rate on government borrowing will also help. The evidence reported above suggests that where lending is difficult, making lending to the government less lucrative can strongly encourage bankers to make loans to the private sector. Thus it is the less obviously creditworthy firms that suffer most from the high rates of government borrowing.

Comment and Discussion

Urjit R. Patel: The Banerjee, Cole, and Duflo paper presents a series of hypotheses that, strictly speaking, relate to banking *performance* in India rather than to reform, except in the limited sense of decisions taken regarding dilution and embellishment of stringent administrative dictates imposed earlier. More important, it does not adequately address the issue of *how* to proceed with even the limited changes that the authors suggest. Although the paper addresses the micro-behavior of the bank from which the data are drawn, the systemic "macro" implications of that behavior remain tenuous at best.

Most of my comments will deal with the paper's conclusions and recommendations rather than the mechanics of the models themselves. As to the models, I will focus on the first one, not just because it is the most detailed but also because it is the most contemporary. Since the practice of banking changed so vastly in the latter half of the 1990s, conclusions regarding differences in the 1970s and 1980s, though interesting in themselves, are likely to have little "predictive utility" for policy in the current environment.

The results obtained by the authors are congruent with intuition—that is, there is little about them that is surprising. A statistical deconstruction of the estimation procedure, however, turned out to be surprisingly difficult, especially given the apparent simplicity of the estimation equations. I have to admit that although the language is a bit dense, the modeling steps are crafted methodically, and I enjoyed trying to second-guess the authors' underlying reasoning. A clearer picture of the rationale of the constructs emerged on reviewing the authors' 2002 working paper. Even then, the rationale and intuitiveness of the multiplicative term as an instrument for growth in credit is not completely convincing, but I suppose, in an elliptical way, it could capture the interaction of spatial and temporal distribution of firms. The periodicity of the dataset (1997–99) that the authors use is not self-evident: are the data periodic (annual, quarterly, or something else), or are they sporadic, in the sense that they were available when the bank made the loan decision and were then aggregated by the authors?

A brief description of the procedure the authors used to test their hypothesis of underlending is warranted. They look at under-lending from the viewpoint of firms, a clever "turning on its head" of the normal approach to credit constraints. If firms are not credit constrained, there is no under-lending. A testable hypothesis is the corollary that for constrained firms revenue growth should be greater than growth in subsidized credit, and this is the hypothesis that the authors test. Equation (1) tests whether credit growth differed across types of firms (BIG or small), over time (POST) or as a combination of the two (BIG * POST). In my understanding, the sequence is as follows: they filter out the differential treatment, if any, of "small" and "big" firms, of lending before and after the ("inclusion" of) policy change, and of interactions between the two. These are essentially the results in tables 1 and 2.

Were there some other extraneous policy changes during this period (apart from the higher credit limits that allowed segmentation of the sample) that might have changed the bank's decisionmaking and thereby interfered with the control structure of equation (1)? Looking at the *Economic Survey of India* for 1998–99, one finds that indeed there had been changes in 1998 relating to loans to small-scale industry (SSI) units. For instance, ceilings for working capital (subject to 20 percent of annual turnover) were doubled from Rs. 2 crore to Rs. 4 crore. The powers of bank managers of specialized SSI branches had been "enhanced" to allow them to make credit decisions at the branch level. Following the report of a high-powered committee in June 1998, measures like enhancing composite loans from Rs. 2 lakh to Rs. 5 lakh, delegating more powers to branch managers for granting ad hoc facilities, and so forth were implemented. These policy relaxations are likely to have had an impact on banks' lending decisions regarding both firms that were below and firms that were above the changed exclusion limit.

As for column (2) in table 2, where the effect of borrowing from the market by small firms (that is, the substitution effect) is incorporated, it is unclear what it means by small firms borrowing from the market. It is unlikely that small firms are accessing the capital markets; maybe the authors mean loans from SIDBI, state finance corporations (SFCs), or other similar sources. Other financing modes available to SSIs—for example, bill discounting—also should be included in the definition of credit. Various directives and notifications from the RBI regarding these channels have the potential of distorting credit aggregates if all the components have not been factored in.

TABLE 10.   Business Loan Rates, 1996–99

	Minimum general loan rate of scheduled commercial banks	Prime lending rate of Industrial Development Bank of India	Rate charged to small-scale industries by state financial corporations	Cost of scheduled commercial bank funds (deposits)
1996–97	14.5–15	16.2	12–27.5	11–12
1997–98	14.0	13.3	12–18	10.5–11
1998–99	12–13	13.5	12–18.5	9–11
Average 1997–99	13.3–14	14.3	12–21.3	10.2–11.3

Source: Reserve Bank of India (2003, table 63, pp. 99–100).

There are multiple references to subsidized credit, and in some ways the key to identifying credit-constrained firms is their behavior on being able to access "subsidized" credit. We normally associate subsidized credit with priority sector lending; in this case, small firms (SSIs) would be the typical candidates for being credit constrained. At what rates have they been granted credit? Some figures from the 2003 RBI *Handbook of Statistics* are given in table 10.

In light of these numbers, it is rather difficult to judge whether SSIs indeed have had access to "subsidized" credit. One then has to be very careful about benchmarking these rates with banks' published prime lending rates (PLRs), as the authors later seek to do for the interest rate spread with respect to the PLR of the State Bank of India (SBI). PLRs in Indian banking, unlike in other counties, are quite deceptive, with significant sub-PLR lending often taking place.

In the model for testing the effect on credit growth of vigilance activities, causality effects that could bias the coefficient estimates cannot, prima facie, be ruled out. For instance, higher credit growth could have been the result of increased "extra-commercial" considerations for disbursement, thereby leading to more vigilance investigations.

So much for the technical aspects of the models. Now let me address the authors' conclusions and comments on the future of banking reform. I could not agree more with them about the need for privatization. Many of the incentives and disincentives that the authors mention, test, and attempt to quantify are considerably more likely to be correctly aligned with the goals of banking reform in a privatized environment.

Some of the authors' observations might have benefited from elaboration of the underlying processes. For instance, it is not surprising that priority sector lending of private sector banks surpassed that of public sector banks in 2003. This is patently due to the growth of individual housing loans (less than Rs. 10 lakh)—which, for urban areas, had already been included as part of priority lending since 1999;[1] as of April 2003, loans of less than Rs. 10 lakh in rural and semi-urban areas also were included. For private banks, the *Report on Trends and Progress in Banking in 2002–03* shows that the share of "others" (that is, other than agriculture and SSI) in priority sector loans—which include home loans—was the highest. Moreover, as of 2003, loans to NBFCs toward their SSI lending also count as priority sector loans. (This last measure, incidentally, is close to the authors' prescription that banks be empowered to lend to specialized companies.)

The authors state that for the period between 1977 and 1990, studies have shown some improvement in rural poverty and output because of the increase in rural branch bank openings. Remember, though, that this was precisely the period when a whole slew of "development" programs rendered the public exchequer bankrupt. In addition, the tapering off of rural branch additions, especially for nationalized banks, after the "4 for 1" scheme was abolished does not tell us much about what—other than the high base levels—might have led to this phenomenon in terms of underlending. It is instructive that as of March 2003, despite the fact that 49 percent of bank branches were in rural areas, their share of credit was only 10 percent.[2] One can but conjecture that rural areas could, in fact, be considered "overbanked" in some sense.

The authors' contention that "privatization will make it harder for the government to get private banks to comply with [agricultural lending subtargets]" cannot be ignored. In this context, a proposal that merits consideration is a suitably designed mechanism to use "minimum subsidy bidding" to provide rural credit. Acquisition of financial resources from rural and semi-urban areas has already been accomplished quite efficiently through the various small savings schemes, which can be ramped up through greater collaboration with the extensive network of post offices. The problem is credit delivery. Some corporations are now beginning to explore underdeveloped rural markets to tap their latent purchasing power, and these markets might also be profitably explored as avenues for the use of funds from small savings schemes. Besides, an extensive network of regional rural banks already exists. While there are likely to be problems in

---

1. RBI Master Circular (March 2004), paragraph 1.8.1.1.
2. RBI Banking Statistics, Quarterly Handout (March 2003).

ensuring suitable deployment of funds, credit delivery mechanisms other than through commercial banks should be explored.

I have some disagreement with the authors on their seeming perception of a heightened risk of bank failure following privatization. First, is there something inherent in the risk profile of their portfolios, their lending processes, or their incentive structures that makes private banks more prone to failure (in the sense of bad loans eroding their net worth)? Prima facie, the lending processes of some public sector banks that I am aware of make them more vulnerable to bad decisions. Second, presuming that this is so, is it an empirically validated phenomenon, especially for India? Remember, we are talking of commercial banks, not the relatively less regulated cooperative banks or NBFCs.

Ownership of public sector banks remains a fundamental barrier to establishing the "correct" incentives in risk management—for instance, as the authors say, in making "lending rules more responsive to current profits and projections of future profits." In a properly enforced regulatory environment and with the enhanced commercial discipline increasingly being demanded by shareholders, a focus on (risk-adjusted) return on equity is best achieved through profit maximization by intermediaries.

There can be no quarrel as such with the apparent remedial prescription for more tightly enforced prudential regulation. However, reading through the authors' approach to regulation, I get a lingering "feeling" that they advocate a more intrusive ratio-based oversight, although admittedly I may be mistaken. I am a bit ambivalent about this; tighter enforcement is a must, but the approach should devolve risk management toward the banks. Regulation is moving away from stifling ratiocentric approaches toward a more decentralized risk management system (the Basle II approach), and, to its credit, the RBI already has embarked on a prompt corrective action approach—which ensures that regulators act in a timely fashion—with a pilot under way. Furthermore, both shareholder and depositor scrutiny need to be augmented, to bring greater commercial discipline to banks. One area that deserves rethinking in this regard is deposit insurance, which thus far has contributed to lulling depositors into an unwarranted, false sense of security.

The observations on establishing processes to give more discretion to public sector loan officers are very sensible, and the approach in my own institution points to taking collective responsibility in approving loans; in fact, all banks have credit committees, with various degrees of empowerment. While one may completely agree with the authors about banks' need for internal bureaucratic reforms to advance loan disbursement, there have to be concomitant reforms in bankruptcy and foreclosure laws to allow them to turn distressed assets around expeditiously.

The prescription regarding making holdings of government securities by banks less attractive is more open to criticism. Artificial tampering with interest rates is not desirable, interfering as it does with an authentic interest yield curve formation. Besides the obvious injunction to reduce government borrowing, the role of the RBI as sector regulator on the one hand and investment banker to the government's borrowing program on the other—and the consequent potential conflicts of interest—is what needs to be examined more closely.

General Discussion

Suman Bery raised the issue of how the microeconomic analysis of the Banerjee paper could be related to macroeconomic questions, such as those about capital account convertibility and financial vulnerability. The question is whether India would be well served or badly served by the fact that public sector banks dominate the banking sector and private sector banks operate in their shadow. In response, Banerjee said that regarding financial vulnerability, when nothing responds to anything—for example, firms get the same loans whatever happens—the system is actually going to be pretty stable. This is a system that is going to be hard to hit through exchange rate changes. The way the economy gets hit in typical financial-flow crisis models is through the credit channel: if banks do not have enough liquidity, they stop lending. But if the situation is one in which banks keep lending and firms keep borrowing regardless of the liquidity position, it is going to be a very static system that does not have the unstable dynamics of a more responsive system.

Surjit Bhalla returned to the issue of nonperforming assets (NPAs), arguing that in view of the capital gains on the public debt held by banks, no matter how the level is calculated, the low level of NPAs reflected in the official figures is quite accurate. Rakesh Mohan joined in, making the point that whatever the definition used, NPAs are definitely coming down. The low level of lending to the industrial sector has helped in this.

Responding to other comments, Banerjee said that the paper did mention privatization as one of the options being discussed. Maybe the authors were too cautious, and they will state it more forcefully in the future. That said, the most important steps that need to be taken are to ensure better enforcement of loan contracts, better loan service history, and stiffer penalties. Any other measures would be just a Band-Aid. Banerjee noted, however, that he had not given enough thought to what happens when public sector banks have to compete against private sector banks. Maybe such competition will transform public sector banks, but the outcome will very much depend on the stance the government takes. If it just raises salaries as it has done recently, fails to exercise forbearance, and refuses to close down banks that are unable to compete, that will be the worst deal possible.

In closing the session, Rakesh Mohan made several comments. First, the paper is about banking sector performance rather than banking reforms; in light of that, the authors might want to reconsider the title. Second, a very interesting experiment has been under way in India over the past dozen years. On one hand, private sector entry has been opened up; on the other, there has been a very conscious movement toward adoption of what might be called best practices in regulation and supervision. Today, the second-largest bank, ICICI, is a private sector bank that is very aggressive and is expanding fast. The interesting question is how this development interacts with the systematic introduction of such regulation and supervision. Third, under-lending is a real issue. The impression that there is under-lending is widespread, as evidenced by the recent proposals of the Ministry of Finance for large funds for agriculture, small-scale enterprises, and infrastructure lending. Fourth, based on Mohan's personal experience, even large banks seem not to have the credit histories of their borrowers. Finally, regarding vigilance, there is active discussion on making a clearer distinction between when the Central Vigilance Commission (CVC) goes into action because there is a prima facie evidence of wrongdoing and when it does so just because some loan has gone bad.

References

Banerjee, Abhijit. 2003. "Contracting Constraints, Credit Markets, and Economic Development." In *Advances in Economics and Econometrics: Theory and Applications, Eighth World Congress of the Econometric Society, Volume III,* edited by Mathias Dewatripont, Lars Hansen, and Stephen Turnovsky. Cambridge University Press.

Banerjee, Abhijit, Shawn Cole, and Esther Duflo. 2003. "Bank Finance in India." Mimeo, MIT.

Banerjee, Abhijit, and Esther Duflo. 2001. "The Nature of Credit Constraints. Evidence from an Indian Bank." Mimeo, MIT.

————. 2003. "Do Firms Want to Borrow More? Testing Credit Constraints Using a Directed Lending Program." Working Paper 2003-005. Cambridge, Mass.: Bureau for Research in the Economic Analysis of Development.

Banerjee, Abhijit, and Kaivan Munshi. 2004. "Networks, Migration and Investment: Insiders and Outsiders in Tirupur's Production Cluster." *Review of Economic Studies* 71: 19–42.

Berger, Allen, Nathan Miller, Mitchell Peterson, Raghuram Rajan, and Jeremy Stein. 2001. "Does Function Follow Organizational Form: Evidence from the Lending Practices of Large and Small Banks." Mimeo, Harvard University.

Bernanke, Benjamin, and Mark Gertler. 1989. "Agency Costs, Net Worth, and Business Fluctuations." *American Economic Review* 79 (1):14–31.

Bertrand, Marianne, Antoinette Schoar, and David Thesmar. 2003. "Banking Deregulation and Industry Structure: Evidence from the French Banking Reforms of 1985." Mimeo, MIT.

Blanchflower, David, and Andrew Oswald. 1998. "What Makes an Entrepreneur." *Journal of Labor Economics* 16 (1): 16–60.

Burgess, Robin, and Rohini Pande. 2003. "Do Rural Banks Matter? Evidence from the Indian Social Banking Experiment." Mimeo, Yale University, June.

Cole, Shawn. 2002. "Corruption, Vigilance, and the Supply of Credit." Mimeo, MIT.

————. 2004. "The Effect of Ownership on Banking." Mimeo, MIT.

Das-Gupta, Arindam. 1989. *Reports on Informal Credit Markets in India: Summary.* New Delhi: National Institute of Public Finance and Policy.

Dixit, Avinash. 1996. *The Making of Economic Policy: A Transaction Cost Politics Perspective.* Munich Lectures in Economics. Cambridge: MIT Press.

Fazzari, Steven, R. Glenn Hubbard, and Bruce Petersen. 1998. "Financing Constraints and Corporate Investment." *Brookings Papers on Economic Activity,* no. 1: 141–95.

Government of India. 2000. *Cases Referred to the Central Vigilance Commission by Public Sector Banks: A Critical Analysis.* Delhi: Central Vigilance Commission.

————. 2001. *Special Chapter on Vigilance Management in Public Sector Banks.* Delhi: Central Vigilance Commission.

Kaplan, Stephen, and Luigi Zingales. 2000. "Investment-Cash Flow Sensitivity Are Not Valid Measures of Financial Constraints." *Quarterly Journal of Economics* 115: 707–12.

La Porta, Rafael, Florencio Lopez-de-Silanes, and Andrei Shleifer. 2002. "Government Ownership of Banks." *Journal of Finance* 57: 265–301.

Lamont, Owen. 1997. "Cash Flows and Investment: Evidence from Internal Capital Markets." *Journal of Finance* 51 (2): 83–109.

Mian, Atif, 2000. "Creditor Incentives and Privatization." Mimeo, MIT.

Reserve Bank of India. 2000. *Directory of Commercial Bank Offices in India (Volume 1)*. Mumbai.

———. Various issues. *Statistical Tables Relating to Banks in India*. Mumbai.

———. Various issues. *Report on Trend and Progress of Banking in India*. Mumbai.

Tandon, Prakesh, 1989. *Banking Century: A Short History of Banking in India*. New Delhi: Viking.

Tannan, Mohan. 2001. *Banking Law and Practice in India*. New Delhi: India Law House.

Topalova, Petia. 2004. "Overview of the Indian Corporate Sector: 1989–2002." Working Paper 04/64. Washington: International Monetary Fund.